PENTAGON PRESS

COMMITTED TO SERVE THE ARMED FORCES

Emerging Trends in West Asia

Regional and Global Implications

Emerging Trends in West Asia

Regional and Global Implications

Editor

MEENA SINGH ROY

idsa
INSTITUTE FOR DEFENCE STUDIES & ANALYSES
NEW DELHI

PENTAGON PRESS

Emerging Trends in West Asia: Regional and Global Implications
Meena Singh Roy (Ed)

First Published in 2014

ISBN 978-81-8274-771-5

Published by
PENTAGON PRESS
206, Peacock Lane, Shahpur Jat,
New Delhi-110049
Phones: 011-64706243, 26491568
Telefax: 011-26490600
email: rajan@pentagonpress.in
website: www.pentagonpress.in

Branch:
Prime Arcade
Office #11
1154 Saifee Street
Opp. M.G. Road, Camp
Pune-411001
Email: pentagonpresspune@gmail.com

In association with
Institute for Defence Studies and Analyses
No. 1, Development Enclave,
New Delhi-110010
Phone: +91-11-26717983
Website: www.idsa.in

Printed at Avantika Printers Private Limited.

Contents

Preface

Trapped in a political tsunami, the West Asian region has been weathering waves of volatility and instability for the last five years. The political storm that slammed into Tunis in late 2010 gradually engulfed the entire region under the umbrella of 'Arab Spring', a journey that has been nothing short of turbulent. Several countries witnessed a street show of public dissatisfaction against existing despotic regimes, paving the way for change. Initial experiments with democracy have altered the strategic landscape in significant ways. Reverberations of the 'Arab Spring' have made the region a hub of global attention. As the old political order changes, sectarian clashes in several countries have taken place. The regional rivalries have accentuated. Radical Islamist groups have risen to power in several countries. Another significant dimension of the fluctuating geo-politics is the growing Pan-Asian economic linkage. With the rise of India and China as the economic power houses and the deepening of oil-energy ties between Asia and the Gulf, several Asian nations have developed major stakes in stability in the West Asian region. A key question on every one's mind is the direction of developments in West Asia and its regional and global implications.

The Gulf region is critical for India. It remains India's largest socio-economic partner and the main source of India's hydrocarbon imports. Therefore, any developments in the region will inevitably have major implications for India. Given the strategic significance of the region India is working towards exploring new ways of forging strategic cooperation with the West Asian region. The questions are how should India prepare to meet the challenges of instability in the region and what role can it play to safeguard its interests?

Against this backdrop, the Institute for Defence Studies and Analyses organized the 15thAsian Security Conference on February 13-14, 2013, to stimulate discussion and debate on contemporary socio-economic and political developments in the region. The last such conference on West Asia was held in 2006. The desire to understand the West Asian region from a global perspective has been at the heart of inquiry into this subject. The diverse and rich exchange of information on the subject helped to envision a holistic landscape of the region, with well-defined focus on regional and international repercussions of recent developments.

The present book brings together the papers presented by the international scholars at the conference. The book provides an in-depth assessment of socio-political and strategic trends unfolding in West Asia. The complexities of West Asia have been systematically explored by scholars, diplomats and specialists to advance the understanding of West Asian issues and share Asian perceptions regarding evolving political, economic and security dynamics of the region.

The book is expected to inform the reader about West Asia's political and strategic architecture. It is hoped that this book would contribute to the ongoing debate on the subject and cater to needs of scholars, academicians as well as the policy-makers for more information and analysis of the unfolding situation in the region.

Arvind Gupta
Director General,
Institute for Defence Studies and Analyses.

Acknowledgements

This volume is an outcome of the Asian Security Conference organized by the Institute for Defence Studies and Analyses in February, 2013. The aim of the conference was to extract Indian and West Asian perspectives on issues of mutual interest, and augment the understanding of emerging regional and global challenges.

First and foremost, I would like to extend my sincere thanks to all the Indian and foreign contributors for giving their worthy insights and adding immense scholarly value to this work. Most of the papers presented during the conference were duly updated by the authors.

Compilation of this volume would not have been possible without the unconditional support of my colleagues and administrative staff at IDSA. I am immensely grateful to Dr. Arvind Gupta, Director General IDSA for his wholehearted support while completing the conference proceedings.

I take this opportunity to express my gratitude to Brig (Retd) R. Dahiya, Deputy Director General IDSA, and my centre members – Col Rajeev Agrawal, Dr. P.K. Pradhan and Dr. Mahtab Alam Rizvi for their constant support and feedback in organising the event which led to the publication of this volume. Ms. Divya Malhotra deserves a special recognition for her immense help in bringing out this volume.

Special thanks are due to copy editors – Mrs Radha Joshi and Dr Kiran Sahni for their timely assistance in refining the volume. I would like to thank Mr. Vivek Kaushik, Associate Editor, IDSA for his support during the finalisation of the manuscript.

Views expressed in the book are those of the authors in their individual capacity.

Meena Singh Roy

About the Editor/Contributors

Editor

Meena Singh Roy is a Research Fellow and Coordinator of the West Asia Centre at the Institute for Defence Studies and Analyses. She has done her Ph.D. from University of Delhi and has been senior research scholar in the Department of African Studies, Delhi University.

Contributors

Talmiz Ahmad joined the Indian Foreign Service in 1974 and served as Indian Ambassador to Saudi Arabia (2000-03; 2010-11), Oman (2003-04), and the United Arab Emirates (2007-10). He was also Additional Secretary for International Cooperation in the Ministry of Petroleum and Natural Gas from 2004-06.

Ahmed Salem Saleh Al-Wahishi is currently serving as Executive Director of the Yemen Centre of International Affairs. He has served as Chief Representative of the League of Arab States in New Delhi.

Atul Aneja is currently the West Asia/Middle East correspondent for *The Hindu* newspaper and is based in Dubai. He has reported extensively on West Asia from the region for the last 10 years.

Waiel S.H. Awwad is a journalist based in South Asia since 1979. He has covered Sri Lanka, Kashmir, Afghanistan, West Asia and the Gulf Region as a war correspondent.

Shebonti Ray Dadwal is a Research Fellow with the Institute for Defence Studies and Analyses, New Delhi. She has worked as Senior Editor in *The Financial Express* and she has also served as Deputy Secretary at the National Security Council Secretariat.

Sami Al Faraj heads the Kuwait Centre for Strategic Studies (KCSS), which he established in 1997 as the first private consulting centre on strategic issues in the Gulf region.

Muhammad Abdul Ghaffar served as Ambassador of the Kingdom of Bahrain to the European Union and as the non-resident Ambassador to Luxemburg.

Serhat Güvenç is Associate Professor in the Department of International Relations as well as Coordinator for Graduate Studies in International Relations at Kadir Has University, Istanbul, Turkey.

Efraim Inbar is a Professor in Political Studies at Bar-Ilan University and the Director of its BESA Center for Strategic Studies. He serves on the Academic Committee of the History Department of the Israeli Defence Forces (IDF).

Ephraim Kam is the Deputy Director of The Institute for National Security Studies (formerly The Jaffee Center for Strategic Studies), Tel-Aviv University. He served as a Colonel in the Research Division of Israeli Defence Forces (IDF) Military Intelligence.

Mahmoud Karem served as the Ambassador of the Arab Republic of Egypt to Japan, Belgium and Luxembourg, Head of Mission of Egypt to the European Communities and Permanent Representative of Egypt to NATO till 2009.

Mohammad Hassan Khani is Associate Professor of International Relations at Imam Sadiq University (ISU), Tehran, Iran. He has been a Staff Member of the Faculty of Politics and Islamic Studies at ISU since 1998.

P.R. Kumaraswamy is Professor, Centre for West Asian Studies at Jawaharlal Nehru University (JNU), New Delhi. He was a research fellow at the Harry S. Truman Research Institute for the Advancement of Peace, Jerusalem from 1992-99.

Fyodor Lukyanov is Editor-in-Chief of the *Russia in Global Affairs* journal published in Russian and English with participation of *Foreign Affairs*.

Timothy C. Niblock is Emeritus Professor, Chair of the Management Board of the Institute of Arab and Islamic Studies (2008-11), and Special Adviser to the Vice-Chancellor on the Middle East, University of Exeter (2008-present).

Girijesh Pant is Dean, School of International Studies, Jawaharlal Nehru University (JNU), New Delhi. Professor Pant has been Director of Gulf Studies programme and Chairman, Centre for West Asian and African Studies, JNU.

Rajesh Rajagopalan is Professor in International Politics at Centre for International Politics, Organization and Disarmament, School of International Studies, Jawaharlal Nehru University, New Delhi.

Ahmed A. Saif is the director of the Sheba Centre for Strategic Studies. Dr Saif received his PhD (2000) in Politics from the University of Exeter, UK. He taught at Exeter, AUS and Sanaá universities.

Amin Saikal is Professor of Political Science and Director of the Centre for Arab and Islamic Studies (the Middle East and Central Asia) at the Australian National University, Canberra, Australia.

Adel Soliman is Director of the International Center for Strategic Dialogue and Future Studies, Egypt and Executive Director of the International Center for Future and Strategic Studies, Egypt.

Julie E. Taylor is a political scientist at the RAND Corporation. She served as a trustee for the American Institute for Iranian Studies from 2005 to 2008, and was a Strategic Studies Fellow at Harvard's Olin Institute.

Ranjit Gupta is a retired Indian Foreign Service officer and is currently a Distinguished Fellow of the Institute of Peace and Conflict Studies, New Delhi and a Visiting Fellow at the Institute of Chinese Studies, New Delhi.

Welcome Address by Director-General, IDSA

*Dr. Arvind Gupta**

I extend heartiest greetings to the participants of the 15th Asian Security Conference at the IDSA.

We are grateful to the Honourable Raksha Mantri and the President of the Executive Council of the IDSA, Shri A K Antony, for agreeing to deliver the key note address. His support and encouragement to the IDSA has been invaluable for us.

This conference is being held at a time of transition in West Asia. The old order is giving way slowly to the new one. Popular protests that began in December 2010 in Tunisia spread to several other countries in the region, bringing in hope of reform and change. However, two years down, the promise of 'Spring' in the West Asia North Africa (WANA) region has given rise to forecasts of long 'winter' and more 'turmoil'. Regimes and governments have changed in a few countries, while in others, reforms are on hold; and in some few adjustments to the political systems have been made. Overall, this is a period of transition and uncertainty.

Islamist Forces: The political vacuum created by the passing away of old regimes is being filled up by new forces. In many countries Islamist forces with Islamist agendas are resurgent. We can expect new domestic and foreign policy agendas being unfolded in these countries.

Violence: One striking feature of the transition has been the widespread violence. Syria is in the middle of a civil war with no end in sight. More than sixty thousand people have reportedly been killed. Libya has seen a bloody end to the earlier regime. Protests in Egypt are continuing despite the ushering in of new political dispensation. In Tunisia, the security situation has become tense after the recent assassination of an opposition leader. There is no consensus as yet on the national dialogue in Yemen. It is becoming clear that the so called Arab Spring has not yet run its full course. The danger of violence remains stark.

MEPP: Domestic changes have led to exacerbation of exiting faultiness. The Middle East Peace Process has been stalled. Tensions between Israel and the Hamas are rising dangerously. A new round of violence has begun as reflected in the recent hotting up of conflict between Israel and the Hamas.

*Delivered on 13 February, 2013.

Sectarian fault line: The region has long standing sectarian fault line which has been exposed during the Arab uprisings. Sectarian tensions in the region can also rise. If these tensions go out of control, the region could suffer grievously.

Security Situation: This transition is taking place in the backdrop of global economic crisis, sharp decline in economic growth and rise in unemployment in several countries in the region Political uncertainty and low economic growth will cause hardships for the people who are expecting fundamental reforms and improvement in living standards. As a result of these changes the regional order is under great stress. The future of the peace treaties between Israel and Egypt, between Israel and Jordan is uncertain. The relations among key regional players will have a great bearing on the future of the region. Regional rivalries can undermine stability in the area.

Intervention: The role of external actors is important but ambiguous. The principle of non-intervention and non-interference is being questioned. Are external interventions motivated by the hidden agenda of regime change, or, are interventions governed by humanitarian considerations alone? The jury is still out. The external intervention in Libya has set the precedent for similar interventions elsewhere. Syria is a test case.

Extremism: The rise of extremist elements is a matter of great concern. Al-Qaida type of terrorist outfits can gain foothold in the emerging vacuum. The situation in Mali, where extremist elements gained control of the capital briefly, is a case in point.

Defence: The geopolitical significance of the reform cannot be overstated. The uncertainties in the region have an impact on the security situation. In the last couple of years, there have been accretions of military forces in the area. In view of the great importance of the SLOCs, several countries have joined in a variety of naval exercises and deployment. The defence budgets of the regional powers have also been increasing in the recent years. The dangers of piracy and WMD proliferation remain ever present.

India: India has deep interests in the region. India cannot be indifferent to these major changes in its extended neighbourhood. India's key national interests are at stake: energy security; well being of the Diaspora; economic and commercial ties, inward remittances and so on. India's security interests are closely intertwined with the security situation in the Gulf. Therefore, India has a stake in the security and stability in the region. At the same time, as the largest democracy, India cannot be insensitive to people's aspirations.

There are varying perspectives on these matters. This conference will discuss these and other issues in depth in the next three days. We look forward to a productive and constructive exchange of views.

Thank you and Jai Hind.

Inaugural Address by Honourable Defence Minister

*Shri A.K. Antony**

It is a pleasure to address this distinguished gathering that has come together for the 15th Asian Security Conference being organised by IDSA. Over the years, the Conference has attracted eminent strategic experts and scholars from across the world. This is the 15th year in a row that the IDSA is organising a conference on themes pertaining to Asian security.

The response of the international strategic community to this year's theme, 'Emerging Trends in West Asia: Regional and Global Implications', has been encouraging. In the context of West Asia, the theme is highly relevant, as developments in West Asia have a major impact on regional and international security. Many distinguished speakers from West Asia, North Africa, United States, United Kingdom, Europe, Australia, Pakistan, Japan and China will be sharing their views during the Conference.

Since December 2010, the Middle East has been experiencing tumultuous changes. These changes have ushered in fundamental political and socio-economic transformation in the Arab world. New political dispensations have taken over in Tunisia, Libya, Egypt and Yemen. Such transition, unfortunately, has been accompanied by large-scale violence. The ongoing violence in Syria is a matter of concern for the region, as well as the world. Moreover, recently, extremists believed to be linked with the Al Qaeda elements took over the government in Mali. Meanwhile, France has sent its military forces for intervention.

The recent developments in all these countries offer a few lessons: Firstly, no government, or regime, can afford to ignore the popular aspirations anymore. The common strand running through all these protests and demonstrations has been the youth. The voice of the youth is a universal message that is strongly echoing across to governments in all regions of the world. The strong urge for change is clearly visible across the region.

Secondly, the process of transformation is far from complete and on the contrary, has just begun. The journey ahead will be long, tortuous and full of

*Delivered on February 13, 2013.

unexpected twists and turns. Thirdly, the developments in West Asia have the potential of changing the regional and geopolitical landscape. The West Asia region is critical for energy security. Instability in the region will have an impact on global oil prices, availability of oil and gas and shipping of these resources. Fourthly, though traditional political and socio-economic structures have been transformed, new structures that will replace them have not yet got consolidated. While fundamentalist forces have got a fillip, democracy is yet to be consolidated. New political equations are emerging in Iraq and Afghanistan, which has heightened regional and global uncertainties. Lastly, social media has emerged as a potent and vibrant force. The social media has served as a 'force multiplier' in the hands of the protesters.

For India, in particular, West Asia is a critical region. People-to-people contacts have existed between India and West Asia for centuries. These links have got deepened and further strengthened in the era of globalisation. Our stability and prosperity are affected by the developments in the region. First, the Gulf region is vital for India's energy security. The region has about 48 per cent of the world's total proven oil reserves and almost 16 per cent of the world's natural gas reserves. Nearly two-thirds of our hydrocarbon imports are from this region. This will continue to be so in the near future. In addition, nearly 6.5 million Indians live and work in different countries of this region. A World Bank report says that India received US $ 70 billion in remittances during 2012 and a majority of the remittances came from the Gulf region. These remittances support nearly 40-50 million families in India and at the same time, contribute to local prosperity. During 2011, India evacuated nearly 19, 000 Indians working in Libya. The safety and security of Indians working in the region is a sensitive concern for the Indian government.

India's trade with the region is expanding. During 2011-12, India's trade with Gulf Cooperation Council (GCC) was more than $145 billion (with exports and imports from the region standing at 20 per cent and 14 per cent, respectively). India also offers a destination for surplus funds in GCC countries. India has a long tradition of democracy and it is home to a diverse, pluralistic society. The democratic processes have managed its vast regional, cultural, linguistic and regional diversity. At a time when several West Asian nations are in a state of transition, India can share its experiences with the governments and civil societies.

Recent developments have complicated the security situation in the region. Given India's vital stakes in peace and stability in the region, it is natural for India to have an interest in abiding peace and security in the region. At the same time, long-standing conflicts in the region cannot be ignored.

India can ill-afford to remain aloof from the transformative changes taking place in its immediate and extended neighbourhood. We have centuries old linkages with the Arab world. Our civilisations have closely interacted and influenced each other in the past. We have excellent bilateral relations and the relation can be placed on an even stronger footing in the new phase that has set in recently in West Asia.

Ladies and gentlemen,

This conference is holding deliberations on several themes. The discussions will explore the causes behind the ongoing transformation; look into the future and make an attempt to assess the regional and global impacts of these changes. I have been told that several sessions will also explore India's relations with this region. I am sure that the delegates will come up with crucial inputs and practical recommendations during these discussions.

With these words, I hope that our foreign guests will have a pleasant and an enjoyable stay. I wish the deliberations at the Conference all success.

Thank you. Jai Hind.

Special Address by National Security Advisor

*Amb. Shiv Shankar Menon**

Thank you for asking me to speak at the annual Asian Security Conference organised by the IDSA. The Conference, like the IDSA, has developed a formidable reputation for excellence in terms of content and participation. You have also chosen a very topical theme.

There is, today, no region which impinges on India's security with as much immediacy as West Asia. This is not surprising or new. For centuries our extended neighbourhood in West Asia has been a part of our lives in India, beginning with the four thousand-year-old trading relationships evidenced by sailing ships on Indus Valley seals found in archaeological sites in Iraq. These are truly historical, cultural, linguistic, religious and civilizational links.

The strong Indian interest in West Asia continues to this day. You know the facts. Over 6.5 million Indians live in the region, the largest concentration of the Indian diaspora abroad. In several countries they constitute the largest expatriate group. The diaspora in West Asia remit home over US$ 35 billion every year. India's trade and economic ties with the region of about US$ 160 billion are growing, as is our dependence for energy. About 60 per cent of our oil and gas is imported from the region. It is also a factor in our food security as a major source of phosphatic and other fertilizers. Major maritime lines of communication carrying our westward trade and our energy supplies pass through the region. We share common cause with the people of the region in fighting extremism and terrorism. In sum, India's interest lies in a peaceful and balanced strategic environment in West Asia which is such an important part of our extended periphery. (Notice that I do not say stability. This is even though it has become a mantra in Delhi that stability in the region is vital to India's national interest. I am not sure that obstructing or preventing change is practical or sensible policy, though helping or nudging change in the right direction might be. But that is something for you to discuss.

*Delivered on February 15, 2013.

India's Contribution

It is in the quest for regional peace and security that India has sought to contribute to West Asian security within the limits of her capacities.

We have done so politically, encouraging the solution of the region's conflicts and differences through dialogue and by peaceful means. On the Arab-Israeli conflict our support for peace in the Middle East has been principled and consistent. India was the first non-Arab country to recognize the state of Palestine.

We have opposed the proliferation of weapons of mass destruction and their delivery systems in the region. For instance, we have recognized Iran's right to the peaceful uses of nuclear energy while urging that the international community be convinced that she is fulfilling her international commitments, and arguing that the only effective way to do so is through dialogue and by using the IAEA's expertise.

We have contributed to anti-piracy efforts off the Horn of Africa and developed maritime cooperation with the countries of the Gulf to protect the sea-lanes that are vital to our trade and energy flows.

We have worked to promote defence cooperation with the countries of the region, bilaterally and through cooperation among the Indian Ocean rim countries. Our first defence cooperation agreement with a Gulf country was signed with Qatar during Prime Minister Manmohan Singh's 2008 visit.

We have built effective partnerships within the region to combat terrorism and extremism, working with our partners against terrorist groups which are increasingly interlinked across South and West Asia.

We have sought to build energy security through long term arrangements and mutual investments, both upstream and downstream, in the energy industry of the region and India, building the mutual interlinkages that assure both producers and consumers of stability.

While the list is long, it is our hope that it could and should grow in time, in accordance with our mutual interests, as our countries develop their capabilities.

The Situation Today

The immediate question, however, is how recent dramatic developments and changes in West Asia will impact on our security and on what we have been trying to achieve with the countries of the region.

It seems to me that the turbulence in the region poses short-term challenges but also opens up longer term opportunities in terms of our security.

The challenges are well-known. They include the space that domestic changes in several countries have opened up for extremist groups to pursue their agendas. They include the possible regional instability and the sectarian divide that seems to be opening up. They include the disruptions and dislocations that accompany processes of fundamental change in the way these societies and nations are run.

The opportunities are less easily evident. But in the long run, what we are seeing could result in the people of West Asia taking control of their own destinies and choosing their futures and leaders. We in India have strongly supported the democratic aspirations of the people, but have not supported externally enforced change. We have called for restraint in the use of coercive measures against the people. But we are clear that societies cannot be reordered from the outside through military force. As recent experience shows, external interventions have uncertain and unstable outcomes. We only have to look at the instability radiating out of Libya into the Sahel region and the prolonged conflict in Syria, with spill over effects in Mali and the wider region.

Beyond specific situations in individual countries, we are witnessing deeper and longer term changes with profound security implications. The changes in the world energy scenario, for instance, and its geopolitical effects in terms of great power interests in the region. What political and security effects will the West's diminished dependence on Middle East oil have? Demographics, communications, the political role of religion, and cultural factors are all changing rapidly and in ways that affect the politics of West Asia very deeply. But these factors have yet to work themselves out and their implications are still far from clear.

For practitioners, the issue is how to navigate the short-term with its challenges to arrive at a more positive long-term future. Frankly speaking, we had all got comfortable dealing with West Asia in ways set by habit. That is no longer possible. I do hope that your deliberations will map the uncharted territory that we have entered. We are in a time when scholarship and increased engagement with the region is needed more than ever before. Your discussions could help us to see where we are and what we should do.

I wish you success in your deliberations.

PART I

Political Transformation in West Asia: Prospects for Peace, Stability and Prosperity

1

Islamist Politics after the Arab Spring

Talmiz Ahmad

The aftermath of the Arab spring is witnessing the interplay of the Islamist discourse with domestic and regional politics in an environment that is fraught with the promise (or threat) of change. This interplay embraces the three principal expressions of contemporary Islamism—the Wahhabiya of Saudi Arabia; the activist tradition of the Muslim Brotherhood in Egypt and its affiliates in other parts of West Asia-North Africa (WANA), and the radical worldview and agenda of Al-Qaeda and its affiliates. The ramifications of this scenario of competition for space, influence and power over the next few years are examined in this paper.

The second anniversary of the Arab Spring witnessed none of the euphoria of two years ago, not even the quiet self-confidence and sense of achievement of a year later. In Tunisia, where it all started, there was an air of dissatisfaction with the political and economic situation. The economy had been particularly badly hit by the recession in Europe, the country's main economic partner, and the government was seen as pursuing populist policies. But, the deeper divide was between the liberal and Islamic sections of the population. The former, products of several decades of a secular order and significant Western influence, saw increasing efforts by the Al Nahda–led government to Islamicise the nation, a major concern being the politicisation of the civil service with the induction of Islamists. This led to deep anxieties about personal rights and liberties in an Islamist order.[1]

These fears, enhanced by the assassinations of prominent liberal political figures led, over the last year, to an even greater distancing of liberal elements from the government, and deep political polarisation across the country.

On the positive side, the Tunisian economy was in far better shape than that of several of its neighbours, and was expected to see a rebound in the near future. Again, Al-Nahda was careful to include in the government setup non-Islamist partners as also an apolitical president. Its constitution-making process, though tardy, was reasonably accommodative of non-Islamist views. The optimists at that time felt that the process of reform, would be slow and painful, but would ultimately be achieved.[2] However, Al-Nahda could not promote national reconciliation, and on September 28, 2013 agreed to step down in favour of a non-partisan government of national unity.

The picture in Egypt is more gloomy. Not only was there no euphoria on the second anniversary, there were in fact large scale demonstrations, police firings and, finally, on January 27, 2013, a declaration of emergency in selected towns. The president sought a "national dialogue" but was rebuffed since opposition leaders saw no reason to bail out the person they held responsible for the acute mess in the country and his failure to build a consensus.

Morsi's critics in the GCC media had a field day. Dr. Hamad al-Majid said:

> During the "era of President Mursi", prices have risen, Egypt's currency has fallen to record lows, the tourism industry has sunk to new depths, capital has fled abroad, the fragile security situation prevails, and the president is suffering from a lack of genuine prestige.[3]

The Saudi writer, Tariq Al-Homaid, criticised the Brotherhood as a whole:

> The Brotherhood's problem, not only in Egypt but in all countries of the Arab Spring, is that they offended everyone with their greed for power and their overwhelming desire to seize everything, from the trade unions to the presidency, the People's assembly, the Shoura Council, and the government.[4]

The Egyptian politician and commentator, Hassan Nafia had been critical of the government even before the riots when he had said: "The Egyptians are shocked by the scale and grave nature of the Brotherhood's mistakes."[5] Later, with the rioting at its peak, he said: "Dr. Mursi has become part of the problem and not the solution."[6]

Commentators now saw a civil war situation in the country and even the possibility of an armed forces intervention, effecting another regime change in the country, wrought by the same forces that had unseated Mubarak two years ago. Elias Harfouche provided the most sober and severe indictment of the rule of the Brotherhood in Egypt:

> The Egyptian Revolution was supposed to mend the rifts in society between the former president and those benefiting from his rule on the one hand, and the remaining sectors of society. The hope was that the Revolution would unify most Egyptians behind the same aims and aspirations, regardless of their political affiliations, religious creeds, and where they come from. What happened, however, was a monopoly over power despite the tiny majority by means of which power was gained. The road to dialogue was blocked and religion was used as a political cover with the aim of declaring those who disagreed with the regime as 'apostates'.[7]

The deep polarisation in the country throughout President Morsi's one-year rule culminated in the ouster of his government by Egypt's armed forces on July

3, 2013, the suspension of the constitution, and the arrest and incarceration of the Brotherhood's leadership.

Not only did the military rule end Egypt's brief encounter with democratic politics, it also had an immediate impact on the regional strategic scenario. The GCC countries, with the exception of Qatar, welcomed the change and promised to extend generous financial support to the regime. On the other hand, the coup led to Egypt's estrangement with Qatar, Turkey and Iran, which had had good ties with Morsi's government.

The other countries in the Arab world that experienced regime change or armed insurrection, such as Libya, Yemen and Syria, continue to be in turmoil. Two monarchies, Kuwait and Jordan, that had gone in for elections but without the principal opposition parties (mainly Islamist in both cases), are witnessing agitations against the royal family—sponsored national assemblies that have emerged from restrictive electoral laws, though for now the leaderships have succeeded in maintaining domestic order.

The UAE has strongly struck back at the Brotherhood elements, both national and foreign, in its polity, while Saudi Arabia's apparent calm camouflages simmering sectarian tensions and burgeoning dissent from an activist clergy (the Sahwa)[8] in association with non-religious liberal elements.

The broad trends in the principal areas of contemporary Islamist discourse are examined in the following paragraphs.

Islamist Parties

Oliver Roy has made the astute observation that, after the Arab Spring, Islamism and democracy had become interdependent and "neither can now survive without the other."[9] This is because Islamists can maintain their legitimacy in the political process only through elections, even as the democratic process in the Arab world cannot be consolidated without the participation of the mainstream Islamic groups. He is confident that participation in the democratic political process will give the Islamists experience of governance and will in due course blunt some of their slogan-based posturing. In fact, even two decades before the Arab Spring, Islamist groups, frequently in exile, had already begun to move towards democracy and human rights, recognising that "democracy was a better tool to fight dictatorship than the call for either jihad or sharia."[10]

The electoral success of Islamist groups as against that of their liberal/leftwing opponents is the result of their long history of active presence at the national and local levels, albeit in an oppositional situation but which provided them the opportunities to consolidate grassroots presence and establish close ties with local communities. Thus, after the toppling of authoritarian rulers, the Islamist groups were best placed for success in these first free elections since they had a sophisticated political apparatus in position, which included mobilisation networks, a clear political outlook, and a settled leadership and hierarchy.

At the same time, to enhance their allure, Islamist groups approached the electorate with the message of moderation, inclusiveness and openness, even conveying their readiness to work with non-Islamic groups. They were reassuring in the social area as well, particularly with regard to the interests of women and ethnic and religious minorities. Above all, they made very effective use of traditional and new media: well before the uprisings, the Islamists had begun to make extensive use of social network platforms as also their own TV channels. Their leaders were also active on the important regional channels such as *Al Jazeera* and *Al Arabiya*.[11]

However, both the Brotherhood and Al-Nahda faced serious difficulties in government. They had no previous experience of governance—lacking qualified human resources, vision, leadership, and a national development agenda. Above all, they failed to build a national consensus around their parties by pursuing enlightened accommodative policies.

The early electoral success of Islamist groups had obviously raised concerns regarding the nature of the state and society that would emerge under their leaders, who had had no experience of governance. Naturally, the Islamist groups are expected to insist on a central role for Islam in the reformed polity. However, as Oliver Roy asserts, this core commitment need not necessarily result in an Islamic state.[12] Islam, he believes, defines the national identity and imbues in the Islamic political leaders the need to espouse traditional values. However, these values are not likely to be projected as Islamic, but as those that have their basis in public order, public health or decency. In short, a "conservative modernisation of public life", articulated in terms of universal moral values, can be expected over the long- term. Not surprisingly, such an approach could, in due course lead to the separation of religious and civil institutions. In any case, the continued competition between different Islamic groups, particularly the tradition ulema, the Salafi[13] groups and the Brotherhood, will ensure that no single entity will enjoy a monopoly of influence in the religious field.[14]

The main contest in the nascent political order is likely to be between the mainstream Islamist parties and their more hardline Salafi cousins.

Most Sunni-majority countries have some Salafi streams, though their strength varies widely from country to country: in Morocco it is estimated at 17,000; in Tunisia at 10,000; in Jordan at 7,000; while Egypt has the largest number, between 3-5 million.[15] Obviously, the Salafis have limited strength in the different countries relative to their mainstream competitors, and fewer still among them are likely to veer towards radicalism.

However, they have a high level of commitment to their agenda—that they share with the radicals- for the re-establishment of the "caliphate" and enforcement of the Sharia. Abdel Moneim Said suggests that, given propitious circumstances, the Salafi groups could easily become radicalised. According to him, the following pattern has characterised their evolution in the political order:

> When the state was strong, the Salafis created their bases under a cloak of piety and religious observance. As the authority of the state weakened due to the winds of the Arab Spring, they formed political parties that sought to seize control through democratic means, to be discarded once they were in power. Where the authority of the state was totally absent, they would turn to armed violence against the state and society. The situation is bleak, but it will become grimmer yet unless people open their eyes to the danger and do something about it.[16]

Besides such concerns relating to the Salafis, the liberal/left wing elements in the Arab polities are also aggrieved that, contrary to their assurances on the eve of elections, mainstream Islamist groups have not shown much interest in consensus-building by working constructively with non-Islamist parties. According to them, the mainstream parties are pursuing a relatively narrow Islamic discourse and are seeking both to islamicise the state and retain monopoly over power for themselves.[17]

The failures of Morsi and al-Nahda do not mark the end of Islamist politics in a democratic order. However, in coming years the content and contours of its discourse will be multi-faceted and go through numerous mutations, in an environment where mainstream Islamist parties will have to compete with their more radical Salafi cousins on the right and secular-liberal elements on the left. This competitive democratic politics will demand both accommodativeness and flexibility from the Islamist parties while mobilising varied constituencies and in their vision and agenda for governance. This period when the Islamists are out of power should be used, not to hone visions and weapons of vengeance, but to reflect on past errors and prepare blueprints for mobilisation and governance in a democratic order.

Radical Islam

Abdul Bari Atwan, who published the Al-Qaeda's "Strategy to the year 2020", in *Al-Quds Al-Arabi*, in March 2005, says that Al-Qaeda appears to have met with considerable success in realising its agenda.[18] Its strategic vision had consisted of: widespread confrontation between Western and jihadi forces; the debilitating impact of this conflict on Western economies, and the overthrow of the hated Arab dictators, followed by the establishment of an Islamic caliphate across West Asia. This would culminate in an apocalyptic struggle between the "crusaders" and the believers, ending in the final defeat of the former and the establishment of the "Global Islamic Caliphate".

Given this vision, it is not surprising that, after some initial hesitation, both

Osama bin Laden and Ayman Al-Zawahiri welcomed the Arab Spring. In April 2011, bin Laden celebrated the "unprecedented opportunities" offered by the Arab Spring and the success of the Islamist parties. He urged the jihadis to be "patient and deliberate" and not engage in confrontations with Islamic groups. He pointed out: "A sizeable element within the Muslim Brotherhood and those like them hold the Salafi Doctrine...so their return to true Islam is only a matter of time, Allah willing." Al-Zawahiri saw the uprisings as "the Blessed Revolutions". The Al-Qaeda mouthpiece, *Inspire,* described the Arab Spring events as the "Tsunami of Change", and said that the Arab Spring "has proved that Al-Qaeda's rage is shared by the millions of Muslims across the world." Anwar Al-Awlaki, the spokesman of Al-Qaeda in the Arabian Peninsula (AQAP) based in Yemen, described the uprisings as an "avalanche" which would open "great doors of opportunity for the mujahideen all over the world."[19]

Atwan is of the view that the Spring provides valuable opportunities to Al-Qaeda:[20]

- Al-Qaeda welcomes the emerging confrontation between the liberals and mainstream Islamist groups, being convinced that this would yield weak governments and clear the path for itself and its affiliates.
- Similarly, the failure of mainstream Islamist groups to provide effective governance and reform would also discredit them, paving the way for an extremist upsurge.
- On the other hand, if the Islamist groups were to be denied full access to power through elections, there would again be an extremist upsurge, as had occurred in Algeria, in the early 1990s.
- Finally, the burgeoning sectarian divide between Shia and Sunni, which is in accord with Al-Qaeda's own views would also benefit the radical groups.

So far, the Al-Qaeda and its affiliates have been most successful in failed or failing states, where the central authority is either non-functional or is extremely vulnerable, so that the security apparatus and normal political and economic life in these states have collapsed or are very fragile. Thus, these movements have been most effective in Afghanistan, Iraq, Somalia, Yemen, Libya and Mali. In Pakistan, too, the central authority has been non-effective, in that, major players in state structures, particularly in the security apparatus, have actively supported the proliferation of radical groups and/or have failed to suppress them when called upon to do so. In the face of this governmental pusillanimity, large areas of Pakistan, particularly the tribal areas on the Pak-Afghan border, have become important sanctuaries for radical forces. These sanctuaries have mutual support connections with the Taliban in Afghanistan.

The symbiotic Al-Qaeda–Taliban relationship had been cemented between bin Laden and Mullah Omar, sometime in 1998, when bin Laden announced he had sworn *bayat* (allegiance) to Mullah Omar, the Amir of the Faithful. Later, all the other principal leaders of Al-Qaeda and its affiliates had similarly sworn *bayat* to Mullah Omar.[21] The heart of jihadi activity today is the alliance between the Taliban, Al-Qaeda and the Tehrik-e-Taliban-Pakistan (TTP). The Haqqani network, which has a presence on both sides of the Pak–Afghan border, maintains close ties with the Afghan Taliban and has encouraged the rise of the TTP in Pakistan. "Al-Qaeda Central" remains in Pakistan, with a strong presence in Yemen where it is referred to as "Al-Qaeda in the Arabian Peninsula" (AQAP), with Saudi and Yemeni membership. It keeps itself well-informed about the activities of various Al-Qaeda-oriented groups in different parts of the world, though it maintains varying degrees of association with them. As Atwan has noted, "there is the congratulatory nod, the wholehearted support, the expression of commonality, an alliance and, for some groups, the full-scale merger."[22]

It appears that for a group to move up the scale, in terms of its affiliation with "Al-Qaeda Central", it should manifest the ability to carry out effective and lethal assaults on "strategic" targets. Both Osama Bin Laden and Al Zawahiri had been deeply unhappy with Al-Zarqawi's mindless violence in Iraq as also his wanton assaults on the Shias.[23] Earlier, they had had similar reservations about GIA's extensive violence in Algeria. A top Al-Qaeda leader had then said:

> [In] Algeria, between 1994 and 1995, when [the GIA] was ...on the verge of taking over the government...they destroyed themselves with their own hands with their lack of reason, delusions, ignoring the people, their alienation of them through oppression, deviance and severity, coupled with a lack of kindness, sympathy and friendliness.[24]

Arab states, such as Syria and Libya, where political structures have collapsed after the Arab Spring, have attracted a large number of Al-Qaeda militia, whose intervention could mean either, that the Al-Qaeda will play a larger role in the political order that emerges there, or, failing that, it will continue to promote turbulence and chaos in the country. It has been seen that, when the Arab Spring causes authoritarian regimes' collapse, the state splinters on tribal and clan lines, with specific areas being dominated by well-armed warlords, who divide the country and assert local autonomies. There are legitimate concerns that, at least in the short-term, a viable democratic process that would reconcile the various warring factions with incompatible agendas is unlikely to emerge in Yemen, Libya and post-Assad Syria, and that the countries would remain united and their sharp internal animosities blunted only under the authority of a radical grouping. In fact, Atwan believes that, after the Arab Spring, Al Zawahiri seems to be moderating his position to avoid alienating popular opinion, and further suggests that Al-Qaeda could in time even develop a political wing to become a more effective role-player in the prevailing regional scenario.[25]

Two prominent Arab observers, Mohammed Abu Rumman and Hasan Abu

Haniya, believe that Al-Qaeda has already commenced a process of "ideological adaptation" in terms of which some of Al-Qaeda's public positions have changed to reflect the new realities of the Arab world, without of course compromising on its fundamental beliefs. According to them, the "Ansar Al-Sharia" is the new more moderate face of Al-Qaeda. The setting up of Ansar Al-Sharia was announced in Yemen in April 2011 and is part of AQAP. From there, it has spread to Tunisia and Libya, where it has carried out the demolitions of Sufi tombs and shrines. Its "theorist" is the Mauritanian preacher, Abu Mundher Shanqeeti, who sees the Ansar as an instrument to impose Sharia and to compete with the mainstream and Salafist parties for popular support, while not participating in democratic politics. Without giving up on the Al-Qaeda's core demand for the setting up of an Islamic caliphate and the rejection of democracy, this new body could become a pressure group to persuade the mainstream Islamist parties in power as also Salafi groups to enforce the Sharia in their polities.[26]

Sectarian Divide

The deepening sectarian divide is one of the most pernicious results of the Arab Spring. On the Islamist side, it feeds into a long tradition of anti-Shiism in the Wahhabiya[27] sections of the Sahwa and radical Islamic traditions. Given that all the GCC countries have a Shia minority, the sectarian divide is a matter of grave concern since it threatens national unity and diminishes the prospects for political reform. If not stemmed quickly, the divide could lead to the increaseing radicalisation of Shia youth.[28] Sectarianism has been given a strident regional geopolitical value as well in terms of the Saudi/GCC *versus* Iran strategic rivalry across West Asia but most urgently in Syria, where the civil conflict is now firmly anchored in the sectarian divide.[29]

Even if the Al Assad regime in Syria were to fall in the near future, the aftermath in that deeply divided country can hardly be benign. What is certain is that, over the next two years or so, Syria will be the battleground between the mainstream Islamists led by the Muslim Brotherhood and the more radical elements represented by Jabhat Al-Nusra and its Iraq-based affiliate, the Islamic State of Iraq and (Greater) Syria, ISIS.

The Arab Monarchies

In Jordan and Morocco, the rulers are likely to promote a monarchy-sponsored reform agenda, in the hope of retaining control over the political process, so that the agitations led by mainstream Islamists do not topple their regimes, with street support. Both regimes are under considerable stress and the outcome of their attempts to manage political matters cannot be safely predicted.

The leaders of the GCC believe their political order is resilient because it is in tune with popular aspirations, while the leaderships themselves have access to sufficient financial resources to discourage agitations for significant reform. However, this scenario could change. Thus, a UAE-based political commentator, Mishaal Al-Gergawi, has pointed out that some of the GCC regimes "evoke specific ethnic and pre-state alliances" to justify the legitimacy of their rule, while others invoke a specific interpretation of Islam to obtain legitimacy.[30] He believes that all of these bases of legitimacy have serious shortcomings, in that, they privilege small groups in the national order and exclude several others, both in terms of familial or ethnic groups or exclusivist religious groupings. Al-Gergawi concludes:

> The notion of constitutional legitimacy served Kuwait well in its hour of need. And while it is unlikely that other Gulf States could suffer its fate [i.e. the ongoing political crises], the Gulf Co-operation Council as a whole faces daunting political, economic and social challenges in this decade. It will need all the unity it can get, and *only the singular upholding of constitutions can recognize all citizens as individuals—regardless of sect, race or any other divisible factor—and unite them as such.* (Emphasis added.)

Given its very different history of political participation, from the rest of the GCC, Kuwait can be expected to break ranks in the near future. The confrontation between the Amir and parliamentary members, with the leitmotif of elections and parliamentary dissolution, is not sustainable, particularly when parliamentarians have begun to mobilise street support. In this context, it would appear that a move towards constitutional monarchy in Kuwait in the next few years cannot be ruled out.[31]

In Oman, the public agitations in the Sultanate in early 2011, the heightened political consciousness of the people and the accommodative approach of the ruler, would suggest that participatory politics could become a reality in the near future.

The situation in Bahrain continues to be grave and uncertain, with indications that at least some sections of the royal family favour entering into a dialogue with the Shia-majority opposition, and would countenance a degree of political change. It would appear that some degree of reform is possible within a two-three year time frame.

Saudi Arabia has shown remarkable flexibility and dexterity in handling the challenges it has had to face over the last fifty years or so. Thus, in the 1960s, its rulers used the services of the Muslim Brotherhood to counter the secular allure of Nasser. Later, faced with the challenge of the Islamic revolution in Iran, it gave full support to the "global jihad" in Afghanistan, shedding its quietist character in support of Islamic activism on the regional and global stage. After the events of 9/11, domestically, its leaders turned against the ulema and the education system shaped by them, and appeared to support a liberal Islamic agenda that included political participation and wide-ranging social and cultural reform, and even some overtures to the marginalised Shia. The King initially seemed to support the criticisms of the Wahhabi order by the "Awakening Sheikhs", but came down heavily upon them and their Brotherhood mentors when their demands came to include political change, including a constitutional monarchy. In short, the Kingdom has repeatedly exhibited the ability to correct course swiftly and make dramatic U-turns whenever the interests of the royal family and the state so demand.

As of now, Saudi Arabia seems to be confident about its ability to weather the fallout of the Arab Spring. In this challenging period, the royal family has turned to its traditional bastion of support, the Wahhabi establishment, and is extending political and financial support for the augmentation of its authority in the country's social, cultural and educational domains. This obviously contradicts the king's avowed desire to accommodate the modernist aspirations of his people, particularly the young, and to project the country as a moderate, accommodative and attractive partner for regional and international engagement. The Kingdom has so far managed this contradiction by robustly challenging Iran and its "hegemonic" intentions.

But, under this façade of bravado and self-confidence, certain fragilities are apparent: the leadership has to manage the twin challenges of maintaining the unity of the royal family and the strident demands of the ulema, while accommodating the expectations of the people, many of whom are anxious for change. But, can their dissatisfaction translate into the organised dissent that would pull people out on to the streets in a collective popular demand for change? There is no evidence to support this. In the alternative, could some modicum of change trickle down from the top, as the monarch or his successor, with the consensual support of senior royal family members, initiates a programme of systematic political reform? This seems to be the most likely scenario, but it would have to contend with elements in the Wahhabi establishment, both quietist and Sahwi, who would actively challenge any attempt to tamper with the unique Islamic character of their state order.[32]

The Regional Scenario

The Arab Spring has had a significant impact on the regional political order which today consists of the following aspects:

(i) a deepening sectarian divide, resulting from Saudi Arabia's challenge to Iran's influence in the region, which has domestic implications for each GCC country and broader regional geopolitical implications;
(ii) GCC support to the military regime in Egypt, with Qatar staying aloof;
(iii) continued hostility between Egypt and Iran paralleling the Saudi-Iran estrangement and improving ties between Turkey and Iran; and
(iv) dramatic changes in the regional scenario following the thaw in US-Iran ties in November 2013.

The Saudi-Iran Competition

The ongoing turmoil in most countries of the Arab world has been complicated by the larger geopolitical competition between Saudi Arabia and Iran that has religious, ideological, political and military dimensions, as well as regional and global implications.

In the context of demands for reform in Bahrain, which has a substantial Shia population, Saudi Arabia moved quickly to play the sectarian card. The uprising in Bahrain was attributed to Iranian "interference", after which Saudi Arabia geared itself to confront the Iranian presence and influence in different theatres in West Asia. This confrontation with Iran was given an ethnic and sectarian hue, which was reflected in the Saudi and sections of the Gulf media. Thus, in response to the Iranian Shoura Council's National Security Committee's demand for the withdrawal of Saudi troops from Bahrain, *Al-Watan* in its editorial said:

> Iran has ignored the realities of its intervention into the affairs of the region, its attempts to ignite sedition and its hostile policies, brushing aside international laws and good neighbourly principles. Since this state came into existence, Saudi leaders have been keen on non-intervention into affairs of others. Similarly, they have never allowed others to intervene into their affairs.[33]

Al-Madinah, in its editorial, applauded the unified position taken by the GCC at the Foreign Minister's Conference in Riyadh, in April 2011, saying that this had blocked Tehran's attempts to disturb the region, while contributing to the restoration of peace and stability in Bahrain.[34] *Okaz* commented that Iran had been continuously pursuing the policies of expansionism, i.e., by occupying the islands belonging to UAE; encouraging sectarianism in Bahrain, and, more recently, using spy cells in Kuwait to undermine the leadership there.[35]

This strident tone of the Saudi media was echoed in other sections of the Gulf media as well. Thus, the distinguished Kuwaiti editor, Ahmad Jarallah, said in *Arab Times*, that the Iranian regime "has become a viral disease attacking all countries except those supporting its ideologies or (those) in its bondage."[36] Recalling the pernicious role of Iran in encouraging sectarianism in Iraq, Lebanon and Yemen, Jarallah said:

> Iran's relationship with GCC nations is on the brink of collapse, because the regime has been pushing the region towards an armed offensive, thinking it is the region's power bloc in control of the situation.

This aggressive posture continued all through 2012. In May 2012, an editorial in the Saudi *Al-Watan* said:

> Quite simply, the Iranian nuclear program is proceeding as the leadership in Tehran wishes. It is based on the dream of reviving the Persian Empire and reinstating its control over the region, subjecting its nations by force to

> an agenda that is no longer secret to anyone. This agenda is based on territorial/confessional [Shiite] expansionism, digging up the past from its grave in the service of this expansionist policy.
>
> The Iranian project in the region is no longer a secret. Even if it assumes different forms and adopts various guises such as 'backing the resistance against Israel' it ultimately aims at ensuring Tehran's control over the so-called 'Shiite Crescent'. This is the prelude to taking over the rest of the region—something that the region's states and nations should be wary of.[37]

The Arab Spring has thus set the stage for a fundamental transformation in existing postures and alliances, sharpening the edge of intra-regional competition and creating opportunities for the restructuring of the old West Asian order, primarily on sectarian lines.

The principal area of conflict, however, is Syria. In the early days of the Syrian uprising, the Saudi agenda was quite modest: the Kingdom saw the ferment as an opportunity for far-reaching reform in the Syrian political order or, failing that, regime change, either of which would serve to break the longstanding strategic ties between Damascus and Tehran. Thus, the Saudi commentator Tariq Al-Homaid wrote in *Ashraq Al-Aswat* that, in Syria "the time for reform has come."[38] He added that, "repression may buy the regime-any regime—more time; but it will not rescue it", and went on to say that:

> The time has come for Damascus to pay greater attention to its domestic affairs and work seriously on providing decisive solutions on the issues of political parties and the peaceful transfer of power. A republic remains a republic. There is no magical solution for this predicament.

Again, the position taken by the government of Nouri Al-Maliki on the developments in Syria evoked serious criticism in Saudi Arabia, which saw in this posture, another evidence of sectarianism. Tariq Al-Homaid said that the present regime was "worse and more dangerous than Saddam Hussain's Iraq" since it was based on a "detestable sectarianism and its export." According to him, "the events in Syria (and in Bahrain before that) have proven that the Iraqi regime has less to do with democracy and more to do with sectarianism and the establishment of Shiite rule."[39]

The Syrian conflict quickly acquired a sectarian character with the Assad regime mobilising support by projecting a threat to Älawite power in the country, while Saudi Arabia nöw "discovered" the Shia character of the Alawi regime in Damascus. Regime-change now became the principal Saudi demand, in the expectation that an emerging Sunni-dominated administration would detach Syria from Iran, thus denying Iran an access to the Mediterranean and tó its protégé, the Hezbollah in Lebanon, a double strategic advantage for the Kingdom. Thus, over the last year, the Saudi-Iran competition has played out most viciously in Syria, where over a hundred thousand people have been killed, millions have become refugees, and historic cities and shrines have been destroyed. Islamist militias, consisting of Brotherhood, Salafi and Al-Qaeda elements, fight each other with the same ferocity they use against government forces, with no possibility of any side emerging victorious. Following the use of chemical weapons in August 2013, the US and Russia have now begun to work together to pursue a political solution, a daunting task given the Saudi and the rebels insistence on regime change and Assad's refusal to abdicate under "terrorist" pressure.

The Saudi/UAE—Brotherhood Estrangement and Support for the Coup

Saudi estrangement from the Brotherhood, that became public in 2002, with the strident criticism of the Brotherhood by then interior minister, Prince Naif bin Abdul Aziz, has yet not been bridged; in fact, in the wake of the Arab Spring, as the Brotherhood in Egypt and its affiliates in other countries obtained political power, the distance between the Brotherhood and the Kingdom became greater. This was clearly seen in the hostility with which commentators wrote about the Brotherhood and the Morsi government in the Saudi and other sections of the GCC media and the two pan-Arab Saudi-owned papers, *Al Hayat* and *Asharq al-Aswat.* In fact, the non-Saudi pan-Arab paper, the liberal *Al Quds Al-Arabi,* in an editorial said that Saudi Arabia had given "a green light to some of its commentators to publish a series of articles attacking the Muslim Brotherhood harshly, accusing them of ingratitude and trying to topple certain regimes."[40]

The Saudi-Brotherhood divide has deep ideological moorings: while both occupy the common space of Salaf, the (selectively) "quietest" aspect of Wahhabiya is entirely at odds with the robust activism of the Brotherhood in the political domain. Again, the Al-Saud see Wahhabiya as the basis of their legitimacy both as rulers and as the "Guardians of the two Holy Mosques"; while the Brotherhood has a political agenda that is much broader in content and geographical space. As the Saudi experience of the Sahwa movement has shown, the Brotherhood has been able to engender a movement at the heart of the Wahhabi establishment that poses a real challenge to the monopoly of power that the Al-Saud enjoy on their own home turf. The recent activism of the Sahwa in the aftermath of the Arab Spring in the Kingdom, the emergence of its liberal elements who are espousing constitutional monarchy and democratic rights, and their active association with Shia activists on a common platform of reform; all of these developments have convinced the Al-Saud that the Brotherhood poses a threat to its domestic order and its regional influence.

Abdul Bari Atwan, editor of *Al-Quds Al-Arabi*, has pointed out that the GCC nations had every reason to feel vulnerable in the face of the electoral successes of the Brotherhood, and referred specifically to the following:

(i) the Brotherhood was now a global organisation;

(ii) it had considerable influence among the GCC youth whom it had mentored earlier in local educational institutions;
(iii) it was well-funded; and
(iv) its links with Islam gave it a strong base of support among the local population.[41]

But, there was a major crack in the usually solid phalanx of the GCC-Qatar. Both Arab and Western observers watched with some bemusement as Qatar strode robustly on the regional stage, "bankrolling a new generation of Islamists across the "Middle East", while showing "eagerness to retain influence in the West."[42] Commentators were unable to figure out the motive force behind Qatar's activism: in Libya, it was seen supporting Islamist factions over the liberal transitional government; it had links with the radical Al-Shabaab in Somalia, and, above all, it was most active in backing the Brotherhood elements in the Syrian uprising, though there were even suggestions that some of its military aid could be going to more extremist groups.[43]

One explanation for the role of Qatar, came from a Nigerian diplomat who said: "They want to be seen as a big player, an important player that is respected and willing to bring peace to distant lands."[44] James Dorsey made the interesting point that Qatar, a Wahhabi state, in fact "offers young Saudis a vision of a conservative Wahhabi society that is less constrained and permits individuals, irrespective of gender, greater control over their lives".[45] Whatever the explanation, Qatar certainly caused some exasperation in Saudi Arabia. The Saudi columnist, Tariq al-Homaid, commenting on Qatar's cosy ties with the Brotherhood in Egypt, categorically asserted that: "Backing a particular current in Egypt at the expense of another is tantamount to sabotage."[46] Al-Homaid was also truly puzzled because:

> For one thing, Qatari society is Salafi and follows the school of Sheikh Mohammed bin Abdelwahab, and more so than many people believe. And this renders Qatar's backing for the Brotherhood in the media and in political terms genuinely surprising and strange. Moreover, this is taking place not only in Egypt, Libya, and Tunisia, but also in Syria, Jordan, and as mentioned earlier, in certain Gulf States—in fact, in states where no Brotherhood presence was known before.

The change of the Amir in Qatar at the end of June 2013 and the fall of the Morsi government a week later have over-turned the regional scenario, so that, Saudi Arabia is now playing the lead political and economic role in Egypt (and Syria) even as Qatar has lost its high profile influence in GCC and regional affairs.

A Kuwaiti writer, commenting on the "plots" in the UAE with which the Brotherhood is said to be linked, bemoaned the absence of a "unified strategy" among the GCC countries in spite of the serious threat to them: While Saudi

Arabia was cautious and watchful; Kuwait had to take into account its own Brotherhood-affiliated political party, the Constitutional Islamic Movement; while Qatar was host to the Brotherhood's very public figure, the cleric Sheikh Yusuf Al-Qaradawi, even as its government supported the forces of political Islam in different parts of the Arab world Libya, Tunisia, Egypt and Syria.[47]

Egypt-Iran Ties

The GCC's ideological divide from the Brotherhood and its increasing political distance from Egypt, had set the stage for Egypt and Iran, to come closer to each other. These ties were given a boost by the January 2013 visit to Cairo by the then Iranian foreign minister, Ali Akbar Salehi, who was known for "his well-measured statements and composed demeanour", besides being a fluent Arabic speaker.[48] This was followed by the visit of President Ahmadinejad to Cairo in early February 2013, for the OIC summit—the first visit by an Iranian President since 1979. As expected, these visits and the general warming of Egypt-Iran ties caused considerable unhappiness in the GCC.

Several GCC commentators noted with concern that Iran could be assisting Egypt in setting up a cadre for the Brotherhood on the lines of its own Islamic Revolutionary Guard Corps (IRGC). This news perhaps originated, in a British paper which reported that the head of the IRGC, Major General Kassem Suleimani, had paid a secret visit to Cairo at the end of December 2012, though several sources on both sides asserted that the visit had not taken place and no such plan was being pursued.[49]

The GCC commentators gave a hostile response to the foreign minister's visit as well. *Asharq al-Aswat's* Ahmad Othman wrote somewhat confusingly that the Egypt-Iran rapprochement was bringing together a party that sought "to re-establish the Persian Empire's hegemony over the Arab countries, and a group [the Brotherhood] that aims to recreate the Caliphate in order to bring there some countries under its control."[50] Ahmad Youssef Ahmad, writing in the Abu Dhabi-based *Al-Ittihad* said, that the Iranians were offering "generous economic aid to Egypt with the secret aim of sabotaging relations between Egypt and the UAE."[51]

Relations between Iran and the Brotherhood go back to the 1950s when Iranian religious figures, who gained prominence during the Islamic revolution, had first met Brotherhood leaders in Cairo in 1954; these links continued in later years. Sayyid Qutb's writings were translated into Persian and were very popular. There has been considerable overlap between the Brotherhood and the Iranian religious establishments, in that, both accept the leadership of a "supreme guide" and the practice of *taqiyya* (religious dissimulation) to avoid persecution; they both support elections and the rule of the Sharia, with oversight by the clergy. As Hassan Hassan has pointed out, we should draw a distinction between the ideology and the organisation of the Brotherhood, in that, while its members reflect a wide variety of views on religious matters, from extreme Salafi to moderate, as an *organisation* the Brotherhood takes a very cautious position on sectarian matters, thus facilitating its ties with Iran.[52]

The Arab Spring, which aggravated the sectarian divide because of the Saudi-Iranian rivalry, seemed to have, simultaneously served to bridge this divide, to some extent, by bringing together Iran and Egypt under Morsi. Morsi's rejection of the sectarian approach was a breath of fresh air in the fraught West Asian scenario, and was at that time seen as a possible precursor of a "post-sectarian foreign policy"[53] that would challenge the primacy accorded to the sectarian wedge by Saudi Arabia. However, the ouster of the Morsi government and Saudi assertiveness against Iran in Egypt and Syria have meant that sectarianism remains the principal factor in the regional divide, with little evidence that the two Islamic giants are willing to re-engage politically to stem the tide of violence and stabilise the region.

US-Iran Thaw: Regional Implications

The West Asia-North Africa (WANA) region had barely come to terms with the coup in Egypt and the heightened violence in Syria (with the strong possibility of a US military intervention) when, on the sidelines of the UN General Assembly session in September 2013 there was a palpable thaw in US-Iran ties, culminating in a telephone conversation between Presidents Obama and Rouhani. This was quickly followed by Iran concluding an interim agreement on the nuclear issue with the P5+1 countries in November 2013.

The US-Iran engagement has the potential to change the regional strategic scenario, with the US's traditional allies, Israel and Saudi Arabia, feeling betrayed and isolated, and fearful of an enhanced Iranian role in West Asia. Saudi Arabia's entire strategy of keeping the Arab Spring at bay by demonising Iran and confronting it across the region now faces a serious challenge. While Saudi Arabia's first reactions have been petulant (i.e., refusing to speak at the UNGA and rejecting its hard-won UN Security Council seat), it is quite likely that the Kingdom will soon revert to its traditional pragmatism, and, realising the utter futility of the ongoing sectarian and strategic competitions with Iran, will respond to Iranian overtures and seek an engagement with the Islamic Republic to address matters of common interest such as: the sectarian divide, the renewed challenge from radical Islam, pursuit of regional security through credible and consensually accepted confidence-building measures, and the issue of shared energy-related challenges in the face of the shale revolution in the US.

Conclusion

The principal competition in the domestic arena among the WANA countries is between the mainstream Islamist parties and the Salafi groups that are seeking to occupy the space vacated by the increasingly moderate mainstream parties.

Both the mainstream Islamist and Salafi parties will continue to be challenged by the jihadi vision and activist programme of the Al-Qaeda. As its recent penetration in Northwest Africa has shown, it will send in its cadres wherever it senses fragility and internal dissonance in a state system.

At the regional level, the situation is more complex. Saudi-Iranian competition has exacerbated regional insecurity, already a matter of concern due to Iran's nuclear ambitions and its political and military influence across West Asia. While this competition could stem the tide of the Arab Spring in the GCC countries, the price to be paid over the long term, in the form of a burgeoning sectarian divide, promises to be quite high. This will have immediate implications for the future of polities in Iraq, Lebanon and post-Assad Syria, but it will over time also poison the national order within the GCC countries themselves. As the Moroccan writer, Hicham Ben Abdullah El-Alaoui has said:

> The confrontation between Sunni and Shia will be crucial to the future. However much it may be manipulated from outside, it is a clash which is likely to multiply the fault lines and cloud the horizon of the Arab Spring.[54]

Institutionalising Democracy

Two years after the Arab Spring, several commentators in the Arab world had written with dismay about how the Arab Spring had been "hijacked" by Islamic parties, which had in fact played a relatively marginal role in the demonstrations that brought down the Arab potentates. There are grim forebodings that the spring of hope would become (or had already become) the winter of despair. They feared that the Arab world, excluded for several decades from the promise and structures of freedom and dignity, would now slide back into the miasma of authoritarianism, this time under the dictatorship of "Islam" and its votaries, shaped on the lines of the early Muslim "caliphate" or even on the Iranian theocratic model—the nightmare rule of the Mullahs.[55] Now that the Brotherhood has been replaced by military rule in Egypt, and in Tunisia the Al-Nahda has been replaced by an apolitical technocratic government, do these seemingly bleak scenarios have a silver lining?

The concerns relating to Islamists in power display an inadequate understanding of the significant changes taking place across WANA. The Arab Spring is an expression of the collective will of the Arab people to re-order their polity and recover their dignity so that they no longer have to live under authoritarian rulers who have thus far subordinated national interest to personal and Western advantage. No part of the Arab world is excluded from this aspiring "collective will": indeed, most Arab writers in the early days of the Spring saw the WANA countries as an integrated whole, experiencing the same political, economic and cultural malaise, and seeking the same freedom and dignity in reformed democratic polities.

Though Islamist movements today are under siege, given the pervasive religious ethos across the Arab world, there can be little doubt that they will continue to be significant role-players when normal democratic politics re-surfaces in the region. Hence, not surprisingly, the principal challenge before the region in the aftermath of the Spring has been to replace the mindsets and institutions of the authoritarian era with the values and structures of a functioning democratic system based on Islamic rules and principles. It should be noted that the emerging state order is already "civil" since there is no institutionalised rule of the clergy, as in Iran. Again, the Islamic movement is not, and has never been, a monolith, so that no single party or grouping in the state order can:(i) claim a monopoly over "Islam" in terms of its principles, values and institutions; (ii) decide what aspects of Islam's historic texts should be influential in contemporary affairs and who should decide and pronounce on this; and, above all, (iii) determine what aspects of the Arabs' encounter with the West over 200 years should find a place in the new order. These and other issues will remain subjects of debate *within* the Islamic family as the national constitutions are formulated and democratic institutions are given concrete shape. These intra-Islam debates will also have to accommodate the views of liberals, both within and outside the Islamic order as part of the national consensus.

Commentators, Arab and Western, who see the ongoing domestic political competitions in terms of liberal *versus* traditional, or, more specifically, secular *versus* Islamic, are on the wrong track. As Tariq Ramadan has pointed out, the historical experience of Western and Arab societies in regard to secularism has been quite different. While in Western political evolution, secularism meant democracy and religion pluralism, in the Arab world, secularisation "became identified with the threefold experience of repression, colonialism and assault on Islam."[56] While the Arab authoritarian regimes projected themselves as separating state and religion and upholding women's rights, they were:

> in reality...dictatorial regimes. There was no alliance of democracy and pluralism in the name of separation of religion and state; religion was subjected to the state, with no democracy and no pluralism.[57]

Beyond the fact that, even in the West the "no public sphere is entirely culturally and religiously neutral,"[58] the Islamic *versus* secular debate in this context is quite unnecessary, since Islamic law has consistently distinguished between *ibadat* (worship) and *muamalat* (public or social matters): rules in respect of the former are eternal and immutable, while the latter are always subject to review, on the basis of the well-established Islamic principle of *ijtihad* and the process of *Shura*(consultation). Numerous scholars with different political orientations, both medieval and modern, have upheld this important aspect of Islam. Thus, the recourse to Islam, in this period of political transition, as Ramadan asserts, can provide the "means to liberate minds through the acquisition of knowledge, autonomous rationality, critical thinking and freedom of thought: the very definition of pluralism, responsible citizenship and of civil society..."[59]

Three years is too short a period to judge the content, direction and resilience of revolutions. Almost all revolutions and revolutionary efforts are painful, both those that effect change and those where change is thwarted. The old order remains under threat while the new order that emerges is rarely representative of the totality of the forces that brought about the change and is usually unable to build a consensus in the short-term. It also has little experience of governance or even of deal-making that constitutes the stuff of politics. And, of course, all its mistakes and they are many, are magnified, not least by the vestiges of the old order that seek a restoration, however misguided their aspirations might be. Three years ago, the French intellectual, Jean-Pierre Filiu had already warned us that:

> This Arab revolution will suffer backlashes, betrayals, defeats and vicious repression. Once the initial enthusiasm fades away, this uprising and its actors will be slandered, vilified and caricatured. Even if its most radical demands are to be fulfilled in the political arena, the rehabilitation of governance will be only part of a daunting challenge to cope with the deficits in the labour market, in the housing sector or in the public infrastructure.[60]

The principal point to be noted is that, following the Spring, the Arabs' "wall of fear" has been pulled down, and, though there might be several setbacks due to inexperience, short-sightedness or ineptitude, this tide will not be stemmed. The Arab revolution, as Filiu has said, is an "Arab Renaissance". [61]

NOTES

1. "Tunisia After the Spring", University of Tunis El-Manar-Brookings Joint Workshop, Event Summary, September 20, 2012, at: www.brookings.edu (Accessed on Jan 30, 2013)
2. Ibid.
3. Dr. Hamad al-Majid, "The Brotherhood's Mistake", *Asharq al-Awsat*, Jan 29, 2013, at: http://www.lebanonwire.com/1301MLN/13012903AWST.asp (Accessed on Jan 29, 2013)
4. Tariq Al-Homaid, "A Long Night for Egypt", *Asharq al-Awsat*, Jan 29, 2013, at: http://www.lebanonwire.com/1301MLN/13012905AWST.asp (Accessed on Jan 29, 2013)
5. Hassan Nafia, "Correcting the Course of Revolution", *Al-Masri al-Yawm*, translation at *Mideast Mirror*, Jan 24, 2013.
6. Hassan Nafia, "Veering towards chaos", *Al-Masri Al-Yawm*, translation in *Mideast Mirror*, Jan 29, 2013.
7. Elias Harfouche, *Al-Hayat*, translation in *Mideast Mirror*, Jan 29, 2013.
8. This movement, translated as "Awakening Sheikhs", emerged in Saudi Arabia in the 1980s as a result of the influence of Muslim Brotherhood intellectuals who at that time dominated the Saudi educational institutions. The Movement's leaders went public in the early 1990s with severe critiques of the Saudi political, economic, social and cultural order, and demanded wide ranging reform. It died away under state pressure in the late 1990s, but re-emerged a few years ago. For details see: Stephane Lacroix, *Awakening Islam—The Politics of Religious Dissent in Contemporary Saudi Arabia*, Harvard University Press, Cambridge, MA, 2011.

9. Olivier Roy, " The New Islamists", *Foreign Policy*, April 16, 2012, at: http://www.foreginpolicy.com/articles/2012/04/16/the_new_islamists?page=full(Accessed on December 13, 2012)
10. Ibid; for details of "Islamic Constitutionalism" in Egypt before the Arab Spring, see Charles E. Butterworth, "What do Egypt's Islamists Want?" in Mehrzad Boroujerdi, *Mirror for the Muslim Prince: Islam and the Theory of Statecraft*, Syracuse University Press, New York, 2013, p. 240-78.
11. A.E. Kadoussi, in his article "Islamist Resurgence and Arab Spring", *Islam and Politics*, July 16, 2012, at http://newageislam.com/Print.aspx?ID=7938 (Accessed on October 22, 2012), provides an excellent summary of the reasons that were responsible for the success of Islamist parties in the recent elections.
12. Olivier Roy, "2011 Raymond Aron Lecture: Interpreting the Arab Spring", *Brookings Institution*, December 13, 2011, p.7-8, at www.brookings.edu/in/media/events/2011/12/13/aronarabspring/20111213_arab_spring (Accessed on Dec 31, 2011).
13. This is derived from *Salaf*, "pious ancestors", and goes back to the first sources of Islam, the Quran and the Sunna, in order to reform or renew present-day Islamic belief and practice with the removal of aberrations and corruptions that have crept in over the years. For details see: Bernard Haykel, "On the Nature of Salafi Thought and Action", Roel Meijer (Ed.), *Global Salafism—Islam's New Religious Movement*, Hurst & Co., London, 2009, p. 33-57.
14. Roy no. 12, p. 14.
15. Will McCants, "A new salafi politics", *Foreign Policy*, October 13, 2012, at: http://lebanonwire.com/1210MLN/1201305FP.asp (Accessed October 21, 2012).
16. Abdel Moneim Said, "Salafist Spring", *Al-Ahram Weekly*, October 4-10, 2012, at http://weekly.ahram.org.eg/print/2012/1117/op9.htm (Accessed on October 23, 2012).
17. See for instance: Nathan Brown, "Can Egypt's Democratic Uprising Be Redeemed?", December 24, 2012 at: http://carnegieendowment.org/2012/12/24/can-egypt-s-democratic-uprising-be-redeemed/ewbv (Accessed December 26,2012); "Egypt building on sand", *The Guardian*, December 25,2012, at: http://www.lebanonwire.com/1212MLN/121222509GDN.asp (Accessed December 26, 2012);AlaaAswani, "The Practice of the Brotherhood and Salafists contradicts the teachings of Islam", *The National*, Abu Dhabi, December 27,2012.
18. Abdel Bari Atwan, *After Bin Laden – Al-Qaeda, the Next Generation*, Saqi Books, London, 2012, p. 12-13; for a summary of Al-Qaeda's vision and strategic thinking see Talmiz Ahmad, *Children of Abraham at War—The Clash of Messianic Militarisms*, Aakar Books, New Delhi, 2011, p. 270-74.
19. Atwan, no. 16, pp. 37, 58-60.
20. Ibid, pp. 37-38.
21. Ibid, p. 134.
22. Ibid, p. 177.
23. Ibid, p. 210.
24. Ibid, p. 172.
25. Ibid, pp. 264-65.
26. Mohammed Abu Rumman and Hasan Abu Haniya, "Ansar al-Sharia: Al-Qaeda's Response to Arab Spring", *Al-Monitor*, January 9, 2013, at: http://www.lebanonwire.com/130IMLN/13010910AM.asp (Accessed on January 13, 2013)
27. *Wahhabiya* refers to Islamic beliefs and practices advocated by Mohammed Ibn Abdul Wahhab, who flourished in the Najd area of the Arabian Peninsula in the 18th Century. Drawing inspiration from Ibn Taymiya, Ibn Abdul Wahhab sought a sweeping reform of Islam by insisting on *tawhid* (oneness of God) and getting rid of aberrations such as revering saints and worshipping at their tombs. His austere teachings constitute the state doctrine of the Kingdom of Saudi Arabia
28. Frederic Wehrey, "Shia Days of Rage" *Foreign Affairs*, December 10, 2012, at: http://

carnegieendowment.org/2012/12/10/shia-days-of-rage/essf(Accessed on December 20,2012); for the burgeoning sectarian divide in West Asia see: GeneiveAbdo, "The New Sectarianism: The Arab Uprisings and the Rebirth of the Shia-Sunni divide", Analysis Paper, Number 29, The Saban Centre for Middle East Policy at Brookings, April 2013;Talal Salman, "Arab World Enters Age of Sectarian Wars", June 9, 2013, http://www.al-monitor.com/pulse/politics/2013/06/arabism-fall-intra-arab-wars.html(Accessed on June11, 2013); RamzyBaroud, "Sectarianism and the Irrational Discourse: Why Arabs Must Worry", June 14, 2013, http://www.lebanonwire.com/1306MLN/13061412RB.asp (Accessed on June18, 2013); and David Gardner, "A schism in Islam is ripping the Middle East apart", *Financial Times*, June 15, 2013, http://www.lebanonwire.com/1306MLN/13061507FT.asp (Accessed on June 18, 2013).

29. In regard to the geopolitical aspects of the Syrian scenario, Steven Heydemann has noted: "Syria sits at the intersection of every major strategic axis in the Arab East. It is a key member of the strategic alliance linking Iran, Syria, and Hezbollah, with support from Iraq's Shia-dominated government in Baghdad. Syria is also deeply enmeshed in regional axes of competition and confrontation: between Turkey and Saudi Arabia for influence in the Levant; between Iran and the Gulf Cooperation Council (GCC) states; and between Turkey and Kurdish groups seeking greater autonomy from both Arab and Turkisg governments. Additionally, Syria is a long-term strategic ally of Russia and an equally long-term strategic adversary of the US."
(Steven Heydemann, "Syria's Uprising: sectarianism, regionalisation, and state order in the Levant", Fride and Hivos, 2013, p.3; www.fride.org/publication/1127 (Accessed on June 19, 2012);
Asserting the primacy of strategic competition in the Syrian conflict, Toby Matthiesen says: "Sayyida Zainab—a shrine whose status as a site of Shia religious pilgrimage was largely created in the 1980s and 1990s—lies at the heart of a strategic relationship between the Assad regime, Iran, and Arab Shia groups. This relationship uses religious symbols and sectarian language but it is driven far more by geo-strategic interests than faith. The various groups that profit from a further sectarianisation of the conflict, this time on the Shia side, are to blame. These include Iran, which is trying to re-establish its influence over all Shia political movements and groups, whether in the Gulf, in Iraq or elsewhere."
(Toby Mattheisan, "Syria Inventing a Religious War", newsletters@nybooks.com (June 18, 2013), p. 5.

30. Mishaal Al-Gergawi, "Gulf rulers should rely only on constitutional power", *Financial Times*, February 2, 2012.

31. Explaining the Kuwaiti political scenario, Shafiq Nazem al-Ghabra has pointed out:
"But the current impasse (in Kuwait) is linked to a series of changes that took place in Kuwait in the past decade. The mechanisms of social, political and cultural change have affected Kuwaiti society. Education, the growing population, and the effects of globalisation and social networking have jointly contributed to the emergence of new forces, consisting of the youth and their movements. Meanwhile, these contributed to the emergence of qualitative development in the tribal political role. The categories that previously refrained from openly claiming their rights became more determined to gain recognition of their rights. These categories include youth, tribes, Shiites, women, professional and business groups and different political groups."
"Thus, what used to be appropriate and acceptable in the 1960s is no longer appropriate in 2013, because the changes in the structure of Kuwaiti society both socially and in terms of education."
(ShafiqNazem al-Ghabra, "Kuwait's Coming Constitutional Revolution", *Al-Hayat*, June 6, 2013; English translation at http://www.al-monitor.com/pulse/politics/2013/06/kuwait-society-constitution-amendments.html (Accessed on June 11, 2013)

32. On the gradual passing of power to the next generation of the Saudi royal family, see: Bruce Riedel, "Saudi Arabia's Quiet Transition", *Al-Monitor*, June 5, 2013, http://www.al-monitor.com/pulse/originals/2013/06/saudi-arabia-succession.html (June 9, 2013); for some details of the dissident movement in Saudi Arabia, see: Frederic Wehrey, "A New Saudi Arabia?", http://carnegieendowment.org/2013/05/22/new-saudi-arabia/g5em (Accessed on May 23, 2013).
33. *Al-Watan*, April 2, 2011.
34. *Al-Madinah*, April 4, 2011.
35. *Okaz*, Riyadh, April 5, 2011
36. Ahmad Jarallah, *Arab Times*, Kuwait, April 4, 2011
37. *Al-Watan*, May 29, 2012
38. Tariq Al-Homaid, *Asharq Al-Awsat*, March 28, 2011
39. Ibid, April 27, 2011
40. *Al-Quds Al-Arabi*, translation in *Mideast Mirror*, January 17, 2013
41. Abdul Bari Atwan, "What's behind Gulf's Brotherhood moves?",*Al Quds Al-Arabi*, translationin *The National*, p. 15.
42. Colum Lynch, "Qatar's support for Islamists muddles its reputation as neutral broker in Mideast", *Washington Post*, Nov. 30, 2012, at: http://lebanonwire.com/1211MLN/12113002WP.asp (Accessed on Dec 6, 2012)
43. Ibid; Nicola Nasser, "Qatar and US: Collusion or Conflict of interests" at: http://www.lebanonwire.com/1301MLN/13012503MOL.asp (Accessed on Jan 30, 2013)
44. Colum Lynch, no. 42
45. James Dorsey, "Qatar's Challenge to Saudi Arabia: An alternative view of Wahhabism", *RSIS Commentaries*, No. 017/2013, dated January 30, 2013
46. Tariq al Homaid, "Qatar and the Brothers", *Asharq al-Awsat*, translation in *Mideast Mirror*, January 10, 2013.
47. Dr. Shamlan Yussef Al-Essa, *Al-Ittihad*, translation in *The National*, Jan 14, 2013.
48. Richard Javad Heydarian, "Iran tries charm-offensive in Cairo", Jan 18, 2013, at: http://www.atimes.com/atimes/printN.html (Accessed on Jan 20, 2013.)
49. Ahmad Youssef Ahmad, *Al-Ittihad*, Abu Dhabi, Translation in *Mideast Mirror*, Jan 16, 2013; Ahmad Eleiba, "Relative Values", *Al-Ahram Weekly*, Jan 16, 2013 at: http://weekly.ahram.org.eg/Print/1056.aspz (Accessed on Jan 22, 2013)
50. Ahmad Othman, "Common ground between Cairo and Tehran", *Asharq al-Awsat*, Translation in *Mideast Mirror*, Jan 14, 2013.
51. Ahmad Youssef Ahmad, no. 49.
52. Hassan Hassan, "Iran-Brotherhood Ties: rooted in history, with eye on future" *The National*, Abu Dhabi, Jan 15, 2013, p. 14.
53. Heyderian, no. 48.
54. Hicham Ben Abdullah El-Alaoui, "Arab Spring Act Two—Are the Arab monarchies next?", *Le Monde diplomatique,* January 2, 2013, at: http://mondediplo.com/2013/01/02arab (Accessed January 8, 2013).
55. See for instance: Yasmine El Rashidi, "Egypt: Whose Constitution?", *New York Review of Books,* January 3, 2013, at: http://www.nybooks.com/blogs/nyrblog/2013/jan/03/egypt-whose-constitution/?utm_medium=email&utm_camp... (Accessed January 8, 2013); Hassan Hassan, "As Al Azhar is thrown to politics, extremists are the only winners", *The National*, Abu Dhabi, January 2, 2013, p. 12; Khalil Al-Ani, "Re thinking the Muslim Brotherhood", *Foreign Policy*, December 17, 2012, at: http://mideast.foreignpolicy.com/posts/2012/12/17/rethinking_the_muslim_brotherhood (Accessed December 27, 2012).
56. Tariq Ramadan, *The Arab Awakening—Islam and the New Middle East,* Allen Lane, an imprint of Penguin Books, London, 2012, p. 82-83.
57. Ibid, p. 85.

58. Ibid, p. 89.
59. Ibid, p. 91.
60. Jean-Pierre Filiu, *The Arab Revolution—Ten Lessons from the Democratic Uprising,* Hurst and Co., London, 2011,p. 147-48.
61. Ibid, p. 135.

2

West Asia in Transitional Period of International Order

Ahmed Salem Saleh Al-Wahishi

The sweeping effects of Arab turmoil have been felt all over West Asia and North Africa. The reasons for these developments are said to be many but "regime failure" is one of the important factors that gave legitimate cause to the people to demand change, with the aim of changing the unbearable conditions. West Asia has entered a phase of transition where governments are crumbling, new social forces are emerging, and international tensions are rising. The non-transitional countries to some extent remain stable and secure because of the continued investments of their governments in infrastructure and security. However, they are surrounded by this great turmoil.

The Gulf States are exposed to new set of challenges despite them using their vast resources to help their neighbours to deal with the difficult conditions. The Gulf remains focused on difficult realities such as the strife in Yemen. The "Failed State Index" of the "Fund for Peace" ranked Yemen 13th among 177 states, in 2011. Due to inefficiency, under-developed state institutions and corruption, the state lacks the power to fulfil its key tasks i.e. ensuring security, an effective civil administration, basic services for the people, and the rule of law. Because of this the Republic of Yemen faces various political challenges that are endangering its stability.

The Yemeni experience in the face of recent developments represents, a political solution that saved the country from civil war and brought about change in accordance with the GCC initiative, which facilitated the stepping down of the president and resulted in peaceful transition. It also helped in resolving the South Yemen issue through national dialogue. In addition to the above, increasing international and regional support in terms of developmental help, and political and security support contributed to the solving of problems within Yemen.

It is important to note that any discussion on security and stability in the Gulf, inevitably draws attention to the issues relating to global energy. Pipelines and shipping lines run throughout the region threatened by terrorism and piracy, crossing areas of great contention and conflict as reflected in the statements about the closure of the Strait of Hormuz. The perceived stability of the region plays even more important role in oil markets and the price of oil, which inevitably affects almost every economy in the world. Among the alternatives for overcoming the threats of the closure of the Strait of Hormuz are the Emirati pipelines diverted to seas other than the Gulf including the pipeline to Fujairah, UAE. This pipeline however does not have the capacity required for carrying the required volumes of oil. Thus more pipelines need to be extended particularly to the seas linked to the Indian Ocean, which means extension of pipelines to Oman, the southern coast of Yemen and the Fujairah coast of UAE.

As one looks at the wider global energy market through the prism of the Arab turmoil, one sees another phase of transition. In this context two important developments merit attention: first the plans of the Gulf governments to work together with the international community to guarantee an energy mix that comes from a variety of stable sources and second, the plans of UAE and Saudi Arabia to play a major role in building nuclear reactors for peaceful power. In this regard, it is important to know that the Middle East Weapons of Mass Destruction Free Zone (MEWMDFZ) must include an incentives regime for member countries, that include not only technical and economic support for developing civilian uses of nuclear energy, but also a nuclear security umbrella for the zone's member countries guaranteed by the five permanent members of the Security Council. It should also have a sanctions regime for countries that refuse to join MEWMDFZ.

The turmoil that swept across West Asia and North Africa, had an impact on the Palestinian-Israeli conflict as well. The West Bank and the Gaza Strip witnessed marches calling for an end to the political split between Fatah and Hamas. The agreement, which followed two years of Egyptian efforts, to promote inter-organisational reconciliation, was signed by the leadership of the two competing organisations. It focused on the holding of elections for presidency and the parliament "legislative council". The questions to be raised here are: Will the election take place? Which political party will win? The already minimal willingness of the Israeli leadership to take responsibility for stopping the building of settlements in the West Bank will further diminish the possibility of reviving the Israeli-Palestinian negotiations. This could lead to the renewal of violent confrontations between Israel and the Palestinians.

Indeed, measures that would demonstrate a readiness to fundamentally change the political and territorial realities in the conflict region, remain a prerequisite, for the Palestinians to negotiate with Israel. The international solidarity with the Palestinian cause, the Palestinian political representation at the United Nations will strengthen the position of those Palestinians in the region, who strive for a compromise, through peace negotiations with Israel.

An attractive peace initiative for the Palestinians, is the Arab peace initiative, provided that some political steps that may serve as a basis for a solution are taken. This initiative offers several advantages: First, to stop Israeli settlements which it would extricate Israel from its growing isolation in the international and regional arenas. Second, it would strengthen Fatah and Abbas in their struggle for legitimacy and leadership. So far, the political party, which supports peaceful solutions, has not been rewarded for its moderation.

Two years after the fall of some leaders of the region, those who created the winds of change out of the anguish of being denied a future, it is the university educated jobless young people, who are facing greater challenges than before. Unemployment has doubled since then. Foreign investment and tourism- the mainstay of the economies of these transition countries, have come to a standstill and it was not long before people were out on the streets again, demonstrating for food and sustenance.

The return of hundreds of thousands of labourers because of the global economic crisis has also increased demands for job opportunities. The question which merits attention is: Will the new political Islamist leaders be able to achieve economic stability for their people? In this context the concerns are more about the economic hardship that the people of the region will be facing in the coming years, than the kind of constitution they will have.

On January 5, 2012 President Obama summed up the United States attitude with respect to Arab Spring: "Not every country will follow our particular form of representative democracy, and there will be times when our short-term interests do not align perfectly with our long term vision for the region." Still, it is important to highlight some of the main features of the evolving US policy:

- There is no single policy towards all uprisings in the Arab world. The United States of America deals with each case, based on its unique circumstances. Thus, American policy towards Syria, Libya, Egypt, Tunisia, and Yemen varies significantly.
- The US has approached all important players in the region including the Islamists.
- The US prefers to let domestic forces and regional powers take the lead.
- The US has supported peaceful and transparent democratic change.

In January 2013, Hilary Clinton declared, in the US Congress, that the Arab Spring had led to instability, extremism, and inexperienced governments. While the transition towards reform and change needs to be appreciated and people of the region applauded for their courage in challenging their political masters to gain freedom, it is equally important to voice some concerns, because though the tyrants of yesterday may be gone, but it appears that a new form of tyranny has been let loose and the people who brought the Spring into being, may very well be the ones who will suffer most. It is unclear how the regimes in the region will deal with a form of political Islam that is tolerant of people of other faiths and those who want to live in a civil modern state. The hope is that the youth and women of the region will find a way to share the freedom and dignity they fought for. This, will be the real barometer of the success of the Arab spring.

3

The Future of Political Transformation in West Asia and North Africa[1]

Timothy C. Niblock

The past two years have posed important questions about the manner in which observers of the Arab world analyse the developments taking place in the region. Many of the observers may now seek to present the Arab uprisings as a natural outcome of the inherent injustices and failings of the regimes. However, none of them predicted the Arab Spring. Neither the ability of popular movements to mobilise and challenge the regimes, nor the weakness of regimes in the face of such challenges, was envisaged in writings prior to the events. The emphasis of much of the analytical study of Arab regimes in the previous decade, indeed, had been on trying to understand what made the regimes so seemingly impregnable. The failure of observers, in this respect, applies not only to external observers (whatever national background they came from) but also to regional Arab or wider West Asian and North African observers. It was not limited to any professional category. Academics, journalists, diplomats, think-tank analysts and military strategists were all taken by surprise.

A lot of analysis has been done on this element of surprise by various scholars.[2] In particular, it is significant to focus on the mistaken assumptions which underpinned much of the analysts' thinking about the Arab world. This paper, however, will move on from that analysis and focus on how specialists have interpreted the events over the past two years, in order to examine the assumptions which strengthen the current analysis. The objective is to consider whether the mistaken assumptions of the past may now simply have been replaced by another set of mistaken assumptions—leading to similar surprise when events turn out differently than expected.

In order to understand the present political transformation of the Arab region, it is important to have a clear recognition of the conceptions and assumptions for an observer, before undertaking such an analysis.

To recap briefly on the mistaken assumptions prior to the Arab uprisings, it is suggested that analysts were harbouring five misconceptions about the political, social and economic dynamics of the region. These were:

1. "The age of popular protest in the Arab World is past". Specialists well-acquainted with Arab history were, no doubt, aware that popular protest had been a key ingredient in Arab political development over a prolonged period in the first half of the 20th century (and a bit beyond). The structuring of the relationship between the Arab people and the rulers seemed to have become entrenched: power, force and authority were exclusively in the hands of the regimes; while fear and submission were inherent in the attitudes and conduct of populations. It seemed natural to assume that the pattern was fixed for the foreseeable future. Change through popular protest did not figure in assessments of future political development. This assumption was dramatically undermined in the first three months of 2011.
2. "The levels of inequality and injustice, while substantial, are nonetheless tolerable". The existence of substantial social and economic inequality and of injustices in the exercise of political power in the Arab world was acknowledged by external as well as domestic observers. The possibility that this was of an extent and character to lead on to regime-threatening unrest, however, was not given serious attention. The uprisings indicated that inequality, corruption and injustice (which were in fact increasing, not declining) were not tolerable for significant sectors of the population—in fact for the majority of people.
3. "The regimes are internally solid, based on the perceived common interests of key elites". Most regimes in the Arab world clearly, were kept in power by the close collaboration of presidential, military, security and sometimes business elites. Observers assumed that these elites were effectively and inevitably bound together by common interest. They were forced to "hang together, otherwise they would hang separately". The uprisings revealed that this pattern did not hold universally. The outcome of the uprisings, indeed, has in part been dependent on the nature of the relationship between presidential and military/security elites—and how this has varied from country to country.
4. "The regimes retain a significant degree of 'secondary legitimacy' at the popular level". Analysts believed that although regimes had lost most of their primary legitimacy (i.e. belief among the population that the regime constituted their preferred and proper system of government), there remained a basis of secondary legitimacy underpinning them: a belief that whatever the regime's failings, it was better than a feared alternative. People supported the government, then, not because they

liked it but because they thought any likely alternative (or the break-up of the country) would be worse. In practice, however, secondary support was steadily waning. There was a strengthening conviction that it was the regimes themselves which were the problem, and not the potential alternatives.

5. "Pan-Arab identification has ceased to be of any relevance to the Arab political scene". The inter-Arab conflicts of the 1970s, 1980s, and 1990s had led most observers to give diminishing attention to Arab identification. Arab nationalism was seen as a spent force, and the conclusion was drawn that Pan-Arab identification carried no political significance. The Arab uprisings put Arab identification back on the political map. Events in one Arab country clearly had a major impact on the developments in others. The Arab world was shown to constitute a common ideational space, with information and opinion resting in a shared cultural pool. Satellite television channels (especially Al-Jazeera and Al-Arabiya) had played a key role in the re-creation of this ideational space. State oppression in one country, therefore, created echoes and vibrations across the region.

Perceptions of the Uprisings: New Assumptions, New Misunderstandings?

While the events of the Arab Spring have acted as a corrective to the perceptions of specialist observers of the region, it is (as noted above) important to ensure that one set of misconceptions is not simply offset by another set of similarly misguided assumptions. This section will examine the dominant assumptions which observers have made since the outbreak of the uprisings. In practice they can be divided into two phases, which are the 2011 assumptions relevant mostly to the phase during and after the uprisings and the 2012 assumptions relevant to the phase which followed.

The 2011 Assumptions: The Arab Spring

At the beginning of the Arab uprisings outside observers (at least in the Western world) saw the developments in predominantly positive terms. There were three, interlinked, assumptions which they were making about the events which were unfolding, and each of them was seen as the harbinger for a brighter future for Arab countries. The term "Arab Spring" itself conveys this positive projection. The assumptions were:

1. "The Arab Spring has brought a democratic revolution to the countries concerned". This conception placed the uprisings in the context of Huntingdon's "waves of democratisation".[3] The "third wave" of democratisation had begun in 1974, with the Carnation Revolution in

Portugal, and continued through the democratic transitions in Latin America in the 1980s, Asian countries such as the Philippines, South Korea and Taiwan in the 1980s, and Eastern Europe and Central Asia after the collapse of the Soviet Union. The most recent phase of this process of democratisation included the "coloured revolutions" and "flower revolutions" in such countries as Georgia (the "rose revolution" 2004), Ukraine (the "orange revolution" 2005), and Kyrgyzstan (the "tulip revolution" 2005).

The Arab Spring, then, was frequently portrayed by observers as a continuation of the third wave, or possibly as a separate Arab "fourth wave".[4] The core element was that these were popular uprisings aimed at the creation of democratic systems of government.

2. "The weaknesses of authoritarianism has been revealed, and authoritarian regimes in the region are doomed (whether in short or medium-term)." There was, among observers, a strong belief that something fundamental had changed in the region, and that even those regimes where no uprisings had occurred would find themselves impelled to change. Among some observers, there was a belief that Western countries would be increasingly prepared to give direct assistance to support the transition of regimes to democracy. The Western position could be an outcome of their guilt for past association with non-democratic authoritarianism in the region, or could be deliberate so as to strengthen or maintain their strategic presence there.
3. "The liberal democratic regimes expected to follow from the uprisings will provide a sound basis for resolving the social and economic problems which have faced Arab countries". The extent and gravity of these problems was evident prior to the uprisings, and it was further highlighted by the uprisings themselves. The focus on mismanagement, elite corruption and wide-ranging inequality which existed under the outgoing regimes linked these to the form of government. Authoritarianism enabled regimes to manipulate economies in their own interests, with no concern for rest of the population. A democratic system of government, it was assumed, would not have the same scope for corruption and mismanagement.

Therefore, the Arab Spring, in 2011, was conveyed in the context of a global march towards democracy, carrying with it all the presumed benefits of democratic principles and practice.

The 2012 Assumptions: The Arab Winter

In the course of 2012 (and into 2013), the views of the same outside observers have become much less optimistic, to the extent that many now talk of an "Arab

Winter" and the "failure of the Arab Spring". The foreign ministries of a number of Western countries have begun studies on "what has gone wrong".

A number of perceptions have shaped this view:

1. Some uprisings have either failed to achieve their objective of overthrowing the regime, or have led to a level of civil conflict and destruction which has cast a shadow over any possible achievements of the uprisings. At the time of writing, this scenario clearly applies to the case of Syria, where a UN-sponsored report has suggested that as many as 60,000 people may have already lost their lives in the conflict.[5] Other organisations have reported lower death tolls, around 40-45,000. However, there is no indication that the conflict is about to end—at least not with the establishment of a stable democratic state. The uprising in Yemen resulted in a transition of power, but with key elements of the previous regime still in positions of power and not reconciled to conceding space for new political structures. In Bahrain, similarly, the objectives of those who took part in the demonstrations in February and March 2011 are no closer to realisation now than they were then—and perhaps further away.
2. The regimes of the Arabian Peninsula, with the exception of that of Yemen, have mostly proved adept at remaining in power, and indeed in some cases of reinforcing control over their societies. A combination of factors has supported this scenario: the introduction of substantial new packages of welfare for the population (increased subsidies, higher salaries for civil servants, unemployment pay etc), the absence of aggressive external pressure for change, and in some cases the introduction of incremental political change or the ability to depend on primary and secondary support among parts of the population. In the case of Bahrain, there has of course been the presence (and the significant symbol) of Saudi Arabian military support for the regime. In Kuwait, the ability of the regime to control the expression of popular discontent has been weaker than elsewhere, partly due to a more long-standing tradition of representative practice and perhaps due also to divisions and political mismanagement in the leadership.
3. Where uprisings have led to elections, the general trend has been for Islamist movements to gain political ascendency, which some observers see as likely to lead to the pursuit of socially-restrictive policies, and to embody a long-term threat to democratic practice. Whether the latter perception is realistic, is questionable, but there is little doubt that significant sectors of opinion in the Western world hold that view. The "general trend" certainly exists: in Egypt, Tunisia, Libya and Morocco governments supported by Islamist political movements now wield

governmental power, even though in some cases a "deep state" (with a military dimension) remains in existence—constraining the actions of the governments.

4. The new governments which have come to power are seen as failing to address effectively the social and economic problems facing their societies. As the uprisings were in part shaped by the failure of previous regimes to improve the social and economic conditions of their people, it was assumed that this would be the immediate focus of attention for new governments coming to power. Yet in practice the central focus, as perceived by observers, has often been constituted by petty wrangles over constitutional niceties, intense in-fighting between different political groupings, and a failure to establish the institutions, structures or climate necessary for economic growth, the provision of welfare, and the redistribution of wealth. Key indicators on employment, investment, poverty and growth are mostly less positive than they were before the uprisings.[6]

Future of Political Transformation: Towards Some Realism in Predictions

The contention of this paper is that both the initial optimistic perspectives, and the later pessimistic perspectives, reflect faulty assumptions about the social, political and cultural forces which are at work in the region. An accurate assessment of the future of political transformation which is occurring in West Asia and North Africa needs to be based on realistic assumptions. The paper puts forward five points which are considered critical to making an accurate realistic assessment.

First, putting the uprisings into pre-conceived categories ("democratic revolutions", or more recently "Islamist revolutions") leads to distorted expectations and understandings. At present we do not know what kind of revolutions they were, are or may be. The crowds who demonstrated on the streets were motivated by many different interests, emotions and beliefs. Some were showing their despair at prolonged unemployment or at the rising cost of living; some were moved by anger at the wealth being accrued and flaunted by the elite; some felt marginalised or side-lined by the ethnic or religious composition of the political leadership; some had been alienated by the secularism or un-Islamic practices of the society and polity in which they lived; some were motivated by the oppressive conditions imposed on women; and some were rebelling against the authoritarianism of those who held political power in the country, nationally or locally.

No doubt, all the demonstrators wanted more political space in which to express their own views and pursue their political, social and economic objectives. It was natural that the slogans raised in the demonstrations called for freedom and (to greater or lesser extent) democracy. Yet, that does not mean that there was any commonality in the views of demonstrators either about the political structures which should be instituted, or about the kind of social milieu in which they wanted to live.

By labelling the uprisings as "democratic revolutions" observers set a standard by which to judge them, and thereby to dismiss them as failures. What is important, rather, is to abandon preconceptions and focus on what has actually changed. This will provide a surer basis on which to assess how the uprisings and their outcome may affect the political development of the countries concerned.

The regimes which are emerging may not follow a liberal democratic pattern (at least not one which fits Western conceptions of liberal democracy), but the character of political power has changed. Despite some of the journalistic comments (for example, describing the Egyptian President, Mohamed Morsi, as "a new Pharaoh"), the government does not—and is no longer likely to—take the form of a single integrated oppressive force. The exercise of political power has, increasingly, to be negotiated among different sectors of society. The sense of popular empowerment coming out of the uprisings, moreover, shows no sign of diminishing. Elections are one channel through which popular interests and wishes achieve expression, but they are not the only one. Demonstrations, strikes, journalistic activism and social media expression form part of the new scenario. Parts of the population which were politically quiescent for years have come together to voice their interests. The secular liberal intelligentsias, previously critical of the authoritarian regimes but ineffective in mobilising popular support for a political alternative, are now engaging in practical politics necessary to pursue their objectives. Others are doing so on the basis of religion, ideology, social mores, or class interest.

The pattern of government in Tunisia, Egypt, Iraq, Libya and Morocco over the next decade is most likely to be that of "negotiated power, with popular involvement". It may be neither stable nor democratic (in Western eyes) but it will not simply constitute a "reversion to type", as some have suggested. The sense of popular empowerment achieved in the uprisings limit the extent to which power could be re-assembled in the hands of a unified oppressive state.

It is, also, worth noting that the composition of the political elite in those countries where uprisings have been successful has changed. Many of those, who are now holding positions of authority centrally, and to some extent regionally, have not held such positions before. Some of them have served time in prison, others have been in exile. They come from backgrounds which are less secular, more Islamic and often lower-class and less associated with capital cities than the previous office-holders. This may or may not be significant to the social and economic policies pursued, but it does mean that the governing circles may be subject to influences from different directions than before.

Second, the political systems of the Arab world will become more diverse in character and dynamic than they were prior to the uprisings. This may seem contrary to current developments and expectations, inherent in the trend toward moderate Islamist movements taking power, with support from conservatively-inclined Gulf States. Yet, the surface differences between Arab States prior to the Arab Spring—some republics and some monarchies—concealed far-going regime commonalities. They were all authoritarian in character, with a tightly-knit ruling group wielding power through a combination of military and security services support, cooperation with key social elements crucial to the operation of the state, and representative or consultative bodies which gave the appearance of parliamentary forms but with limited ability to hold policy-makers to account. It was significant that the republics were themselves moving towards hereditary leadership, copying the pattern of the monarchies.

Despite the commonalities in the governing practices of Arab regimes prior to the uprisings, and the apparent commonality represented by the moderate Islamist trend emerging as the main beneficiary of the uprisings, in practice the social, cultural and economic bases impinging on government in different Arab countries vary greatly. The fluidity which the uprisings have induced in some of the political systems of the region will mean that the differing social, cultural and economic bases will articulate themselves in terms of institutional and structural differences.

The dynamics which impinge on the oil-rich monarchies of the Gulf, for example, are distinctively different from those of the less resource-rich republics. Despite the considerable problems which the oil-rich monarchies face, their resource-base has enabled them to maintain a level of welfare which significant parts of the population fear may be lost with political change. This creates an element of eudemonic[7] legitimacy (and allied secondary legitimacy) which may be lacking in less well-endowed polities. Gulf monarchies, moreover, may also benefit from residual elements of primary legitimacy based on ethnic, historical or religious factors: parts of the population supporting the regime because they see their own identity as linked to that of the ruling group. Deficiencies in government conduct or policy will undermine a regime if its legitimacy is based on what it offers the population, but not necessarily if the perceived legitimacy stems from ethnic, historical or religious identification. The influences from the Arab Spring have affected, and will in significant ways continue to challenge, the monarchies of the Gulf, but there is no good reason to expect the imminent demise of these regimes.[8]

Even among the republics where uprisings have successfully overthrown authoritarian regimes, the pattern of political development will not be uniform. The balance between, and the identity of, the different sectors of society and institutional groupings which will take part in the negotiation of political power vary greatly from one state to another. The political formations which emerge will be affected by the size and influence of different class, ethnic, cultural and religious groupings, as also by the linkages which exist between military, security, business and other elites. The characteristic of "negotiated power with popular involvement" may be common to all these emerging systems, but the political and institutional outcomes of this characteristic are bound to be very different from one country to another.

What can be said about the likely diversity of political systems, however, does not necessarily apply to foreign policy. The greater popular involvement in government will render governments more responsive to popular opinion, which on some issues (such as that of Palestine) may well create a greater commonality of policy. With regard to the positions which Arab countries adopt towards Iran, on the other hand, there could be more diversity of policy.

Third, ideological positions should not be regarded as fixed and unchangeable. The statements of ideological principle made by Islamist movements which were not tolerated under the authoritarian regimes of the past are, as they stand, often difficult to combine with the values associated with liberal democracy. Yet, participation in a political process where movements/parties are competing for popular support—however deficient these may be by Western standards—is likely to have a conditioning effect. Even participation in elections was previously condemned by the Salafi figures which formed the Al-Nour party in Egypt, yet they are now actively engaged in Egyptian parliamentary politics. When exposed to competitive politics, practical realities, and the need to gather international and domestic support, even the most radical ideological positions can prove malleable. Strident and militant professions of political position do not necessarily indicate an inability to compromise when the need arises.

Rather than reacting to Islamist involvement in politics by questioning the long-term objectives of the Islamist groupings concerned, it is more productive to integrate them into the political process and allow that process to shape and inform (an in practice change) their ideological rigidity. Fears about the long-term objectives are little different from the fears which some quarters of Western opinion had about the role of Communist parties at the time of the Cold War. It was in the countries of Western Europe (particularly Italy) where Communist parties were strongest, and were able to compete most effectively in the political process, that the ideologically-flexible "Euro-communist" strand developed.[9]

Fourth, the extent of social and economic inequality in West Asia and North Africa has been, and remains, an unstable basis on which to build participative and representative political systems. The concentration of economic power as well as political power in the hands of the pre-uprising regimes meant that any genuine measures towards democratisation threatened their wealth as well as their political power. The pressures which Western governments exerted on them to institute political reforms, therefore, were never likely to bear fruit—even if the pressure was exerted intensively and consistently (which it seldom was). Reform and liberalisation could involve dismantlement of the most savage dimensions of the security apparatus, greater latitude for the criticism of state policies in the media, and managed elections limited to parties whose challenge could be contained, but it was bound to stop at the point where the regime's control on power was threatened. The accountability of government personnel to representative institutions would have crystallized that threat.

The impact of inequality on the wider population was equally inhibiting to democratisation. The business class had the resources and usually the education to play an independent political role, but no inclination to risk their well-being in risky political activity. Travel and contacts abroad linked them to the wider global environment, providing some release from the restrictions of authoritarianism. The poor, marginalised by the all-pervading state and its associated elites, sought respite in the communal and religious values, which gave meaning to their lives. Emigration to gain employment elsewhere constituted a possible avenue of escape for them.

While the setting has now changed, continued inequality could again distort political processes and limit the range of options available. The outcome would depend on the specific conditions in each country—perhaps the growth of extremist activity (built on the despair and resentment of the poor), perhaps an increasingly authoritarian trend (whereby the wealthier elements in society seek to protect their interests), or perhaps a tendency towards political apathy (stemming from a lack of hope that the revolutions can bring change). All such outcomes would be damaging to the future of the countries concerned.

Fifth, the impact which the Arab Spring has had on the domestic politics of non-Arab West Asian countries has been limited. While the Arab Spring has created interest and discussion within the wider region (and outside) there have in practice been few developments elsewhere which have directly drawn inspiration and political dynamic from the uprisings. In the case of Iran, whose proximity to the region and involvement there create the strongest likelihood of impact, the Arab uprisings appear not to have affected the country's political dynamics. Iran's own "Green Revolution" (the militant political activity and demonstrations in 2009, against the government's alleged misconduct in the presidential elections) had no significant impact on the domestic politics of the Arab world. Similarly, there has been no noticeable impact in the reverse direction from the Arab uprisings of 2011-12.

In a wider region, significant impact has been observed in regional and international politics. The position of Turkey has been strengthened, while the regional roles of both Iran and Israel have become more problematic. As with most cases where a rebalancing of regional (or global) power occurs, there are considerable risks to regional stability which could ensue in the short-term—before the countries concerned grow accustomed to operating within a changed configuration of power and influence.

Conclusion

In practice, the central issue for Arab countries (as for most countries with less well-established political institutions) remains what it was before: how to create and maintain political systems where those who govern are accountable to the population, where social and economic problems can be addressed effectively, and where the population feels a sense of common purpose and common identity. When the previous regimes first came to power in the 1950s and 1960s they sought legitimacy on the grounds of being able to resolve these issues. Their means of resolution envisaged rapid development through state-sponsored industrial and agricultural development, measures to bring relief to the poorer parts of society and create greater equality, accountability through fostering popular participation in supposedly all-encompassing single parties, and projecting a national identity which created among the population a feeling of common endeavour. There were times when these objectives seemed capable of bringing success, but ultimately the regimes failed to deliver what had been promised.

The new regimes represent a new approach to resolving the same problems. Their success will be measureable over the long-term, not the short-term. It is, at present, too soon to draw negative conclusions about the outcome of the uprisings. A sense of hope remains the correct approach.

Notes

1. In practice it is within the Arab world that the crucial changes have occurred, so the analysis in this paper will refer mainly to the Arab world. Nonetheless, reference will later be made to some of the implications which these changes have for West Asia more broadly.
2. Tim Niblock, "Explaining the Arab Uprisings and Predicting their Future Course", in David Mulrooney (ed.), *The Situation in West Asia and North Africa and its Impact on the International Strategic Configuration,* Institute for Security and Development Policy, Stockholm, 2012, pp. 20-34.
3. Samuel P. Huntingdon, *The Three Waves of Democratisation in the Late Twentieth Century,* University of Oklahoma Press, Oklahoma, 1991.
4. One possible difference with the "third wave" was noted. The role of the West's human rights agenda, and the support of Western governments for NGOs promoting democratisation, were said to have been characteristic of the third wave democratisation, whereas it was more difficult to detect evidence of that in the Arab "fourth wave" uprisings.
5. UN News Centre, available at http://www.un.org/apps/news/story.asp?NewsID=43866.
6. For the case of Tunisia, see World Bank, "Tunisia Overview", September 2012; or for a more extensive analysis, International Bank for Reconstruction and Development, *Interim Strategy Note on the Republic of Tunisia for the Period FY 13/14,* IBRD, New York, May 2012. The more positive aspects of the Tunisian experience are brought out in an article written by the Nahda leader, Rachid Ghannouchi, "We'll Create a Tunisia for All", in *The Guardian,* January 14, 2013. For the case of Egypt, see Joel Beinin, "All Unionised and

Nowhere to Go", available at http://carnegieendowment.org/sada/2013/01/08/egypt-s-unions-in-wake-of-new-constitution/f04r. Also see Ibrahim Saif, "The Economic Agenda of the Islamist Parties", *Carnegie Paper*, May 2012.

7. The word "eudemonic" comes from the Greek "creating happiness", and thus eudemonic legitimacy refers to people viewing a government as legitimate by virtue of the beneficial conditions which government policies have created for them.
8. For a different view on this see Christopher Davidson, *After the Shaikhs: The Coming Fall of the Gulf Monarchies,* Hurst & Co, London, 2012. The writer of this paper would concur with Davidson with regard to the problems faced and weaknesses inherent in some of the regimes. His assessment, however, is that Davidson's analysis underplays the strengths which regimes also have at their disposal.
9. Writing on this subject, set within the context of how "anti-system" parties can operate within a democratic framework, and how this process gradually moderates their ideologies, has been extensive. The literature first developed in the 1970s and related in particular to European communist parties. See, for example, Giovanni Sartori, *Parties and Party Systems: A Framework of Analysis,* Cambridge University Press, 1976; Giovanni Capoccia, "Anti-System Parties. A Conceptual Reassessment", in *Journal of Theoretical Politics*, vol. 14, no.1, 2003, pp. 9-35; and Ignacio Sanchez-Cuenza, "Party Moderation and Politicians' Ideological Rigidity", in *Party Politics*, vol. 10, no. 3, 2004, pp. 325-349.

PART II

Future of Political Transformation in West Asia

4

Potential Strategic Cooperation among Pivotal States in Western Asia in the Light of Current Changes

Muhammad Abdul Ghaffar

Introduction

Given the current regional and international changes, the GCC countries are becoming aware of the strategic importance of Gulf-Asian relationships in general and Gulf-Indian relationships in particular. The GCC countries can establish a cooperative model for security and stability, based on economic development and commercial cooperation, distinct from the strategy of power politics. In other words, the desired cooperation among the West Asian countries is based on three principles: **firstly,** historical and cultural links that were a prerequisite for commercial prosperity throughout the various phases of history in addition to the geostrategic realities; **secondly,** common security challenges facing West Asian countries such as illegal trade and piracy, and **finally**, the current changes at the regional and international level, that require close cooperation among West Asian countries.

The goal is to achieve security and stability in the region through cooperation, because of its strategic importance, not regionally, but also internationally. However, this cooperation will not prove fruitful until the problems responsible for the current state of instability are resolved, the foremost among these being: the Palestinian conflict; proliferation of nuclear weapons in the Arabian Gulf and the Middle East; plus the regional and international conflict in Syria.

On the other hand, the security and stability of the pivotal states in West Asia cannot be ensured except on the basis of certain principles notably: non-intervention in the internal affairs of other countries; adhering to principles of cooperative security rather than strategic security; in addition to developing cooperative frameworks for regional cooperation that are largely on going.

The current international situation is undergoing profound and historical changes that will have unpredictable consequences for the strategic international balance of powers. This is apparent from the economic structural problems facing the United States and Europe and the implications of their policies, as for example, the changes in US defence policy over the next ten years. Foremost among these changes is the revival of the concept of "regionalism". West Asia is deemed to be the model for a strategic region that consists of pivotal states, i.e. the GCC which is a regional organisation, India and other countries such as Iran and Pakistan. Cooperation among them may lead to creation of a new geostrategic reality and a more positive, regional environment.

The Concept and Types of Pivotal States in Western Asia

The Concept of Pivotal States

A pivotal state refers to a country or group of countries with power and influence within a specific region, on the basis of several criteria, such as the level of social, economic, political and organisational integrity.[1]

As per these four criteria, the Kingdom of Saudi Arabia and the GCC as a regional organisation, are deemed as being pivotal states because they possess a unique social harmony in addition to similar political regimes and economies. Organisationally, they fall under the umbrella of the GCC.

These characteristics give them regional significance, and positive and balanced international relationships with various influential countries.

Types of Pivotal States in Western Asia

Pivotal states in Western Asia can be divided into three categories: (i) Countries engaging positively with their regional and international milieu (ii) Countries engaging negatively at the regional and international level (iii) Countries that vacillate between positive and negative engagement, due to certain or specific circumstances.

To elaborate, we can say that countries engaging positively with their regional and international milieu base their external policy on principles of good-neighbourliness, peaceful coexistence and sanctity of state borders. Countries engaging negatively with their regional and international environment, intervene in the affairs of their neighbouring countries and create tensions in their regional and international relations. With regard to some countries in Western Asia, "influential balance" can be deemed to be the criterion for controlling the imbalance between positive and negative engagement, which explains developments in some of these countries.

Cooperation among Pivotal States in Western Asia

Historical Background

Cooperation has prevailed in Western Asia since ancient times, both in the period before Christ i.e. B.C. and through modern history i.e. from 1258 to 1498. Despite the flourishing trade, 1258 saw a transition in the land trade from India and China to the Indian Ocean through Egypt after the Mongols invaded and captured Baghdad. The year 1498 marked the discovery of the Cape of Good Hope route, hence, reducing the importance of the Indian Ocean.

Based on the history of trade via the Indian Ocean, we can conclude three facts:

> **First:** The importance of Arab ports for trade in the Indian Ocean, including the Omani Coast, because of their important location at the entry of the Arabian Gulf that made them the hub for the inbound trade from the East and West. Sohar was one of the major trading ports at the time as it was a point of departure for travellers to China. It was at its peak from the fourth to the seventh century Hijri. The ports of Basra and Bahrain were also very important.
>
> **Second:** The various commercial powers that significantly contributed to the trade movement were the Arabs, Indians, Africans, Chinese and Persians.
>
> **Third:** Despite the tremendous volume of trade through the Indian Ocean there was no attempt by any party to exercise control over such trade. There was good understanding among the Indian Ocean parties; therefore, everyone worked towards contributing to and benefiting from it.[2]

These facts should be the basis for drafting any future vision of a regional community where security and stability prevail and trade flourishes. In other words, cooperation between pivotal states in Western Asia does not mean creating something from nothing; rather, it is a continuation of the shared historical and cultural heritage of these countries.

Geostrategic Background

The Arabian Gulf nestles between the Arabian Peninsula and South West Asia. This is connected to the Arabian Sea via the Strait of Hormuz through which around 17 million barrels of oil pass daily, i.e. around twenty per cent of the global demand for oil. The Arabian Gulf also connects with the North West Indian Ocean which means that the security of the Gulf region is closely related to security in Western Asia.

Current International Changes

The international scene is currently undergoing important strategic changes; foremost among which is the US withdrawal from several parts of the world, including Iraq in 2011 and Afghanistan in 2014, in addition to changes in the energy market. In this context, it is worth highlighting three issues:

> **First:** The nature of the US role abroad in light of the announcement by the US administration that it will be reducing US military expenditure by nearly $487 billion over the next ten years.[3] This announcement followed the US economic crisis as the total US domestic debt reached $16 trillion in 2012.[4]
>
> **Second:** The evolving role of the Asian pivotal states at the regional and international level at present, and the role of India and China in the future.
>
> **Third:** The World Energy Outlook 2012 issued by the International Energy Agency (IEA) forecast that by 2020, the US will surpass Saudi Arabia as the biggest oil producer in the world. The report also indicated a continued fall in US oil imports, to the extent that North America becomes a net oil exporter around 2030. It also mentioned that the United States currently imports around twenty per cent of its total energy needs.[5]

These are all indicators that the US role in the world might undergo change.

> In this context, the economic analyst Gideon Rachman, in his book *Zero-Sum World: Politics, Power and Prosperity After the Crash* (June 2011), stated that after the economic crisis, the US is no longer the world's super power, which means that the current international system and its regional extensions, are giving way to new strategic formations- including geostrategic ones—in Western Asia, which has a long history of commercial and economic cooperation. Therefore, it is time for pivotal states in Western Asia to have their say at the regional and international forums since they wield considerable political, economic and strategic clout.[6]

Areas of Cooperation among Pivotal States in Western Asia

At the Strategic Level

Given the presence of regional frameworks, with which some pivotal states are affiliated in Western Asia, such as India's membership of the South Asian Association for Regional Cooperation (SAARC; established in 1985) and its membership, along with some of the GCC countries, of the Indian Ocean Rim Association for Regional Cooperation (established in 1995; approved in 2000), in addition to the establishment of the GCC in 1981, there is still a dire need for evolving new frameworks for regional sustainable development and security in Western Asia. In this context, the establishment of a forum for the Western Asian countries, can be examined by think tanks, to crystallise the insights and thoughts relating to the present and future of regional cooperation among the region's pivotal states. Such a forum can become the nucleus for forums at the country level to lay the foundations of regional security, on the principle of the sanctity of borders with the aim of achieving joint security and interdependency.

At the Security Level

The Kingdom of Bahrain is a member of the Combined Maritime Forces (CMF) which has 27 member nations. This coalition consists of three principal task forces: CTF-150 (maritime security and counter-terrorism), CTF-151 (counter piracy) and CTF-152 (Arabian Gulf security and cooperation).

This joint international force with its command headquarters located in the Kingdom of Bahrain forms part of the US Navy Fifth Fleet. It is noteworthy that Bahrain has twice commanded the CTF 152.[7]

These forces are very important in light of the security challenges facing Western Asian countries that require mutual cooperation for checking illegal trade, smuggling and piracy. According to estimates sea piracy costs the international community around $8 billion annually. Due to the gravity of piracy in the Indian Ocean region,[8] the UN Security Council (UNSC) passed several resolutions to address the issue between 2008-2012. Most notable of these was Resolution 1816 which allows countries and various organisations to send naval forces to waters off the coasts of Somalia and the western Indian Ocean to combat piracy as per which India sent several ships to counter piracy. Reports indicate that piracy was lower in 2012 as compared to 2011.

At the Economic Level

In the light of the substantial intersection of economic interests, the proposed cooperation among Western Asian countries would best be achieved by resurrecting commercial and economic ties between such countries, by developing a framework, based on these countries' economic competencies. This is reflected in the following indicators:

Regarding the GCC Countries

The GDP of the GCC countries as percentage of global GDP went up by around 24 per cent in the period from 1999-2012. The Gulf economy currently constitutes 2 per cent of the world economy[9] although the GCC population is only 0.5 per cent of the world population.[10]

International Gulf investments rose from $12 billion in 1999 to $350 billion in 2012, the most important of these are concentrated in oil importing countries. This is associated with a current account surplus between the Gulf countries and key importing countries.[11]

The GCC countries are considered to be rising economic powers as the Gulf sovereign wealth funds plays an increasing role in the world economy. The total value of their assets touched $2 trillion in 2012. The following table gives the financial breakup of the countries of the region:

Total Size of the Gulf Sovereign Funds in 2012

Assets $ Billion	Sovereign Fund Name	Country
627.00	Abu Dhabi Investment Authority	UAE-Abu Dhabi
58.00	International Petroleum Investment Company	
48.20	Mubadala Development Company	
70.00	Investment Corporation of Dubai	UAE-Dubai
532.80	Saudi Arabian Monetary Agency	KSA
296.00	Kuwait Investment Authority	Kuwait
100.00	Qatar Investment Authority	Qatar
9.10	Mumtalakat Holdings	Bahrain
8.20	State General Reserve Fund	Oman
1,749.30	**Total**	

Source: Sovereign Wealth Fund Institute, 2012; http://www.swfinstitute.org/wp-content/uploads/2012/04/SWF-asset-allocation-2012sample_1.pdf

India

The Indian economy underwent structural transformations following the economic reform programme undertaken in the early nineties. The average Indian GDP growth in the period from 1980-1991 was 5.1 per cent and it then rose to around 6.7 per cent in the period from 1992-2012 as a result of the economic liberalisation. This significant growth was reflected in the contribution of the Indian economy to the global economy, increasing from 2.5 per cent in 1980 to 5.7 per cent in 2012.[12]

One of the main drivers of the growth of the Indian economy is the increase in the average external trade of India. In the period from 1997-2011, the exports went up from $33 billion to $251 billion and average imports went up from $39 billion to $370 billion.[13]

Based on the tangible economic achievements made by the GCC countries and India, there are many examples of cooperation between the two sides including:

- A 1500 per cent increase in trade between India and the GCC in the period between 2001-2010 as total bilateral trade between the two sides was $5.6 billion in 2001 and it rose to $88.8 billion in 2010. The GCC countries have become India's most important trade partner in 2010, constituting 18 per cent of India's total external trade.[14]
- The number of Indian workers in the GCC exceeded 6 million in 2010 and international remittances of Indian workers reached $55 billion in 2010—30 per cent of which was from GCC countries. This workforce contributed to various GCC developmental plans.[15]

  There is still scope for increasing economic cooperation between the two sides, apart from the Gulf energy products, which constituted around 40 per cent of Indian imports in 2011, especially considering that Indian demand for these products will grow over the years, due to population growth and the increasing needs of India's industrial sector.[16]

- The Indian economy still needs investments in infrastructure, and this presents an opportunity for the GCC countries, which are still seeking for new foreign investment opportunities. India offers one of the promising opportunities in this regard. There is no doubt that the Gulf Ministerial Council's decision in 2004, to enter into negotiations with the Indian government to establish a free trade zone, provides a solid foundation for furthering economic and commercial relationships between the two.
- In addition, estimates indicate that the trade between the GCC countries and Pakistan will increase from $59 billion to $350 billion by 2020.

Current Changes in the GCC Countries

At the Internal Level

The GCC countries are undergoing a political transformation as reflected in the current media discourse in the Arab region. This is a positive indicator, as such a phenomenon precedes the movement of the Gulf official institutions and complements them.

The modernisation and reforms taking place in the GCC countries are not necessarily a corollary to the transformation being witnessed in the region. For example, the protests in the Kingdom of Bahrain in early 2011 did not stem from the political or economic situation of the country. Bahrain has an elected parliament, a national action charter and a constitution, that all reflect the level of political development in the Kingdom. It also has mechanisms through which any popular demands can be met. However, when facing the 2011 crisis, Bahrain took the dialogue approach, for conflict resolution. In addition, the political regime's openness to undertaking more development, in accordance with the National Action Charter, reflects its flexibility and capacity for adopting a positive approach with regard to the internal and external developments. In other words, policymakers in the Kingdom—quite early—realised the need to accommodate new changes in its economic and social structures following globalisation and taking into account the external interference, with its ideological extensions.

At the Regional Level

There were two important developments, relating to cooperation and integration, in the past two years in the GCC countries:

> **First:** The new strategic trend of the GCC countries was in keeping with the Saudi King's proposition at the 2011 Gulf Summit to move from "cooperation" to "confederation." This is believed to be an important step towards balancing the regional powers. It will even translate into increasing the influence of the GCC countries at the regional and international levels.

Second: The agreement among GCC countries at the Manama Summit 2012 to establish a military command, to plan, coordinate and lead the allocated and additional land, air and naval forces in the GCC countries. This is considered to be a positive development in the field of military integration.

Principles and Foundations of Future Cooperation Among Pivotal States in Western Asia

The current state of affairs in the GCC countries, the West Asian countries in general and India in particular does not reflect the extent of their common interests. Despite the nearly 51 visits exchanged between India and the GCC, especially between 2010 and 2012, that included 31 visits from India to the GCC and 20 visits from the GCC to India, there were very few visits by state presidents, governments and foreign ministers. These were two visits by state presidents, 17 visits of foreign ministers, one visit by the Bahraini Crown Prince to India and one visit of the UAE Vice-President to India.

On the other hand, there is still a need for greater cooperation among pivotal states in Western Asia to resolve the problems that threaten regional security and stability. These are:

Non-Proliferation of Nuclear Weapons

The GCC countries are concerned about the likelihood of war in the region because of the Iranian nuclear issue. Therefore, the key blocs in Western Asia should play a role in urging Iran to deal positively with the international community regarding its nuclear ambitions. The main problem lies in Iran seeking the technology necessary for manufacturing nuclear weapons. According to some reports, Iran currently has about 240 kg of the 20 per cent enriched uranium necessary for manufacturing a nuclear bomb. It is should be noted that modern nuclear bombs require less quantities of enriched uranium. The nuclear arms race among nuclear powers in Western Asia is a matter of huge concern for the GCC.[17]

The Palestinian Conflict

Previously as part of the early peace process and with the improvement of communications between the Arabs and Israel, the Arab countries made a peace proposal to Israel in 2002 which it rejected. Further, the Oslo Accords are also about to expire. It should be noted that Israel will not feel secure in the future if it does not enter into negotiations with the Palestinian and Arab side to create a habitable Palestinian state with Jerusalem as its capital, as per the Security Council Resolutions 242 and 338. Since its inception, and till today, Israel has been isolated from its regional surroundings, especially at the Arab popular level. If such tensions continue, the region will witness another bout of instability.

Principles of Future Cooperation among Western Asian Countries

Non-Intervention in the Internal Affairs of Countries

It is necessary for the pivotal states in Western Asia to reach a consensus on the essential, internationally-accepted principles, such as, non-intervention in the internal affairs of countries; and not using religions as engines of extremism, especially given, that most religions essentially call for tolerance and moderation. Iran is an important country but it still has problems with the international community and regional countries. It seeks to intervene in the internal affairs of independent countries by creating organisations and militias in the heart of these countries, often by exploiting circumstantial instability. Thus the concluding declaration of the December 2012 GCC summit in Manama, included the clear message, that the GCC's interaction with Iran in the coming period will be different from the previous pattern, which was characterised by conventional methods of accommodation and maintaining common interests and failed to prevent Iran from interfering in the internal affairs of the GCC states.[18] The main problem lies in Iran's external policy, since 1979, which focuses on ideology for advancing interests. This has created a vicious cycle of tension in the Iranian-regional and international relations. It is incumbent upon Iran to redefine its external policy so that it is based on reciprocal interests rather than ideology.[19]

Cooperative Security Instead of Strategic Security

The strategic cooperation among the West Asian countries must not rely on traditional patterns based on geostrategic influence and conventional and unconventional military power. There must be cooperation based on common interests, especially economic and commercial interests, which promotes peaceful coexistence among the different peoples.

The Presence of Continuous Cooperative Frameworks

These include security forums that can meet regularly to address West Asian security developments and formulate suitable responses. This can be done at the official and unofficial levels.

Future of Changes in Western Asia

At the Level of the GCC States

Internally

The GCC states are aware of the importance of continuing the political reform and modernisation that they started long ago, and which in themselves are not necessarily related to the current transformations in the Arab world. Policymakers in the Gulf states are fully aware of the ambitions of the present young generation, mostly created by social and economic development and globalisation. Therefore, they strongly believe in the youth's rights to political participation and to decision making. However, this reform and modernisation must take place gradually keeping in mind interests of the Gulf, and based on national criteria, detached from any external agendas.

Externally

The GCC are studying the Saudi King's 2011 proposition to move the GCC from "cooperation" to "confederation", which they regard as an important strategic option. On the one hand, it will be one step forward in the Gulf's partnership, and on the other hand, it is a response to current regional challenges. In its preface, the GCC charter as well as Article Four thereof, states that integration and union are two of the GCC objectives. Therefore, implementing the proposal will represent a blossoming of the Gulf integration vision and it will reinforce the GCC states' regional and international position.

Regionally

The GCC states believe it is imperative to clear the Middle East and the Arabian Gulf region of weapons of mass destruction, as the proliferation of these weapons threatens regional and international security and peace alike. In this context, Iran must respond positively to the efforts of the international community to end the Iranian nuclear crisis peacefully.

At the Level of Developments in Western Asia

The GCC states believe that there is close correlation between security in the Gulf region and the security of the Indian Ocean. Therefore, the features of the Gulf vision for the development and future of cooperation among the Western Asian countries are:

1. The GCC states seek broader relations with the pivotal states in Western Asia, notably India, which is an important strategic partner. This calls for the development of a mechanism for partnership between the two sides that reflects the economic weight of the GCC states and India's status as a rising economic power at both the Asian and international levels.
2. The GCC states realise the importance of developing relations with Pakistan, especially at the strategic and economic levels.
3. The need for the Afghanistan government to establish security and stability following the withdrawal of foreign troops from Afghanistan in 2014 to prevent the future emergence of extremist groups, something that can threaten all West Asian countries.
4. In the light of the reliance of Indian Ocean trading routes on a number of strategic international straits, maintaining maritime security must be

one of the objectives of cooperation among pivotal states in Western Asia especially in light of the growing security threats to waterways, most notably piracy.

To recap: since countries are seeking to cooperate under the umbrella of regional organisations West Asian countries must consider new frameworks for cooperative security. Many principles, notably good-neighbourly relations and coexistence, rely on the one hand on geostrategic inputs and shared cultural heritage and on the other hand on dealing with the current security challenges.

NOTES

1. Dr. Mohammed Al Saeed Idris, *Study on the Principles of International and Regional Relations. Cairo*: The Centre for Political and Strategic Studies, Al Ahram 2011, pp. 61
2. Dr. Shawky Abdul Qawi Othman, The Indian Ocean Trade under the Islamic Rule.: *Alam Al-Marefa Series* No. 151, Kuwait pp 7, 8, 41, 55, 66, 124 & 125.
3. See US Presidential address at http://www.telegraph.co.uk/news/worldnews/barackobama/9816372/Barack-Obama-Inaugural-Address-2013-full-text.html
4. See US Treasury website at http://www.treasurydirect.gov/NP/BPDLogin?application=np
5. International Energy Agency. *World Energy Outlook 2012.* 2012.
6. Karen Abul Kheir, Asia and the New World Order: International Politics, Al-Ahram Centre for Political and Strategic Studies.
7. For more details on this coalition and its tasks, check the following link http://combinedmaritimeforces.com/about/ Also check http://www.cusnc.navy.mil/articles/2011/cmf001.html
8. Abeer Abu Shamala, *Sea Piracy and its Effect on Global Economy*, June 2012 at http://www.alkhaleej.ae/portal/f31d8e8c-f122-49c0-be33-a5f903311bf5.aspx
9. World Economic Outlook Database, 2012, International Monetary Fund.
10. World Development Indicators Database 2012, World Bank.
11. World Economic Outlook Database, 2012, International Monetary Fund.
12. Ibid.
13. P.R. Kumaraswamy. Persian Gulf-2012: India's Relations with the Region, Middle East Institute in New Delhi, 2012.
14. Alpen Capital: *Trade and capital flows—Gulf Cooperation Council (GCC) and India* 2012.
15. Ibid.
16. P.R. Kumaraswamy, *op cit.*
17. Henderson, Simon; Heinonen, Olli; Technical Issues Overshadowing Iran Negotiations *Policy Watch* 1993 http://www.washingtoninstitute.org/policy-analysis/view/nuclear-iran-technical-issues-overshadowing-negotiations
18. See the concluding declaration at www.library.gcc-sg.org
19. Nia, Mahdi Mohammad; Holistic Constructivism: A Theoretical Approach to Understand Iran's Foreign Policy Perceptions *Journal of International Affairs*, Vol. XV, No. 1-2, pp. 1-41, Spring-Summer 2010.

5

Global Elites and Media in West Asia

Atul Aneja

Media, across the world and particularly in the West has been undergoing a profound and unique transformation. Mainstream media especially print and television have long ago departed from their role as the fourth estate—a vital and supposedly independent cog in the preservation of a healthy democracy.

On the contrary, it can be argued that some of the most influential sections of the so-called international media have allied themselves among others with the "globalists"—a cabal of some of the most powerful people on earth, residing on either side of the Atlantic. These globalists include some of the world's top business magnates, bankers, financiers, former diplomats, intelligence officials and ideologues, who have been mostly drawn from the trans-Atlantic world. At their core, these individuals envision "international governance" and the formation of a federated world government as their final, many would say utopian, objective. These globalists include hyper-influential people such as David Rockefeller - banker, philanthropist and patriarch of the Rockefeller family that commands stratospheric wealth. Its other luminaries include George Soros, the Hungarian-American businessman, who manages the cash-rich Soros Fund that supports "progressive liberal causes". Soros is also the chairman of the Open Society Institute-a network of institutions that is funded to promote "democratic governance, human rights, economic, legal and social reform". After the end of the Cold War, the globalists have aggressively pursued promotion of democracy, including support for colour coded "revolutions" in strategically significant parts of the world.

One of the leading ideologues of this group is Zbigniew Brzezinski. Brzezinski has continued to remain a highly influential thinker, and there are enough write-ups on the internet to suggest that he has President Obama's ear, to say the least.

Early in his career, Brzezinski recognised that technology, in which lay embedded the new avatar called electronics, had begun to integrate the globe as never before. He reasoned that the advancement of what he called "technotronics" presented a unique and unprecedented opportunity to break down the walls of national sovereignty, and, over time, lay the foundations of a supra-national state. In his book, *Between Two Ages*, published in 1970, Brzezinski wrote: "Today we are again witnessing the emergence of transnational elites ... [Whose] ties cut across national boundaries....It is likely that before long the social elites of most of the more advanced countries will be highly internationalist or globalist in spirit and outlook....The nation-state is gradually yielding its sovereignty... Further progress will require greater American sacrifices."

In terms of institutions, the globalists are represented in three major interlocking forums. These comprise the Bilderberg group, the Council for Foreign Relations (CFR) and the Trilateral Commission (TC). Out of three organisations listed, the Bilderberg group is the most secretive. The group was formed on May 29, 1954 as a result of the efforts of a number of people on both sides of the Atlantic who wanted to bring together leading citizens, not necessarily connected with government, for informal discussions of problems facing the Atlantic community. Robert Gaylon Ross Sr., who has studied the three organisations in detail, points out in his study, *Brief Description of... The Elite Conspiracy*, that in the early 1950's, "a number of people on both sides of the Atlantic sought a means of bringing together leading citizens, not necessarily connected with government, for informal discussions of problems facing the Atlantic community". He adds: "Such meetings, they felt, would create a better understanding of the forces, and trends affecting Western nations, in particular. They believed that direct exchanges could help to clear up differences, and misunderstandings that might weaken the West." According to Ross, a pioneering role in this enterprise was played by the late Joseph H. Retinger. In 1952, he approached His Royal Highness Prince Bernhard of the Netherlands for support. After finding considerable backing in Europe, the idea was proposed to a number of Americans, including C.D. Jackson, the late General Walter Bedel Smith and the late John Coleman, who agreed to cooperate.

Bilderberg members, according to this study, are largely drawn from Western Europe, Turkey, Greece, the Scandinavian countries, the US, and Canada. Says Ross: "When they meet, they clear out all the guests, and employees in the buildings in which they are to meet, they completely debug all the rooms, bring in their own cooks, waiters, housekeepers, heavily armed security guards, etc., and do not allow 'outsiders' anywhere near the meeting place just before, during, and immediately after they meet." Their meetings in the US have always been held in a Rockefeller-owned property.

Complementing the Bilderbergers is The Council for Foreign Relations—an elite organisation that is another favourite haunt of the globalists. In his 1991 book *The New World Order*, Pat Robertson, quotes long-time insider Rear Admiral Chester Ward as saying that the CFR is quite open about its advocacy of the "submergence of US sovereignty, and national independence into an all-powerful one-world government."

The shadow of David Rockefeller, the arch-globalist overhangs the formation of TC. The formation of TC was the brainchild of Rockefeller, who roped in Brzezinski to develop the concept. In his article published in Foreign Affairs in 1970, Brzezinski argued that the time had arrived to include Japan in the world's ruling elite. By the mid-nineties, TC included around 325 members drawn from "The European Community, North America (US and Canada), and Japan. The power, influence and the imperial ambitions of the globalists acquires a new turbo-charged momentum after the collapse of the Soviet Union and the emergence of a unipolar world. Where does the media fit into this broad one-world paradigm, and what role does it play as a result of its alliance with globalists in West Asia?

In his investigations, Ross has listed some of most influential media owners and personalities who have participated in meetings of the either of the Bilderberg, TC and the CFR if not of all three organisations. He points out that the late Katharine Graham, owner of the Washington Post was a regular at the meetings of the all three—Bilderberg, CFR and TC. The same goes for Thomas Friedman, columnist for the New York Times, the late Robert L. Bartley, and Vice President of the Wall Street Journal.

Others such as William Kristol, founder and editor of the political magazine *The Weekly Standard* and a regular commentator on the *Fox News Channel* has been attending Bilderberg meetings. The list of the media Moghuls who support the globalists is vast and insightful. However, it is important to note that during these meetings, representatives of the media elite do not participate to report on proceedings, which are invariably open, frank, and agenda setting. On the contrary their role is to advance the broad intellectual lines that emerge from these meetings. That would mean highlighting certain themes and avoiding others so that the agenda decided by the ultra-rich and the powerful can resonate in the public domain.

For instance, the war in Yugoslavia, which included the demonising of the Serbs, appears to have been the test-bed in the extensive use of the media as a tool to help break-up a nation-state, undermine the concept of sovereignty and experiment with the doctrine of "regime change". The media played an essential part to justify a "humanitarian intervention", by extensively and graphically reporting at a break-neck speed on regime atrocities that on many occasions proved exaggerated if not blatantly false. It is also important to note that by the mid-nineties, the media, including the increasingly powerful international satellite channels have been sensitized to promote concepts such as soft power, democracy and human rights in the medium of a unipolar global system—a half way mark in the globalists project of establishing a supra-national state.

While the media has been shaped by the globalists, they do not represent the only game in town. The neoconservatives in the Bush era, more inclined to support hard power than soft power, have had their own aggressive vision of the assertion of American power on a global scale, especially in West Asia after 9/11, and with the inauguration of the Global War on Terror (GWOT). One neocon institution that has been playing a leading role in "shaping" the media is The Henry Jackson Society (HJS), which, of late has been particularly active in Syria.

A glimpse to the disposition of the HJS can be caught from the people that the organisation represents. These include neocon icons: James Woolsey, William Kristol, Robert Kagan, Joshua Muravchick, and Richard Perle.

The society's director of communications and public relations is Michael Weiss. Through his writings in the online publication "Lebanon Now" which has a section called "Syria Now," Weiss has been a relentless advocate of military intervention in Syria. In his insightful comment in *The Guardian*, Charlie Skelton says that Weiss is the author of the influential report "Intervention in Syria? An assessment of Legality, Logistics and Hazards." It is not surprising that the publication has been endorsed by the Syrian National Council now Syria National Coalition. Another HJS associate is Ausama Monejid, who has been regularly appearing on satellite television in active support of the Syrian opposition. Monejid runs the anti-government Barada satellite television out of Vauxhall in South London, according to Skelton. Barada TV is closely affiliated with the Movement for Justice and Development, a London-based network of Syrian exiles, says a *Washington Post* report. The pattern that emerges out of this is clear. A network of globalist organisations, think tanks, experts in strategic communication and media has been playing a leading part in setting the international information agenda as part of a larger project of establishing control in the post-cold war world. It would therefore be highly flawed to view media as an isolated institution. On the contrary, it is a component of an assembly line of well integrated institutions, which aspire to manipulate thought perceptions on an industrial scale.

Like Syria, Iran has also been in the cross-hairs of the information war unleashed chiefly by influential globalists, neocons, and others with or without the backing of the State. For instance, Radio Fardais one of the main instruments in winning the hearts and minds of ordinary Iranians. Interestingly, it is the Iranian Branch of Radio Free Europe/Radio Liberty's broadcast services. It beams its messages out of Prague. Radio Farda and the Voice of America Persian are reportedly funded largely by the $ 66 million Iran Democracy Fund, which was established in 2006 by the Bush administration.

In recent years, the globalist, democracy-promoting counter-sovereignty media campaign has begun to meet stiff resistance, in several parts of the globe, including Iran. Iranians believe that they are targets of a media backed "soft war" unleashed by what they call cultural-NATO. Consequently, they have concluded that an aggressive response is required to defeat this assault. As a result, Iran has established a special military force called a "Unit of the Soft War" (Setad-e-Jang-e Narm). Its probable role is to disrupt foreign organised soft attacks, possibly by jamming and other similar techniques. The Iranians also started Press TV in 2007—their own satellite channel in English. Its effectiveness is apparent, for Press TV seems to have been deliberately targeted in conflict zones, including Syria and Gaza, in the region.

While state-backed media such as Press TV in Iran or Russia Today in Russia are doing their bit to counter the globalist media onslaught, the real game changer has been largely uncontrolled instant messaging on the internet the emergence of social media, YouTube and Vimeo. The citizens' media from below has emerged as an extremely powerful force, which is difficult to control. In Egypt, documentation of protests on video, creation of credible blogs and tweeting of stories to influence international and domestic journalists has had a powerful impact on news creation. Even a strike in relatively remote Mahalla can no longer be ignored by the media, for activists are avid at videotaping the event, blogging about it and using their Facebook/twitter accounts to force the mainstream coverage of the subject. In turn mainstream media culture is now in a real and tangible flux. In the words of Brzezinski, the world, especially the developing world is experiencing a "global awakening," channelled by the media. Says Brzezinski: "The nearly universal access to radio, television and increasingly the Internet is creating a community of shared perceptions and envy that can be galvanized and channelled by demagogic political or religious passions. These energies transcend sovereign borders and pose a challenge both to existing states as well as to the existing global hierarchy, on top of which America still perches."

In conclusion, the collapse of the Soviet Union set in motion a real media upheaval. Globalists and subsequently the Neoconservatives, among others, for more than a decade, have networked with mainstream media and sought to monopolise it in an attempt to consolidate unipolarity and undermine the concept of national sovereignty. But, their path did not go unchallenged on account of the emergence of alternative state-backed media such as Press TV of Iran, RT from Russia, and a string of low-budget private alternative media outlets in the West. However, the explosion of the media from below powered by the internet and social media has begun to seriously challenge the hegemony of conventional media directed from the top. With the spread of "global awakening," fanned both by alternative and social media, the demand for a new social contract driven by newly empowered people with their State is rising, forcing governments to consider altering their mentality of control with a real policy of public engagement. However, the emergence of a new people-responsive social contract is still a work in progress. The challenge posed by non-western alternative media, as well as media from below, especially in West Asia, as seen during the course of the Arab Spring, is sought to be countered by status quo regimes through new tools of surveillance and technology. These are imparting totalitarian characteristics to nation-states that are being tested by youthful demands for change.

6

Emerging Trends in West Asia: Regional and Global Implications

Ahmed A. Saif

Introduction

The Arab region has been the least responsive to the third democratic wave which took place in 1989. Since December 2010, however, a number of the Arab countries witnessed an unprecedented popular uprising to call for not only socio-political reforms and transparency in governance, but also for regime changes. Evidently, the year 2011 was a decisive moment in the modern political history of the Arab world.

These uprisings have profoundly altered the regional order in West Asia. While revolution in Tunisia and Egypt paved a way for change in regimes, in other Arab countries, the authoritarian governments have resorted to either co-optation or violence to impede or resist the transformative changes. Historically, revolutions have been capable of orchestrating new domestic political orders and foreign policies. What is evident in all the cases is the Arab Spring's capacity to reshape relations between major state and non-state actors in West Asia, and redefine the role of external players in geo-politics of the region.

The advances of liberalisation have been more limited in the Arab world than in (other parts of the world), say, Eastern Europe or Latin America.[1] Recent elections have produced many new leaders in the latter two regions, whereas Arab political leadership has not undergone any such change by democratic means for a generation, except in Lebanon. The average tenure of an Arab leader is twenty-three years. Arab parliaments and consultative assemblies that have become more pluralistic, including those of Morocco, Yemen, Jordan, and Kuwait, remain toothless by the standards of countries generally considered democratic.[2]

The region is definitely in a political ferment, but whether that presages transitions to democracy remains to be seen.[3] The popular demands for democracy which echoed in the Arab world in the last two years gave a rise to the expectations of the people for a genuine change. However the Arab dream of democracy and sound political governance is unlikely to materialize unless legal institutions of the state are liberated from the political, tribal, clienteles or family partisanship. The evident drama of these events makes it difficult to discern those changes that are superficial and transient from those which will be far-reaching and long-lasting.[4] It is therefore essential to understand that a democratic movement in the Arab world should essentially aim at changing and reforming the larger socio-political and legal institutional framework.

The battle to change and reform the institutions ought not to be delayed until after the triumph of the democratic movement. However, there must be work at the level of these institutions and departments in order to realize these reforms, which constitute important instruments of leverage in democratic work.[5] The spread of demands for democracy in the Arab world in 2011 and 2012 gave a rise to the expectations of the people for a genuine change. But the imagery is not just premature but also misleading.[6] The evident drama of these events makes it difficult to discern those changes that are superficial and transient from those which will be far-reaching and long-lasting.[7]

Refining the Terminology[8]

Many phrases have been used in describing the events of 2011 in the Arab countries, yet no academic consensus has been reached. Thus, there is a need to refine the terms used because of connotation, consequences and analysis they entail.

Revolution

Revolution, in social and political science, is a major, sudden and hence typically violent alteration in government and in related associations and structures. The term is used by analogy in such expressions as the Industrial Revolution, where it refers to a radical and profound change in economic relationships and technological conditions.

A revolution constitutes a challenge to the established political order and the eventual establishment of a new order radically different from the preceding one. The great revolutions of European history, especially the English, French, and Russian revolutions, changed not only the prevailing system of governance but also the economic set up, the social structure, and the cultural values of those societies. In this sense, what is happening in the Arab countries does not qualify to be labelled as a revolution, or at best can be termed as an "Unfinished Revolution".

The Awakening

The series of precise issues in dispute were blurred by a tendency to equate awakenings with peaks in revival activity, at best an imperfect measure. The "Arab Awakening" as we see it today has its roots in the history of West Asia (Roots of the recent Arab Awakening can be traced to the history of the West Asian region). In the landmark 1938 book titled "Arab Awakening", George Antonius; a Greek Orthodox Lebanese and British official in Palestine extolled the rising of a renewed pan-Arab political and cultural consciousness after decades of European, principally British, machination and domination. But setting aside the historical elements of Antonius' original work, reference to his book "Arab awakening" conjures up precisely the wrong imagery for what has been happening in Arab countries over the past three years.

So, like the romantic term "Arab Spring", the equally romantic term "Arab Awakening" obscures more than it explains.

Arab Spring

'Arab Spring' refers to the ongoing crop of pro-democracy uprisings that swept the West Asia and North Africa (WANA). 'Arab Spring' finds an ideological consonance with the democratisation wave that swept Eastern Europe after 1989, which was called "Democratic Spring". Originally used to describe a hopeful movement in Prague that was crushed by Soviet tanks in the 1960s, the phrase "Arab Spring" was borrowed and applied to the West Asian context in 2011. The "spring" in West Asia is in contrast to the "winter" of oppression that many of these countries have experienced in the past. So, Facebookers and youth who celebrate the Arab Spring of 2011 recall the days of old regimes. Thus, in comparison with other pro-democracy uprisings the term "Arab Spring" is unreflective.

Renaissance

It is the theory of continuity applied to the middle ages; which exhibits a restless phase full of exuberance, stimulated by many problems, interests and aspirations. It connotes and distinguishes between every-day-life and the life of mind; the theoretical formulation of man's thoughts and ideas, which is primarily: artistic; literary; cultural and religious. Thus, the renaissance in essence is considered as an "intellectual" reality, not as a "physical" one, hence, political change.

Transformation

Transformation is the process of changing from one qualitative state to another. Transformation; therefore, as a process of transmutation from one state to another can apply to an individual or an organisation, or the product or service supplied by the organisation. In South Africa, transformation has a particular meaning related to the political transformation of society: political change having a transformative role in moving from apartheid to an inclusive society. Transformation, also, entails a long and gradual process of political change; therefore, transformation may be the most pertinent term to describe what is happening in the Arab countries.

Pre-Revolutionary State

Past Models of Change in Pre-Independence State

Islamist Evolutionary Model

During the reign of the Ottoman Empire, there were efforts to internally transform the Ottoman state as the "Caliphate State". In Islamic political thought the concept of state does not exist, instead there is the "Rule" or "Politics" and the core of concern is the group and justice and not individualism and law. The early scholarly works produced by Jamaludin Al Afghani and Mohamed Abdo focused on religious and ethical unity vis-a-vis the western colonial powers, and shed light on this model of Islamic governance.

Nationalist Revolutionary Model

Instead of religious and ethical bonds, this Arab nationalist trend had linguistic, cultural and ethnic affiliations; with the ultimate vision of an independent Islamic nation state. The Arab nationalism was led by Qustantin Zuraiq, Zaki Arsozi, Michele Aflaq and Sata Husari in the Levant. Most of them were Christians who believed that the minority Christians had melted in a large Islamic pool. A secular national state was therefore considered to be the most suitable model for equal citizenship, and the model consequently called for independence from the Ottoman State. Nonetheless, this idea of nation state was based on the Islamic conception of freedom, and was fundamentally distinct from the western liberal concept that is based on law and individualism. Therefore, the latter created nation-state paved way for authoritarianism.

Landlords and Aristocrats' Model

During the post-Ottoman era of British colonialism in the region, social reforms received an impetus from the colonial powers. Therefore, reforms in the legal and administrative institutions, and economic arenas like agriculture and infrastructure were designed to serve the colonial powers and foster the power of local elite.

Post-Independence State

In post-independent state, regardless of the nature of the regime, whether republic or monarchy, all reform models were characterised as elite-led projects. Moreover, changing process adopted top-down direction and embraced mass politics and populism.

Revolutionary Regimes

The revolutionary regimes adopted three tools for change:

Agrarian Reforms

To weaken the opponent landlords and to mobilize the masses, agrarian reforms were introduced by new revolutionary regimes. Arable land was confiscated from the landlords and redistributed among peasants who were previously waged-farmers. The populist move, though well received by masses, had serious economic implications. While the fragmentation of land into small and uneconomic shareholdings negatively impacted the macro economy by impeding mass production and disturbing the cropping patterns, it also failed to improve the living standards of poor peasants.

Mass Politics

Due to low representational level of the new regime, they heavily relied on a security centric approach that overshadowed economic and political issues. Thus, there was a clear preference for single party rule over multi-party system, and the same was institutionally imbibed via means of media, education etc... In this context, unprecedented dictatorship was established in this part of the world.

Import-Substitution based Industrialisation

In the absence of legal legitimacy, these regimes tried to engender their legitimacy by adopting a populist economic agenda/adding socio-economic achievements to their credit. For instance, regimes in Egypt, Syria, Iraq and Algeria launched the import substitution endeavour in heavy industries. This orientation, that was meant to be the leverage for development, involved heavy investments in this industry in a propagandist fashion, without due consideration of domestic and foreign markets. The outcomes of this strategy were catastrophic in terms of quality of industrial output and export competition, and led to unnecessary industrial expansion and oversized the public sector.

Monarchical Regimes

In comparison, the Arab monarchies in order to survive had adopted different models to compete with neighbouring countries which were undergoing change. The models adopted by oil rich countries and non-oil rich countries were not the same. However, with variation, the monarchical regimes embraced: Mineral Based and Renteirism Strategy.

The Gulf Co-operation Council (GCC) countries are exposed to two contradictory situations; while on one hand they are highly dependent on external world and are vulnerable to outsiders, at the same time they are privileged with absolute domestic independence. This phenomenon assures absolute independence in managing financial revenues flowing from (exploration, production, refinement and marketing of) oil resources by foreign companies. As suggested in the well-known theory of rent, the citizens have no bargaining power vis-à-vis the state. The state also enjoys autonomy in allocating/managing its workforce which ensures inflow of remittances from expatriate community, while the citizens have no power to organize themselves in syndicates and unions or to exert enough pressure on the government through strikes. Finally, defence and security establishments are also state monopolies, and are largely dependent on external powers for protection.

Even though the state appears extremely powerful against its citizens, it is weak and less influential against the external powers. Against this backdrop context, it is unlikely that a powerful and despotic state/regime would recede and promote democracy, unless there is a strong and consequential civil movement for political transformation.

The Current Model of Change

Tunisia took the lead in such popular uprisings against one of the most oppressive Arab regimes. Interestingly, the popular Tunisian revolt to overthrow the despotic regime had reverberations in Egypt, where the uprisings also led to regime change. Libya also witnessed fall of monarch and rise of democracy but the future of the new democratic state remains uncertain. Gaining such irresistible momentum, these three successful revolts have prompted more popular uprisings in the region; popular protests became commonplace in Bahrain, the Sultanate of Oman, Yemen, in addition to considerable bloodshed in Syria.[9]

It is pertinent to understand that besides unremitting political oppression, difficult socioeconomic circumstances, the lack of freedom and the rampant spread of corruption were the primary drivers for the public protests. However access to education and modern means of communication via social networking websites etc... mobilized the masses, united them for a common cause, and inspired public display of discontent. No one can deny the significance of moral values but that of institutions is certainly more important in the long term. Thus unless there is a change in power sharing accompanied by rebalancing between society and government, ensuing political change would be of no avail.

So far three models of change have been identified: the radical change, the evolutionary consociational change and the demand for authentic reforms.

The first model aims to radically change the incumbent regime without having alternative to replace beforehand, such as the case in Libya. This model may lead to political uncertainty and anarchy.

The second model seeks to avoid the destiny of the former model by adopting an evolutionary approach. Gradual change of the incumbent regime is preferred.

This model, however, embraces consociations and compromises that offer the regime incentives to step down, such as the case of Yemen. Because of sequence of compromises, the case of Yemen shows taking unconstitutional measures, such as having a sole presidential candidate, enacting an immunity law for the former president and extending the tenure of the parliament.

The third model is based on public demands for introducing authentic reforms without toppling the regime, such as the cases of Kuwait, Bahrain, Oman, Morocco and Jordan. Interestingly, the reform-oriented model has existed only in Arab monarchical regimes, while the other two models of change have existed in Arab republics only. This observation addresses the suitability of monarchy or republic for the Arab countries based on their respective harmony with the cultural and political developments in the countries.

Important Features of the Arab Transformation

Role of the Muslim Brotherhood

At the first glance, no concrete political, religious or ideological movements can be identified among the protestors. Instead, there is a surge in web activism; such that social media websites like facebook and Twitter are being used as a platform to harness the public opinions. The two conventional players; political parties and the ideologically motivated popular movements are no longer important actors in the contemporary geo-political theatre. Instead, the traditional players have been replaced with apolitical movements that focus on definite socio-economic demands. We see a civilian phenomenon whose dynamics are connected primarily with the city, but it has no definite political agenda. Seemingly, the current debate can be detached from the confines of ideologies dominating the Arab politics for decades. Yet, a close scrutiny shows that the Muslim Brotherhood, which is a transnational movement, dominates and directs the events in all cases with abundant Qatari resources at its disposal.

The recent developments in West Asian can be seen as an offshoot of the constraints imposed by the international players on the Arab regimes; which has led to the emergence of new and unprecedented forces in the region and replaced vertical dialogue with horizontal dialogue. As a result of the weakness of civil society organisations and the fragility of the nationalist and leftist parties, the political stage has been dominated by the Islamist powers; precisely the Islamist rhetoric of the authorities and opposition in Iran; Hezbollah in Lebanon; the Islamist currents (Shiites and Sunnis) in Iraq and the Hamas Movement in Gaza. The domineering Islamist influence of is due to the dramatic metamorphosis of mosque as a powerful organisation/institution for mobilisation and sensation. Today, the young protesters have found their own "mosque" on Facebook, Twitter and blogs. Since youth comprise the majority of bloggers and social media users, the young Arab populace is rightly perceived as an influential player in initiating the revolutions. Thus the so called "BLOG culture" has added a fresh/unique dimension to the revolution. The young people demonstrated high degree of collective consciousness and enthusiasm in expression and action alike (in expressing their discontent and demanding a change).

The age-old convention of offering mass prayers on Fridays has become a source of annoyance for all the Arab rulers. On Fridays the protesters make use of the normal gathering of people who come to perform their prayers and call for regime change, exploiting the spiritual aspect of this day. Recently, the role of the mosque as a platform for a weekly conference to discuss the issues of concern has been revived. This role of the mosque had been hijacked and suppressed according to late Sadiq al-Naihum. The involuntary collective action of masses on Fridays has resulted in unbeatable influence.

The slogans of 'freedom', 'justice' and 'dignity' that have been raised or are still being touted in the face of authoritarian regimes do not appear to transcend the threshold of demands possessed within a liberal frame of reference. Thus, democracy has not only become a civilisational choice on account of its ability to resolve differences and produce social benefits, but is also viewed as the best alternative to transcend systems of subjugation and tyranny. In fact, we find political parties and groups, particularly those affiliated to political Islam, have begun to present more than one justification for appearing in 'democratic' guise, even if that exposes them at a certain stage to distortion, and divests them from their significance, especially given that most of its constituents 'want restricted democracy that does not contradict Islamic *shari'ah*', and put preconditions on the principle of freedom demanded by the youth as well as other sensitive issues.[10]

Accumulated Protests

The protests and demands were not sudden and abrupt; rather they kept accumulating and ascending in terms of time and space. In Egypt, for instance, trade unions staged over 1000 sit-inns from 1998 to 2004. After that, economic liberalisation coupled with decline in social security networks led to a radical rise in protests. In 2006, over 222 sit-ins and protests were staged, going up to 580 in 2007. Like Egypt, Tunisia witnessed similar protests to defend freedom and civil rights; such protests peaked on December 17, 2010, and did not stop until Zain Al Abdin bin Ali was ousted from power on January 14, 2011. Likewise, Shiite-Sunni tension also escalated over years. The Shiites, who make up the majority in Bahrain, protested against marginalisation and tortures, as well as against granting the Sunnis the Bahraini nationality, which was aimed at altering the "demographic equation". The primary cause of discontent in Bahrain was the lack of good governance and the abuse of human dignity. Even as the grievances in Bahrain were intensified by rapidly growing prices, there were few slogans protesting against high prices. This is a lesson to be learned from all other Arab regimes.

Characteristics of the Protesting Powers

The protesting powers in the Arab countries are characterized with unique features that have not been seen in the region. First, the Arab citizens have realized the significance of overcoming fear, which in turn has encouraged peaceful demonstrations in the region and eased the overthrow of the regimes once the psychological barrier is broken down. Second, when a group of protesters take to streets, they double in number the next day. Thus there is a mass appeal. Third, the revolutions of the youths have been characterised by the absence of a charismatic leader; there is no particular individual leader. Fourth, the protests clearly lack any political affiliation, for the protesters who belong to a wide political and civilian spectrum which encompasses the Islamists, the liberals, the leftists, the poor and the rich. Fifth, the revolutions have been characterised for the first time by the absence of ideologies that simultaneously mobilize, regulate, impose frameworks and put restrictions on people. During modernism and post-modernism periods, ideologies melted away by virtue of intellectual and human convergence created by the technological revolution, so participation and globally-accepted human values such as human rights, public freedoms, and the right to a clean and safe environment have gained a universal unanimity and legal power in line with the international conventions.

However, the revolutions have a critical shortcoming that is the lack of a post-regime agenda. Also, there are other certain deficiencies in the revolutions such as the absence of a cohesive regulatory entity. We find in each Arab experience, spatially/geographically scattered protests and lack of harmony and coordination among the protesters to rely on each other in a coordinated process to overthrow the regime.

Another distinctive feature of these revolutions is that the influence of the opposition parties is marginal (despite of the role played by the Muslim Brotherhood movement and Islah Party in Egypt and Yemen, respectively). The demands of the protesters have gone far beyond the agenda of these parties, and the opposition parties find themselves running behind the momentum gained by the protesters while trying to reap the fruit of the revolutions. Perhaps the most noticeable characteristic of the revolutions is the revolutionary tool which has been used by the young people and is different from the one used by the opposition parties. It is clear that there are no particular forces to organize the youth on the ground and the channels of dialogue and communication with the other political powers are weak and virtually non-existent. Furthermore, there is no communication with and support by the external world. Maybe the fastest impact or outcome of the revolutions is embodied in the termination of extension or heredity in office power in Libya, Egypt and Yemen.

The weakness of the opposition parties in the Arab states is one of the most important reasons contributing to the survival of the authoritarian regimes; these parties have failed to form a united front capable of putting sufficient pressure on the government and forcing it to respond to their demands. In addition, a charismatic inspiring leadership is absent, and the trade unions have failed to fill this vacuum and lead the protests for structural and cultural reasons. Naturally, the revolutions have been accompanied by increasing oppression, looting, and bullying acts against the protesters. But, the media's focussing on such events has helped limit such acts as the perpetrators fear being brought to justice later on.

In the cases of Tunisia and Egypt, the military forces took a neutral position and played a decisive role in the success achieved by the two revolutions. In contrast, the Libyan and Syrian cases were different. Because of the weakness of civil society and intricacies of the tribal structure (whose influence affected the military)[11] there was bloodshed in the revolutions. Comparatively, it is possible to extrapolate the political future of Yemen.

The six cases (Tunisia, Egypt, Bahrain, Libya, Syria and Yemen) have showed the failure of the regimes to handle the events; reflected in the contradictory statements issued by the regimes day after another, which exacerbated the situations in all these countries. The revolutions have exposed the inability of these regimes to manage crises. This can simply be accounted for by the fact that the cadre of these regimes are based on kinship and alliance, not on merit and experience. Quick defections on the part of the regimes were also witnessed wherein regime supporters, in a bid either to find a safe haven or to re-position themselves, embrace the political change as an opportunity for political survival.

The most noticeable outcome of these revolutions is the swift collapse and fragility of the state and this may be attributable to the fact that the state is built on traditional structures. The political elites from the rural areas/with rural affiliation have traditionally dominated the state institutions and this has led to inculcation of rural heritage, values and legacies within the state institutional framework. Thus, once the ruling elite are changed, the state apparatuses fall down as a result of the downfall of the kinship and patronage monopolizing the state decisions. We can say that all the Arab states, apart from Egypt, are mere ruling authorities and the statehood in its political and academic sense has not established yet.

Finally, patience, the war of nerves and willpower have proved decisive factors in quickly changing the regime or resisting the regime to change it; the longer time the protests take to realize their objectives, the more chance the regime stands to survive, whether by forging new alliances, defections of the protesters, or the regime's success in reaching international agreements that help it survive; and when regime change happens, it is more likely that the vacuum left will be filled by the military or the political Islam or an alliance between the two.

Some Lessons Learned[12]

There are a number of lessons that the Arab regimes should consider. First, although the socio-economic situation and reforms are important, but good governance and citizens' dignity should be given precedence over anything else. Thus, it is necessary to pay as much attention to the issues of administration and governance as to those of economy and freedom.

Second, no Arab regime is still secure and immune to change. Tunisia, for example, fared well at the economic, legal and civil levels, with the existence of weak opposition and firm security forces; however, this did not prevent change.

Third, the common rumour that if the states resort to political liberation, Islamist forces will dominate the political stage has become unacceptable to justify authoritarianism. Although the Islamists still enjoy wide influence, the two cases of Tunisia and Egypt show the hegemonic tendency of Islamists; nonetheless, it is unacceptable to impede democracy under this justification.

Fourth, the Western states have always adopted a hypocritical and dubious approach towards democratisation of West Asian nations. As a matter of fact, they have supported autocratic and authoritarian regimes in the Arab world, which hampered democratic transformation. Thus, the Arab states should reconsider their policies and overcome their fears that democratic transformation would lead to the triumph of the political Islam over other political powers. If the Western states stop their support for the dictatorial regimes, the weapons and security forces of these regimes will be of no consequence, as the Arab populations have discovered that mass protests are capable of endangering the regimes. The rise of Islamist powers to the office cannot be ruled out due to fragility of the civil society, the weakness of the opposition political parties, and the total dependence of the private sector on the state. This makes it possible for old elites to revive through Islamists or the military or both.

Thus stepping down of the dictators does not necessarily imply democratic transformation. Some dictatorial leaders leave the office just to help their regimes survive. So, the genuine evidence of democratic transformation will be reflected in the power sharing arrangement. In other words, there should be a fine balance between the state and society. If this is not realized, any change in the regime; in names or personalities, will be merely a façade.

External Catalyst Factors: Redrawing the Maps

The Arab state along with its known boundaries was established as a result of the Sykes-Picot Agreement after the First World War, the agreement which served the then Great Powers (Britain and France). With the end of the Cold War and the emergence of a new international order, these borders do not render any service anymore, particularly for the US interests. This assumption carries the seeds of division based on religious, sectarian and doctrinal differences under the guise of human rights, minorities and democratisation. This is enhanced by the diminution of state sovereignty due to the economic and financial dependence of the Arab states on US and increased incidence of terrorism in Arab states.

In 2005, the then-US Secretary of State Condoleezza Rice famously told a Cairo audience that "for 60 years, my country, the United States, pursued stability at the expense of democracy in this region, here in the Middle East, and we achieved neither."[13] It is pertinent to note that the current 'Arab Transformation' began in 2002 in line with *the US-Middle East Partnership Initiative for Democratisation* in the Arab states which imposed several constraints on the Arab rulers. In latter half of the decade, revelations made by "wiki leaks" weakened the political legitimacy of many Arab regimes. Finally, all this culminated in a warning that these regimes shall not use violent force against the protesters and access to cyberspace (Internet, cell phones, satellites) must not be disrupted. As Joshi points out succinctly, "How much democracy is too much, and how much pursuit of immediate stability is too much?" it becomes obvious that idea of democracy still remains abstract in West Asian nations. Thus, the consensus among all the protesters about the regime change without any post-regime agenda will open the doors for differences, leading probably to division of the already fragile and fragmented societies along the ethnic and sectarian lines.

Western states remained unwilling to put the same degree of pressure on either Bahrain or Saudi Arabia as had been placed upon Mubarak in the days before his departure. This may avoid the many pitfalls of a volatile democratic transition, but it does nothing to address the pent up demands of activists who remain unsatisfied with the severe backsliding in Bahrain's modest liberalisation over the past ten years."[14]

On closely monitoring the behaviour of the international players towards the on-going events in the Arab states, one observes that these powers took a neutral position at the outset but as the events tilted towards a particular direction, the powers drifted from their stated position. For instance, there was a change in the American and European political discourse towards Zain al-Abdin Ben Ali and Hosni Mubarak once the domestic equation became unfavourable on the ground. Some of the determinants influencing the superpowers' position are; how important the geopolitics of the concerned state is, how important that state is for the regional stability, and to what extent the regime can resist the revolution to survive?

Perhaps some of the factors making regime change more difficult are reflected by the two cases of Ben Ali in Tunisia and Hosni Mubarak in Egypt: the difficulty in attaining political asylum; frozen bank accounts; delayed delivery of justice/ disruption of judicial machinery/set up; domestically and internationally. This is a lesson which other regimes in the region have learned and are therefore resorting to violence to resist/impede any political change. This is evident from Libya and Syria cases.

On the other hand, pan Shiism is another cause of concern for the Arab world and Western stakeholders in the region. The notion of an emerging 'Shia Crescent' under Iranian leadership stems from the historical Shia-Sunni rivalry and has been fuelled by Iran's escalating influence and attempts of political penetration in Arab states through their local Shia allies, such as in Iraq, Bahrain, Syria, Lebanon, Yemen, Saudi Arabia, including Pakistan.

Iran's current regional strategy has four main priorities: preserving its Islamic regime, safeguarding Iran's sovereignty, defending its nuclear ambitions, and expanding its influence in the region and the Islamic world. There are a number of factors that shape its efforts to achieve these strategic goals and its actions in dealing with its Arab Gulf neighbours. Most senior leaders in the Iranian regime still seem to believe in the justification of the Iranian Revolution and this belief colours their actions and policy regarding their Sunni neighbours.[15]

Another notable observation is a profound regional and foreign policy shift by Qatar; towards an assertive and interventionist approach.[16] The newly emerging tendencies in the global geo-politics enabled small states to project greater power internationally. During the 1990s and 2000s, the acceleration of globalising forces integrated states and societies in worldwide systems and networks of interaction. This represented 'a significant shift in the spatial reach of social relations and organisation' as the constraints of 'distance' and 'geographical space' weakened and shrank. Therefore the notion of power and its manifestation by nation states underwent drastic change in an intensely interconnected world and this reconfiguration generated a distinctive form of 'global politics' that accounted for the intensity and extensity of global interconnections.[17]

Regime Change: Rising Fragmented Powers

The Arab regimes which collectively constituted, what can be labelled as, an Arabic bloc at the regional and international arena now is now shaking. This bloc has been notably fragmented due to disintegration of key states in the Arab world. The Middle Eastern balance of power has witnessed considerable shifts since signing the Camp David Agreement in 1977 that neutralized Egypt *vis-à-vis* Israel. In 2003, Iraq was also dropped from the balance equation in light of the US invasion that consequently brought Iraq under Iran's shadow. Bashar al Assad's Syria is currently at the verge of elimination from the balance equation and Assad's ouster is only likely to fragment and destabilize Syria furthermore. It is important to understand that Assad's departure from Syrian politics would not transform the political institutions built on overlapping networks of political, military and business elites.

Similarly, Saudi Arabia because of political and structural shortcomings is on the horizon. The Arab transformation that began in the spring of 2011 has added a new dimension to Saudi perception of US-Iranian equation in the region. Saudi Arabia initially saw such instability as threatening, while Iran saw it as opportunity. Saudi Arabia has maintained the policy of supporting its allies through public statements, increased funds, and military support.[18] Saudi Arabia sought to maintain the stability of its GCC allies, while supporting uprisings that are costly to Iran.

Geo-political dynamics of West Asia can therefore be seen as a concoction of external factors, and regional pressures. Following the end of the Cold War and the disappearance of the Soviet Union, this regional dynamics have become more independent, in spite of the fact that the states in the region have started to look upon the United States as the point of reference, with the only exception of Iran. By the eve of the Arab Transformation the Arab Ummah, as a whole, is likely to lose its relevance; while Israel, Turkey and Iran will be the three power centres in the region. This tripartite axis is presumed, after resolving the Iranian nuclear issue, to form a new troika under the US umbrella to administer the region.[19] In such fragmented and volatile context, the scenarios given below are the most expected outcomes.

The Potential Scenarios[20]

Based on responses from 47 experts, in a conference recently held at Wilton Park,[21] potential scenarios were measured on scale from 1 (the least scenario) to 6 (most likely scenario).

Scaling	Potential Scenarios	Grades
Most Likely	Mideast Mosaic	196
	Arab Spring on Steroids	169.5
	Things Fall a Part	163
	Re-Drawing the Territorial Borders	162
	Resurgence of Authoritarianism	156
Least Likely	Federated Sunni Caliphate	133

It is important to note that some of these scenarios may overlap and have some cross points. These scenarios, however, have been explained in greater detail in the diminishing order of their probability;

First Scenario: Mideast Mosaic

There have been many external players who have intervened in the contemporary regional developments in the Arab world, resulting in fragmentation of societies and division of political powers in congruence with the views endorsed by the external supporter. At times, the vulnerable nature of the Arab state gave the international actors and organisations more leverage in Arab domestic politics at the expense of local agendas. These scenarios led to domestic and regional fragility, such that no group or political entity dominated the political scene. In such context, the state may retreat due to its inability to provide a national identity and security, and failure to execute the state functions. Thus, people in such states would turn to sub-national domains, which would strengthen sectarian and ethnic feelings. Consequently, this would further fragment the society and deteriorate the socio-political fabric of states and intensify the need for the external support. Regardless of the external intervention and influence, the Arab states would not slide into anarchy, however change within these countries would be uncontrollable and unexpected. The changes in the states would vary because of the population size; that is change in smaller countries would be controllable and stability would be more viable as compared to countries with bigger population.

Second Scenario: Arab Transformation (Spring) on Steroids

This scenario suggests that good governance would gradually get robust in the Arab countries concomitant with economic prosperity and human rights. In the light of the ascendency of political Islam, this scenario hints at the evolution of Islamic democracy in the region; the cornerstone for such possibility would highly depend on how successful Islamists would be on economic issues. This rosy vision exhibits North Africa proceeding positively towards more democracy while the Levant, despite the Syrian conundrum, is also expected to change positively just as the Israel and Palestine peace talks.

On the other hand, a successful transition to constitutional monarchy in the Arab monarchical entities, particularly in Jordan and Morocco, would function smoothly. The GCC, in contrast, would join the democratic change but in a slow motion. Finally, the US is supposed to play the crucial role in this scenario as the main facilitator for democratisation in the region.

Third Scenario: Things Falling Apart

This scenario demonstrates pessimistic trends unfolding in the region. The school of thought is rooted in the wave of instability, triggered by economic failures, population growth, sectarianism and the Iran-Saudi rivalry in the region. The possibility of proxy wars remains very high under such disturbing circumstances. This scenario would led to revival of rigid ideologies in the region, turning West Asia into a terror exporting zone, thus causing further instability and geo-political disequilibrium. More dangerously, the region could witness a nuclear struggle at the expense of democratisation and development; that could inaugurate a new Cold War era. On one hand, the western powers would use the opportunity to weaken Iran and absorb the extra oil revenues made by the Arab oil rich countries, and on the other hand, western competition with China over energy would further threaten regional stability and revive the global politics of polarisation.

Fourth Scenario: Re-Drawing the Territorial Borders

In this gloomy scenario, two factors are of exceptional importance: first, to assess whether the means of change should be diplomatic or violent and; second, to evaluate the influence of regional developments on West, given West's historic engagement in the region. According to this scenario, dramatic permutations and combinations can be identified. The Berbers of Nile valley may get partial autonomy but certainly not full independence because of geopolitical complexities. Kurdistan is also likely to gain some degree of independence and annexation of areas densely inhabited by Kurds (densely populated Kurdish areas) in Syria cannot be ruled out.

In this scenario, two countries are likely to disintegrate; the first is Sudan; that is more prone to further disintegration. Separating South Sudan has proven that Darfur can claim independence under the same justifications that South Sudan has made but this time it would not be velvet separation.

Geographically uneven distribution of resources and the US competition with China over energy would make this scenario more probable. The second country likely to disintegrate is Yemen. There have been grievances of inequality in the southern areas for long time. Moreover, there are also several sub-national identities that claim sufferance from the hegemonic rule of the centre-north, let alone the dilemma of eastern Yemen province of Hadramawt. Therefore, Yemen is at a high risk of split up into more than two states, with some pockets having sort of autonomy.

The complicated political mosaic in Syria, defined by sectarian hegemony and prolonged single-party rule makes the Syrian borders flimsy and susceptible to change. Similarly, the fragmented Iraq, de facto autonomous Kurdistan and the crucial Iranian influence places Iraq in a very precarious situation. Such a scenario would involve the eastward expansion of Jordanian Hashemite kingdom to include some Iraqi Sunni areas within its territory. It has been argued, for long time, that this would enable Jordan to provide some concessions for the creation of state of Palestine on Gaza Strip, the West bank and small areas of western Jordan.

These dramatic changes, coupled with Iran regional supremacy may compel the GCC countries to orchestrate a Gulf Union. Another possibility is the redistribution of population based on sectarian lines, and consequent emergence of the Arab Shia' federation and the Arab Sunni federation.

Fifth Scenario: Resurgence of Authoritarianism

This scenario studies the possibility of revival of authoritarianism in the region. The trigger for this would lie in the economic failures that could evoke nostalgia for reasonable standards of living, at the expense of freedom and democracy. Authoritarianism would also benefit from the competing balanced but divided powers. According to this scenario Egypt, Syria, Iraq and Libya are the most likely cases to bounce back to military dictatorships because of their past experiences with the rule of single party and military hegemony.

Other possibility is the emergence of the Islamic dictatorship. Political Islam comprises of various competing and contradictory factions that are fragmented and hostile to each other. Also the Islamist tendency to adopt the monolithic approach based on the pure orthodox interpretation of Islam is an exclusionary way of thinking and practices. Therefore, if in power, political Islam with its predominantly totalitarian orientation would lead to religious impositions over society and prosecution of other political players, all in the name of God. In the light of weak institutional structures in the region, this scenario expects sort of alliance between military and newly emerging dictators to fill the void. Hence, political Islam is likely to emerge as an ideological justification for despotism under this scenario.

Sixth Scenario: Federated Sunni Caliphate

This least likely scenario largely overlaps with the "re-drawing of borders" scenario with some variation. It suggests that the GCC plus would adopt the model of unity to challenge security issues and to counter rising Iranian influence. Also a stable Syria is likely to unite with Jordan and western Iraq under the auspices of Turkey, which may form a confederation between Iraq and the Levant. Essentially, Arab Israel peace remains indispensible for establishing a stable regional order.

Regional and Global Implications

The Arab Transformation that began with Tunisia in early 2011 gradually engulfed major parts of West Asia and North Africa. The dilemma of democracy still dominates the subject of Arab Transformation in one or other form. The series of mass protests have toppled four governments in Tunisia, Egypt, Libya and Yemen so far and the threat lingers over the Syrian regime.

Whatever the context of origin and nature of Arab Transformation, it predominantly reflects people's flight from culture of authoritarianism and their aspiration for democratic participation in governance. To this extent, Arab Transformation retains the capacity to challenge the political status quo and the political culture of the Arab world. A democratic Arab world is bound to alter the political equations and re-orchestrate the balance of powers in the region.

But the most pertinent question is; will these Arab Transformations result into the democratic governance? Or is it a mere collective expression of historically accumulated grievances without any democratic vision? The issue of SUSHI, a new geo-political parlance to express the Sunni-Shia division, is central to this debate. The political transformation may shift the focus of conflict from conventional Arab-Israeli Diaspora to regional sectarian conflict. The dual sword of Arab-Persian divergence and Sunni-Shia conflict hangs over the West Asian region, which may flare up the entire region. Given the sensitive nature of domestic issues, coupled with West Asia's oil and energy basket, the global stake holders are extremely concerned with the progress of Arab Transformation.

Qatar and the GCC

One of the main beneficiaries of the Arab Transformation is Qatar, though the country had also expanded its regional influence prior to 2011. With security assistance from the US military and boom in oil and gas sector, Qatar has used both its wealth and media influence, to rise above its political stature. The Al-Jazeera news channel has helped in spreading the reporting of unrest across the region. It is essential to note that Qatar led Arab League against Qaddafi and Assad, and also directed the GCC against Saleh in Yemen. Some accuse Qatar of hypocrisy for being vocal about unrest in Libya and Syria, while maintaining silence on Bahrain, its ally. Qatar is also being accused of using the Arab Transformation to spread an Islamist agenda. The region is changing and Qatar has been among the fastest to realise that it is well placed to shape a future that will enhance its own interests.

Yet, the Arab Transformation has had a relatively limited impact on the governance and internal politics of the Gulf States, largely due to their ability to use oil money to suppress dissent. Bahrain, with the least oil money, has witnessed the biggest protests.

Saudi Arabia has seen its position in the Arab world weaken in recent past, due to the Arab Transformation, losing its most important ally, Hosni Mubarak. Some elites in Saudi Arabia consider playing the sectarian card as the best way to limit the perceived Iranian influence in the region. Saudi Arabia primarily intends to maintain the status quo and ensure continued stability, and as a result it has maintained a pragmatic stance towards its neighbours. Saudi Arabia's support for President Saleh in Yemen until his position became untenable proves the point.

Non State Actors

The Arab Transformation has finally brought together the rival Palestinian factions, Hamas and Fatah, in a unity agreement, which however remains tenuous and in permanent danger of collapsing. Furthermore, the success of the Muslim Brotherhood as a result of the events in Egypt is likely to strengthen Hamas furthermore.

Hezbullah is at a risk of losing one of its closest allies: Bashar al-Assad. Without al-Assad, Hezbullah is likely to lose its legitimacy as an "Arab organisation" and thus will be reduced to the notorious status of an Iranian pawn. Already, Hezbullah has become unpopular in the Arab streets due to its unequivocal support for al-Assad and its threats to those who oppose him. Ousting Syrian president Assad and weakening Iran are two unsettling issues. Since Iran, along with Syria, has been the main supplier of money, weapons and ideological inspiration to Hezbullah in Lebanon and Hamas in the Palestinian occupied territories, it remains crucial to any discourse of the subject.[22]

In Yemen, the Huthis emerged as the strongest faction after two years in the transformation there. The struggle for power has made the Huthis to be sought by other disputed factions as a potential ally. The Huthis have capitalized this to expand their presence all over Yemen. The state vulnerability, the fragmented military and security establishments have allowed the Huthis to freely receive enormous quantities of weapons from Iran via the uncontrollable Yemeni shores. The real risk, however, is emanated from the predominance of sectarian discourse that embraces both Iranian and Saudi Arabian schools of political thought

Israel

Israel is most worried by the sea-changes that are occurring in its Arab neighbourhood. The list of Israeli concerns over these changes is almost endless and they will reshape and redefine Israeli regional policies and threat perceptions. The biggest worry for Israel is what has happened in Egypt since the overthrow of its partner in peace and regional stability, Husni Mubarak. The regime change in Egypt has the potential to bring about a serious re-evaluation of the peace treaty signed in 1979. Israel may soon be entirely surrounded by unfriendly Islamist governments, forcing it to either compromise or become even more insular. There is very little chance of a break-through in Israeli-Palestinian 'peace' negotiations in the coming years. Although Syria is an enemy, it was at least predictable and stable: it is a known fact that a civil war in the land of Sham may threaten Israel's north-eastern border. Even the friendly Hashemite regime in Jordan may have to make concessions to its revived Muslim Brotherhood, which wants to abrogate the Jordan-Israeli peace.

Turkey

Turkey has also come to occupy an important place in West Asia in recent years. Turkey under the leadership of AKP has become a major player in West Asia. Turkish model of democracy has been heavily debated in the Arab media, intellectuals and policy makers in the context of Arab Transformation.

Turkey certainly is one of the major winners of the current events. In the years preceding the Arab transformation, Turkey's 'zero problems with neighbours' policy had considerably expanded its political, economic and cultural influence in the region. Turkey was the first country to call for resignation of the authoritarian Arab leaders in the protested countries in favour of pro-democracy protestors. Moreover, most of the moderate Islamist parties that are now likely to dominate the Arab world subscribe to the international Muslim Brotherhood.

These Islamic parties regard the Turkish ruling party, the AKP, as their model. There is also a belief that the Arab Transformation is a Turkish project. Therefore, Turkey is expected to translate its support for the new regimes into strong relations and is expected to have enhanced influence over them.

Iran

The Arab Transformation opens opportunity and challenge for Iran. It enables Iran to extend its influence in Bahrain, Saudi Arabia and Yemen. Nonetheless, when the uprisings would reach Syria—the main Iranian ally in the region, Iran's interests will have to be jeopardized. Similarly, Hezbullah will also face a significant shrinkage in its power due to loss of Syrian support; such a scenario is likely to pacify the Iranian influence from the regional politics. With new balance of power unfolding in the region and Iran nuclear talks underway, Iran might as well get a chance to play a crucial role alongside Turkey and Israel to stabilize and manage the region in favour of the international interests.

India

India has a heavy stake in the stability of the region, particularly the stability of the Arab Gulf and Gulf of Aden. The close Oil and Gas linkages/trade connections, market for investment and flow of remittances make the region crucial for India from an economic and strategic angle.

For India the region has been a major source of raw materials, the incubator for violent extremism, the main theatre for the proliferation of weapons of mass destruction, the home to large number of failed and failing states and an important economic partner. Then and now, the big question is about the meaning and consequences of a power transition in the region.[23]

For India, the Gulf of Aden is a crucial sea lane of communication and trade, which, in its interests, should be secured. The same applies for the Straits of Hormuz of the Arab Gulf and of Malacca in the Far East. For India, a nation billed to be one of the highest energy consumers in the coming decades, energy security is of prime concern to the government.[24]

South-East Asia

The US and Europe were not the only ones surprised or worried by the upheavals in the Arab world. The events of 2011 in the West Asia and North Africa (WANA) region forced South-east Asian polities to pay greater attention to this physically distant yet economically important region. The events in the Arab countries forced South-east Asian governments to take action to repatriate their expatriate citizens working especially in violence-torn Libya. Given the large numbers of their nationals elsewhere in oil-rich WANA countries, they will have to take into consideration another series of repatriation of nationals if the regional situation worsens.

Moreover, several South-East Asian countries, facing economic pressures, legitimacy crises, and the presence of religious extremist groups, have been alarmed by the events in the region and by the seemingly rising star of Islamist movements in the WANA. Therefore, Thailand, Indonesia, Malaysia, the Philippines and Myanmar, all of which have serious political and socio-economic problems, have paid close attention to these events. They have warned their populations against any attempts to emulate the 'chaos' and vacuum occurring in the region, and are scrambling to immunize themselves politically and socio-economically from the contagion of violence by trying to resolve their deep-seated internal issues.

US

A combination of military overstretches after both the Iraq and Afghanistan wars, an economic slump and a revived isolationism in domestic politics were clear signals to indicate weakening US position in the region. The Arab Transformation has exacerbated the US policy of distance, costing the US one major regional key ally, Hosni Mubarak, and deeply unnerving another, Saudi Arabia.

The events that ushered the hopes for unprecedented political transformation have turned into a chaotic "Islamist Winter" in many Arab countries. These disturbing developments increasingly threaten US national interests. Washington not only lost a key strategic partner in Egypt, and is at the risk of losing other regional allies in Bahrain, Jordan, Kuwait, Morocco, Saudi Arabia, and Yemen in face of rising Islamist-dominated political opposition movements.[25]

EU

The European Union's operating assumption while dealing with countries of the southern Mediterranean is that there are reciprocal relations between the security and stability of Europe and the situation in the region. The Arab Transformation leaves the region in a transition period whose end is not in sight, a period that will include uncertainty about the direction of developments, which will escalate instability with repercussions for Europe as well. As part of the lessons learned from the outbreak of the events, the EU has decided to reorder its future relationship with the region, on the basis of a partnership founded on the assumption that states in the region must choose a socio-political and economic model for themselves. The European Union will make an effort, within the framework of the budgetary constraints to adopt new rules of the game that conform to universal and democratic values.[26]

Russia

Russia under Vladimir Putin has already revived some of the former prominence in the region, expanding its economic, military and diplomatic presence in Syria in particular; but this is unlikely to continue, if and when Assad falls from power. The reluctance to approve UN resolutions on Libya and the steadfast refusal to do so on Syria suggests that Russia seeks to guard its expanding strategic regional position. Russia will increase its strategic heft but it still has little to offer in terms of economic benefits. As Islamist governments take over, there is a possibility, however, that its arms relationship with regional states may take off.

From the start of the events, Russia worked to adapt its policy in order to preserve its prior achievements and even benefit from the new situation. In this context, Russia cooperated with the international community and with the new regimes in the region while turning its back on collapsing authoritarian regimes. It even supported international intervention in Libya, a decision it later regretted.[27] Russia still identifies itself as an important player in West Asian affairs and will work to stabilize its weakened status. It appears that its willingness to compromise with the West on the WANA is now great, given that its strongholds are in the process of collapsing and it is being pushed into an uncomfortable position.[28]

Conclusion

The advent of the year 2011 represents a critical juncture in the modern political history of the Arab world. Since December 2010, a number of the Arab countries have witnessed an unprecedented popular uprising to call for not only reforms, transparency and the enforcement of law but also regime changes. The parameters of the Middle East's regional order have undergone profound changes on a scale not seen in the Arab contemporary history. Revolutions make possible new domestic political orders and substantial reorientations of foreign policies. Imitative uprisings have far resulted in widespread violence, regime retrenchments and even foreign interventions, although prospects do remain for more positive outcomes. The region is definitely in political ferment, but whether that presages transitions to democracy remains to be seen. The spread of demands for democracy in the Arab world in 2011 and 2012 rose up expectations of the people for a genuine change. But the imagery is not just premature but also misleading. The evident drama of these events makes it difficult to discern those changes that are superficial and transient from those which will be far-reaching and long-lasting. More importantly, these events have shifted the power balance in the region; thus, make key global players to reconsider their policies towards the region.

NOTES

1. Ahmed A. Saif, "Paradox of Regional and International Intervention in the Democratic Transformation Countries", Al Jazeera Center for Studies, Doha, 2012
2. Timur Kuranimur, "The Vulnerability of the Arab State: Reflections on the Ayubi Thesis", *The Independent Review*, Volume III, Number 1, Summer 1998, p. 113
3. Robert Springborg "Whither the Arab Spring? 1989 or 1848?",*The International Spectator: Italian Journal of International Affairs*, 46:3, 2011, 5-12, p. 5
4. Shashank Joshi, Ibid, p. 60.

5. Ghalyūn, B., "Al–Dimuqrā ṭiyah min Manzū ral–Mashrū al–Ḥaḍā ri", Paper presented at NaḥwMashrū Ḥaḍāri Nahḍawi, Arab studies and discussions of a seminar held at the Centre for Arab Unity Studies, Beirut, 2001, p. 442.
6. Shashank Joshi, "Reflections on the Arab Revolutions", *The RUSI Journal,* 156:2, 2011, 60-67, p. 60.
7. Shashank Joshi, Ibid, p. 60.
8. This section is based on a previous work; see Ahmed A. Saif, "Historical Background and Observations of Political Change in the Middle East", Second International Middle East Congress, "Change in the Middle East", 7-9 December 2011, Hatay, Turkey.
9. Ahmed A. Saif, "The Arab Spring", *Madarat Istratijiyah,* Issues 7-8, January-April 2011.
10. Mohammed Noureddine Affaya, "The 'Arab Spring': Breaking the Chains of Authoritarianism and Postponed Democracy", *Contemporary Arab Affairs,* 4:4, 2011, 463-483, p. 467
11. Christian-Peter Hanelt and Michael Bauer, March–June 2011, p. 1.
12. This part is based on a previous work; see Ahmed A. Saif, "Democratic Transformation in the Middle East and Potential Scenarios", "Revolution and Democratic Transformation in the Arab World: Towards a Road Map", Center of Arab Unity Studies and Swedish Institute in Alexandria, February 6-10 2012, Tunisia.
13. *BBC News,* "Rice Calls for Mid-East Democracy", June 20, 2005.
14. Shashank Joshi, No. 7, Ibid, p. 62.
15. Peter Alsis, Marissa Allison and Anthony H. Cordesman, "US and Iranian Strategic Competition in the Gulf States and Yemen", CSIS, March 16, 2012, p. 5.
16. Kristian Coates Ulrichsen, "Small States with a Big Role: Qatar and the United Arab Emirates in the Wake of the Arab Spring", Durham: Al-Sabah Number 3, October 2012, p. 3.
17. Kristian Coates Ulrichsen, Ibid, p. 8.
18. Ibid, p. 21.
19. Ahmed A. Saif, "The New Turkish Orientation Towards the Middle East: The New Ottomanism", Third Think Tanks Forum of the OIC Countries, "Change and Transformation in the OIC Countries", Center for Strategic Studies (SAM-Azerbaijan) and TASAM Institute of Islamic Studies, March 2-3, 2012, Baku-Azerbaijan.
20. This section is based on a previous work; see Ahmed A. Saif, "Rethinking the Arab Spring: Potential Scenarios", *MadaratIstratijiyah,* Issues 12-13, March-June 2012.
21. Analyzing the suggested scenarios is solely author's work.
22. Rosemary Hollis, "Britain and the Middle East from 9/11 to 2011", in Conservative Middle East Council the Arab Spring: Implications for British Policy, October 2011, p. 58.
23. C. Raja Mohan, "India's New Role in the Indian Ocean", available at http://www.indiaseminar.com/2011/617/617_c_raja_mohan.htm
24. Abhirup Bhunia, "India will Expand Global Geostrategic Clout by 2022", August 12, 2011, available at http://globalpolitician.com/27216-india-geostrategy-china-usa
25. James Phillips, "The Arab Spring Descends into Islamist Winter: Implications for US Policy", The Heritage Foundation, *Backgrounder,* No. 2754, December 20, 2012, p. 2
26. Shimon Stein, "The European Union and the Arab Spring" in YoelGuzansky and Mark A. Heller (eds.), *One Year of the Arab Spring: Global and Regional Implications,* Institute for National Security Studies, Memorandum No. 113 March 2012, p. 27
27. Zvi Magen, "Russia Faces the Results of the Arab Spring", in Yoel Guzansky and Mark A. Heller (eds.), *One Year of the Arab Spring: Global and Regional Implications,* Institute for National Security Studies, Memorandum No. 113 March 2012, p 29.
28. Ibid, p. 31.

7

West Asia: The Changing Political and Strategic Environment

Amin Saikal

The political and strategic environment of West Asia—usually designated as the region that stretches from Afghanistan to the Gulf and Levant states—is changing dramatically. The old regional order and co-relation of forces, which until recently exemplified the remnants of the Cold War era, are now vulnerable to greater political and strategic shifts than ever before. At this stage, one cannot be certain about the depth and intensity of the changes and their consequences, in the short term. A host of interconnected variables are at work and shaping the environment. However, by examining the most salient of these variables in the context of parallel or conflicting ideological and *realpolitik* objectives, interests and capabilities, it is possible to gain some degree of insight into the direction the regional strategic environment might take, in the medium to the long term.

As the situation exists, the main indicators point to a West Asia, whose political and strategic landscape is most likely to be dominated by four contrasting variables. The first is the Afghan, Iraqi and Syrian conflicts. The second is the growing popular drive in the region for greater political pluralism and accountability rather than authoritarianism, and a more *Ijtihadi* or reformist (that stresses on a creative interpretation and application of Islam, based on independent human reasoning), rather than *jihadi* or combative Islamism. The third promotes political and sectarian splits as for example the Saudi-Iranian rivalry, rather than across-the-board political and social reconciliation. The fourth is the festering Palestinian problem, and serious economic concerns, with regional actors and outside powers scrambling for leverage to influence the strategic shifts in their favour, in one way or another.

Political and Strategic Environment

Although there is no precise and concise definition of what constitutes a political strategic environment, in broad terms, it is the geopolitical space, within which grand strategies encompassing the calculation and projection of military, economic, diplomatic and moral resources are formulated by various actors, from within and outside that space, in times of both peace and conflict.[1] The issues taken into account include 'the importance of geographical configurations and location within which political power is exercised',[2] geographical centrality, balance of power and security parameters, and spill-over effects, where the conflict or politics in one state, directly affects the political organisation and behaviour of adjacent states.[3] It is in this context that West Asia's political and strategic environment is currently undergoing a metamorphosis.

The Afghan, Iraqi and Syrian Conflicts

Afghanistan, Iraq and Syria are in the throes of long-term structural disorder. They can all be best characterised as weak states with strong societies, that lack the necessary solid institutional foundation, national cohesion and effective ruling elites. There is no regional consensus on how to stabilise any of them. The future of each hangs very much in the balance.

With most of the US forces and those of its NATO and non-NATO allies slated to depart by the end of 2014, Afghanistan faces three scenarios. First is the continuation of the current situation. Backed by American air power and special forces from safe bases, Kabul may be able to hold out against the Pakistan-backed Taliban and their affiliates for some time before the situation becomes untenable, for either side. This was true in the case of the Soviet-installed Najibullah's government, from the time of the Soviet withdrawal from May 1989 until the government's collapse nearly three years later. Second, the Karzai leadership may succeed in striking some kind of power-sharing deal with at least elements of the armed opposition to install, a more or less, ethnic Pashtun-dominated government. This scenario could materialise, especially if China leverages its strategic relationship with Pakistan in its desire for a stable mineral-rich Afghanistan. However, this development would have an in-built high risk, of challenging Afghanistan's non-Pashtun clusters, which form the majority of the country's population, and alarming Afghanistan's neighbours (other than Pakistan) as well as India. It could result in Afghanistan relapsing into a situation similar to that, which existed prior to the US-led intervention more than 11 years ago. Third, the central government could implode, creating a greater political and strategic vacuum and resulting in violent fragmentation of Afghanistan, with Afghanistan's neighbours seeking to advance their regional interests by supporting favourable groups.

However, the scenario that could enable Afghanistan to avoid these possibilities is one where the Karzai leadership moves fast to put essential political and electoral reforms in place and holds free and fair presidential elections by mid-2014. Yet, this can only be achieved if the US and the international community sufficiently pressurise Karzai to do so, and remain fully engaged, albeit with reduced troops in Afghanistan. Otherwise, Karzai's record of poor leadership and governance, and his reluctance to hold an election at all, does not inspire much confidence. The direction Afghanistan takes and how its neighbours react are likely to have a profound impact on the regional political and strategic situation.

The same holds true of Iraq. The majority Shi'ite-dominated government in Baghdad may continue to hold on to power, with support from the Islamic Republic of Iran. But this would be at the cost of alienating the Saudi-led, Arab supported, Sunni minority and creating space for the US-backed but Turkish and Iranian-opposed Kurdish enclave in northern Iraq, which for all practical purposes has become as autonomous as it can, short of declaring independence. On the other hand, given the degree of elite fragmentation, and ideological and ethnic divisions, Iraq is at serious risk of violent disintegration, with regional actors, most importantly, Iran, Turkey, Saudi Arabia and its Gulf Cooperation Council (GCC) partners waiting to pick up the pieces. Unless the Iraqi ruling elite manages to get its act together, and reconciles national differences, and unless there is a regional understanding over Iraq, neither of these scenarios, leaves much room for a stable Iraq to emerge in the foreseeable future.

Syria's predicament is even more disconcerting. Whilst the minority Alawite-centric regime of Bashar al-Assad is in tatters, it still commands sufficient firepower and sectarian support to hang on to power for some more time. The popularly backed opposition forces, lack the necessary degree of unity and military resources to bring an end to the carnage in Syria. As long as this remains the case, and regional actors and major powers (Iran, Turkey, Saudi Arabia, the US, Russia and China in particular), pursue their divergent geopolitical objectives, the Syrian conflict is set to get more bloody and destructive until such time that one of the parties runs out of steam. The end result may not be a stable and democratically pluralist Syria. At best it could be a badly patched up and poorly governed country, or at worst a country fragmented along ethnic and sectarian lines, with various local overlords controlling different parts of the country.

The Syrian crisis has already proved to be extremely costly for Syria's neighbours. In addition to the humanitarian burden following the flow of refugees, it has wrecked Turkish-Syrian relations and strained Turkish-Iranian ties, that had been carefully nurtured since the rise of the, moderate Islamist Justice and Development Party in Turkey, which had become a stabilising factor in the region. Meanwhile, Iran's support of the Assad regime, followed by the Iranian-backed Hezbollah in Lebanon, has undermined the standing of Tehran and Hezbollah, in the Arab world, which is backing the opposition in Syria. Whilst labouring under crippling UN and Western sanctions, Iran's regional isolation has intensified. In the event of the collapse of the Assad regime, Tehran's overall political and strategic influence could further diminish—something that the US, Israel, Saudi Arabia and its GCC partners would very much welcome.

The Arab Revolts and Political Islamism

Along with the power shifts and uncertainties in West Asia, the Arab people's anti-authoritarian uprisings, since January 2011, have altered regional dynamics. Although popularly dubbed as the 'Arab Spring', the uprisings are more in the nature of an 'awakening, given the accompanying carnage that however varies from country to country. This awakening denotes a higher political and social consciousness and the inter-connectedness of the many segments of the Arab world, that is greater than at any other time in history.

The uprisings, spearheaded by pro-democracy elements, were for genuine self-determination against the backdrop of: chronic political repression; the substantial demographic changes in favour of younger and more connected generations; high unemployment and inflation; climatic changes, including long periods of drought; rising food prices; widening socio-economic inequalities and injustices; intellectual stagnation and outside interference.[4] The toppling of Ben Ali in Tunisia followed shortly by Hosni Mubarak in the Arab world's most populous and pivotal state, Egypt, highlighted the power of diffusion between Arab peoples and, more importantly, opened the way, for the first time in Arab history, for political activism and pluralism at the grassroots. The Tunisian and, more importantly, the Egyptian revolt encouraged the opposition in other Arab counties, which resulted in the bloody overthrow of Qaddafi's dictatorship in Libya, uproar in Syria, Bahrain and Yemen, and pressure on Algeria, Morocco, Jordan and most of the oil-rich Gulf Arab states, including even Saudi Arabia, to promise, and in some cases, even undertake, some political reforms.

Whatever the future course of developments, the Arab uprisings have altered the correlation of forces on the ground, across the wider West Asia. They have provided a stimulus for political pluralism, enabling political Islamists in the Sunni dominated Muslim Arab countries, where the dictatorial rulers have fallen or been weakened, to gain unprecedented electoral legitimacy and political ascendency.

Of course, not all the Islamists are of the same ideological texture. In general, political Islamists are those who believe, Islam to be an ideology for the political and social transformation of their societies. Some, like the Al-Qaeda, believe in violence, but most reject the use of any form of violence as a means to achieve their objectives. The bulk of Muslim thinkers, intellectuals and activists belong to the second category. Even so, they are of different ideological and political shades.[5]

Tunisia's Al-Nahda party, led by Rashid al-Ghannushi, falls in the *Ijtihadi* category. It has already proved to be moderate, pragmatic and inclusive, with a serious commitment to Tunisia's democratic transformation.[6] In this, it parallels the ruling Turkish Justice and Development Party (AKP).[7] On the other hand, the Egyptian Muslim Brotherhood has proved to be more complex and unpredictable. Whilst under President Mohammad Morsi it made a public commitment to a democratic transformation of Egypt, some of its Islamist actions caused much anxiety among the liberalists, secularists and Coptic Christians in Egypt. As a result, Egypt's transition has moved along a more turbulent and unpredictable path than that of Tunisia.

The Libyan situation appears to be heading in an even more uncertain direction. Although the pro-democracy elements gained the upper hand in 2012 parliamentary elections, Libya is in the throes of a long-term political and social division, the complexity of which is compounded by virtual disintegration of the state, as occurred in Iraq in the wake of the 2003 US invasion that toppled Saddam Hussein's dictatorship.[8] There is a need for serious compromise between the various political, social and ideological groupings to ensure the establishment of a non-extremist political order.

The Arab awakening has created a climate, in which people are no longer afraid to voice their demands and aspirations, and to fight for these demands if necessary. Whilst it is not possible to be exact about its implications at the regional level, in general the empowered political Islamists can be expected to advocate, as some of them have already done, a foreign policy posture which would be more in line with their Islamic ideological disposition. But this has to be in consonance with their domestic compulsions of maintaining power and authority, although largely through political competition and contestation.

In the years ahead, the political Islamists may press for a more independent foreign policy that is less accommodating towards Israel and less accepting of the traditional US geopolitical dominance in the region. It would be ideologically remiss of them not to sympathise with Hamas, the Palestinian Islamist group, that controls Gaza, and up the ante for a resolution of the Palestinian problem, involving the Israeli withdrawal from East Jerusalem, which is the third holiest site for Muslims, after Mecca and Medina. They can count on popular Arab support in this respect. The tide of such sentiment has already been on display, with the Islamists' taking a series of anti-Israeli steps over the last year. Prominent among these, is been the increase in the number Egypt's border openings into Gaza, in breach of Israel's blockade of the Strip;[9] the September 2011 storming of the Israeli embassy in Cairo as a reaction to the Israeli killing of three Egyptian border guards, for which Israel apologised;[10] and the most recent unilateral and politically induced cancellation of the Egyptian-Israeli gas contract, which had provided 40 per cent of Israel's gas needs.[11]

Does this mean that one could expect the Arab Islamists to follow Iran, in their approach to power and disposition towards the West?

In broad terms, the answer is no. Despite all its public posturing that the Arab revolts are essentially a confirmation of the Iranian revolution of 1978/79 that toppled the Shah's pro-Western regime, and paved the way for the establishment of Ayatollah Khomeini's Islamic government, with its anti-US and anti-Israel policy, Tehran has not been immune from the Arab developments. In reaction to them and Western pressure over its nuclear programme, the Iranian regime has become even more theocratic, clamping down on all forms of opposition, including that arising from within its own clerical ranks. Whilst the Iranian Shi'ite Islamic order is uniquely based on an unelected supreme political and religious leader, representing the 'sovereignty of God', and an elected president and National Assembly, representing the 'sovereignty of people', the majority of the Arab people want only a popularly mandated exercise of power and authority. They uphold Islam as their religion, but want good governance, based not on religious dictates, but on evolving internal and external realities. In other words, they challenge their political Islamists to be *Ijtihadi* rather than *Jihadi*. This applies not only to the countries that are undergoing political transformation, but also to those where such a transformation has not yet commenced, in a substantial way. Most Arab political Islamists have been put on notice, as the case of Egypt has demonstrated. Outside powers need to be very understanding of the nature of developments in the Arab domain and must respect their popularly mandated outcomes.

Sectarian-Political Splits and Saudi-Iranian Rivalry

Another variable that partly springs from the Arab Awakening is the deepening and broadening of sectarian-political fault-lines and the Saudi-Iranian proxy conflict for regional influence. As several Arab states, most importantly Egypt, have been seriously disrupted, and their economic conditions weakened in varying degrees, the oil-rich conservative Islamic Saudi monarchy, which claims leadership of the Sunni Muslim world, has become more assertive as a regional player, because it has two main objectives. The first is to ensure that Saudi Arabia, together with its Arab partners within the GCC, all of whom (with the exception of Bahrain) are also oil-rich, are not contaminated by the popular revolts in other parts of the Arab world.[12] The second is to steer a foreign policy course that prevents other regional actors to take advantage of the transformative developments in the Arab world, to expand their interests, at the expense of Saudi Arabia and its allies.

With regard to the first objective, whilst presiding over a sovereign fund of some $500 billion, the Saudi leadership has been engaged in subtle resource diplomacy and geostrategic activities to support the Islamist and secularist forces that are aligned with its national interests and security, including preserving the status quo within the GCC.[13] For example, it has provided some backing to the Salafists and the Military Council in Egypt to 'balance' the Muslim Brotherhood and some of the other groups, which it regards as undesirable.[14] In Yemen it has backed a transition that leaves Saleh's regime largely intact, but without Saleh.[15] Meanwhile, it has deployed troops in Bahrain,[16] reportedly channelled arms and money to the opposition in Syria, and stood shoulder to shoulder with the Arab monarchies, whether in the Gulf or Jordan or Morocco, to maintain the status quo within their own borders.

With respect of the second objective, Riyadh has been careful not to allow, any strategic space created as a result of changes in the Arab world, to be filled by other regional powers. Two countries that have come under its spotlight are the predominantly Sunni Muslim, Turkey and Shi'ite Islamic Iran, although, more the latter than the former. Riyadh has harboured some irritation with Turkey, because of the popularity that Turkey has gained among the Arabs, including among a number of non-Salafist Islamist groups. In addition to emerging as an attractive model for many Arabs, Turkey's moderate Islamist AKP has proven acceptable to the US and its Western allies. Led by the charismatic prime minister, Tayyip Erdogan, Turkey has not only downgraded its past close relationship with Israel and made common cause with the Palestinians, but has also been quick to lend moral, political and humanitarian support to the Arab popular uprisings, based on democratic principles and values.[17] In spite of making common cause with Ankara in condemning the Assad regime in Syria, Riyadh cannot be pleased about Turkey's growing role in the region. There is lingering suspicion in a number of Arab circles regarding Ankara's motives, as Turkey is now more influential in the Middle East, than it was in the heyday of the Ottoman Empire, when it ruled most of the Arab world.

Saudi-Iranian Rivalry and the Iranian Nuclear Program

However, it is Iran that Riyadh views, as the real regional protagonist. It has demonstrated increasing concern, about what it perceives as, Iran's expanding regional influence and ambitions. It is troubled, not only by Tehran's strategic partnership with Assad's regime in Syria and its organic links with the powerful Hezbollah in Lebanon,[18] but also by its close sectarian cum political relationship with Nurri al-Maliki's Iraqi government and certain Iraqi sub-national groups, most importantly that of firebrand Muqtadr al-Sadr and the Islamic Supreme Council for Iraq (ISCI), not to mention some Shi'ite groups in Afghanistan.[19] Hence the Saudi deployment of forces in Bahrain, the strong support for the Saad Hariri-led Sunni opposition in Lebanon and certain Sunni groups in Iraq, the Sunni opponents of the Assad regime in Syria, and the strenuous efforts to ensure that Yemen has a post-Saleh government that is receptive to Riyadh and has the capability to prevent Iran from providing support to Yemen's rebellious Shi'ite minority, right on the border with Saudi Arabia.

An additional dimension of the volatile Saudi-Iranian relationship is Iran's nuclear programme, over which Saudi Arabia shares concerns with its GCC partners as well as the US and some of its European allies, and paradoxically even Israel. Whilst circumspect in its public utterances about what should be done to ensure that Iran does not acquire military nuclear capability, King Abdullah reportedly supports the use of force by the US, as a last resort.[20]

At this point, it is important to note that neither the International Atomic Energy Agency (IAEA) nor the US and its allies have so far produced any solid proof that Iran has a secret military nuclear programme. The IAEA has only raised questions about such a programme, based largely on an assessment of the number of centrifuges and the Arak heavy water reactor that Iran has made operational, as well as the Iranian refusal to allow the IAEA free access to all its nuclear facilities.[21] In fact, the Barack Obama administration's position is that Iranian nuclear ambitions can be contained by coercive diplomacy, involving sanctions and negotiations. By the same token, in contrast to the repeated warnings by Israeli Prime Minister Benjamin Netanyahu and some of his ministers, that Iran is determined to produce nuclear weapons and that Israel will not allow this to happen; several credible serving and retired Israeli military and intelligence figures have confirmed the American position and questioned the efficacy of an Israeli aerial assault on Iranian nuclear installations. The latest person to do so is the Israeli Chief of Staff Lt. Gen. Benny Gantz, who has now publicly stated that Iran will not develop nuclear weapons and that the Iranian leadership is rational.[22]

The Obama administration and like minded groups and individuals have been influenced by two considerations. The first is that according to credible Iranian sources, the Iranian leadership has not yet taken the decision to acquire military nuclear capability. Three competing views seem to be current within the defused leadership and wider Iranian population. One favours nuclear weapons for deterrence purposes. Another argues that possession of such weapons will mean more international pressure and isolation, and could make Iran the target of an Israeli conventional or nuclear attack. The third postulates that Iran should acquire nuclear technology but refrain from crossing the threshold.[23]

The second consideration is, that a military attack could only set the Iranian nuclear programme back by a few years, but would at the same time mobilise the Iranian public behind an unpopular regime, and make the regime renew its efforts to produce nuclear weapons. Moreover, in the event of an Iranian retaliation—both military and non-military—the region could become an inferno,[24] with far-reaching international political and economic implications, at a time when

Western economies are in serious difficulties and US-Russian and US-Chinese relations are fragile. However, whilst an Israeli, US or for that matter combined military attack on Iran is not inevitable, if the international talks between Iran and the five permanent members of the UN Security Council, plus Germany, fail to produce tangible results, the risk of a military confrontation and its consequences may result in a major regional strategic upheaval. It is unfortunate that the nuclear fuel-swap deal, brokered by which Brazilian President Lulada Silva and Turkish Prime Minister Erdogan, in May 2010, whereby Tehran agreed to send 1200 kg of uranium to be enriched in Turkey, was condemned by the US and its allies.[25] The Obama administration could have capitalised on this deal to test Tehran's stance.

Yet, all this does not suggest that a direct Saudi-Iranian military confrontation is looming. The constraints under which both sides operate are significant. The Iranian regime has not only to contend, with a fragile political system, that has pitched the 'sovereignty of God' against the 'sovereignty of people',[26] but also with severe Western sanctions and isolation, exacerbating Iran's deep-seated economic and social problems.[27] Saudi Arabia faces a daunting leadership succession problem and its limited capabilities do not allow it to spread itself too thin.[28] Yet, the two protagonists can be expected to enhance their involvement in proxy conflicts. This is already evident in Bahrain, Iraq, and Lebanon, and has taken a sharper dimension in relation to Syria.

Major Power Involvement

The scene is set for a heightened Saudi-Iranian rivalry, dominating the changing regional strategic landscape in the coming years. Intertwined with this would be a conflicting major power interest and involvement in the Middle East. Irrespective of its renewed emphasis on the Asia-Pacific, the United States can be expected to remain deeply engaged in the region to preserve its traditional geostrategic dominance. Thus, its policy may continue on its present and past contradictory course. At present, while on the one hand Washington has been keen to project a public profile in support of democracy, stability, peace and self-determination in the region; on the other hand, it has also remained steadfast in supporting those forces with whose cooperation it can maintain its influence. Hence, for example, the US support for Saudi Arabia and its GCC partners despite the authoritarian nature of their regimes, and its commitment to Israel within a strategic partnership, regardless of the Israeli government's intransigence in negotiating a settlement with the Palestinians, within the framework of the internationally-backed two state solution.[29] In this context, the Palestinian issue is most likely to persist as a festering problem and as a source of anti-American feeling within the Arab and Muslim world, preventing the empowered Arab Islamist forces from being favourably disposed towards the United States and its allies. By the same token, Israel runs the risk of wider isolation in the region, and should the Arab countries around it, take a democratic trajectory, it will not be able to claim the higher moral ground as the only democracy in the region.

At the same time, Russia and China can be expected to remain supportive of Iran, and indirectly, some of its allies, for both strategic and economic reasons. This is already apparent in relation to Syria. Russia's interest in backing the Assad regime is shaped not only by lucrative arms deals and the use of Syria's Latakia port, but also by a desire to maintain a strategic foothold in the unpredictable and changing wider West Asia, to counter-balance the US and prevent the rise of a Sunni Islamic crescent that could benefit its historical rival, Turkey. It is also influenced by a policy consideration not to see a weakening of Iran, with which it has $4 billion annual economic and military trade.[30] Similarly, China has good economic reasons to have a strategic niche in the region. It imports eleven per cent of its oil needs from Iran, with the volume of trade between the two sides reaching some $45 billion in 2011.[31] Beijing also seems to be uncomfortable with changes in the regional *status quo*, specifically if they involve pro-democracy developments, as well as, what it views as, America's efforts to pursue a policy of containment vis-à-vis China.

The Economic Variable and Youth Unemployment

Another variable in the overall calculation is the economic situation in the countries, undergoing leadership changes or embroiled in popular turmoil. This is nowhere a greater issue than in Egypt. The Egyptian economic situation is dire. The country's national treasury is depleted, with sources of income, ranging from tourism to industrial production, falling. Its economy needs an injection of some $80 billion to enable it to reach an annual growth rate of 7 per cent, as was the case prior to the overthrow of Mubarak, as a minimum requirement for creating more employment opportunities for the swelling ranks of unemployed youth. That capital is not available from anywhere.[32] Demographic changes in favour of the younger generation have been phenomenal across the region. Overall, 60-70 per cent of the population in each Arab state (not to mention Iran) is below the age of 25.[33] The demand for job opportunities and better standards of living has grown exponentially in most of the Arab states and this trend is set to continue for the foreseeable future, with national consumption outstripping national production. Whoever is in power, along with outside interested actors, will have to focus paramount attention on the economy; and the unemployed youth which are the main reasons for the chronic social unrest and political instability.

The same is true in the case of Iran, whose economic and social woes are also deep seated. Unless Tehran reaches a settlement over its nuclear programme, its economic situation can only get worse. Despite the interim agreement between

P5+1 on Iran's nuclear programme, final outcome of this agreement is yet to unfold. Indeed, another option would be to arrive at a settlement within the context of a region-wide regime of disarmament to include Israel—but it is highly unlikely that the Israelis and the US would embrace this idea.

Conclusion

A number of variables are now set to determine and influence the evolving strategic environment over at least the next five years. Critically, they include political pluralism and accountability, *Ijtihadi* political Islamism, demand for better standards of living, sectarian-political divisions and conflicts, Saudi-Iranian strategic competition, the Iranian nuclear programme, the Palestinian problem and the policy attitudes and actions of the major powers toward the region. All indicators point to a changing, although not necessarily less volatile, strategic environment, with major powers playing their part in seeking to influence it according to their geopolitical preferences. West Asia is on a rollercoaster ride. How the regional leaderships and international actors handle this will be critical for the overall outcome.

NOTES

1. For more on grand strategy, see B. H. Liddell Hart, *Strategy* (London: Faber & Faber, 1967).
2. Geoffrey Sloan, 'Sir Halford J. MacKinder: The Heartland Theory Then and Now', in Colin S. Gray and Geoffrey Sloan (eds), *Geopolitics, Geography and Strategy* (Abingdon: Frank Cass, 1999), pp. 15-38 at p. 20. For a discussion on geopolitics, see Saul Bernard Cohen, *Geopolitics: The Geography of International Relations*, 2ndedn (Lanham: Rowman & Littlefield, 2009) and Colin S. Gray and Geoffrey Sloan (eds), *Geopolitics, Geography and Strategy* (Abingdon: Frank Cass, 1999), esp. chs 1, 2, 6, 7, 9 and 11.
3. Kemal Kirisci and Gareth M. Winrow, *The Kurdish Question and Turkey: An Example of a Trans-State Ethnic Conflict* (London and Portland: Frank Cass & Co., 1997), p. 19.
4. See Amin Saikal, 'Authoritarianism, Revolution and Democracy: Egypt and Beyond, *Australian Journal of International Affairs*, 65(5) 2011: 530-544.
5. Amin Saikal, *Islam and the West: Conflict or Cooperation?* London: Palgrave Macmillan, 2003, pp. 20-23.
6. See Alfred Stepan, 'Tunisia's Transition and the Twin Tolerations', *Journal of Democracy*, 23(2) 2012: 89-103.
7. For a discussion on the AKP, see Umit Cizre (ed.), *Secular and Islamic Politics in Turkey: The Making of the Justice and Development Party* (Abingdon: Routledge, 2008).
8. See Brookings Institution, *Iraq Index: Tracking Variables of Reconstruction & Security in Post-Saddam Iraq*, Saban Centre for Middle East Policy, 30 September 2010.
9. Donald MacIntyre, 'Egypt Softens Stance on Hamas with Move to Open Gaza Border Crossing', *The Independent*, 30 April, 2011.
10. Harriet Sherwood, 'Egypt Declares State of Alert after Israeli Embassy Broken into', *The Guardian*, 10 September, 2011.
11. Avi Bar-Eli, 'Egypt Cancels Natural Gas Deal with Israel', *Haaretz*, 22 April 2012.
12. The GCC was founded as a defensive alliance primarily against Iran in 1981, and is composed of Bahrain, Kuwait, Oman, Qatar, Saudi Arabia and United Arab Emirates.

13. For an overview, see See Mehran Kamrava, 'The Arab Spring and the Saudi-Led Counterrevolution', *Orbis*, 56(1) 2012: 96-104.
14. Saudi Arabia sees the Muslim Brotherhood as a competitor for its religious leadership of the Islamic world.
15. Michael Peel, 'Saudi Arabia Pledges $3.25bn aid to Yemen', *The Financial Times*, 23 May, 2012.
16. Ethan Bronner and Michael Slackman, 'Saudi Troops enter Bahrain to Help Put Down Unrest', *New York Times*, 14 March 2011.
17. See Ziya Onis, 'Multiple Faces of the "New" Turkish Foreign Policy: Underlying Dynamics and a Critique', Center for Globalisation and Democratic Governance, GLODEM Working Paper Series, April 2010; and Meliha B. Altunsik and Lenore G. Martin, 'Making Sense of Turkish Foreign Policy in the Middle East under AKP', *Turkish Studies*, 12(4) 2011: 569-587.
18. On Hezbollah, see Augustus Richard Norton, *Hezbollah: A Short History* (Princeton: Princeton University Press, 2007). For more on Hezbollah's perspectives, see Nicholas Noe (ed.), *Voice of Hezbollah: The Statements of Sayed Hassan Nasrallah*(London: Verso, 2007).
19. On Iran's foreign policy and growing role in the region, see Amin Saikal, 'Iran's New Strategic Entity', *Australian Journal of International Affairs*, 61(3)2007: 296-305 and FarhandMorady, 'Iran Ambitious for Regional Supremacy: The Great Powers, Geopolitics and Energy Resources', *Journal of the Indian Ocean Region*, 7(1) 2011: 75-94 at p. 81. On the Syria-Iranian relationship, see Jubin M. Goodarzi, *Syria and Iran* (London: I.B. Tauris, 2006).
20. The GCC and Egypt are unlikely to stand by idly if Iran develops a military nuclear capability. See Eric S. Edelman, Andrew F. Krepinevich and Evan Braden Montgomery, 'The Dangers of a Nuclear Iran: The Limits of Containment', *Foreign Affairs*, 90(1) 2011: 66-81.
21. For more on Iran's nuclear capability, see Amin Saikal, 'The Iran Nuclear Dispute', *Australian Journal of International Affairs*, 60(2) 2006: 193-199 and *Implementation of the NPT Safeguards Agreement and Relevant Provisions of Security Council Resolutions in the Islamic Republic of Iran*, Report by the Director General, GOV/2011/65, International Atomic Energy Agency, 8 November 2011, p. 10.
22. Gabrielle Rifkind, 'Iran Nuclear Talks: Signs of Cautious Optimism Emerge', *The Guardian*, 22 May 2012.
23. See International Crisis Group, *US-Iranian Engagement: The View from Tehran*, Middle East Briefing No. 28, 2 June 2009.
24. For a discussion on Iranian military capabilities in the Strait of Hormuz, see Caitlin Talmadge, 'Closing Time: Assessing the Iranian Threat to the Strait of Hormuz', *International Security*, 33(1) 2008: 82-117 and Anthony H. Cordesman, 'Iran, Oil, and the Strait of Hormuz', Discussion Paper, Center for Strategic and International Studies, 26 March 2007.
25. Trita Parsi, 'The Turkey-Brazil-Iran Deal: Can Washington take "Yes" for an Answer?',*Foreign Policy*, 17 May 2010.
26. On this confrontation, see Amin Saikal, 'The Roots of Iran's Election Crisis', *Survival*, 51(5) 2009: 92;RaminJahanbegloo, 'The Two Sovereignties and the Legitimacy Crisis in Iran', *Constellations*, 17(1) 2010: 22-30 and Jamsheed K. Choksy, 'Is This Really The End for Ahmadinejad?', *Foreign Policy*, 26 November 2010.
27. On Iran's faltering economy, see 'Preface' in Amin Saikal, *The Rise and Fall of the Shah: Iran from Autocracy to Religious Rule*, 2ndedn(Princeton: Princeton University Press, 2009); Jahangir Amuzegar, *Iran's Economy in Turmoil*, Carnegie Endowment for International Peace, March 2010 and FarnazFassihi, 'Iran's Economy Feels String of Sanctions', *The Wall Street Journal*, 12 October 2010.
28. For more on Saudi Arabia, see Tim Niblock, *Saudi Arabia: Power, Legitimacy, and Survival* (New York:Routledge, 2006) and Anthony H. Cordesman, *Saudi Arabia: National Security in a Troubled Region* (Santa Barbara: ABC-CLIO, 2009).

29. For a discussion of the US-Saudi relationship, see Parker T. Hart, *Saudi Arabia and the United States: Birth of a Security Partnership* (Bloomington: Indiana University Press, 1998).
30. Nevertheless, it is considered that a triangle of regional competition exists between Russia, Turkey and Iran. See HoomanPeimani, *Regional Security and the Future of Central Asia* (Westport: Praeger Publishers, 1998) and Alvin Z. Rubinstein and Oles M. Smolandsky (eds) *Regional Power Rivalries in the New Eurasia: Russia, Turkey and Iran* (New York: M.E. Sharpe, 1995).
31. For more on China's complex relationship with Iran, see John W. Garver, 'Is China Playing a Dual Game in Iran?', *Washington Quarterly*, 34(1) 2011: 75-88.
32. For more on the Egyptian economy, see Hanâ' Khayr al-Dîn (ed.), *The Egyptian Economy: Current Challenges and Future Prospects* (Cairo: American University in Cairo Press, 2008). On some perspectives on the global financial crisis's effect on the Egyptian economy and recent Egyptian policies, see Robert Bowker, *Egypt and the Politics of Change in the Arab Middle East* (Cheltenham: Edward Elgar, 2010) and American Chamber of Commerce in Egypt, *The Report: Egypt* (Oxford: Oxford Business Group, 2010).
33. For instance, on the youth in Egypt, see RaguiAssaaad, 'Unemployment and Youth Insertion in the Labor Market in Egypt', in Hanâ' Khayr al-Dîn (ed.), *The Egyptian Economy: Current Challenges and Future Prospects* (Cairo: American University in Cairo Press, 2008) pp. 133-176 and Bowker, *Egypt and the Politics of Change in the Arab Middle East*, Ch. 3.

PART III

West Asia's Security Dynamics-I: Role of Extra-Regional Powers

8

Russia in the Middle East: Battle for Principles?

Fyodor Lukyanov

In mid-2012, when a new round of diplomatic activity began in Syria, a French journalist sought an interview with me to discuss Russia's position on this severe conflict in the Middle East. He began the interview without any preface. "Why does Russia support the criminal dictatorship which kills its own people aspiring to democracy?" "And why does the West support terrorists and Islamists who seek to take power in one Arab country after another, relying on material and ideological support from the most reactionary governments in the region?" I parried. Having exchanged civilities, we began to speak to the point.

The Western and Russian perspectives of the events in the Middle East, are poles apart. The reason is not propaganda or fundamental differences in interests, although both exist. Moscow and Western capitals have basically different views of what is going on in the world. Russia, which recently experienced the catastrophe of economic and simultaneously geopolitical collapse, is very sensitive to destructive tendencies and related threats, and it knows—from experience—how great is the difference between intentions and their implementation. The West, despite many upheavals of the last decade, still lives on its triumph of the late 20th century, analysing developments in the world through an ideological prism.

The Middle East is a complex and diverse region, where one can find signs of all possible processes. In the near future, it will become clear who was right—Moscow with its down-to-earth pessimistic view of the upheavals, or Paris and Washington, which prefer to see manifestations of the "right side of history" in the changes.

Mercantile and Geopolitical Interests

It seems that no one abroad, understands Russia's position on the Syrian issue, which encapsulates the quintessence of the developments in the Middle East and, possibly, in the entire Muslim world. In any case, none of those who are directly involved in doing anything about this bloody conflict.

Initially, Moscow's stance was explained in purely mercantile terms: Bashar al-Assad's regime is a major customer of the Russian defence industry, so the latter, frustrated by its losses in the Iranian market (the cancellation of a contract for the sale of the S-300 missile system) and in the Libyan market (the overthrow of Gaddafi following Russia's refusal to veto a UN Security Council resolution), has taken a last ditch stand to save its last partner. However, the cogency of this reasoning soon began to be doubted. According to recent estimates by the Centre for Analysis of Strategies and Technologies, arms sales to Damascus in 2011 accounted for only five per cent of all Russian arms exports. The so-called Russian "naval base" in Tartus, which is described as the only Russian military base outside the former Soviet Union, has only a token value, because in actual fact it is nothing more than a berth for ships and a ship-repairing workshop. In addition, Syria has paid Russia only $1 billion since 2006 out of the $5.5 billion it owes Russia for various contracts. And, finally, it quickly became clear that, regardless of the scenario that unfolds in Syria, "business as usual" with the Assad regime was no longer possible.

In view of this, Moscow's policy seems especially puzzling. Commentators wondered why Moscow should so stubbornly refuse to acknowledge the facts, cling to a doomed figure, and thus burn its bridges, because the incumbent regime will go, and its stubborn support by Russia will only mean hostile relations with any future government of Syria. Therefore, in late 2012 the statements of Russian officials were closely examined to see whether there were any signs that the Kremlin and the Russian foreign ministry were "waking up to reality." A statement by Deputy Foreign Minister Mikhail Bogdanov, not intended to be broadly cited, to the effect that the opposition may win in Syria, created a sensation: Russia seemed to be changing its point of view under the pressure of the inevitable and giving up its support for Assad.

Clearly, no one ever believed the continuously repeated statements of Putin, Lavrov, Bogdanov and others, that Moscow's is not supporting Assad in Syria, but certain principles. Meanwhile, sceptics should give the Russian position a second thought. In order to understand what really motivates Russia's policy in the Middle East at the height of the Arab Spring, one should know that for Russia, the Syrian market, or the future of Bashar al-Assad and his regime (in descending order) are not decisive factors.

Its policy should be viewed from a different angle—one not so much related to the Middle East as to Moscow's general view of how international relations should be organised. This view has been repeatedly expressed, publicly and officially, by Foreign Minister Sergei Lavrov: "If someone wants to use force by all means, we will hardly be able to prevent that," Lavrov said at an annual press-conference on January 18, 2012 in Moscow, "But let this happen on their own initiative and let it rest on their conscience. They will not receive any authorisation from the UN Security Council." The minister's statement set the framework of parameters for Russia's position. Another crucial and even more explicit statement was made on July 16: "A model of the international community's reaction to internal conflicts in the future will largely depend on how the Syrian crisis is resolved."

Russia's persistence is directly related to what happened in Libya in 2011. Following President Dmitry Medvedev's personal decision, Moscow at that time had backed away from its usual position, on the inadmissibility of outside interference in countries' internal affairs and actually agreed to a military operation against the Gaddafi regime. That "goodwill gesture" is now almost officially considered a mistake—both in practical and conceptual terms, and Moscow's tough stance on Syria is intended to disavow it, and not let the "international community" take the Libyan model as an example to follow in future conflicts. From the point of view of Russian strategists, the Libyan model is as follows: external forces choose the "right" side in an internal conflict and help it come to power by their interference.

As a matter of fact, events in the Middle East have revealed that the Russian leadership is divided by conceptual differences over the country's place in the world and ways in which it should be gained. This is not the stereotypical opposition between "pro-Western" and "anti-Western" approaches, between "Westerners" and "nationalists." Generally speaking, the West as a reference point in Moscow's coordinate system is slowly and painfully receding into the background—it makes no sense to be guided by this reference point in a world where the East is becoming the main determinant factor. In these circumstances, a different logic comes to the fore—allocation of priorities in world affairs, assuming that Russia is not (and will never be) the Soviet Union, and that therefore it cannot claim equal participation in all international processes.

Structural Realism of Putin

Dmitry Medvedev's unusual decision in early 2011 to not oppose a military operation against Libya may be explained in different ways—but one of the reasons was simply—Russia's priorities. During the years of his presidency, there was a tendency to view Russia as a regional power. Of course, given the region in which Moscow intends to retain its leadership, a global dimension is inevitable —actually, this is almost the whole of Eurasia, stretching from "Old Europe" to the Pacific Ocean. And yet, this is a territory that is geographically limited.

The high-profile statement made by Dmitry Medvedev in August 2008, immediately after the Five-Day War against Georgia, to the effect that Russia would defend "the sphere of its privileged interests" by all means was taken as a declaration of intent to start a new Russian expansion. Later it became clear that the statement had a somewhat different meaning, and that "the sphere of interests" implied some boundaries. For example, the Soviet Union had no well-defined sphere of interests; rather, it encompassed the entire globe, as did the United States. Libya was not included in Russia's sphere as Medvedev saw it. Of course, contracts worth $4 billion sound good, but they are nothing more than just business. They are not worth risking a new confrontation with the US and Europe, with whom interaction in other areas is very important.

Putin, like Medvedev, does not view Russia as a global power in the former sense. His priorities encompass the same "sphere of interests," and his favourite idea is a Eurasian Union that would link the markets of Europe and the Asia-Pacific region. However, unlike Medvedev, Putin does not think Russia should concentrate exclusively on its own region. The incumbent president views the ability to influence the situation in other parts of the world as an instrument for bargaining, namely, exchanging the opportunities available there for privileges in the sphere of Russia's immediate interests. In other words, it is only by playing the entire field (even if sporadically) and maintaining global coverage that Russia can secure its priority right in its sector of the planet. From this point of view, the Middle East is not an area of Russia's immediate interest but the arena of an important regional game, where holding the trump card would enable it to feel more confident at other gaming tables.

In international affairs, Medvedev proved to be a liberal, consciously or unconsciously. According to him, internal development was primary and determined the foreign policy (Medvedev spoke about this in detail in his speech before the diplomatic corps in July 2010). Various processes and events should be viewed individually, and one should take decisions on a case by case basis, rather than view everything as interlinked. This is a typical liberal approach.

Vladimir Putin views the world differently and is committed to structural realism according to which, the environment determines countries' behaviour; the system is a single whole and everything in it is interlinked. An impact on one part affects the other part. Hence his constant criticism of the West's interventionism—not only because it calls into question the "sacred" principle of sovereignty. Any interference in the system disrupts self-regulation and exacerbates the general chaos in the world, which, he believes, will sooner or later provoke chaos in countries to which Russia is also vulnerable.

Putin's tenure as president coincided with a period when Russia, willy-nilly, was already an integral part of the global world system and could not isolate itself from the processes taking place in it. He came to power under the banner of stability in Russia when the world was swept by uncertainty and when the habitual institutional structure was falling to pieces. Feverish attempts by the West to bolster the world system, built according to Western templates, rendered the entire construct unstable. And since it is a single whole, as it has never been before, the consequences of someone's ill-considered moves affect everyone. Internal stabilisation cannot deal with the increasing external destabilisation. In other words, Putin has found himself out of phase, which disturbs him. He does not understand the policies of the leading powers, whose actions seem to be intended to throw the international situation off balance and knock out the props keeping it in place.

Putin is not alone in opposing this state of affairs, but it has so happened that he is leading the resistance—first of all, because Russia, despite its decline after the Soviet Union's break-up, remains one of the most active countries, with clear ambitions. Secondly, because of Russia's nuclear and raw material potential, it is impossible to ignore its opinion. And finally, because of the president's personality—which is characterised by straight forwardness and frankness, not typical of top-level politicians. Political correctness is a concept deeply alien to him. Taken together, these factors have turned Putin into the poster child of the anti-Western opposition, although he is not going to lead any "fronts". He does not want a world geopolitical revolution, and he is rather concerned about shutting himself off from external pressures.

During Vladimir Putin's first two terms as president in the 2000s, there was much speculation in the West about Russia: one committed to the status quo, or a revolutionary revisionist state. It has now become obvious that Russia is a status-quo power, but in a somewhat different sense. Moscow is trying to preserve the principles, that would help structure the international environment, which is becoming increasingly chaotic, uncontrollable and therefore dangerous. The point is not about influence but self-preservation.

No Use Changing the Position

Russia has a basically different view of the happenings in Syria (and in the Middle East in general) than the West and the Arab world. It sees it as a bitter civil war driven by religious (Sunnis vs. Shiites) and geopolitical (Gulf monarchies vs. Iran) motives. At stake in this war is not democracy in Damascus but a balance of power in the Middle East. The majority of the forces involved in the war, especially external ones, do not care about the future of Syria. Moscow understands that, given the scale of the foreign interference in the developments in Syria, Bashar al-Assad will hardly be allowed to stay. Yet, all Russian experts, specialising in the Arab East, are of the unanimous view that a large part of the Syrian population (it is difficult to get precise figures in the war conditions) is behind Assad.

In this situation, Russia's logic is simple. There is no point in changing its position, because, after Assad is removed from power, Syria will either lose its territorial integrity or will be controlled by forces that view Russia as their enemy.

(In Libya, Gaddafi was overthrown largely due to Moscow's non-veto. Had it taken a different position, the extravagant dictator might have suppressed the opposition in Benghazi and still ruled in Tripoli. However, Russia has not received even small thanks in return from the new authorities.) But even in the second scenario, the example of Iraq (the $4.2-billion-dollar contract for the purchase of arms, signed in the autumn of 2012,) and, partly, the example of Libya show that over time the winners need to diversify their contacts, including in favour of Russia. Participating in a settlement imposed from abroad is dangerous—the results will most likely be disastrous, while Russia will find itself among countries that will have to bear moral responsibility for the future chaos. Proposing a political process in which the Syrians themselves should determine their own destiny is safe: the idea is obvious, and if this proves impossible... "Well, we warned you".

Russia is greatly concerned about the Islamisation of the Middle East, because the strengthening of radicals and dogmatists will inevitably affect the Muslim regions of Russia. This was already proven by the sad experience of the Chechen war during the 1990s-early 2000s. This is a particularly burning issue; now that Russia's Soviet and post-Soviet identity is dissolving, concerns regarding inter-religious relations in the country are on the rise. Russian Muslims are gradually becoming aware of their rights, and this may trigger opposition from Russian Orthodox believers.

As for Russia's geopolitical outlook, it is the main mystery for those who are trying to interpret the Russian position. Russia has one advantage over the United States, which claims global leadership, and over Europe—which is dependent on it for energy supplies—in a worst-case scenario, Moscow can simply leave. That would be vexing, but not fatal. Neither the US, nor the EU can afford to do this. Moreover, not being a global power and being more focussed on its interests as a regional power, Russia can afford to leave the game in the Middle East, if things get really hot there, "entrench itself" on distant approaches and watch the West trying to cope with the "Arab Awakening." And it will only need to wait until the situation changes again, which will inevitably happen when it turns out, yet again, that things have not gone the way, the initiators and participants of the changes had planned.

How to Capitalise on Stubborn Position

Throughout 2012, Russia did not yield from its position on the Syrian issue—that the conflict must be resolved politically within the country, with no outside interference. Moscow endured sharp criticism, strong pressure, and bewildered questions about the reasonableness of its approach: why knowingly make a losing bet on a doomed dictator? At least three times, Russia was declared as being fatally intransigent, and others promised to resolve the problem without it, but then again after reaching a stalemate on the battlefield, they turned to Moscow once more for help. It seems that the West and the Arab countries are only now beginning to understand that Russia is actually standing on principles and not simply pursuing its own mercantile interests. This means that the successful result of Russian diplomacy will not be keeping Bashar Assad in power, but ensuring a smooth transition of power without external intervention or internal collapse. And in general, it is not of fundamental importance who will lead Syria in the future. The previous, hugely profitable commercial relationships will no longer exist, but new relationships will surely be built, simply because certain things in the region still depend on Russia.

The overthrow of Bashar Assad, of course, will be a political defeat for Russia; at least it will be seen as a defeat by all. Both from the point of view of prestige and in the practical sense: all of Russia's enormous diplomatic efforts will come to nothing, and Moscow will be seen as having bet on the wrong horse. Therefore, it is in Russia's interests to support and advance the political process, in order to capitalise on its two years of intensive work.

The Russian diplomats working on resolving the Syrian conflict are more and more frequently using the word "Dayton". The Dayton Accord of 1995, which ended the war in Bosnia, has faced much criticism since that time, because it has not provided the basis for stable statehood in that country. It is unpopular in Russia, because it was signed during the period when Moscow's influence in international affairs was at its low point. However, the model itself is being discussed now, because Bosnia is similar in some ways to Syria. A diverse, multicultural society with a harsh history, a fierce internecine conflict involving religious strife, active outside interference from both neighbours and great powers, and finally, one side considered by international public opinion to be "most at fault" (in Bosnia, it was the Serbs and Slobodan Milosevic). Of course, the parallels are not exact. The Syrian situation is more complex, but the arrangement worked out in the Balkans could be applied in the Middle East with appropriate modifications.

The most influential outside players, representing what might be called the various opposing groups, would use diplomacy and pressure to get them to the negotiating table, where they would not only formulate a transitional government, but develop a new system of government for Syria. On the one hand, this would distribute power among the various religious and ethnic communities in order to establish a balance of interests, primarily in the name of security. On the other hand, there would be a system of external guarantees, in which all of the involved countries would participate, even those that have antagonistic relations with each other. (In an interview with the author of this paper, Sergey Lavrov confirmed back in November that Russia favours Egypt's initiative, in the format of the "Four Neighbours"—Egypt, Turkey, Saudi Arabia and Iran—as an important tool in resolving the Syrian conflict.) The most important aspect of this is the participation of all actors that affect the situation, and in this sense the achievement of Dayton was that Slobodan Milosevic was included in the negotiations even though he was already considered a war criminal in the West.

One approach has been and will be firmly rejected by Moscow: the assertion that Assad's resignation is the solution to the Syrian crisis. On all other matters, Russia could certainly be flexible, for example, on the parameters and format of a hypothetical Syrian "Dayton." Of course, the "peace conference" proposed by Bashar Assad in his speech in early January implies something very different which is sweeping aside the opposition that is primarily conducting military operations against him. But even this idea might have some merit, if Damascus actually carries it out. Such a forum would unite the internal forces that are trying to avoid the destruction of the entire system. If the regime is willing to compromise with its moderate opponents within the country, it could create a "party" for future negotiations. With support that would be hard to deny, this party would be capable of holding talks with the implacable opposition from the National Coalition, which is also more consolidated now than in the past.

This is all still in the realm of speculation, but the deadlock of violence in which Syria is currently trapped is forcing everyone to look for different ways out. And this cannot be done without Russia.

* * *

Since the disappearance of the USSR, Moscow's policy in the Middle East has actually been in a state of inertia. It has not acquired any new features in that very important part of the world. Formally, Russia is in a unique position, as Russian diplomats and Orientalists keep saying. Unlike the Soviet Union, it has (or at least had before the Arab Spring) normal relations with all Middle East players, including the Gulf monarchies, Israel and the Hamas movement. In reality, however, Moscow has not benefited much from them and has had meaningful contacts only with rulers with whom it has maintained ties since Soviet times—Saddam Hussein, Muammar Gaddafi, and the Assad family. They all have had their roots in a different era, and their fall was predestined. The new authorities may have some interest in Moscow, but they will not orient themselves towards it: Russia is no longer a patron. Yet, Moscow may have value as an important international (not regional but global) factor for countries that have enough clout to claim a role in the world game (for example, Egypt will most likely do that).

Meanwhile, the Middle East is changing dramatically. The Arab Spring, which has swept away authoritarian republics, is only the beginning; sooner or later, the transformation will reach the other countries, too, including those Gulf regimes that today are assisting revolutions in Syria and other secular dictatorships in the hope of channeling the social energy outwards. No one can say what the geopolitical map of the region will be like in five years. Of course, it is an attractive idea to maintain one's strategic positions in the region, but no one knows yet how to do it.

The future Middle East may become a source of growing dangers for Russia —the fall of secular regimes and the Islamisation of the region may lead to more active interaction with Muslims in the North Caucasus. A serious destabilisation in Syria, Lebanon and Jordan can cause local ethnic minorities to leave these countries—Armenians and Circassians have already begun to return to their historical homelands. Violent clashes between Sunnis and Shiites and an acute crisis inside and around Iran may result in chaos spilling over into the South Caucasus, destroying the fragile status quo in Nagorno-Karabakh, and involving Russia in a severe conflict as a major regional power. So, of course, Russia will not be able to simply forget about the Middle East, but it will likely change the vector of its policy to find ways to insulate itself from the impending danger. Paradoxically, if things continue the way they are now, in a couple of years Israel may end up as the most reliable partner of Russia in the Middle East. Russia is gradually expanding cooperation with this country in various fields, and there is only one serious disagreement between them, namely, Iran. But the Iranian issue will soon be resolved, one way or another and the situation will change. Meanwhile, the United States, Israel's strategic patron, already feels the burden of the need to coordinate all its moves with Israeli interests. The Arab world also is undergoing a tectonic shift and the US needs to urgently and flexibly adapt its strategy to these changes.

But this is a medium and long-term matter. Meanwhile, Russia is playing its Syrian game with one goal on its mind: to prevent the worst—which it believes the fascination with the Arab Spring may bring about.

9

US Foreign Policy in the Middle East: Combatting the Realist Resurgence

Julie E. Taylor

We are a little more than two years into the start of the Arab uprisings, and after the Obama Administration's initial enthusiasm for supporting Arab aspirations for democracy, there already appears to be a resurgence of realism within US policy circles. This shift is evidenced by the recent spate of articles by senior policy analysts, appointments to the Administration's second-term foreign policy team,[1] and by an interview in January, in which the President said that US involvement in Syria could be of little effect and would not directly serve US national interests.[2] This change of heart is prompted by the many setbacks that Arab democracy movements have faced. Demonstrations in Bahrain were crushed by internal security and Saudi forces, while in Syria, Bashar al-Assad used indiscriminate violence to halt protests, escalating the civil unrest into an all out civil war. Even in countries where "successful" revolutions occurred, outcomes have ranged from disappointing to alarming: a suspended parliament and Muslim Brotherhood Presidency in Egypt; little to no change in Yemen; the rise of Salafi extremism in Tunisia, and a terrorist attack on the US consulate in Benghazi, Libya. According to the realist interpretation, these events are evidence that conditions in Arab societies are not ripe for successful democratic transitions, that the political chaos is empowering extremists, and that the leaders who are coming to power are more anti-American than the dictatorships they replace and will work against US strategic interests. Realists contend that rather than supporting democracy, the US should continue working with its traditional allies, despite the authoritarian make-up of their regimes.

It would be a mistake, however, for the US to give up, so easily, on Arab democracy movements. While there is an obvious moral argument to be made for supporting the uprisings, they also further US national and security interests—indeed, much more so than a return to relying on authoritarian allies. This paper will refute realist arguments in the reverse order, arguing that US allies in the region are not as helpful as they may appear, that new, democratically-elected leaders do not substantially threaten US interests, that the instability wrought by democracy movements is less harmful to America's position in the region, than not supporting them would be, and that there are distinct social trends in the Arab World that auger well for democratic development.

US Strategic Interests

To assess whether its policies further US interests, it is best, to first, clarify, what they are. The main strategic interests of the US in the Middle East are: maintaining the flow of oil and other commerce; protecting US citizens at home and abroad from terrorist threats emanating from the region; ensuring the security of Israel; and preventing Iran from acquiring nuclear weapons and using its regional influence to undermine US interests. This paper does not argue for a change in US interests, but instead focuses on how to best achieve them.

With Friends Like These...

There is a considerable overlap of interests amongst the US, the countries of the GCC, and other Middle East monarchies. The presence of the US Sixth Fleet at a base in Bahrain is the clearest indication of the value that both the GCC and the US place on checking Iran's ability to disrupt the free flow of oil and to threaten Gulf counties. On the whole, the monarchies present the least threat to Israel. And, according to most realists, they cooperate with the US in counter-terrorism efforts, and are less anti-American than other Arab countries.

What the realists overlook, however, is the role that GCC countries have played in nurturing the terrorist threats that confront the US today. Instead they focus on anti-Americanism. The level of anti-Americanism in official government rhetoric is a poor barometer of the level of anti-Americanism in a country, and the level of anti-Americanism in a country is not a measure of the level of threat a country poses to US interests. Indeed, anti-Americanism in various forms is so rampant in the Arab World today that it hardly distinguishes US allies from its enemies. But, while it is certainly a barrier to promoting US interests, anti-Americanism does not in, and of itself, constitute a direct threat to those interests: global jihadism does. This intolerant world view—that paints the West as the enemy of Islam and legitimates violence against it—is propagated more by US allies in the Gulf than by most of its enemies or allies elsewhere in the region. Though these regimes do not espouse or agree with global jihadism, they make considerable efforts to ensure that their populations perceive the West as their enemy, and thus lay the foundation for those, who take this line of thinking, a step further and target the US. And it is not just their own populations that they seek to influence. Throughout the Muslim World they have supported the spread of this intolerant strain of Salafism, actively undermining the influence of other schools of Islamic thought. Currently in Syria, it is the US allies who are arming the Jabhat al-Nusra and manoeuvring to ensure that they will have an important role in post-Assad Syria. GCC governments often refuse to crackdown on individuals and organisations that are known financiers of jihadist organisations, despite frequent US requests for them to do so. Gulf countries do occasionally work with the US when extremists have turned their attention to attacking their monarchies, but this is only evidence of their pragmatism, not that they are dependable allies in the US counter-terrorism efforts.

Elected Arab Leaders Cannot Abandon Strategic Interests

Realists fear that Arab democracies will be a greater threat to the US because they will want to appease the anti-American sentiment of voters to gain at the ballot box. While it is likely that democratically elected Arab leaders will speak more frankly with the US and will be less accommodating, the strategic interests that they seek to maintain will not differ substantially from those of their predecessors. A change in regime-type does not impact whether an economy is based on oil exports, a military needs foreign assistance, or a country fears Iranian intentions. Realists are forgetting one of their main tenets: that strategic interests remain relatively constant. Also, while elected Arab leaders may want to demonstrate their autonomy from the US and diversify their foreign relations, it is unlikely that they will sour their relations with the US or become its enemy, solely because the US champions democracy. This is because when it comes to protecting their core national interests, they have limited options. For instance, if GCC governments were no longer monarchies, but instead were democratically elected, they would be no less concerned about protecting energy transport and keeping Iran from realising its nuclear ambitions. Are they going to turn to China or Russia to protect those interests, when those concerns are of much greater importance to the U.S? Ironically the country where realist concerns most apply is Iraq, the country whose transition to democracy was orchestrated by the United States. Given Iran's proximity and ties to the Iraq's Shiite community, it is understandable that its relations with Iraq would grow closer, but even in this case, electoral pressures have not caused the Iraqi government to turn against the US.

Democracy Movements are Less of a Threat to US Interests Than Not Supporting Them Would Be

There is no doubt that the wars in Libya and Syria, and the inability of newly elected Arab regimes to maintain order and project power, have created new opportunities for Muslim extremist groups. They can operate freely in ungoverned areas, borders are easier to cross, and weapons are plentiful. Conditions for recruitment have improved: with internal security apparatuses in disarray, the individual-level costs of joining such groups have plummeted and the potential benefits are greater. Groups like the Jabhat al-Nusra are enhancing their popular legitimacy by spreading resources and fighting to topple a ruthless tyrant. The Arab uprisings have come with clear security concerns and democratisation will remain a messy and disruptive process.

But these dangers would not be alleviated by relying more on authoritarian regimes, or by standing on the sidelines, as democratisation is thwarted by those, seeking to consolidate power in their own hands. The genie cannot be put back in the bottle, and efforts to do so are the main source of instability, not the process of democratisation. Taking a realist position would also hurt US interests by deepening anti-American sentiment. Though anti-Americanism is not a direct threat per se, the US would obviously benefit if it were reduced. And yet, there is no greater source of anti-Americanism than the hypocrisy of its foreign policy. The Obama Administration's perceived abandonment of democracy movements is fodder for greater anti-Americanism, not the solution to its security concerns.

Certain Social Trends Auger Well for Democratic Development

Realists cite macro-economic indicators as evidence that the Arab World lacks the conditions necessary for democratic development. But this type of mile-high perspective—looking at the conditions of the population as a whole—is not useful for assessing a movement's prospects for success. Popular political movements are, almost always, driven by a narrow segment of the population that is strongly committed to its ideals, feels disenfranchised, and wants a complete reordering of the society. Countries such as Egypt and Tunisia have this critical mass, though it is less obvious in other Arab counties.

This vanguard—for lack of a better term—has emerged as a result of distinct social trends, eroding the paternalistic order upon which Arab authoritarian regimes were built. Arab youth are demanding that their rights as individuals be respected—in the home, in the work place, and in the political sphere as well. They want to make their own choices and are not abiding by traditional social expectations. Arab youth have new spaces (civil society organisations, the internet, fast-food restaurants, etc.) in which to exchange ideas and intermingle with those from another class, viewpoint, or gender. It also helps that they are a generation that feels disconnected from the government: unlike their parents generation, they do not feel cared for by the state, nor are they vested in it through public sector employment. As Arab regimes evolved into security states, they increasingly perceived the state to be their enemy. Whether they are secular liberals or Muslim Brotherhood youth, young people are demanding greater accountability, participation and protection. And demographic trends are on their side: though these views do not reflect the views of the majority- who still cling to traditional, collectivist views—demands for individual liberty are growing fastest among the younger cohorts of Arab societies, and these cohorts are growing fastest within

Arab societies. This social transformation makes it less likely that anti-democratic setbacks can be long-lived.

Conclusion

As the political situation in the Arab World grows increasingly unpredictable and complex, many observers of the regions are claiming that the United States can do little to influence the course of democratisation in the region. Realists cite this reasoning when building their case for why the US should pull back from its efforts at democracy promotion and continue "working with some authoritarian governments and accepting the Arab World for what it is today."[3] While it is their case that a sustainable democracy can only be built by its own citizens, and that the US can do little to directly shape the process, what is often overlooked is the extent to which the US—as the world's greatest power—can derail political liberalisation. By praising and supporting its authoritarian friends, the US deflates activists' hopes that they can significantly change the status quo, by providing anti-democratic forces the political cover—and often the means—for cracking down on perceived challengers. Even sitting on the sidelines while human rights are violated and liberalisation is reversed, has a chilling effect on democracy proponents and provides a boost of confidence for those who work against them. What realists fail to recognise is that support for democracy does not have to mean direct US intervention, nor does it require abandoning allies who are not democratic. It does require however, that the US strongly advocate for democracy and try to bring its rhetoric more in line with its deeds. Security cooperation may become increasingly awkward and relations will cool if the US praises democracy activists within authoritarian states or expresses disappointment when they violate human rights, but alliances with those regimes are unlikely to collapse because they are based on mutual security interests. The US cannot return to its previous modus vivendi and wait for the Arab World it "wishes to have"[4] to arrive: this very modus vivendi has in fact been one of the greatest impediments to political liberalisation, and returning to it in the name of pragmatism will only serve to increase the threats to US interests for a long time to come.

Notes

1. The nominations include: John Brennan to head the Central Intelligence Agency, John Kerry as Secretary of State, and Chuck Hegel as Secretary of Defense.
2. Franklin Foer and Chris Hughes, "Barak Obama is Not Pleased: The president on his enemies, the media, and the future of football," *The New Republic*, January 27, 2013.
3. Seth Jones, "The Future Promise of Arab Uprisings," *Foreign Affairs*, January/February 2013, pp. 1-9.
4. Ibid, p. 9.

10

Emerging Trends in West Asia: A Syrian Perspective

Waiel Awwad

The political assassination of the Tunisian activist, Chokri Belaid, the general coordinator of the Democratic Movement, marked the commencement of the second phase of the Tunisian Revolution. The outrage was evident throughout Tunisia and the world at large, that witnessed the birth of what was popularly labelled the 'Arab Spring'. It triggered a wave of unrest in most of the Arab capitals, toppled regimes and is still simmering in many capitals and threatening to engulf others.

The ruthless killings–though an on-going process after the toppling Zine Abidine Bin Ali regime in Tunisia—exposed the true face of those who claim to be "revolutionary guards" of political intolerance. This will have repercussions within the international community and well-wishers, which will lead to a loss of sympathy for those who tried to hijack the true demands of the masses.

The shock wave was strong enough to shake the establishment in neighbouring countries, especially the Egyptian opposition, across the political spectrum. The call was denounced and condemned by a vast majority of Egyptians. The Al Khaleej newspaper interviewed Chokri, few hours before his assassination, where he said among other things, that the attack on Syria was a conspiracy and there was no revolution there.

The Plight of the Arabs

In the Arab region it was a transformation from feudal agricultural society to a modern industrial society. After the fall of the Ottoman Empire, the Arab world was divided into small countries by Britain and France (Sykes-Picot Treaty) to retain it under their influence and dominance. In the middle of the last century and when Europe was witnessing an internal conflict, the Arab countries gained independence and started political and economic reforms and inward restructuring. Their efforts to stand once again as independent and sovereign nations in different capitals led to the birth of a Pan-Arab movement that was challenged by the UK, France and the US, who encouraged more nationalist movements for each country to topple any prospect for Arab world unification which extended from Qatar to Morocco.

The Rise of Arab Nationalism

In 1956 the Nasser Era helped in consolidating the autocratic regimes. Many would believe the birth of Israel as a state at the cost of Palestine reinforced this tendency. But, over the years, it contributed to despair and resentment against the Arab governments that failed to solve the conflict and give the Palestinians their legitimate right to establish a sovereign state in their homeland alongside Israel and live in peace. In addition, it was the discovery of oil and gas which added to this rise of nationalism where the Arab League helped in defining each Arab country within the given borders by France and Great Britain.

There was a mass exodus of manpower from the Arab world to the US and Europe in search for a better future as the unemployment ratio was very high—14.4 per cent as compared to the international figure of 6.3 per cent. The manpower was 30 million in the 1990s and reached 100 million in 2009 and instead of being a force to reckon with it became a burden on successive governments and miscalculated economic reforms.

The population explosion was another challenge that faced the region. From 317 million in 2007 the population is expected to rise to 395 million by 2020. The Arab world would require another 100 million new jobs in the near future.

In 2009 the poor numbered 65 million and the gap between the food securities widened and reached US \$ 27 billion in 2010. It is likely to reach US \$ 44 billion by 2020.

The role of women was very limited in the region. Thirty-three per cent of the women in the region contributed to the economy against the global figure of 55 per cent of the global figure. The participation of women in political life was also limited and neglected in general.

Political reforms in the Arab world were minimal and many political parties were barred, especially those with a Pan-Arab manifesto. Gathering of people was only allowed in mosques which did not leave any scope for the revolutionaries in the Arab world to hope for any reconciliation with the ruling elite. It also led to the belief that all the sufferings of the masses were due to one individual, the head of the state. Hence, the people united against the regimes and called for a regime change.

The lack of political reforms in the Arab world and the onset of the process of democratisation led to the decline in popularity of the regimes' heads. What complicated the matter were the economic reforms of a new liberal economic policy or "King Lear Syndrome". Roger Owen in his book *The Rise and Fall of Arab Presidents for Life* (p.121) argues that as the gap widened between the rich and the poor and benefited only the upper echelons surrounding the leaders, the slogan for reforms and lack of accountability, led to the increase in corruption, appeasement, lack of trust and anger. The economic transformation of the state into liberal capitalism put a brake on political liberalism. Democratic elections were a farce and fruitless exercise that failed to create an alternative and inculcate democratic ideas in politics.

The US Interest in the Middle East

The Pan-Arab national movement witnessed a decline in the 1970s which led to internal and regional conflicts and further divisions, that kept the prospect of any development hanging in balance. This was followed by the two Gulf Wars, and the US and the West focussed on a "New Middle East and North Africa Order". It is believed that the US's intention was to promote human rights values, democracy, and civil societies so as to bring the region under American influence. In reality, it was "Re-shaping the Middle East" which started with the invasion of Iraq when Colin Powell, former US Secretary of State said: "Overdrawing the Middle East in ways that enhance the US interests and political landscape".

Despite resentment against the Iraqi regime, the US invasion of Iraq led to more anger on the Arab streets, which was aggravated by the global financial crisis and economic recession and the rise in prices of essential commodities.

The youth, exasperated with the policy of puppet regimes that did not carry out reforms to meet the minimum requirements of the people, decided to take the law into their hands and get rid of those regimes that suppressed them and denied them their basic rights.

The 'Arab Spring'

The turmoil on the Arab streets was a reflection of the anger among the middle class that had been piling up for decades and had been ignored by the ruling elite. Later, all strata of Arab society expressed their anger and suffering. Some analysts called it a lesser secular revolution in Tunisia, others added economic and political angles to the revolt in Egypt where the people were kept away from the decision-making process in matters that directly affected their daily livelihood.

What is more astonishing is the quick success of these peaceful movements that toppled regimes. The masses formed a people's committee, opened dialogue with the army and adhered to legitimate demands like political freedom, free and fair elections, a new Constitution, economic development and social justice.

Despite the war propaganda and the large-scale diplomatic offensive by the West to justify the invasion of Iraq in 2003 by the US and the UK, the vast majority of the international community believed that the reason behind the invasion was the thirst for Iraqi oil and natural resources and never the Weapons of Mass Destruction, in a campaign that was led by a Weapon of Mass Deception.

Iraqi occupation and the outcome clearly brought out the fact that the US and its allies were never interested in bringing democracy to West Asia but chaos and destruction—a total anarchy that will ensure hegemony of the great powers in the new game played out since 2010 under the pretext of what is called the "Arab Spring".

The US was leading a war quietly in the region to define its role in the third millennium in a region rich with natural resources in an era of global economic recession, financial crisis, and a bankrupt Europe.

Targeting Syria

Syria occupies a strategic position in the Middle East. It is considered the cradle of civilisation which goes back to the Bronze Age. It is a heterogeneous society with Arabs in a majority. It is also a multi-linguistic society with Arabic, Armenian, French, Kurdish, Assyrian, and Aramaic, the oldest language (of Jesus Christ) still being spoken in Syria in small villages like Maalloula, Jabaadin and Bakhaa and many other Christian-dominated areas.

When the US invaded Iraq, the Colin Powell paid a visit to Syria carrying terms to Damascus which included among others: ending of Syria-Iran alliance, withdrawing forces from Lebanon, dismantling the Hezbollah Party, ending support to Hamas and opening of the Syrian market. However, Damascus gave a cold shoulder to Powell much to the chagrin of the US. Former NATO Director, General Wesley Clark, said in 2007 about the Neocons' plans, that NATO was planning to occupy seven countries in five years including Libya, Yemen, Somalia, Sudan, Syria and Iran.[1] Wikileaks revealed the US plan of a military coup in Tunisia and Egypt to gain logistic support to invade Libya.

The drawing new boundaries of the New Middle East and North Africa is meant to divide the region into small countries on ethnic and religious basis. The Islamic parties gaining power in most of the Arab states held elections in Morocco, Tunisia, Libya and Egypt. Many have accused Qatar and Saudi Arabia of pumping billions of dollars to let the Islamist parties gain control. The general perception is that the departure of the US from Iraq will lead to a vacuum that a growing regional power Iran will fill and this will lead to strengthening of resistance forces against Israeli occupation. The US and Israel believe that Hezbollah Party in Lebanon, Syria and Iran will be a threat to their strategic partnership. By toppling the regime in Syria, the West and the US believe, Iran will lose a strong ally in the region and will be further isolated. It will lead to a defeat of the Lebanese national resistance forces represented by the Hezbollah. Russia feels that with the fall of Syria it will widen its Islamic influence in the region and will be a part of the containment plan of the US and the West.

The new maps of the Middle East were drawn by the US scholars and military experts and published in military journals and books.[2] Many in the US felt that its image in the Arab world, led to the setting up of a programme by the Neocons, who were advocating "the New Middle East Order" to glorify the American image in the eyes of the masses. Millions of dollars were spent on social networking, media institutions, and programmes were launched in the US. The Arab youth was invited to attend seminars and get trained in networking and organizing protests and leading demonstrations to meet the aspirations of the people, and hence ensure a "regime change" to meet the socio-economic demands in countries infested with malpractices of unchallengeable regimes, lack of democracy, unemployment, poverty, illiteracy, fanaticism and the sectarian divide.

The "Constructive Chaos" project was launched in the Arab world. Balkanization started in Sudan which was divided into two, regimes were overthrown in Tunisia and Egypt, but all eyes were on Libya which was attacked by France-led NATO forces under the "Humanitarian Intervention" which compounded the problems and prompted other superpowers to prevent similar action in other countries like Syria. In fact, even Silvia Berlusconi, the former Prime Minister of Italy, accused the French President Sarkozy of initiating a war on Gaddafi who was loved by his people, on the request of his friend Bernard Livy Henry, even though Libya was peaceful and there was no revolt against the Libyan president.[3]

War on Syria

Undoubtedly, the winds of change in Tunisia and Egypt reached Syrian shores sooner than expected since the general perception was the revolts were against pro-Western regimes. However, the demands for internal economic and political reforms were common in the other Arab countries that led to people's anger spilling out onto the streets. The Syrian president formed a committee to investigate the reasons that led to the uprising and changes in Tunisia and Egypt and tried to expedite the political and the economic reforms to meet the aspirations of the people. But as it is said in Arabic, "the winds do not blow as the vessel wishes", Syria was aware of the plot planned for her from neighbouring countries and struggled to calm down the street and compromise with the demand of the demonstrators but the armed infiltrators' took advantage of the genuine demands of the demonstrators and tried to settle scores with Syrian regime

The movement which ignited in Daraa was largely peaceful. It was focussed on toppling the regime from day-one as the rebels refused to accept the reforms that the government offered. Slogans like, "No Iran no Hezbollah...We want a President who fears Allah" were raised in Daraa city. Such slogans indicate that the masses were being incited about sectarian division rather than evoking a genuine revolt for economic and political reforms. It was repeated in different parts of Syria, Talkalakh, Jisr Alshougor, Idlib, Aleppo and Homs.

Jihad Declared on Syria

Three years have passed since the uprising and Syria continues to bleed. With at least 25 nationalities supported by the EU, regional players and monarchs are active in Syria according to UN Secretary General Ban Ki Moon.

For the US to wage a war is more important and profitable than winning it. Recent reports from the US media suggest that the law-makers in the US are investing their resources in the arms industry and making millions of dollars in profits from waging wars, while the American taxpayers have to bear the cost of wars in Afghanistan, Iraq and Pakistan. Between 2001 and 2005 defence corporations' annual profits climbed 189 per cent. Apparently, it is the military establishment in the US which is dictating its foreign policy, especially the policy that keeps US at war.[4] On February 18, 1819, US Congress rejected the rule of law in foreign policy (Seminole War) and ever since the rule of force was established as a major drive in foreign policy as much as religious belief (Sword of the Spirit, Shield of Faith: Religion in American War and Diplomacy).

The Forces Active on the Ground

With money, arms and trained Jihadis, Syria is turning into a haven for extremists. According to eyewitnesses, thousands of Libyan Zentan tribesmen, Chechen, Turkmens, Tunisians, Pakistani and Cheshans are trained on the borders for three weeks, and then given a gun and a 'key to heaven' before being sent to Syria to fight the "Infidel regime" represented by Bashar Al Assad.

Earlier, it was a variety of people from different strata of the society who wanted to achieve a change in the system and demanded more freedom, social justice and equality in a democratic setup. Gradually, with the arming of the rebels the streets were dotted with different forces which dominated the unrest. Some of these forces were:

1. Islamists Jihadists: Wahhabis/Salafis equipped with money and authority. Led by Qatar, Saudi Arabia and supported by the US, they are anti-Shia and they reject other believers and only adapt to Ibn Taimiya, which does not recognize other sects of Islam. (It calls them Kafir, Infidel, Heretics, Nussairi).
2. Modernized Muslim Brotherhood: Supported by Turkey, the US and the West. This brotherhood is still seeking revenge for the 1982 suppression.
3. Moderate movement: Nationalists, Pan-Arabs, resistance left, liberal and neo-liberal forces supported by Iran and fighting hegemony of the West.

Currently, this is the weakest movement. It lacks finances, media coverage and a strong base.

4. Secular forces: Absence of external support. Most of the secular forces pulled out of the demonstration with the violence reaching new heights and the government giving in more to their demands and agreeable to reforms. The Jihadists became the prominent forces in Syria fighting on different fronts.

Type of War in Syria

The war in Syria escalated and more trained fighters were sent to different parts who found shelter among dissident groups. Local recruitment became easier as economic sanctions and lack of essential medical facilities led to development of harsh conditions. Reports from northern Syria revealed that Islamists militants were forcing people to join their ranks and were implementing strict Islamic rules in exchange for bread and butter stolen from government and private stores.

Knowing that the war in Syria was a long haul the government drew a plan to fight on different fronts simultaneously. The fight became more of a defensive one where the government forces were engaged with Jihadis and foreign mercenaries belonging to Muslim Brotherhood, Salafists and Wahabbis.

According to the Lebanese newspaper *Alakhbar*, the Belhaj Model was defensive and influencial where the government was facing secularists with minimal compromise. "There was many attempts by Saudi Arabia to establish an Islamic front to achieve the following:

1. The call for jihad must be waged under the banner of Islam.
2. Islamic law is to be enforced by setting up specialized councils in the various locales, whose duty it is to apply the law on civilians and combatants alike. News has been circulating recently that a supreme council has also been formed to appoint and oversee the work of local ones.
3. The goal is to establish a state in Syria that is not necessarily religious, with the provision that it is not based on the military and that it implements Islamic law based on the idea that it is the will of the majority.
4. With the toppling of the regime, the military brigades must dissolve themselves and surrender their weapons to the newly established armed forces, integrating competent fighters into the new Syrian army."

Syrian Foes and Allies

The number of killings and destruction in Syria at the hands of terrorist groups helped the government in gaining ground and establishing the support of the people, the army, secular forces and the minorities. Most of the defection from the army was individual which was not a major threat to the establishment.

Syria's Allies

The Russian position supports President Assad, and is based on its determination not to let the US and NATO allies turn Syria into another Libya; hence the support comes from preservation of national interest and an apprehension of a civil war driven by religious fundamentalists. The fear of being engulfed by Islamists and extremists from North Africa and Turkey will have repercussions on its own minorities.

The other important reason is the energy diplomacy with Europe to reduce the dependence of the latter on Russian gas. In addition, the discovery of a new reservoir of gas in the Mediterranean waters has complicated the situation.

China, despite all the lucrative incentives from the Gulf, refuses to relent and remains committed to the policy of non-interference based on the UN charter. Iran and Syria enjoy a strategic relationship ever since the Islamic revolution ended. This strategic relationship consolidated itself through the decades which strengthened the resistance against US-Israel hegemony.

India, as a leader of BRICS, took a firm stand for a peaceful solution by the Syrians and declared that the international community should facilitate dialogue and put an end to violence from both sides. Many other countries such as Algeria, Sudan, Lebanon, South Africa, Brazil, Cuba and Venezuela stood with Syria.

Israel-US-Turkey Axis: Destabilizing the Middle East

The US interference in the internal affairs of Syria goes back to 1949 when they helped Hosni Alzaim to topple the first democratically-elected government led by Shekri Alkuwatly. Undoubtedly, the war in Syria was much hyped by the media and there is no respite from them till date. Headlines like: "West Needs Syria in Turmoil", "Israel See Assad Lesser Evil", "Reshaping the Middle East", "How to Topple Assad", "How to Surpass Russia and China's Veto", "Post-Assad Scenario" and so on, are frequent. But, not a single country has spoken on how to save Syria from a war or even engage the Syrian government to find a solution to the crisis. When the former US Secretary of State Hillary Clinton called the Chinese and Russian veto of the UN Syrian Resolution "despicable", the Chinese questioned the American morality of protecting the Arabs. The world still remembers the Abu Ghraib prison in Iraq and using of Phosphorus bombs in Sunni-dominated Fallujah city of Iraq, which destroyed it. NATO's war on Libya, and the post-Gaddafi civil war, and the latest incidence of burning copies of the Holy Book by US soldiers in Afghanistan are all in media's glare.

Israel never hid its intention of the disintegration of Syria and widely published the plan of how Syria should be divided. Oded Yinon's *A Strategy for Israel in the*

Nineteen Eighties (translated by Israel Shahak) [5] talks of a plan about Syria. With regards to Syria the plan stated:

> "The Western front, which on the surface appears more problematic, is in fact less complicated than the Eastern front, in which most of the events that make the headlines have been taking place recently. Lebanon's total dissolution into five provinces serves as a precedent for the entire Arab world including Egypt, Syria, Iraq and the Arabian peninsula and is already following that track. The dissolution of Syria and Iraq later on into ethnically or religiously unique areas such as in Lebanon, is Israel's primary target on the Eastern front in the long run, while the dissolution of the military power of those states serves as the primary short term target. Syria will fall apart, in accordance with its ethnic and religious structure, into several states such as in present day Lebanon, so that there will be a Shi'ite Alawi state along its coast, a Sunni state in the Aleppo area, another Sunni state in Damascus hostile to its northern neighbour, and the Druzes who will set up a state, maybe even in our Golan, and certainly in the Hauran and in northern Jordan. This state of affairs will be the guarantee for peace and security in the area in the long run, and that aim is already within our reach today".

In his book, former Prime Minister, the late Yitzhak Rabin said that the Israeli government is in fact responsible for the design of American policy in the Middle East, after June 1967.

Israel's Attack on Syria

The provocative Israeli attack on a scientific research centre on the outskirts of Damascus was met with wide condemnation and was considered as a crime and as an act of terrorism, opening a new front and assisting the rebels who failed to achieve their objectives on the ground. The talk of creating a Buffer Zone inside Syria strengthens the belief that Israel is the sole beneficiary of the current unrest in Syria if not behind it with her allies. On February 3, 2013, the *Syrian Arab News Agency* (SANA) said "Israeli Aggression Reveals Israel's Role in Destabilizing Syria." The larger picture, it falls as a part of the strategy of deploying Patriot missiles in Turkey, weakening Syria and encouraging Israel to go for a third war on Lebanon and taking on Hezbollah without much support from Syria and Iran.[6]

Turkey, on the other hand, besides being a NATO ally, has very close ties with Israel and the US. The current government enjoys the best relations with Syria, business is flourishing, there is cross-border trade with no visa requirements. This led to a profit of more than US$ 6 billion annually for Turkey. Syrian industry faced harsh times after the arrival of the surplus from Turkey and incurred huge losses with many employees losing their daily wages.

President Assad declined an offer from Ankara to share power with the Muslim Brotherhood and give them one-third of the seats in the cabinet. Assad told his

Turkish counterpart that the Syrian Constitution is a secular one and does not allow religious parties but they could contest elections in an individual capacity. This did not go down well with Ardogan, the Turkish Prime Minister.

The war on Syria cost Turkey dearly and Damascus accused Ankara of stealing and destroying factories in Syria and dismantling more than 1000 factories in Aleppo, the commercial capital. Evidence regarding the transportation of equipment to Turkey is widely available on the elerctronic media.[7]

Insurgency Groups Active in Syria: 'New Afghanistan'

The Islamic insurgency is gaining grounds in Syria, with the influx of mercenaries from more than 25 countries gaining entry from northern Lebanon, Iraq and Turkey. The insurgents, trying to overpower the prevailing order, are equipped with sophisticated arms (M79 Osa rocket launchers, the RPG-22, the M-60 recoilless rifles and the RBG-6 multiple grenade launchers, Austrian Steyr Aug rifles) and ammunition, and are trained and supervised by the CIA, Mossad, MI5, Qatari and Saudi intelligence. Aron Lund, a journalist and a writer, has done a detailed study of the Jihadi groups active in Syria.[8] The widespread networking and coordination among the insurgent groups is possible with the help of sophisticated telecommunication systems provided by France and the US. They are spread all over Syria under different names and commands. The websites of Al-Qaeda and other global Jihadi outfits display from time to time the names of those killed in different parts of Syria. These groups are:

1. Jabhat Al Nusra: Mainly foreign Islamists linked to Al-Qaeda-Iraqi Style Extremist group. This acts by suicidal operation, execution and training for fresh recruits.
2. Kataib Ahrar Al Sham Al-Islamiah (made of around 50 Jihadi groups) which forms Syria Islamic Front.
3. Soquor Al Sham: Active in Lattakia, Jabal Alzawiah.
4. Liwa Al Tawhid: Damacus
5. Harakat Al Fajr Al Islamia: Active in Aleppo and neighboring areas
6. Kataib Ansar AlSham: Active in Lattakia, Homs.
7. Soquor Al-Islam: In Damascus
8. Kataib al Imam Al muqatila: In Damascus
9. Katibat Hamza Bin AbdulMuttalib: Damascus–Zabadani resort area.
10. Liwa Alhaq, Kataib Al Farooq: Active in Homs
11. Katibat Musab Bin Omair: Rural Alepp-Jamat Altaleea: Idlib
12. Jaish Altawhid: Deir Elzour
13. Jabhat Tahrir Syria
14. Jabhat Alasala wa Al tanmiah
15. Tajamou Ansar Al-Islam fi Qalb Alsham
16. Liwa Ahfad Alrasoul

17. Liwa al-Islam: Damascus
18. Salafi Syria Islamic Front (Eljabha Elislamiah ElSouriah) formed by Ahrar Alsham
19. Fateh Al-Islam (Funded by Lebanese Islamist groups and Gulf States)
20. Amouminoun Yusharikon: Salafist, active in Deraa
21. Firkat Sulieman Al Mukatilah: Active in Hama Abdula Azam, Fajr Al Islam and many of these groups and small factions are fighting under Syria Liberation Front.

Why is Insurgency Islamic in Nature?

This is because it is easy to recruit extremists on the basis of sectarian divisions. Moreover, foreign support from rich Gulf States and Islamic organisations supports the movement against Assad. In addition, President Assad's regional policy made more enemies among the anti-resistance bloc.

The Security Implications

The spread of terrorism in the region has become so evident that the international community cannot ignore the implications of conflicts spreading to neighbouring countries and an all-out war that will threaten global peace and stability. But without cutting the supply of funds and arms to the insurgents, Syrian people will continue to suffer and Syria will remain a battleground for a proxy war between the superpowers.

Syrian Reforms

In spite of the carnage in Syria and the engagement of the Syrian army in the fighting, President Assad went ahead with political and economic reforms and laid out a roadmap that will ensure establishment of a wider base for democratisation of Syria. The programme will be executed in three stages.

Meanwhile, Washington did a diplomatic *volte-face* on Syria and agreed to the Geneva Accord after Moscow succeeded in averting an imminent American attack on Syria because of the alleged use of chemical weapons against civilians. Syria agreed to get rid of its chemical arsenal and sign the treaty banning it, in return.

There was an understanding between the US and Russia to find a political solution to the crisis and avoid spillover of the destruction into neighbouring countries. There was increased apprehension among European countries of the growing danger of terrorism, after thousands of Europeans joined the call for Jihad in Syria, and there was a fallout, with many of them returning to their native countries and participating in terror activities with reports of the Al-Qaida training many of them.

The infighting among different militant groups left thousands dead and fragmented the opposition, which led to Saudi Arabia's former ambassador to the US Bandar Bin Sultan to step in and help in uniting the maximum number of Islamic groups to counter the Islamic State of Iraq and Syria (ISIS) which was gaining ground in northern Syria. This exposed the true nature of the situation in Syria that showed that the struggle was between the government and the terrorist groups led by non-state actors who infiltrated into Syria from 83 countries; their number exceeds 140,000 and any dialogue among the Syrians with the help of the international community may help in drawing up a framework for the future of Syria. But the question remains: What will be the fate of the mercenaries? Will each country accept them back or are they secretly asking the Syrian government to eliminate them permanently?

The war is a long one and no solution is in sight as long as funding, arming and smuggling of infiltrators into Syria continues. It is the responsibility of the international community to bring this to an end and pressurise those countries sponsoring armed conflict in Syria, to facilitate the way forward for the Syrian people to sit across the table and work out a peaceful solution which must ensure that Syria's sovereignty and territorial integrity are retained and secular democratic Syria prevails.

NOTES

1. At http://www.youtube.com/watch?v=9RC1Mepk_Sw
2. Retired Lieutenant-Colonel's book, *Never Quit the Fight, and Blood Borders: How a Better Middle East would look*, in the US military's Armed Forces Journal with commentary from Ralph Peters.
3. At http://www.dailymotion.com/video/xhdrv8_l-appel-de-bhl-depuis-benghazi-libye-en-direct-sur-tf1-au_news#.UPOateTBjFk
4. At http://www.brasschecktv.com/videos/war-is-a-racket/foreign-policy-and-war-profiteering-.html
5. This essay originally appeared in Hebrew in *KIVUNIM (Directions)*, A Journal for Judaism and Zionism, Issue No, 14, Winter, 5742, February 1982, Editor, Yoram Beck, Editorial Committee, Eli Eyal, Yoram Beck, Amnon Hadari, Yohanan Manor, Elieser Schweid, published by the *Department of Publicity/The World Zionist Organization*, Jerusalem
6. At http://www.youtube.com/watch?v=4LBgteyPXo
7. At http://www.youtube.com/watch?v=i9uWKVjY3a4
8. Details are at http://www.ui.se/up/files/77409.pdf

11

Realpolitik of the 'Self-Appointed Frontrunner' for the UNSC Seat

P.R. Kumaraswamy

Self-appointed frontrunners for permanent UNSC membership.[1] When this description, of aspiring countries like India, by US secretary of state Hillary Clinton, was leaked in 2010, there was anger and indignation in India. For long, Indian leaders and its elite have argued that India deserves a seat at the high table of international politics. Its democratic tradition, moral standing and demographic size, they complain, have been ignored because of Western interests and realpolitik. The clamour for being recognised as a great power has intensified since the end of the Cold War. Continuing economic growth and the nuclear tests in 1998 have led to an aggressive campaign for a permanent seat in the UNSC.[2] This desire for great power status, however, has not been accompanied by any political, diplomatic or military initiatives, that are evidence of its willingness to take leadership role in resolving some of the pressing international problems. As in the past, India has been following others rather than taking the initiative. This is most vividly displayed in its reactions and responses to the ongoing Arab Spring.

The strategic importance of the Middle East for India is inversely proportionate to the expertise on the region available, within the country. This is manifested in the common and official nomenclature, of the region i.e. West Asia. This disregards the common expression Middle East that is used not only by the international community but also by the concerned countries of the region. Those harping on the imperial and colonial origins of the expression 'Middle East' too conveniently overlook the geographical roots of the term Persian Gulf. Even in academic discourse, this term, albeit recognised by the United Nations,[3] is discouraged, and one is advised to refer to the body of waters between Iran and the Arabian Peninsula merely as the Gulf. Those unfamiliar with India might mistake this for the Gulf of Mexico. This confusion is compounded by the lack of interest and expertise on the region. One could easily identify a dozen or so scholars, for whom the Middle East is a lifelong passion, while the rest have only a nodding acquaintance with the region and its complexities. The latter's body of knowledge is often confined to the few years they served in the ever dynamic Middle East, or have overseen it in various capacities.

This intellectual inadequacy is further compounded by the lackadaisical official approach towards the region. For example, in November last year, the Indian media announced that the Sultan of Oman Qaboos bin Said would be the chief guest at the Republic Day celebrations in January 2013.[4] In recognition of the historical ties between the two countries, it was to be the occasion to formally confer the Jawaharlal Nehru Award for International Peace on him. Coming in the midst of the Arab Spring, this would have sent a definitive message of India's interest, involvement and commitment to the region. Though the honour was originally announced in 2004, the two countries could not work out a suitable timetable.

Hence the slated January visit was supposed to be a double honour for Oman. This, however, did not happen. A news item in December 2012 stated that for unspecified reasons, the Sultan had cancelled his visit, and India had asked the Bhutanese King Jigme Khesar Namgyal Wangchuk to do the honours. Surprisingly there was no follow up of this *The Indian Express* story, nor was any official explanation offered. It is within these two limitations, namely, India's disconnect with the region and lack of transparency of information, that one must deconstruct India's actions and policies towards the Arab Spring.

Indian Options

India broadly had three possible options with regard to the Arab Spring, namely: democracy promotion; empathy with the protesters; and endorsement of the status quo. All of these were problematic which compelled India to avoid taking any of them. The reasons for this are discussed below.

Democracy Promotion

As the largest democracy in the world, democracy promotion could be an attractive option for India, with regard to the Arab Spring. Its leaders and intelligentsia regularly emphasise the democratic nature of the Indian political system, its ability to periodically elect and 'unelect' governments, and in the process bring about the empowerment of the different marginalised segments of the society. Given the heterogeneous nature of the countries of the Middle East, an inclusive democracy such as India is an attractive option to follow or emulate.

This option, however, has two fundamental problems. Historically, democracy promotion has never guided India's foreign policy. Since 1947, it has had to deal with a neighbourhood where elected governments are more an aberration than the norm. During the Cold War, its larger experience was not different and India could often be found to have closer relations with authoritarian regimes and rulers than democracies and elected governments. For example, it sided with repressive regimes during the crises in Hungary (1956) and Czechoslovakia (1968). The end of the Cold War did not materially alter this historic pattern. As highlighted by its brief bonhomie with the US, India still finds it difficult to deal with democracies, which operate under heterogeneous pressures and interests. Non-democracies are relatively easier to handle: one person, one address and hence, one decision.

Despite some initial interest, India has not been an enthusiastic supporter of the Community of Democracies initiative that was formalised during the final stages of Bill Clinton's presidency in June 2000. It has subsequently found other multilateral political forums such as the ASEAN Regional Forum, BRICS, G-15, G-24 or IBSA more attractive than the Concert of democracy. Some of its experiences, especially in the conduct of elections, can be adapted to local conditions in other parts of the world, including the Middle East. At the same time, Indian democracy is hampered by the weaknesses of the political system, institutional failures, perennial pressures from different segments of the society, the non-democratic nature of most of its political parties and election-associated violence. These prevent Indian democracy from becoming a model for other countries to emulate.

Democracy promotion as a foreign policy instrument faces the additional problem of human rights. There is considerable evidence of widespread human rights violations during the Arab Spring. Under the guise of security and maintenance of law and order, peaceful protesters were brutally attacked in a number of states especially Bahrain, Libya, Syria and Yemen. Though not widespread, the official responses in other countries were also brutal. An official enquiry in Bahrain ordered by the King concluded that, security forces were guilty of widespread human rights abuses.[5] Shias reported similar abuses in Saudi Arabia as well. In Yemen, both the forces loyal to Saleh and the rebels indulged in large scale human rights violations. Similar cases of human rights abuses were also reported in Syria.

The Indian indifference towards human rights violations during the Arab Spring has been for two reasons. At one level, it fears that any response to well-known violations would be interpreted as intervention in the internal affairs of a sovereign country. Historically India has been extremely reluctant to make statements relating to the internal situations of other countries. This is largely due to its apprehension that such a posture would provoke other countries to question India's human rights credentials over Kashmir. Over the years, India has been challenging the right of other countries, especially the collective of the Organisation of Islamic Cooperation (OIC, the erstwhile Organisation of Islamic

Conference) to question its track record in Kashmir. Any statement concerning 'deteriorating' human rights situation in countries under the spell of the Arab Spring, would have exposed India to greater criticism and scrutiny on the Kashmir front.

Furthermore, India's human rights record in general, is not exemplary. Detention without trial, perennial judicial delays, fake encounter killings and misuse of law enforcement machinery are rampant. They inhibit India from taking a strong stand on the human rights situation in other countries. It could not condemn violations elsewhere without being hypocritical. Its consistent refusal to become party to the Rome Statute, which established the International Criminal Court, is partly a reflection of this situation. Though couched in terms of sovereign inviolability, India has been hedging its fears concerning international scrutiny over its human rights violations.

Empathising with the Protesters

There are a number of reasons why India could have empathised with the protestors and openly sided with them in their struggle for change. The general demands of the Arab Spring are in sync with India's continuing struggle for democratic, inclusive and accountable politics. Despite its weaknesses and unfulfilled promises, India has been striving for an inclusive and less oppressive society. The sometimes anarchical, nature of its polity and decision making comes also from its desire to take an accommodative approach, towards the demands and aspirations of different groups within. In this sense the Arab Spring is not different. The absence of a recognisable leadership in most protests could not undermine their core demands. There is a palpable yearning for ending the prolonged authoritarian rule (kept often within the family), spread of crony capitalism, marginalisation of the masses from the socio-economic benefits of the globalising Arab economies, widespread corruption and misuse of power and a political elite that has increasingly alienated itself from the masses. The failure of the post-Ottoman states to evolve an inclusive national identity partly contributed to the popular anger. In the name of national security and unity, minority groups and sections have been excluded from the state apparatus in all the post-Ottoman states of the Middle East, including Turkey. One could interpret these protests as part of the nation-building process whereby the political entities created by colonialism are becoming nations. Hence, it is logical to expect India to be more supportive of the protesting Arab masses.

Furthermore, the peaceful nature of the Arab Spring, at least in the early stages, was more appealing to India and evoked memories of its own non-violent struggle for freedom. It is essential, however, to remember that the Indian leadership advocated non-violence to the Jews, even in the face of Hitler's violence and hence describing the Arab Spring as Gandhian, would mean taking liberties with the Mahatma, and his prescriptive positions. At the same time, one cannot ignore the harsh Middle Eastern reality. Since the end of the Second World War, political changes and transformations in the Arab world have been anything but peaceful. Generally, rulers have either died in office or have been removed through coups or assassinations. Monarchies and republican regimes alike have promoted or sought hereditary succession within the family. Until the election of Mohammed Morsi in July 2012, Yasser Arafat remained the only Arab leader to be elected by popular vote when he won the Palestinian elections in January 1996. Seen within the context of Middle Eastern history, the peaceful nature of the Arab Spring becomes obvious. Under this unexpected, but non-violent public pressure, Ben-Ali fled Tunisia and Mubarak stepped down in Egypt. Similarly the initial protests in Libya, Bahrain and even in Syria remained non-violent.

The non-violent phase did not last long. Prolonged tribal differences, repressive responses of the regime and sectarian divisions soon plunged the Arab Spring into a cycle of violence. Arab regimes were mostly responsible for this violent turn. Unwilling to recognise, let alone accommodate, popular demands for change, these regimes resorted to the traditional use of state machinery to suppress the protests. Regime stability became more important than accommodation with protesters. In the name of national unity, these states, whose national identities were imposed from above, relied on the military and the *mukhabrat* for survival.

Moreover, the quick turn of events in Tunisia and Egypt indicated that change was imminent and the difficulties faced by Qaddafi, Saleh and Assad revealed that they were fighting against popular anger and counting their days in office. Hence, even from a purely narrow national interest calculation, it could make sense to support the opposition, which appears to be gaining not only popularity, but also wider regional acceptance. The region-wide nature of the Arab Spring was an incentive for India to be on the right side of the tide.

However, an assessment of its response to the Arab Spring indicates that India did not empathise with the protesting Arab public. The closest India ever came to taking a pro-opposition position was indirectly urging President Mubarak to 'listen' to the voice of the Egyptians. This remark of External Affairs Minister S.M. Krishna came after entrapped Indians were safely evacuated from Egypt—and interestingly is not available on the ministry's homepage.[6] Its equidistant position towards the Assad regime and the Syrian opposition can also be cited as an evidence of this trend. Even after the Libyan ambassador in New Delhi resigned in support of the opposition, India maintained a formal distance from the National Transitional Council and its contacts remained under wraps until the "Friends of Libya" conference held in August 2011. The prolonged unrest in Yemen also did not evoke any public Indian statement.

Moreover, the non-democratic nature of the Middle East prevented India from establishing contacts with the opposition forces even before the Arab Spring. Indeed, its political as well economic interaction with the Arab world has been confined to the regimes and their supporters. Even when Libya was plunged into the civil war, India was extremely reluctant to engage with the NTC.

This apathy towards the Arab protests was not confined to the Indian government. Various civil rights groups, media pundits and instant experts on the Middle East refrained from openly siding with the protesters. Those who supported the Egyptian revolution were quick to retreat from supporting similar protests in Bahrain, Libya or Yemen. Some Indian intellectuals, who were critical of the Bahraini suppression of the protests, soon turned into apologists for the Assad regime for doing the same: oppression of protests. External interference, interference of satellite channels, conspiracy theories and Western designs were the motifs used to hail the stability of the Assad regime. Indeed, some of the prominent Indian observers did not go beyond highlighting Western 'double standards' regarding popular Arab demands. In their eyes, Western support for the protesters in Libya and Syria was accompanied by their inaction regarding similar protests in the oil-rich countries along the Persian Gulf. The military option pursued in Libya and contemplated in Syria, in their view, was not available in the Gulf due to larger strategic calculations of the West. At the same time, they refrained from openly supporting the protesters in Bahrain or Saudi Arabia. Such a move would have jeopardised India's interests in the Gulf region and hence, even non-official circles in India, did not call for a regime change in Bahrain along the lines of Egypt. In short, except for occasional cases, both official and unofficial India, did not uniformly empathise with the aspirations of the Arab Spring.

Supporting the Status Quo

Despite the widespread nature of the popular protests, the Arab Spring did not offer any viable political alternative to the existing Arab regimes. It also lacked a recognisable leadership. Even in the Egyptian case, the former head of the IAEA Mohamed El-Baradei and former Arab League chief Amr Moussa made their presence felt only upon seeing thousands of protesters in Tahrir Square. The hasty departure of Ben-Ali and the resignation of Mubarak within days of popular protests gave an impression that other Arab regimes too would fall like houses of cards.

Subsequent developments, however, followed a different script. The process for the removal of Qaddafi in Libya and Saleh in Yemen, was long and painful. For close to two years now, the beleaguered Syrian ruler is fighting to retain power. Despite the prolonged protests, often transforming into violent confrontations, the al-Khalifa has been weakened but not eliminated. The Hashemite ruler Abdullah has been resisting the principal Islamist demand for constitutional monarchy in Jordan. The situation is not different in other Arab countries; the tussle between the protesters and regime is dragging on without any endgame. Thus despite the difficulties and protests, most of the Arab regimes appear likely to stay. In this situation, it might have been prudent for India to support the status quo. This option has appeared more attractive, because of the host of political, economic, energy and other interests that India has in the Arab world.

However, for decades, monarchical and republicans regimes have failed to satisfy the minimal aspirations of the Arab masses. The manifestation of the protests, charters of demands and the size of the opposition have differed. But with the sole exception of Qatar, the country with the highest per capita income in the region, the entire Arab world was engulfed by popular protests, often in the heart of the national capitals. They all largely had the same set of demands: good governance, transparency, political reforms and the end of crony capitalism. Even if India were not prepared to support the opposition, openly siding with unpopular regimes, would have been suicidal.

Thus, supporting the status quo does not appear to be a prudent option for India. Despite the longevity of its regimes, the Arab Spring has rattled the entire Arab world. Even economically better off countries such as Kuwait and Saudi Arabia felt rumblings that rattled the ruling families. Even if most rulers manage to stay on, the Arab Spring would still have exposed their domestic unpopularity. Brutal and prolonged use of security forces has not dampened popular opposition in many countries. Thus despite its reservations, regarding the continuing violence, India is not prepared to openly endorse the Assad regime in Syria. This is in contrast to the positions taken by China and Russia. In the name of regional stability and non-intervention, both have rallied around Damascus and prevented the UN from taking stronger measures against Assad. The failure of the UN peace efforts led by Kofi Annan and later Lakhdar Brahimi, was largely due to the lifeline provided by these two great powers, to the Syrian ruler.

Interests in the Middle East

The lack of an adequate number of experts on the region is not an indication of the region's importance for India. The Middle East, especially the Persian Gulf region, is far more important than the immediate South Asian neighbourhood. The widespread official, media and academic attention received by the latter is largely because of the strategic threats emanating from the neighbourhood. The domestic problems of its neighbours have the propensity to spill over into India and become India's own problem. From a realpolitik viewpoint, South Asia is strategically important for India because it is a strategic liability. The ethno-cultural relations that India shares with its neighbours have often spilled over into India and transformed into security problems.

The Middle East however is different. It presents challenges and opportunities. Indeed, there is no other region that is of as much strategic importance for India, than the Middle East. Pigeonholing and neglect has resulted in the under appreciation of the region, not only by the Indian establishment, but also the intelligentsia. Official secrecy and lack of information are the two prominent hallmarks of the foreign policy of a country that seeks to play an important role in the international arena. India's aspiration for great power status is accompanied by its lackadaisical approach to debates on foreign policy. The general apathy with regard to foreign policy debates is more acutely felt in context of the Middle Eastern region. What then are India's interests in the Middle Eastern region that have determined its response to the Arab Spring?

Geo-Strategic Importance: For centuries, the Middle East, especially the Persian Gulf region, has been important to India. Even before the birth of Islam, India had trade and commercial links with the region and their importance increased considerably during the British rule. Trade routes to European mainland and colonial possessions in the Gulf made the region extremely important for British India. Following the partition of the sub-continent, India sought to manage, if not contain, the support of Arab-Islamic countries for Pakistan over the Kashmir issue. The end of the Cold War and economic liberalisation considerably enabled India to delink from Pakistan, when seeking closer ties with the countries of the wider Middle East, including Israel. As an extended neighbourhood, the developments in the region, especially the Gulf, have a direct bearing on India's interests as much of its commercial trade passes through or emanates from the Gulf. Most of the countries of the Middle East are also members of the 57-member OIC, which has acquired great political clout, especially relating to issues concerning the Muslim populations, in different parts of the world, including India. The growing importance of the region is also reflected by the spate of state visits between India and the region and the Republic Day honours bestowed by India upon prominent Middle East leaders. Having ignored the region for decades, India has hosted three leaders during its Republic Day celebrations since the 1990s.[7]

Energy Security: The economic liberalisation that began in 1991 has intensified India's appetite for hydrocarbon resources. The stagnant domestic production could not cope with the galloping demands and hence if 1970s and 1980s saw two-thirds of its hydrocarbon needs being met domestically, the picture has changed since the early 1990s, with increasing import-dependency. There is a general consensus—both within and outside the country—that this dependency would only increase in the years to come and could reach 80 per cent by 2030. A large portion of this demand, is met by the oil-rich countries of the Middle East, especially by those, along the Persian Gulf. Currently the latter meets about 60 per cent of India's imports of oil and gas. The situation is exacerbated by the growing difficulties of importing oil from Iran, which accounts for just over ten per cent of its imports. Energy imports also form the bulk of India's trade with the region and for example, they make up over 80 per cent of India's exports from the UAE. Moreover, since 2001-02, energy products make up a large portion of India's exports. During 2011-12, for example, India exported $57.39 billion worth of oil products or 18 per cent of its total exports. Thus, any upheaval in the Middle East would disrupt the flow of oil leading to shortages, price escalation and have a cascading effect upon an economy that has of late, shown signs of being sluggish.

Growing Trade: Largely due to the import of energy resources, the Middle East has become an important trading partner for India. In 2010-11, the UAE was India's largest trading partner but in the following year, it slipped to second place after China. However, in 2011-12, the UAE was India's largest export destination and imported $33.82 billion worth of goods from India. In the same year, six Persian Gulf countries, the UAE, Saudi Arabia, Iraq, Kuwait, Iran and Qatar, were among the top twenty five trading partners of India. The wider Middle East accounted for about one-fifth of India's total trade during 2011-12. In recent years, India has been looking to the region and its sovereign wealth funds for investments in the infrastructure development programmes. The actual flow of foreign direct investment from the region, however, is minuscule compared to that, from other countries.

Labour Migration: The construction boom in the Gulf region following the 1973 oil crisis has paved the way for large-scale labour migration from India. Scores of unskilled, semi-skilled and skilled as well as professional Indian workers have been migrating to the oil-rich Gulf countries. There are no accurate figures on the size of the Indian community in the Gulf, or the annual flow of migrants. However, it is widely accepted that at least five million Indian nationals, are currently working in the Gulf countries, including about two million Indian workers in Saudi Arabia. In the UAE, Indian workers constitute the largest expatriate community. In many Gulf countries, there is a sizeable presence of Indian doctors, engineers, IT specialists and educationists. Through their presence they contribute to the growth and development of these countries, and this is often projected as India's soft power. Through remittances to their families, the Gulf migrants also contribute significantly to India. The expatriate remittances to India during 2010-11 were estimated at $55 billion and a bulk of this contribution came from the Gulf region.[8]

The large-scale presence of the migrant labourers in the region is not problem-free. During the August 1990 Iraqi invasion of Kuwait, thousands of Indians were trapped, and concerns over their safety greatly hampered India's ability to articulate a clear-headed policy. Until India evacuated over 145,000 of its nationals from the war torn region, it was unable to evolve a policy that opposed aggression and occupation. Likewise, the July 2004, kidnapping of three Indian truck drivers in Iraq snowballed into a major domestic crisis.[9]

The flipside of the expatriate presence became evident when India was forced to evacuate its citizens from Egypt and Libya, following the outbreak of anti-regime protests in these countries. Until the process was completed, India refrained from making any statements that were critical of the unpopular leaders. This was also the most compelling reason that prevented Indian officials from making any statements, even in private, that were sympathetic towards the protesters. After all, with about 300,000 nationals in Bahrain, Indian leaders could not have said anything against the al-Khalifa.

Religious Linkage: According to a PEW study conducted in 2012, India has the second largest Muslim population in the world after Indonesia.[10] During British rule, it had the largest Muslim population in the world. This makes the Middle East an area of considerable importance, not only for India as a whole but also for a sizeable proportion of its population. The upheavals in the Islamic heartland have evoked considerable interest and attention in India's Muslim community. Since the days of the Khilafat struggle in early twentieth century, they have been responsive to events affecting the wider *ummah*. Through rallies, protests and other public activities, they have been reacting to various developments in the Middle East, and the Arab Spring is no exception. Many of these discussions take place in India's Urdu press.

Though the popular protests are more about class discrimination, they also have a sectarian dimension, as the Arab Spring has revealed the Sunni-Shia cleavage within Islam. It is difficult to ignore the sectarian angle, which is most visibly manifested by the protests in Bahrain and Saudi Arabia. The centuries-old Shia-Sunni divide within Islam has assumed the character of political-ideological battle for influence between Iran and Saudi Arabia. This is more apparent in the events, in and surrounding Bahrain, where both these countries have been seeking a greater role for themselves. At the same time, the Shia-bias in the Iranian response to the Arab Spring is also difficult to ignore. The Iranian support for protests in Bahrain was accompanied by its support for the Syrian suppression of similar sets of political demands. India could not ignore the sectarian dimension of the Arab Spring. While most of the Indian Muslims follow Sunni Islam, there is also a sizeable Shia presence in the country. Senior Indian officials maintain that the country has the second largest Shia population after Iran. Thus, the sectarian dimension in the Arab Spring and Saudi-Iran tensions, have resonance within India, and some of this is manifested in the Urdu press that has a partisan view of the Arab Spring, especially with regard to Bahrain.[11]

These political, economic, energy and religious interests would therefore influence and guide India's reading and responses to the Arab Spring. What then were its options?

Salient Features: More than two years after Mohamed Bouazizi, sparked off the popular protests, India has still not made any categorical statement on the Arab Spring. The closest it ever came to taking a stand, was the remark by Foreign Minister S.M. Krishna, urging the Egyptian President Mubarak to 'listen' to the voice of the Egyptian people.[12] Even this remark made during his interaction with the media has not been publicised by the Ministry of External Affairs and is not available on their homepage. Likewise, the Annual Report of the Ministry for 2010-11 did not even refer to the fall of Ben-Ali and Mubarak which took place during its reporting period. If one excludes the Indian expatriate community in these countries, Indian leaders and officials have maintained a studied silence. India did articulate its positions concerning Libya and Syria, but these were primarily due to its membership of the UNSC during 2011-12, when silence was not an option. In this situation one can only interpret various Indian gestures and moves and construct the salient features of India's policy on the Arab Spring.

a. **Travel Advisory:** The safety and well being of its citizens who were caught in the popular protests has been the principal Indian concern. These citizens were trapped in the crossfire, between the unpopular regimes and growing rage of protesters. Hence, its first response was the issuance of advisory against travel to countries in the grip of anti-regime protests. There was, however, no uniformity in this. While such advisories against Egypt and Libya were prompt, it was only in January 2012, that India warned its citizens against travel to Syria. Bahrain, which witnessed much larger disturbances, did not evoke such a move. This was accompanied by the continuing flow of Indian workers to the island nation, despite the unrest. During 2011, for example, 14,323 workers requiring ECR permission went to Bahrain. Likewise, there were no explicit advisories against travel to Yemen.
b. **Evacuation:** When Indians in these countries sought to leave the troubled area, India provided them the required logistical support. Wary of creating precedence for countries where its community was larger, India was reluctant to term this as 'evacuation' but settled for the benign expression 'homecoming.' Through various land, air and naval operations, in 2011 it brought home 750 persons from Egypt, 18,000 from Libya and 850 from Yemen. The round-the-clock helpline for Indians in Yemen, seeking help to leave that country, had to be closed due to poor response.
c. **Regional Consensus:** Far from taking the initiative, India waited for a consensus to emerge before making any moves. Krishna's urging of Mubarak to 'listen' to the people's voice did not come, until it became clear that the vast majority of Egyptians wanted the three-decade-old Mubarak rule to end. A similar consensus against Libya enabled India

> to tacitly support UNSC Resolutions 1970 and 1973. While the former recommended the referral to International Criminal Court, the latter eventually paved the way for the NATO-led military campaign against Qaddafi. Both of these ran counter to Indian positions on the ICC and external intervention, but India's willingness to support the move, emanated from the consensus in the Arab League and African Union who wanted international intervention in support of the Libyan civilians. A similar move, by a majority of Arab countries, forced India to abandon its previously held position and support the Western moves on Syria. Though this was scuttled by the veto of China and Russia, the shift was visible. At the same time, India was not prepared to ignore the role of the opposition, in the continuing violence in Syria and hence abstained from voting on the Saudi-sponsored UNGA vote in August 2012, that condemned the Syrian government for most of the violence in that country.

This minimalist Indian response can be described as a 'studied silence.' India is not a disinterested party but has vital stakes in the political stability and economic prosperity of the Middle East, especially the Persian Gulf region. It appears unwilling to identify with any of the contesting groups of the Arab Spring. By refraining from making any public statement in support of the protests, it has also avoided rallying behind the beleaguered Arab rulers. Continuing political contacts, and visits to and from the region, subtly indicate its preference: regime stability over the rights of the protesters. While there have been no state visits, from India to the Arab world since December 2010,[13] there was a steady stream of visitors from the region. Support for the Arab protests was general and slow in coming, and was visible only when ground realities were decisively against the regime. Such a situation, in its view, had not come to pass in the Gulf region. Thus, short of a far-reaching turmoil, a studied silence would continue to be the golden rule for India towards the Arab Spring. These muted and calibrated Indian reactions to the Arab Spring also challenge the concept of an assertive India, on the international scene. At a macro level, India's calculated and interest-driven positions during the Arab Spring, are also a sign that its aspirations for great power status will be fulfilled through consensus and accommodation, rather than by taking a leadership role—that is, through measured steps, not aggressive public statements. This is the irony of the "self-appointed frontrunner for the UNSC."

NOTES

1. "Reporting and Collection Needs: The United Nations," US Secretary of State, WikiLeaks, 31 July 2009, http://www.wikileaks.ch/cable/2009/07/09STATE80163.html#(accessed 14February 2012). The other three countries named by Clinton were Brazil, Germany and Japan.
2. In the most brazen manner India's Permanent Representative to the United Nations Hardeep

Puri told a media network, "India entered the UN after 19 years, and we have no intentions of leaving," even after its term ends in December 2012. *India Today*, September 23, 2011, http://indiatoday.intoday.in/story/india-may-enter-unsc-by-2012-end-hardeep-puri/1/152474.html, accessed on February 14, 2012.

3. The Persian Gulf: Historical, Geographical and Legally Validity of the Name, (New York, United Nations, Group of Experts on Geographical Names, *Working Paper no.61,* 2006), http://unstats.un.org/unsd/geoinfo/UNGEGN/docs/23-gegn/wp/gegn23wp61.pdf, accessed 20 May 2013.
4. Pranab Dhal Samanta, "R-Day: Bhutan King steps in after Oman Sultan says no", *The Indian Express*, 29 December 2012, http://www.indianexpress.com/news/rday-bhutan-king-steps-in-after-oman-sultan-says-no/1051706/0, accessed 28 March 2013
5. The full report of the Bahrain Independent Commission Inquiry is available at http://www.bici.org.bh/
6. Jyoti Malhotra, "Finally, India supports Egypt's reform desires", *Business Standard*, February 2, 2011, http://www.business-standard.com/india/news/finally-india-supports-egypt%5Cs-reform-desires/423784/. Accessed on February 14, 2012.
7. They were Algerian President Abdelaziz Bouteflika in 2001, Iranian President Mohammed Khatami in 2003 and King Abdullah of Saudi Arabia in 2006. Sultan Qaboos of Oman was supposed to receive this honour in 2013 but India appears to have not managed the issue well.
8. Ministry of Overseas Indian Affairs, *Annual Report 2011-12*, p. 36, http://moia.gov.in/writereaddata/pdf/annual_report_2011-2012.pdf. Accessed February 14, 2013.
9. A detailed account on the abduction and release can be found in V Sudarshan, *Anatomy of an Abduction: How the Indian Hostages in Iraq were Freed* (New Delhi: Penguin Books, 2008),
10. "The Global Religious Landscape," Pew Research Center, 18 December, 2012, http://www.pewforum.org/global-religious-landscape-muslim.aspx, accessed on February 14, 2013
11. Md. Muddassir Quamar, "The Arab Spring and the Indian Urdu Press", *Journal of South Asian and Middle Eastern Studies* (Villanova, PA), Vol.36, no.1, Fall 2012, pp.63-84.
12. "India for Mubarak stepping down", *The Hindu*, February 3, 2011
13. The visit of President Pratibha Patil in November 2010 to UAE and Syria was the last Indian state visit to the region and there have been none after that. No state visit to the Arab countries has taken place in the aftermath of the Arab Spring.

PART IV

West Asia's Security Dynamics-II: Role of Extra-Regional Powers

12

Security Implications of the "Arab Spring"

Efraim Inbar

Introduction

This essay reviews the political repercussions of the events termed as the "Arab Spring" and focuses on the regional security implications, of these developments. The initial optimism in the West has been totally unwarranted and we have to prepare for the strategic surprise; a greater potential for terror; more chances for miscalculation and escalation; the emergence of the East Mediterranean as an Islamic lake; the determination of Iran to pursue its nuclear ambitions. In the absence of a rising modernising Arab elite, which is hardly expected, the deterioration in the security predicament of this region will continue.

The Arab World after the "Spring"

The "Arab Spring" was a series of events that caused great political tremors in the Middle East. Mass demonstrations in many Arab states, challenged the political status quo and the existing political and cultural system in the region. The uprisings were a collective expression of economic and social grievances, but had limited democratic vision. While it is too early to offer a definitive analysis of the impact of the widespread discontent in the Arab world, the trajectory of the events by the end of 2012 indicated regime change in several states, containment of political unrest in most states, rise of Islamic and centrifugal tendencies in a number of political units, and deterioration of economic conditions. In short, in terms of domestic politics the Arab world continues to face the challenge of modernisation. The prospects for the emergence of progressive modernising forces are quite bleak. From an international relations perspective, regional uncertainty has increased following the Arab uprisings, as have the national security challenges that have led to a deterioration in the strategic landscape. So far, much of the old dictatorial order has survived, but its stability has been undermined and the nature of any successor regimes is uncertain. The audacious demonstrations by the Arab masses, against tyranny in a quest for more responsive governments challenged the existing political order. The potential for further unrest in the region and the risk of more states being engulfed by turmoil and civil war and deteriorating into "failed states" has increased significantly. Such political entities are characterised by an absence of a monopoly over the use of force; delivery of very limited justice; inability to sustain a legal and regulatory climate conducive to private enterprise, open trade, and foreign investment; and the inability to meet the basic needs of the population in terms of health, education, and other social services. The harbingers of such a scenario are Libya and Yemen. The possible disintegration of Iraq and Syria, two very different cases, is also not a far-fetched scenario. Inevitably, the governments in the Arab world will be busy parrying the rising domestic challenges in the near future. The unrest in the Arab world, its growing Islamisation, and the greater potential for its fragmentation testify to the socio-political crisis and the general decline of the region—which is a rising trend. At the same time, the foreign policy of these states has created much uncertainty, thus complicating the strategic calculus of policy makers. The issues the decision makers have to deal with are elaborated in the following sections.

Strategic Surprises

Over the years Western states and particularly Israel have built large and sophisticated intelligence services. Nonetheless, the unrest in the Middle East came as a surprise to everybody. For example, Israeli officials had been speculating that the forthcoming succession of an aging Mubarak could turn Egypt into an "Iran next door." But this conjecture was quashed by Israeli intelligence analysts and academic experts, who predicted, a smooth transfer of power. Similarly, Israel failed to gauge the intensity of the opposition in Syria. The Western intelligence community too failed to warn the policy makers about the political discontinuities in various countries. This is a stark reminder of the potential for rapid change and political uncertainty in the Middle East. The new political environment enhances the potential for strategic surprises. Consequently, it is always necessary to prepare for a variety of scenarios, particularly the worst-case ones. Furthermore, regardless of how improbable a scenario is, it is worthy of serious intelligence analysis, if it can have grave consequences.

Greater Potential for Terror

The domestic problems plaguing the weakened Arab states make them more terror prone. As leaders lose their grip over state territory and borders become more porous, armed groups and terrorists gain greater freedom of action. Such problems plague post-Mubarak Egypt, where law and order have become more lax. For example, in the Sinai Peninsula on the Israel border, a pipeline supplying Israel (and Jordan) with Egyptian natural gas has been repeatedly sabotaged. Sinai has also turned into an unimpeded route for Iranian weapons supply to Hamas and a base for terrorist attacks against Israel. Hamas has even set up rocket production lines in Sinai in an effort to protect its assets, as the group believes that Israel will not strike targets inside Egypt, it does not want to damage bilateral relations.

Moreover, as weakened states lose control over their security apparatus, national arsenals of conventional (and non-conventional) arms become more vulnerable, which may result in the emergence of increasingly well-armed politically dissatisfied groups who seek to harm Israel. For example, following the fall of Gaddafi, Libyan SA-7 anti-air missiles and anti-tank RPGs seem to have reached Hamas in Gaza. Similarly, in the event that the Syrian regime collapses, Syria's advanced arsenal, including chemical weapons, shore-to-ship missiles, air defence systems, and ballistic missiles of all types could end up in the hands of Hezbollah or other radical elements.

Greater Potential for Miscalculation and Escalation

The new leaders are strongly motivated by hatred toward Israel and the West, are inexperienced in foreign policy, and might miscalculate their moves. For example, the demilitarisation of the Sinai Peninsula could lead to an undesired escalation. The demilitarisation of the peninsula stabilised the strategic Egyptian-Israeli relations by denying the two sides the option of surprise attacks. The demilitarisation, often seen in Egypt, particularly by the Islamists, as an infringement of its sovereignty, might now be violated, signalling a significant change in Egyptian foreign policy. Such violations would create a heightened threat perception in Israel and might be considered a *casus belli*.

The political vacuum in Sinai has created several new security challenges for Israel along its southwestern border. The area could become a haven for terrorists, as has occurred in parts of Lebanon, or a base for pirates, as in Somalia. It has already turned into a highway for the smuggling of weapons for Hamas. Managing the situation requires a larger military presence in the area facing Sinai. Under duress, Israel might even be forced to recapture parts of Sinai.

Moreover, the neighbouring Arab leaders may decide to divert the attention of their populace from domestic problems by starting a war of attrition with Israel or by initiating terror attacks. For example, in the past, Syria's Assad has organised civilian marches on Israel's borders in order to divert attention from domestic political tensions.

Finally, several of the emerging political entities are not easily deterred. Unstable or failed states, characterised by their complex and decentralised decision making processes, cannot be deterred as easily as states with strong, centralised political control. Moreover, brinkmanship is part of the political culture in the Middle East. Consequently, the regional crisis augments the potential military challenges for Western powers.

East Mediterranean as an Islamic Lake

The turmoil in the Arab world is changing the strategic landscape around Israel, particularly in the eastern Mediterranean basin, where elements of radical Islam could gain control. In this region, Tunisia, Libya, Egypt, Lebanon, Syria and Turkey are displaying Islamist tendencies, threatening the current unrestricted access to this area, for Israel and the West. About 90 percent of Israel's foreign trade is carried out via the Mediterranean, making freedom of navigation critical for Israel's economic wellbeing. Moreover, its chances of becoming energy independent and a significant exporter of gas, are linked to Israel's ability to secure free passage for its maritime trade, and to defend its newly discovered hydrocarbon fields in the Eastern Mediterranean.

The Islamists won the November 2011 elections in Tunisia. Islamists were less successful in the June 2012 elections in Libya, but it is clear that radical Islamic elements will play a greater role in the future of the country than during the rule of Muammar Gaddafi. If the transition to a new regime turns into civil war, the ensuing chaos may allow Muslim extremists greater freedom of action from the shores of this Mediterranean country.

Libya's eastern neighbour, Egypt, saw the dominant role of the Islamist parties in the countries political system during the rule of Muhammed Morsi. Apart from the important ports on the Mediterranean, Egypt also controls the Suez Canal, a critical passageway linking Europe to the Persian Gulf and the Far East, that could fall into the hands of the Islamists. Significantly, Egypt has already opened the Suez Canal for Iranian military vessels, since February 2011. Access to the waterway enhances the ability of radical Iran to supply its Mediterranean allies, Syria, Hezbollah in Lebanon, and Hamas in Gaza. Moreover, it facilitates Iran's access to Muslim Balkan states, namely Albania, Bosnia and Kosovo, thus increasing its influence in that part of the Mediterranean as well.

As noted, the tenuous control of Egypt over Sinai has further weakened since the fall of the Mubarak regime. This could lead to the "Somalisation" of Sinai, negatively affecting the safety of naval trade along the Mediterranean, the approaches to the Suez Canal, and the Red Sea. At the same time, nearby Gaza is currently controlled by Hamas, a radical Islamist organisation allied with Iran. Israel's enforced naval blockade of Gaza is being increasingly criticised by the international community. Despite the current change of regime in Egypt, containing of the Islamist threat from Gaza continues to be a major challenge in the near future.

North of Israel, along the Mediterranean coast, sits Lebanon, a state dominated by radical Shiite Hezbollah, whose ports are inhospitable from a Western perspective. Hezbollah has already laid claim to some of the huge Israeli-found gas fields in the sea, which could diminish Europe's energy dependence on Russia and Turkey. Moreover, Syria, an enemy of Israel and a current ally of Iran, exerts considerable influence in Lebanon. Its Mediterranean shores, north of Lebanon, are also hostile to the West and its ports even service the Russian navy. While the Assad regime in Syria faces great domestic opposition and may fall, any Syrian successor regime could be Islamist and anti-Western as well.

The next state on the eastern Mediterranean coastline is AKP-ruled Turkey. The country has, over the past few years, shifted away from its pro-Western foreign policy, adopting instead a radical foreign policy stance. The Turkish government supports Hamas and Hezbollah, opposes sanctions on Iran, and holds a strident anti-Israel position, which reflects the AKP's Islamic coloration. Moreover, Turkey has displayed huge ambitions for assuming leadership of the Middle East, Central Asia, the Caucasus, the Balkans, and the eastern Mediterranean. A combination of Turkish nationalism, neo-Ottoman nostalgia and Islamic-jihadist impulses has pushed Turkey into taking an aggressive posture on several regional issues. It has, for instance, flexed its naval muscle by threatening Israel that it will escort the flotillas trying to break the blockade of Gaza.

Turkey has also threatened Cyprus over its desire to share the potential energy riches, south of the island. Turkey is interested in gaining control, or partial ownership, of the maritime gas fields in the eastern Mediterranean as this would help fulfil its ambitions to serve as an energy bridge to the West, which would make it dependent on Turkey. This puts Ankara at loggerheads with Nicosia and Jerusalem, who have a common interest in developing the hydrocarbon fields in their exclusive economic zones and exporting gas to energy-thirsty Europe. This conflict of interests with Nicosia, together with the Turkish estrangement from the West, the perceived Western weakness and improbable adventurism, might lead Turkish troops, stationed in the northern part of divided Cyprus, to complete the conquest of the island, that began in 1974. Such a Turkish takeover would not only hurt Western geo-economic interests, but would constitute a significant Western loss of the strategically situated island. The Cypriot island was a bone of contention, in the past, between Persia and the ancient Greeks, and between the Ottomans and Venetians. In short, it represents the struggle between East and West.

West of Turkey is Greece, a democratic Western state with a stake in protecting the Cypriots from Muslim domination. Its current economic crisis, however, might erode its limited military ability to parry the Turkish challenge alone. With the exception of Israel, all other eastern Mediterranean states would likely favour the return of Cyprus to Muslim rule and the ascendancy of Islam in the eastern Mediterranean.

Western influence in the eastern Mediterranean is being challenged by the growing radical Islamic influence in the region. The access of Iran to Mediterranean waters, the disruptive potential of failed states, and the competition between countries for energy resources is destabilising the region. But it is not clear whether the Western powers, particularly the US, are even aware of the possibility of losing the eastern part of the Mediterranean Sea to radical Islam or are, in any way, preparing to forestall such a scenario. Foolishly, they seem to believe that the so-called "Arab Spring" heralds an improved political environment and that Turkey represents "moderate Islam." Such American naiveté and European gullibility could prove extremely costly in strategic terms. Moreover, the American strategic decision to give precedence in its grand strategy to the Asia-Pacific arena and the weakness of the Eurozone states limits the capability of Western powers to respond adequately to the new challenges.

Iran Gets Closer to the Bomb

The upheaval in the Arab world has deflected attention from Israel's most feared scenario—a nuclear Iran. Moreover, the Middle East turmoil has played into the Iranian strategy, to simply buy time in order to present the world with a nuclear *fait accompli*. In the meantime, Iran assiduously continues to work on its nuclear project, hardly impressed by economic sanctions and diplomatic displeasure. Even the International Atomic Energy Agency published a report (November 2011) that raised concerns over Iranian activities that do not conform to a civilian programme. Its report of August 2012 raises even greater concerns.

Israel is very concerned about the ineffective international response to Iran's nuclear progress. This global passivity seems either to indicate an inadequate understanding of its far-reaching implications; or the lack of political will to tackle a difficult strategic problem. A nuclear Iran would lead to nuclear proliferation in the region, as states such as Turkey, Egypt and Saudi Arabia would hardly resist the opportunity to go nuclear, thus turning a multi-polar nuclear Middle East into a strategic nightmare. Iranian nuclear attainment would strengthen its hegemony in the strategic energy sector by its mere location along the oil-rich Arabian Gulf and the Caspian Basin—the "energy ellipse". A nuclear Iran would also lead to the West losing the Central Asian states, which will either gravitate toward Iran, or try to secure a nuclear umbrella from Russia or China, countries much closer to the region. An emboldened Tehran, after nuclearisation, will also become more active in supporting radical Shiite elements in Iraq and agitating such communities in the Arabian Gulf states. Moreover, since Tehran is the main backer of terrorist organisations such as Hezbollah, Hamas and Islamic Jihad, it may be reckless enough to transfer several nuclear bombs to such proxy organisations, which will have no moral constraints about detonating a nuclear device in a European or American harbour. Iran's nuclear programme—coupled with further improvements in Iranian missiles—would initially put most European capitals, and eventually North America, within range of a potential Iranian attack.

The Obama administration has displayed a reluctance to use force in order to stop the Iranian nuclear project. Jerusalem realises, that diplomacy and/or economic sanctions, have been ineffective, and that the time to decide whether to launch a pre-emptive strike against key Iranian nuclear installations or live with a nuclear Iran, is drawing closer. Israel's inclination to unilaterally deal with a potential nuclear enemy is going to be tested.

Conclusion

This paper has surveyed the main security challenges arising from the political upheavals in the Arab world. It is not certain that the political turmoil will not spread to other states in the Middle East. Even if current Arab rulers are able to maintain a modicum of stability, the security challenges to the region and beyond it are very serious. This happens when the strategic attention of the West is focussed elsewhere, which leaves the regional Western allies exposed to the new security challenges.

13

Arab Uprisings as Regional Events with Global Effects: An Iranian Perspective

Mohammad Hassan Khani

In defining, explaining, and analyzing what we know as 'Arab Spring', it is important to see this phenomenon in its real context and understand and envisage its ramifications for the countries it is happening in. This paper is an attempt to identify the main roots and causes of these events in a historical perspective, and then to examine their impact on regional and international orders. It is argued that the Arab Spring domestically will create some kind of confusion and chaos in the short-term, but in the long-term it will bring deep and structural changes to the Arab world and the Middle East. It also will enhance the demand of Political Islam across the Muslim world bringing groups and parties with an Islamic agenda to power.

Introduction

The twentieth century is remembered by Arab historians and intellectuals as a century in which the Ottoman Empire collapsed, which led to the birth of many new Arab states. It is also remembered by the arrival of a new unwanted and unwelcomed neighbouring Jewish state with which they have fought many wars. Despite these wars the conflict still remains unresolved. These significant events of the last century made many observers believe that it was a 'Middle East Century'. However, the 21st century started with a series of event that could win the title of "Middle East Century". These events included September 11, 2001 attacks, occupation of Iraq in 2003, and the surprise advent of the Arab uprisings in the beginning of the second decade of 21st century. The events related to the Arab uprisings arrived unpredictably and quickly that made it hard to find a suitable title for them. Many declared them as revolutions, Arab style and some considered them as waves of Islamic Awakening. For others the events were a part of the 'Arab Spring', something similar to what happened almost three centuries ago in the 1840s and specifically in 1848 at the heart of Europe bringing storms of revolution to the European capitals.

It is now almost certain that the 21st century, or at least the first half of it, will be remembered by what happened in the Arab world. The scenes from Arab capitals, squares and streets, witnessed by millions of people across the globe, are fresh in the minds of the people though they have not been labelled. This article attempts to examine these events in the following manner. First, it would try to identify the roots and causes of these events, and second, it would explore and analyse the impact of these events on national, regional, and international levels.

A. IDENTIFYING THE ROOTS OF ARAB UPRISINGS

In search for the roots and causes of the events leading to the Arab uprisings a variety of reasons can be identified and counted. Scientifically speaking the causes can be categorized in different types including social, political and economic ones. Some of the causes of Arab uprising are as follows:

Political Factors

Lack of Change for a Long Period of Time

The first cause of Arab uprisings was that while the world has gone through tremendous changes in the past century, the countries of the region have almost been frozen with no meaningful change. Looking at the politics and society in the Middle Eastern countries, one can see how things have remained unchanged and intact for over a century since the collapse of the Ottoman Empire at the end of the First World War. There are very few exceptions to this observation and that includes Iran and Turkey. Iran underwent two revolutions which brought deep social and political changes to the country. The first one was the Iranian Constitutional Revolution (1905-7), which caused a lot of political and social changes in Iranian society, and the second one was the Islamic Revolution of 1978 which again transformed the Iranian society in many ways. As Heather Lehr Wanger observed; "The Iranian Revolution brought tremendous change to a people that had known decades of Pahlavi rule. This may explain convincingly that why those who were expecting that Iran follows the Arab uprising in the first few weeks of the uprising were wrong and it didn't happen in Iran. Therefore, in my view the big question when it comes to Arab uprisings should not be that why did it happen but it should be why it happened so late and why it didn't happen sooner".[1] Shibley Telhami agrees with this argument as he writes: "It was hardly surprising to discover that Arabs were angry with their rulers. In fact, every year, after conducting the Annual Arab Public Opinion Poll in Egypt, Saudi Arabia, Morocco, Jordan, Lebanon, and the United Arab Emirates, the question that leapt from the findings was not 'When will Arabs have reason to revolt?' but, 'Why haven't Arabs revolted yet?'"[2] What has happened between 2010 and 2013 is a confirmation of the fact that the change is coming. Toby Dodge agrees with this notion and he writes, "The events of the Arab Spring have given hope to millions of people across the Middle East and beyond that meaningful political change for the better is a distinct possibility."[3]

Dictatorship: Kings, Absolute Monarchies, Life-time Presidents

The second important cause for the Arab uprisings, like any other uprising in other places, was the dictatorships and the tyrannies under which these societies were being ruled. It is interesting to know that almost in all countries hit by Arab uprisings there were dictatorial regimes in power for decades. For instance, in Tunisia, Zeinolabedin Ben Ali was in power for 23 years, in Egypt Mubarak for 30 years, in Yemen Ali Abdulah Saleh for 33 years, and in Libya Moammar Qadaafi for 42 years. When the people do not have a chance to express their demands and their dissatisfaction with the performance of their rulers, their anger and resentment starts to accumulate. Finally, when there is no more room to hold the anger it erupts like a volcano. This is exactly what has happened in all the classic revolutions of the 18th, 19th, and 20th centuries and the Arab uprisings were no exception.

Huge Gap between the Ruling Class and the Masses

The third significant cause of the uprising was the existence of a huge gap between the ruling class and the ordinary citizens in almost all the Arab countries in which the uprisings occurred. It seemed that rulers and the majority of the people were living in two separate worlds. This gap created a vacuum between the two sides and that led to the lack of any viable communication between them. In practice this problem means that there exists no channel through which the regimes can hear their people and can see their true image in the mirror of their nations. The lack of communication also explains why the rulers were shocked with the sudden rise of demonstrations and staging of protests by the people. This deep gap between the ruling classes and the masses resulted in what An Huihou called as "the strong dissatisfaction of the people".[4]

Economic Factor

Corruption and Poverty

Apart from the above political factors, another major factor for the Arab uprising was the high degree of poverty and corruption which these systems have been suffering from for a very long time. For many decades, corruption in all its forms has been the main syndrome and a chronic disease in these countries. High inflation rate, high unemployment rate, incompetent and paralyzing bureaucratic system, huge gap between poor and rich and many other economic problems had caused a deep sense of disappointment, frustration and anger among the majority of the people, particularly the young generations, in these countries. Suzanne Maloney acknowledges this fact and says: "To a considerable extent, the upheaval of the Arab Spring was the product of the prevailing economic order that characterized the region for the previous sixty years (which) is rooted in part in the after effects of colonialism; persistent war, civil violence, and superpower competition; the intellectual marriage of Arab nationalism and socialism; and volatility and market distortion caused by massive influxes of externally generated rents."[5] She goes on and concludes that the Arab Spring was born of economic grievances, and it will be economics as much as any other factor that shapes the outcomes in the individual states. For this reason, policies that successfully address the pocket book will be equally, if not more, essential than elections to ensuring that the transitions to democracy are stable and durable.[6]

Extreme Dependency on Foreign Powers

Independence has always been a matter of dignity and pride for all nations, especially for those who see themselves of different identity and culture. To rely on a foreign power financially, militarily and politically, is an unforgivable sin for the Muslims and even non-Muslim nations and it alienates the people from their rulers.

It brings a bitter sense of humiliation and hurts the national pride of the people. It even appears as an insult to the Islamic identity of a Muslim nation. This is exactly what has happened in Egypt under Mubarak, and in Bahrain under Al-Khalifahs, and to some extent in Tunisia. In these countries people began questioning the competency of their rulers who acted as puppets of foreign powers and received instructions from the US and European capitals.

Timo Behr and Mika Aaltola acknowledge this factor saying, "All of this contributed to a widespread feeling of powerlessness and alienation, which explain the central themes of 'dignity and pride' that permeated the messages of the protesters. Protesters in Egypt were also mourning the lack of principles and the listlessness of their government in the international arena. From being perceived as the proud leader of an independent Arab world under Nasser, Egypt under Mubarak had turned into America's poodle, unable to make independent decisions".[7] Other analysts such as Emina Ademovic recognize this factor and believe that this is an area which will divide the Arab countries into pre and post uprising eras. According to Ademovic, "Revolutions inspire change, or rather change can inspire revolutions. The United States and the European Union have seen that the Arab people were strong enough to fight against their oppressive regimes and that they are not going to be as receptive, as say Mubarak, to outside aid and influence".[8]

Social Factor

Ignoring the Islamic Nature of the Societies

Ignoring the religious nature and the Islamic identity of the people by ruling states and imposing secular regime on a majority Muslim society is another main cause for the Arab uprisings. For decades the religious feelings and passions of majority were hurt by the secular leaders who were violating the basic rules and principles of Islam. A deep sense of anger and resentment was caused amongst the traditional and religious-minded people against the kings, presidents, their cabinet members and other officials who were not committed to Islamic values and rules. In addition to being non-Islamic, the regimes took a harsh stand against individuals and groups with an Islamic identity and tendency. They placed a ban on such groups from having even ordinary social activities and this led to a radicalisation of these groups and individuals.

B. IMPACT AND CONSEQUENCES

No matter what has transitioned in every single country, in which the Arab uprising has occurred, one thing is for sure that the Arab world will never be the same again. The consequences of Arab Spring will reshape the domestic politics of these countries and also reconstruct the regional politics creating a new kind of balance of power in which the role of both regional and international actors will be altered and modified as compared to the pre-uprising era. We can classify the effects and consequences of Arab uprising into short and long terms.

Short-term Consequences

The new governments will face many different challenges domestically and regionally as a short-term consequence of the uprisings. These changes and challenges will include:

Confusion, Chaos, and Instability

The vacuum of power caused by the collapse of old regimes, the lack of experience of new regimes and their weakness and inability to exercise the relative power they have in their hands make fitting conditions for chaos and instability in post-uprising era. This has happened in many Arab countries, weeks and months after the fall of old regimes, including Libya and Yemen. This chaotic and unstable situation is one the dangerous challenges faced by many of the Arab countries after the uprising.

Ethnic and Sectarian Conflicts

Most, if not all, of the countries which witnessed the Arab uprising have been suffering from old and chronic ethnic and sectarian conflicts. During the old regimes these ethnic and sectarian divisions used to be managed in a relatively successful manner due to the powerful central authorities and the iron-fist tactics used by security and military apparatus. However, due to breakdown of security measures and weakening of law enforcement the old problem of ethnic and sectarian division surfaced rather soon. It can remain there as a big challenge for new regimes. Sunni-Shia rift, Muslim-Christian conflict, Arab-non-Arab clash, and even centre- periphery factor, all can be potential sources of conflict in post-uprising era.

Division between Remnants of Old Regimes and Revolutionaries

In almost all classic revolutions the post-victory era has been an era of fighting and clash between the revolutionary forces on one side, and the remnants of old regimes on the other side. History shows that the forces loyal to old regimes, especially if they had influence in the structures and institutions that had remained from old era, would not give up their hope for regaining power easily. They may retreat for a while, but would reorganize themselves and re-emerge when the time is ripe. This possibility of returning of old players in new regimes is among the most critical features of post-uprising era. For example, in Egypt the army returned to power by what they called a democratic and popular coup.

Threat of Disintegration

The peril of disintegration along the lines of ethnicity, geography, and religion remains a valid and risky possibility scenario for post-uprising era. This issue would be more likely and more dangerous if some neighbouring countries come together with extra-regional powers and hasten the disintegration process for their own benefits. What has happened in Libya, Yemen and Syria is a good example of this threat.

Rift between Religious and Secular Factions

Another rift which has the potential to derail the uprising from its path towards progress and normalisation of situation is the quarrel and fight between two important camps of Islamists on one side and the secular and liberal forces on the other. Either side could resort to various means and allegations to criticise each other making it hard to find a solution for this problem. Unless, the two sides are mature enough to prefer the fate of the country and the unity and interest of the nations over factional gains, the prospect for avoiding this conflict remains very dim.

Long-term Consequences

Although the short-term consequences of the Arab uprising do not seem to be positive or promising, the long-term consequences do appear to have a positive impact. Here is a list of these long-term impacts:

Emerging Stable and Democratic States

Analysts believe that after a period of instability and chaos for a short term which may lead to the presence of military rulers for a few years or even a decade, some kind of democratic and stable governments will emerge. It will be very difficult to ignore the collective will of a nation, or let say the majority of a nation and rule against them. Those who take immediate control of the countries after the uprisings, either with the help of military force or with the support of foreign powers, will ultimately have to recognize the will and power of the people and accommodate themselves in social and political mainstream.

Undergoing a Social Transformation

Political changes on the surface will occur in these societies in short-term. However, in the long-term the Arab uprising may lead to many deep and structural changes within these societies, changes that may revolutionise their thinking and their lifestyles.

Rise of Islam as a Determining Factor

Perhaps one of the most significant and durable impacts of the Arab Spring will be the rise of Islam. It means that individuals, groups, and parties loyal to Islam and Islamic agenda, especially those who are moderate and pragmatic, will emerge and will occupy the public sphere and take the political power. Nevertheless, Islamists will be forced to learn how to become relevant to the needs and expectations of modern societies. They also have to learn how to convince their opponents and the people that they can bring growth, development and welfare to the society without imposing their views.

Shadi Hamid recognizes this fact and refers it as 'Learning to Live with Political Islam' saying that: "Political Islam is here to stay. In Egypt and Tunisia, Islamists have only grown stronger in the wake of the revolutions. The opening of political space means that Islamist parties will proliferate and non-Islamist parties, if they want to win, will need to adopt policies and positions that more closely align with the conservative sentiments of voters. Even if Islamists underperform in elections, they will invariably play a major role in the future of their societies. If they are not leading governments, they will be part of them. If they are not part of them, they will influence the course governments take in the coming critical years".[9]

Changes in Foreign Policy

The Arab uprising will bring lasting and important changes, in the long term, in the foreign policy of the countries involved in the uprisings. In this context, following are among the most important changes and impacts as far as the foreign polices of these countries are concerned in regional and international levels:

- Adopting a more independent and balanced foreign policy by new governments.
- Fragile, cautious, and cold relations with the West in general and the United Stated in particular (no more allies for US in the region).
- Moving slowly and steadily towards more regional integration and convergence in form of Islamic Cooperation Organisation of newly established organisations.
- An uncertain future and to some extent a hostile approach towards Tel Aviv (An end to so-called peace process and the possibility of reviewing the previous accords), a bitter and painful isolation for Israel.

Conclusion

To conclude, what is happening in the Arab world will lead to emerging new trends and dynamics in the region with the implications that goes beyond national borders. The effects of these uprisings will be demonstrated, in mid-term and long-term, in regional and global levels. The powerful storm of change will lash and shatter a century or more old and decayed political rules, norms, and institutions paving the way for establishing and building new ones. After a painful period of instability and uncertainty, clash among rivals which may last even a decade or so, an era of relative stability will arrive in which relative democratic governments will come to power.

These new governments if not Islamic in nature, will recognize Islam and Islamic teaching as an important part of the society and legislation in an effort to reconcile Islam and democracy in their own way. As a result, Political Islam as a discourse will be taken more seriously by academia and politicians both within and outside these countries. How successful and how costly this rebirth will be, or how fast this process will take place, remains unknown depending on the challenges faced by each country case by case. Apart from internal political and social transformations in these countries, the region will also witness tremendous changes due to these events. It seems that the nature of power and the kind of relationship among the neighbouring countries will significantly change. After a period of turmoil and chaotic situation the region will move slowly towards more stability and even some degrees of integration in social, political and economic fields. The other significant feature of the revolutions will show itself in the foreign policies of these countries. The next generation of governments in the region will have less dependency on foreign powers making more room for emerging regional powers and regional coalitions. As for its impact on international system, the Arab Spring will boost the role of soft power in world politics discourse. It will also accelerate the decline of American hegemonic role in international relations.

NOTES

1. Wanger, Heather Lehr, *The Iranian Revolution*, Chelsea House, New York, 2010, p. 95.
2. Telhami, Shibley, "Arab Public Opinion: What Do They Want?" in Kenneth M.Pollack, et al., *The Arab Awakening: America and the Transformation of the Middle East,* Brookings Institute, Washington DC, 2013, p.13.
3. Dodge, Toby (2012), "The Middle East after the Arab Spring", retrieved from: at http://eprints.lse.ac.uk/43469/1/After%20the%20Arab%20Spring_conclusion(lsero).pdf, accessed on February 24, 2013.
4. Huihou, An, "The Reasons and Consequences of Political and Social Unrest in Arab Countries", *Journal of Middle Eastern and Islamic Studies,* (Asia) Vol. 6, no. 2, 2012.
5. Maloney, Suzanne, "The Economic Dimension: The Price of Freedom", in Kenneth M.Pollack, et al., *The Arab Awakening: America and the Transformation of the Middle East,* Brookings Institute, Washington DC, 2011.
6. Ibid. p. 66.
7. Behr, Timo and Mika Aaltola, (2011), "The Arab Uprising: Causes, Prospect, and Implications", at http://www.fiia.fi/assets/publications/bp76.pdf, accessed on April 2, 2012
8. Ademovic, Emina (2012), "The Arab Spring and a Liberal Analysis of US and EU Foreign Policies", at http://www.e-ir.info/2012/06/13/the-arab-spring-and-a-liberal-analysis-of-us-and-eu-foreign-policies/ accessed on April 22, 2013.
9. Hamid, Shadi, "Islamists and the Brotherhood, Political Islam and the Arab Spring", in Kenneth M.Pollack, et al., *The Arab Awakening: America and the Transformation of the Middle East,* Brookings Institute, Washington DC, 2011, p. 37.

14

Security Dynamics in West Asia and the Role of Regional Powers: An Egyptian Vision for Gulf Security

Adel Soliman

The entire West Asian region is witnessing rapid and acute changes, along with the rise of emerging regional powers, mainly, India which has a special place in the Egyptian scheme of things. The region is of vital importance—politically, strategically and economically—as it has the largest energy reserves in the world, which drive the global economy. At the same time, the region is in the midst of widespread changes and regional conflicts, this makes the region a main pivot in building any international order. In this context, there comes in scope for competition among the international players to enhance their influence in the region. In the current context global system seems to be governed by the balance of interests rather than the balance of power.

From this perspective, this paper attempts to shed light on the Egyptian vision for the security of the Gulf region and the role of traditional regional powers following the Arab spring and the rise of new national currents that may go beyond their national borders and impact the wider region. These include political Islam that managed to attain power through popular will and also succeeded in gaining international acceptance—that is historically unprecedented. This will change the map of the regional balances and alliances—which everyone should get ready to deal with. The Middle East will not return to what it was before January 2011 when the Arab Spring broke out. The relations and interests will have wider implications for, Asia and Africa—much more than many had expected.

Researchers broadly define regional security as: the group of coordinated and integrated policies adopted by a group of countries in one region that have common interests for cooperation among them.

This paper deals with the shifting situation in West Asia and especially the Gulf region from a security perspective and particularly from an Egyptian point of view. The balance of power principle had prevailed for a long time, as had rules and policies, when the first signs of change began to emerge at the beginning of the 1990s, beginning with, Iraq's invasion of Kuwait and its threat to Saudi Arabia; and the Gulf war to liberate Kuwait. The period after September 11, 2001, marked by the invasion of Afghanistan, the war on terrorism and the US invasion of Iraq, heralded a complete change in the region's security perspective.

Regional security, if it is to be achieved, requires that states must have some commonalities. They should have similar political systems, which will give them the incentive to design a system to achieve regional security, at the economic, military, and social levels, as well as at the international level, based on consensus and common interests. A regional security system is currently acceptable in the international security system, because it bolsters the security systems in the rest of the world.

Political and Security Changes in the Region

While monitoring the shifting and evolving security situation in the Arab Gulf region, as well as the security developments in Iraq, Yemen, Afghanistan, and Pakistan, in addition to the highs and lows of the peace process to resolve the Arab-Israeli conflict, it is necessary to acknowledge the fundamental changes that have swept the world during the last two decades. The old rules have collapsed and new situations have emerged.

The developments in the Gulf region, disturbed the balance of power in the region, which explains the GCC countries' concern and readiness to deal with the possibility of turning the Arab Gulf into a nuclear zone, because of Iran's ambition to become a prominent player in the region, and its nuclear programme, it appears to be somewhat mysterious in its ambitions.

The Arab system, too is no longer what it was two decades ago. The Arab Spring that swept many Arab States is a phenomenon that draws attention, in terms of its timing and the stages that it must go through. Although these changes have not taken final shape yet, but they cast a shadow on regional security relations; particularly the Gulf region and the roles of regional players.

In view of these fast paced events, regional security is acquiring particular importance and centrality in West Asia and the world, in which events are turned into a spectacle on television, while different powers weave secret strategies to take advantage of this media hustle.

There is no doubt that Egypt is witnessing fundamental shifts in its political, economic and social system. Taking into account its geopolitical and geostrategic importance, Egypt seeks strongly to make a return to the regional scene and is being persuaded by local, regional and international parties to play a pivotal role in the region—which it did not for many decades. The real challenge before Egypt is how to play a positive and effective role and consistent with the interests of the various parties, in close cooperation with them, to promote regional security and stability.

The first of these parties is undoubtedly the Gulf countries. There are various aspects of security in the Gulf region. The differences in perspectives are evident on both sides of the Gulf (Iran and the GCC). While Iran criticises the principle of relying on external powers for security and for maintaining a balance of power, the GCC favour relying on external powers (especially the United States) due to their inability to maintain a balance of power and security and peace in the region.

This is not new because the countries in the Gulf that have for centuries relied on the international community, to maintain their security and existence. Since the advent of the Portuguese in the 15th century on the shores of the region, followed by the English in the 18th century and the United States, in the present, the small Gulf countries see the presence of these powers as necessary to maintain security in the Gulf.

This trend was consolidated by several factors including the rivalry between the local major powers to dominate the region, as happened in the past between the Iranians, Ottomans and Wahhabis. This situation continues today because of Iran's desire for domination and control in the region as well as that of some groups in post-Saddam Iraq. The failure of small Gulf countries to create a security structure that can enable them to face regional threats makes them dependent on external powers. The Iraqi invasion of Kuwait in 1990 and the threat to the Saudi Arabia itself, has forced small Gulf countries to review their policy and enter into bilateral agreements with foreign countries, especially the United States.

At present, the Gulf region States' security visions support the United States military presence in the region, and consider that this presence is essential to their inability and to their own balance of power making the United States a key partner in any regional security arrangements in the Gulf.

The GCC countries believe that Europe can complement the US and play a role in maintaining security and stability in this vital region of the world. From this perspective, the GCC countries have focused on developing a strategic partnership with the European Union and discuss issues such as the Middle East peace process, and the issues relating to Iraq and Iran.

There is AN agreement between the EU and the GCC that a lasting and just solution to the Palestinian-Israeli conflict is important for the stability of the region, including the Gulf region, and the wider security situation in the Middle East.

In the pre-war period, both Europe and the Gulf countries agreed that the United Nations should deal with the issue of Iraqi disarmament. The GCC countries contributed to this war in varying degrees, while some European countries led by France and Germany opposed the war in Iraq. Stabilising the situation in Iraq is a necessary condition for a secure and stable and Gulf, therefore it is in Europe's interest to maintain transatlantic relations and participate in the rebuilding a free, democratic and peaceful Iraq.

The same applies to Iran and its attempts to acquire nuclear weapons. The GCC countries see Iran's attempts as posing a security and environmental threat to the entire region. The European Union and the GCC support all efforts to establish a zone free from nuclear weapons and weapons of mass destruction in the Middle East and the Gulf.

In addition to all these powers, the role of Egypt as the largest and most influential Arab power is of great significance for the rising powers in Asia, India and China, for whom the Gulf is of vital interest as it is their main source of energy which they desperately need to maintain their growth and development rates. Egypt is a regional power having relations with all parties involved in the Gulf security from Iran to Israel. Despite differences and contradictions between Iran and Israel, India's relations with both Iran and Israel, China and Japan in the East to the EU in the West and from Russia to the US, Egypt has been trying to maintain engagement with all the countries, bearing in mind the vital importance of the Suez Canal in terms of the movement of oil and gas across open seas and ambitious projects for development of this axis.

Given these factors it is clear that there is need for a multilateral framework for Gulf security. This is possible and necessary, with the participation of the parties who have a vital interest in the security and stability of the Gulf region; and of course, local actors such as the Gulf countries themselves, along with the United States and the NATO which became eligible because of its role outside European continent. This issue needs more in-depth study and a positive and close cooperation that has been lacking for decades. This will lead to security and stability in the region and enable it to catch up with global technological, human and economic development. Perhaps the two powers that are best suited to play a leading role in this are Egypt and India.

PART V

India and the Gulf

15

Reconstructing India-Gulf Relation in the Context of Arab Uprising

Girijesh Pant

Arab uprising is changing the narrative of the Gulf region. It is delineating differentiated social, political and economic processes both across the region and within the countries. Despite shared vision, countries of the region are seemingly defining their engagement with the uprising on their respective assessments reflecting not only in the nature of their domestic reforms but in foreign policy articulation as well. The power relation that the Gulf regimes could construct on the strength of their rentier power and strategic partnership with America within the Arab world is changing. Dialectically while Arab uprising is providing new space for engagement, as illustrated by proactive responses from Saudi Arabia and Qatar on developments in Egypt, its sectarian spill over though nuanced and contained, is likely to impinge upon the political fabric of the Gulf countries in its own way. Moreover the depleting capacity of the rentier state to co-opt its people looking for space with dignity, "to express their views peacefully, including the right to question their government on issues that matter to them, such as corruption or state spending priorities"[1] is likely to manifest in diverse positioning of the Gulf countries on issues and pace of reforms. In other words the "Gulf common" is likely to undergo qualitative shift as uprising unleashes impulses for change. The key assumption of the paper is that these domestic impulses are likely to play more influential role in defining their foreign policy.

Apparently the external stake holders have to reposition themselves to reconstruct their strategic engagement in conjunction with the processes of change. The Gulf rulers are encountering structural limitation of the rentier system in promoting a graduated process of change. They are looking for options illustrated by their Look East Policy. India is on their East. India's engagement with the Gulf region is huge. Apparently it cannot be oblivious to the changing power matrix and its components in safeguarding its interest in the region. How should

India define its Gulf policy in the context of Arab uprising is the central question? It is proposed that a new convergence needs to be constructed, factoring the Look East expectations of the Gulf regime, and the spill over of changes on Indian stakes and constructive engagement in new spaces/ constituencies created by the impulses of uprising. In other words the script of India's Gulf policy needs to be expanded beyond the oil supplies, Indians in the region and remittances. It needs to explore engagement in areas of new convergence in the domain of non-traditional insecurities namely food security, energy security/transition and knowledge empowerment which are going to be the key drivers sustainability in the region. Besides it also needs to forge linkages with the emerging public sphere in the region because in transition from rentier regime and evolving diversified economy, the role of public sphere is going to be critical in medium term perspective.

Uprising and the Gulf Countries: Critical trends

Arab uprising is reconnecting the oil rich Gulf societies to the wider space that it has created by promoting sense of empowerment among the people. It is reconfigrating the power relations both within and across the region. It has clearly underlined the limitation of American influence on the region. It is also manifesting in the new assertion by the Gulf countries in Arab affairs. More significantly it has created new uncertainties, spilling over from the termination of the Syrian crisis. It is observed that the "There's huge nervousness across the region" The nervousness is also caused by the American policy which might re-asses the support to the regimes when the tipping point comes. President Obama's Syria policy and prospects of improvement in US-Iran relations has made the Gulf countries wary of America's Gulf policy. The most vocal expression of this was the decision of Saudi Arabia not accepting the Chair of Security Council. Though both countries are reassessing the dynamics of their engagement, however the strategic imperatives compel them to look for 'progressive engagement.'[2]

Recognising the American posturing, the Gulf regimes are reviewing the construct of their security architecture and looking towards the East to minimise their vulnerabilities. Leading Asian countries are perceived in this role. This is an important geostrategic shift that the region is exploring. Response from Asian countries is going to be crucial. The rising global positioning of China is encouraging them to seek its larger role in the region. "Arabs in varying degrees see China as a potential strategic partner able to counter the influence of an increasingly unpopular United States. Initial Arab hopes for the emergence of a credible check on American influence in the Middle East and across the globe in the shape of the European Union or a rejuvenated post-Soviet Russia have failed to materialize. In this context, China is widely perceived as the only credible alternative to US hegemony."[3] China however recognises the significance of the

Gulf region largely in the context of its search for energy. It has yet to declare its intent to move beyond it. In fact Gulf countries are disappointed by Chinese policy on Syria. Certainly China is not going to replace USA in the Gulf countries strategic calculations but there is strong sense among the GCC countries to expand and extend their energy relation with Asia to security partnership. Apparently none of the Asian countries have the wherewithal to replace American capabilities yet the Asian players collectively can play vital role in deescalating the security quotient and contribute in promoting regional security architecture. Ironically Asian presence in the region is more of competitive in nature if not adversarial, thus undermining the potential of Asian convergence. Asian stake holders need to reconsider their posturing to provide the region the strategic space that the Arab uprising will be pressing for. The five Asian countries- China, India Japan, South Korea, Malaysia, Indonesia, recognised by ADB as the maker of Asian century have the responsibility to contribute to the security interest of the Gulf countries. It may be pointed out that unlike Southeast Asia where the Asian countries have conflict of interest, the Gulf is the region where they can easily synergize their stakes with that of the Gulf countries.

The impact of Arab Uprising is more visible at the domestic level. It is recasting the security-stability context of the region by invoking internal issues on national and regional agenda. "Grassroots changes can be seen quite clearly in the Gulf, even in most conservative Saudi Arabia. The "virtual world" and the internet culture in Gulf Arab societies are opening up unprecedented opportunities for public debate and civil society activities."[4] People in the Gulf region have been voicing their concern against the restricted public space periodically within the accepted norms of the system however subsequent to their connect with Arab street they are pushing the boundaries in diverse ways. They are among the most communicative cohort expressing their concerns and intervening in setting the agenda of change without huge visibility. This is eloquently demonstrated by the award winning movie Wadjda directed by Saudi Women made in the country with local women actors.[5] They are questioning in their own ways the nature of society based on 'shared privileges than shared experiences.' It may be underlined here that the discontent in the Gulf region is going to be defined, not only by the Youth factor but the rise of Islamist (Muslim brotherhood) or political Islam questioning the credentials of the regime. Regimes are concerned of the rise of Islamist hence would not mind to open space in those sectors that will promote 'non Islamist' constituency. Thus the regimes are responding to reform with reference to their perception of protest. Whether their preferred reforms will be meeting the popular aspirations remains to be seen. Apparently the variation in their thrust of reforms lies in the local context.Since Saudi Arabia is perceived to be the pace setter even custodian of stability in the Gulf region, the regime's response has been comprehensive. It can be argued that its strategy has been three pronged, one addressing to arrest the possibilities of street uprising in the region both by financial and coercive power, second responding to domestic impulses by enhancing the share of rent with people and opening strategic space for participation and third by engaging site of uprising to manoeuvre their agenda to contain the spill over and minimise the possibilities of domino effect. In aggregate terms though the regime has been taking calculated moves, it has very few options but to address substantial issues relating to systemic changes. This is very clearly demonstrated by its decision to regulate the labour market and mainstreaming women in Saudi public space. Though the uprising has yet to make any dramatic impact on diverse constituencies in Saudi Arabia, what is certain that it has eroded the capacity of the regime to keep the kingdom insulated from the developments in the Arab world. The necessities of economic reforms on institutional changes both political and social might create and sharpen the differences in Saudi-Wahabi partnership. If this prognosis has any bearing then it may lead to some basic changes in the Kingdom.

In Kuwait the protest is seemingly moving for more substantive institutional changes. Reportedly grassroots groups are actively exposing the suppression by the state thereby changing the quality of protest but the sectarian positioning by the parliamentarian is discrediting them more than contributing to forces of opposition.[6] It is argued that so far fragmented oppositions like youth, Islamists and tribes are trying to forge solidarity and the rulers are sensing the pressure. "The coalition seems poised to become the first properly organized Gulf group to press successfully for significant political reform, with constitutional monarchy as its minimum demand.[7] The popular mobilisation in Kuwait is pointing that the regimes in the Gulf countries are no more immune to the forces of change. Thus addressing to Parliament, Emir of Kuwait Shaikh Sabah Al Ahmad Al Sabah observed, "It is time to launch a new decisive phase and a major qualitative move aimed at achieving comprehensive reform."[8] The regime in UAE has been able to contain the ripple effect of Arab uprising by deft handling not overtly reacting yet monitoring the 'freedom space', restricting social media and providing economic largesse's. Reportedly " dissatisfied with the slow pace of reform, some UAE intellectuals, businessmen, students, and other groups began agitating peacefully—primarily through written editorials and Internet postings—for more political space. Some UAE youth, on social networking outlets such as Face book and Twitter, called for a protest on March 25, 2011. It did not produce a significant demonstration in part because the UAE government blocked some social media sites, although most experts attributed the low turnout to insufficient public support for an open challenge to the regime."[9] However the ascendency of Muslim Brotherhood as political force has been a matter of concern finding reflection in its Gulf policy.[10]

Oman supposedly most vulnerable among the GCC countries due to limited rentier power of the state did feel the tremor epitomised by street protests but the slogans on the street were not against the regime. The protest has been largely on local issues. Nevertheless the Sultan did initiate some political palliatives and initiatives towards job market. Structurally Oman needs to push its economic diversification with a pace that erodes the possibilities of street uprising. The managerial manoeuvrability with the state in Oman is much limited it has to address the issues of popular aspiration decisively. The regime in Qatar has so far been the least vulnerable to the Arab uprising because the power relation between the state and society is highly skewed. Unlike other Gulf countries, the regime enjoys legitimacy to co-opt the social activism in to system. Moreover the succession in the ruling family to younger generation does symbolise the efforts of the regime to connect with Qatari youth. "Qatari youths have been the quietest among their Gulf counterparts—in two recent polls, an average of 83 percent of them stated that their country has been "going in the right direction," the highest figure among a dozen Arab countries surveyed. The limited push for political change thus far has been made by established professionals such as Professor of Economics Ali Khalifa al-Kuwari, who convenes "Monday Meetings" to discuss reform and development in Qatar. This kind of activity could provide an opening for youths to expand their own political activity, including those who created and "liked" the various "Qatar revolution "Facebook pages."[11] Significantly Qatar has been proactively engaged in uprising across the region especially in Egypt and Syria. The political engagement in these two countries with Muslim brotherhood has put the country pitted against the dominant player in the region namely Saudi Arabia. The point of attention is that while the ruling regimes in the Gulf countries have been able to restrain the acceleration of change yet the processes are unfolding.

Though to a significant degree the developments in Arab uprising countries will have bearing on the format and pace of change in the Gulf region, the agenda however is likely to be driven by the new middle class, the educated youth, the divergence pulls of Islamists and the corporatisation of the rentier regime. The changes are constructing a new public sphere and constituencies in the region with global connectivity. These constituencies are going to set the agenda in the coming times. In other words with civil society and social networking emerging as drivers of change, domestic concerns are going to be reflected in foreign policy making, for instance local unemployment is likely to be a factor in regimes outlook towards expatriates. Similarly the question of oil-security trade-off could be in public discourse and may alter its dynamics. The issue of high securitisation of the region and overarching presence of external powers could be yet another issue of citizen's anxiety. The issue of scaling down of securitisation would demand reconfiguration of security architecture and opening new space. Further the security concerns may even migrate to the domain of non-traditional insecurities. The region does face threat to its food security, suffers with knowledge deficit and need for change in its energy mix by exploring its potentials for renewables.

These new factors are going to be the strategic drivers expanding and transforming the security matrix of the region. The uprising thus going to change the security context of the region and it is here India could leverage its position in the region.

Visioning India-Gulf relation in Regional Value Chain: Food, Energy and Knowledge

India and the Gulf countries do enjoy the rich legacy of their historical and cultural ties. The growing economic transactions are making their relations robust, but in the changed context of Arab uprising they need to reflect in embedding their relations structurally to contribute to sustainable development by empowering their respective economies. The high volume and diversified nature of economic engagement from oil to manpower, between the two has enhanced their mutual sensitivities. This precisely is the qualitative shift arriving out of quantitative exchange underlining the potentials of strategic partnership. If India imports more than 70 per cent of its oil consumption and vulnerable to its security so are the GCC countries importing 80 per cent of their food hence susceptible to its security. If GCC is the leading producer of oil and gas so is India the leading producer of wheat and rice. Though India and GCC countries do trade in energy and food but they do not address to their respective vulnerabilities. GCC provides 64 per cent of India's oil needs and India meets eighty percent of rice needs of Saudi Arabia. India's energy insecurity and Gulf countries food insecurity is structurally embedded. In short to medium terms the two will remain import dependent and vulnerable. Strategically, the two cannot leave it to the volatile market to ensure it. They need to construct a food-energy partnership to ensure their energy and food security as strategic engagement. In addition to food –energy complementarities, the two need to visualise their relationship in conjunction with global processes which are essentially knowledge driven. India does enjoy leverage in this sector and the Gulf countries with growing compulsions to engage their youth in nation building project need a robust knowledge based economy. The global knowledge economy is evolving by creating global production net work and global value chain. It needs to be underlined that the global value chain is hierarchical, thus though it enhances the value addition but does not rule out the vulnerabilities emanating from power hierarchy. It is precisely to negotiate with global hierarchy that regional value chain could be conceived at least in strategic sectors like food, energy and knowledge. However to safeguard the dangers of reproducing regional hierarchy, the regional value chain need to be premised on mutually inclusive regional interdependence.

India and the Gulf countries are part of the old economic construct and the newly emerging global simultaneously. Both are under pressure of enhancing returns by moving towards the global value chain though in different economic transactions at different pace. As individual players when they plug into the global value chain their positioning is determined by their capacity quotient drawn from their technological and innovative strength. The convergence of interest India and the Gulf could be to strategize to transform their economic engagement to be part of global chain at higher level not only to withstand the vulnerabilities more importantly to acquire the levers of power to set the very processes of defining the hierarchy of global value chain.

The growing security threat from non -traditional sources is reaching a magnitude that the nation states are finding difficult to negotiate on their own wherewithal and strength. In fact the growing imperatives of non- traditional threat are feeding to traditional security perceptions. The cross border and spatial flows be of people, resources, finance, information both in tangible and in non -tangible ways are creating mutual dependency and vulnerabilities simultaneously. Clearly there is a strong case that to harness the gains and to address the vulnerabilities a regime in the form of strategic framework becomes the logical necessity. At global level supranational bodies like FAO are advocating a case for strategic framework.[12] Countries do need to visualise inclusion of non- traditional threats to their strategic partnership.

India-Gulf Food Value Chain

Conceptually food value chain envisages business relations as strategic partnership where partners add value to supply chain and the chain is framed in win- win terms. It also assumes to treats partners 'with rights and responsibilities' related to information, risk-taking, governance, and decision-making. Further it ensures welfare of all partners including profit, wages etc.[13] The food crisis of 2008-9 has demonstrated that globalising food industry not only eroding the food security of the Gulf countries but made them vulnerable too. "The first noticeable reaction of Gulf monarchies to a changing security landscape came with the sudden spike in food prices in 2008. While the abrupt rise in world market prices was widely acknowledged to be an outcome of the untimely convergence of multiple structural and cyclical actors, sustained high prices, and increased volatility created concerns about food security among the Gulf Cooperation Council (GCC) member states."[14] Their response to buy land in Africa and in Asia for food supplies derogatory described as land grab, is not working well because it is not defined on the premise of inclusive partnership.[15] The regional demand for food is going to go up. The table clearly shows that in next ten tears the region's food imports are going to move up from $ 24 billion in 2012 to $54 billion in 2020. In the context growing global demand coming from Asia and Africa it will be risky not to look for medium term if not long term solution task to meet The move to create strategic reserves can meet the emergencies but is no sustainable solution.

India having successfully completed first green revolution has not only

Table 1: GCC Food Imports, US $bn, 2007-20

	2007	2008	2009	2010	2011	2012	2013	2014	2015	2016	2017	2018	2019	2020
Bahrain	0.5	0.7	0.7	0.7	0.8	0.8	0.9	1.0	1.1	1.2	1.3	1.4	1.5	1.6
Kuwait	1.7	2.3	2.2	2.3	2.5	2.7	3.0	3.4	3.6	3.9	4.2	4.6	4.9	5.3
Oman	1.3	2.1	1.7	2.1	2.1	2.3	2.4	2.9	3.3	3.1	3.5	3.9	4.3	4.8
Qatar	0.9	1.4	1.2	1.3	1.3	1.4	1.6	1.9	2.1	2.3	2.5	2.8	3.1	3.3
Saudi Arabia	12.0	16.7	15.9	16.8	17.9	19.0	20.3	21.7	24.5	27.2	29.0	30.9	33.0	35.2
UAE	2.6	3.8	3.4	3.6	3.8	4.1	4.4	5.1	5.5	6.1	6.6	7.2	7.8	8.4
GCC Total	18.1	25.7	24.1	25.8	27.5	27.2	29.5	33.7	36.3	39.6	42.6	45.9	49.3	53.1

Source: Economist Intelligence Unit. The GCC in 2020: Resources for the future.

acquired self-sufficiency in grains but occasionally supplies to global market. However, given the growing demand it could face food crisis due to low productivity and poor value addition. Consequently Indian agriculture's share in national domestic production has been declining. Indian Prime Minister has underlined the need for a second Green revolution, "We clearly need a second green revolution that is more broad—based, more inclusive and more sustainable; we need to produce more without depleting our natural resources any further."[16] One of the vulnerable point of Indian agriculture and food economy is the lack of post harvest infrastructure and inefficient supply chain management leading to huge loss in value and unequal exchange. According to one estimate India loses five billion Indian Rupees. The twelfth plan recognises the need to link the small farmer as strategic partner of supply chain by enhancing agri and food infrastructure.[17] Putting differently an improvement in post harvest infrastructure would empower the Indian farmers as he can hold on their harvest for better price. This needs huge investment. The Indian state is looking for private investment but there is apprehension that this could lead to corporatisation of agriculture making farmers to lose their asset. Though the apprehension could be relevant on face of it, but if innovative methods and spirit is the guiding force, an inclusive agri-food value chain could be constructed on the basis of strategic partnership as spelled out above. Located in India- Gulf space, a regional food value chain can be visualised on win- win matrix. Indian agri-food economy needs big investment for infrastructure. The Indian state is exploring the possibilities of public private financing. This could be extended to foreign financing in the framework of strategic partnership. Intuitional mechanism can be worked out if the mutual gains are recognised and pursued. The Gulf sovereign fund could be a source of finance. It can be conceived that a dedicated volume of produce could be linked to a dedicated food supply adding value to supply chain without leading to diversion from Indian food market. What is argued here that such engagement leads to trade creation and not trade diversion from the domestic market. It may be mentioned here that Indian companies are exploring the Gulf food market actively. According to newspaper reports a company from UAE, NMC Healthcare has entered an agreement with Radikal, an Indian exporter of food products to introduce Radikal's Basmati rice into the UAE market. India is currently the world's leading exporter of basmati rice, accounting for over 60 per cent of the world's exports and is reported to have exported 3.21 million tonnes of basmati rice in 2011-12, to Saudi Arabia, Kuwait and the UAE retaining their position as the biggest importers of Indian basmati rice.[18] According to ADB study the process is already set in case of staple food in India.[19] In the following section a case study is undertaken to underline the importance of food security as component of strategic partnership between India and Saudi Arabia.

Basmati in Regional Value Chain: India-Saudi Arabia Strategic Partnership

In Saudi Arabia rice is the major staple food and the country imports all its requirements making it the second largest importer. Indian Basmati constitutes more than 80 per cent of Saudi rice imports. Estimates are that Saudi Arabian rice consumption will be reaching at 1.25 million tonnes in 2015. Having faced the food crisis of 2008-9, Saudi Arabia is pursuing an active food security policy with reference to its staple food which includes rice and wheat. Rice exporting countries decision to stop rice exports to meet their domestic demand exposed the vulnerabilities of countries like Saudi Arabia totally dependent on imports. Consequently in 2008 food security plan called, King Abdullah's Initiative for Saudi Agricultural Investment Abroad as conceived encouraging Saudi private sector (companies and individuals) to invest in foreign countries that have comparative advantage in agricultural production. It aimed "nine strategic crops namely; rice, wheat, feed barley, yellow corn, soybean meal, oil seeds, sugar, livestock and poultry meat in foreign countries and export sufficient quantities from these countries to Saudi Arabia in order to meet domestic consumption, as well as building up strategic reserve of the nine agricultural products."[20] The government has formed the East Asian Company for Agriculture Development and Investment with a total capital of SR 100 million with the aim of producing crops, cereal, rice, barley fruits olive vegetables etc.[21] The impact of the scheme is yet to be assessed however meanwhile the country continues to be susceptible to suppliers market. It is reported that the country is having shortage due to rising demand within the exporting countries. Besides exporters like India are looking for better returns in other market thereby impacting on supplies to Saudi Arabia hence leading to price rise as in case of Basmati rice.[22] "The average price of the 40 kg of Indian basmati rice sack, for example, soared from $50 in January 2013 to $70 in the first week of April, an increase of about 40 percent in a three-month period. However, retail prices of rice varieties of other origins such as the United States, Pakistan and Thailand; experience much smaller increases in prices of about 5 percent during the same period. The sharp price increases in the Indian Basmati rice have generated extensive media coverage and raised concerns among Saudi consumers about future prices and availability of the most popular rice variety in the Saudi market. Some newspaper editorials criticized the local rice importers of the price gouging and market manipulation. Rice traders, however, have blamed global rice supply and demand situation for the price hikes, and explained that these price increases are just overdue cyclical price corrections in the global rice market."[23] It is important to note that the Rice importers attributed the tight supply of the India basmati rice in the Saudi market to a huge Iranian demand for the Indian rice varieties, as well as to a switch by the Indian rice farmers towards the production of Basmati rice hybrid

1121 variety, which has a much higher yield and is preferred by Iranian buyers. Iran has reportedly purchased the entire 2012 production of India's 1121 hybrid rice variety estimated at 1.6 million MT (about 40 million bags of unprocessed raw rice). There has been also a big increase in India's exports of Basmati rice to other new market destinations like the EU and China which offer attractive export prices for the Indian varieties. These factors together have resulted in a decline in the available supply of the traditional high quality Basmati rice varieties preferred by the Saudi consumers.

India exports $1.7 billion of agricultural products to Saudi Arabia. The table below provides the details of leading agriculture products exported to Saudi Arabia. Basmati rice accounts for nearly seventy percent of exports to Saudi Arabia.

However India's total exports of Basmati rice are estimated at $ 3.2 billion and Saudi Arabia being the second largest market accounts for 23 per cent of its exports. As the following table shows UAE is the largest market. Demand for Indian Basmati has reportedly gone up with special payment arrangement with Iran "to skirt Western sanctions against Iran which involves exchanging Iranian oil for a range of Indian goods, including rice, soya meal and pharmaceuticals.— Indian importers of Iranian oil deposit their payments in rupees into an Indian bank, while rice traders and other exporters withdraw their rupee payments from Iran once their shipments have been received."[24]

Saudi Arabia in its search for investing overseas for food security perceives India as legitimate source specially for Basmati rice. With Iran and Iraq trading oil for Basmati, Saudi Arabia would like to have regular flow of Basmati without major hike in prices. The interest shown by countries like Qatar to have control over Indian exports of agricultural products is pointer of the new competition that India could visualize and leverage upon.

Though India has made good breakthrough in agri-food specially Basmati yet it is far from the potential. During last ten years there has not been any steady increase in production and area under cultivation has even declined. The production is confined to northern India in seven states where the ecosystem is very fragile, "consisting of rain-fed upland, rain-fed lowland, drought, salinity, hill ecosystem, etc. where the productivity is very low (less than 1 ton per hectare). This brings down the national average."[25] The yield in case of China is reported at 6 to 8 ton per hectare. To augment production and yield, India is working for hybrid cultivation under what is popularly called, Bringing Green Revolution in Eastern India (BGREI) scheme. "Bringing Green Revolution to Eastern India (BGREI)"- aims to address the constraints limiting the productivity of "rice based cropping systems by intensive cultivation through promotion of recommended agriculture technologies and package of practices by addressing the underlying constraints of different agro climatic sub regions.[26] Reportedly the rice production from the scheme has gone up. However in the absence of integrated supply chain

Table 2: India's Exports of Nine Leading Agriproducts to Saudi Arabia

(*Value in million $*)

Product	2009-10		2010-11		2011-12	
	Qty	Value	Qty	Value	Qty	Value
Basmati Rice	64,04,04411.00	695.25	62,27,04,956.00	687.35	72,12,45,483.00	705.15
Buffalo Meat	2,83,72,641.00	69.51	5,37,42,386.00	145.82	6,55,42,572.00	197.50
Non Basmati Rice	1,48,77,290.00	10.78	12,19,759.00	1.14	10,26,80,182.00	58.37
Other Processed Fruits and Vegetables	2,56,76,333.00	21.34	2,55,05,240.00	20.70	4,45,15,194.00	39.82
Mango Pulp	6,34,79,945.00	46.74	4,77,43,775.00	46.42	4,56,85,626.00	32.71
Sheep/ Goat Meet	95,52,657.00	36.77	67,27,430.00	33.63	51,22,342.00	27.22
Other Fresh/Vegetables	1,72,27,297.00	11.86	2,05,61,456.00	14.45	2,31,39,999.00	17.63
Other Fresh/ Fruits	2,17,77,447.00	11.15	193,27,584.00	10.74	1,91,48,732.00	12.08
Miscellaneous Preparations	79,36,968.00	5.22	96,07,894.00	6.46	1,82.,64,728.00	11.71
Total	91,14,93,161.00	952.01	88,56,31635.00	1023.39	1,13,06,87,058.00	1,171.31

Source: APEDA, http://agriexchange.apeda.gov.in/indexp/country_description.aspx?ctry=11351

Table 3: India Basmati Rice Exports to the Gulf Countries

(value in $ million)

Country	2009-10		2010-11		2011-12	
	Qty	Value	Qty	Value	Qty	Value
UAE	61,61,25,134.00	652.88	63,47,69,331.00	623.03	72,88,23,294.00	715.98
Saudi Arabia	64,04,04,411.00	695.25	62,27,04,956.00	687.35	72,12,45,483.00	705.15
Iran	36,46,02,510.00	433.14	45,06,57,163.00	446.24	61,49,22,157.00	593.01
Kuwait	13,94,73,567.00	217.33	19,75,90396.00	239.50	19,98,69,767.00	284.26
Iraq	69,60,478.00	7.57	3,69,07,901.00	36.27	15,19,61,248.00	140.34
Qatar	57,91,638.00	6.96	76,67,738.00	10.03	1,60,12,284.00	19.70
Oman	58,09,422.00	6.68	61,69,878.00	7.98	1,82.92.271.00	19.67
Bahrain	33,49,286.00	3.82	53,71,461.00	7.15	1,38,47,619.00	15.92

Source: APEDAhttp://agriexchange.apeda.gov.in/indexp/Product_description_32head.aspx?gcode=0601

the farmers do not get the legitimate price for their products and post harvest loss along with poor infrastructure support at milling and silos has restricted the potential besides leading to wastage. Apparently the sector needs huge investment for technology and the organising principle of the supply chain providing the farmer the legitimate price. It is observed that by restructuring the supply chain linking to the international market protecting the interest of stake holders strengthening of producer processing linkages, India can augment its capacity to meet the global demand.[27]

Repositioning India-Gulf Energy Relations

Energy will remain dynamic factor in reconstructing India-Gulf relations in changing context. What is required is to provide a more holistic profile to the sectoral relationship. A framework of linking food and energy can be conceived by a comprehensive agreement which entails a certain quantum of their respective needs for food and energy as part of strategic partnership. It is well recognised that increasing energy security imperatives are making countries to look beyond their boundaries. While the global trade in energy is going up what is important that it is reflecting regional shift as the emerging economies are increasingly looking for energy imports. The obvious implication is that the emerging markets are forced to compete which may lead to tension. In other words the shift in direction of energy trade relocating the arena of competition and tension also. Further it is adding the issue of security of energy supply to their national agenda. Chinese move to Indian Ocean or Indian reach to South China Sea illustrate the point, However given their limitations to secure supplies by military means, the emerging markets need to be engaged in finding innovative mechanism of energy security. One way to promote this could be by redefining the organising principle in a way that stakes are spread across the region by transnational ownership. By interlocking the regional interest, the risk could be shared and minimised. The energy domain is moving beyond the national border, towards trans-nationalisation. Trans border projects like the pipe lines, the power grids and transmission are linking national markets to neighbouring regions thereby transforming future profile of energy logistics. Surely the driving force has been the technology which is making energy cheap when produced and managed through efficient distribution system. A strategy of linking ownership and interests on cross border space will certainly ensure more security with relatively less cost not to mention the fact that the confidence building dividend emanated from it will further push the economic boundaries towards cooperation. It is argued that "swapping ownership shares between producers and consumer allows for a redistribution of resources rents and risk sharing: the consumer nation receives a share in upstream equity gas and concomitant production rents and producer nations receive significant downstream assets and profits. At the same time, such joint venture in resource exploitation generates a more equitable distribution of risks associated with investment and price movements as both parties are exposed over the entire value chain."[28]

The Gulf region is major supplier of energy to India and the latter is vital market for the Gulf energy but their energy relations are not sensitive to their supply-demand security. In the changing context when the Gulf energy supplier are experiencing erosion of their strategic leverage and India despite diversifying its sources needs the Gulf oil, their energy relationship needs to be redefined in strategic terms. The framework has to be comprehensive, recognising that the food crisis of 2007-8 that energy security is linked to the food security and water security. If it was the shift in bio fuel production at the cost of maize that pushed the prices in 2008 and 2009, it is the growing demand for clustered beans for fracking that has linked the farmers in remote villages of Rajasthan to global supply. The point made here is that energy security can no more be seen in isolation, more so in the context of the different component of energy mix. To keep pace with changes in energy mix and the linkages of energy with other non traditional security, the new possibilities have to be explored. In terms of illustration it can be argued that with a more comprehensive engagement for non traditional securities which is not confined to concerns around the trading of hydrocarbon alone be visualised by exploring the possibility of creating a regional/spatial value chain in renewable and non renewable along with food sector. Gulf countries are investing in a big way on renewable and on food security. A case of regional spatial value chain in case of renewable is made for three reasons- to share investment in research and development, to provide the volume sale i.e. market and to minimise the burden of subsidies. India can take initiative to create a regional R&D hub and regional manufacturing hub in the format of regional networking. This will create a partnership of stake holders with collective interest hence collective responsibility of ensuring energy security. The Indian Prime minister reportedly talked about creating India as Global hub for solar energy,[29] but without a road path such pronouncement remains no more than press clipping.

Strategic Engagement in Energy Regime Transition

In this section it is argued that strategic salience in energy transition is steered by those who command the technology and have wherewithal to control it. The future of energy security of the Gulf and Asian consumer including India lies in influencing the power dynamics of energy transition leading to making of global energy regime. The processes leading to energy transition are clearly discernible. Transition is complex and lengthy process. It is observed that it was after 100years that coal could acquire a share of 60 per cent in the world commercial energy and oil could become source of fuel supplies accounting by 50 per cent of world's energy in sixty years. Though like coal, oil too will continue to have a significant place in global energy mix however as the transition progresses it will be losing its strategic premium. Looking at the efforts being made by different countries, it is very clear that along with opening up of new oil and gas sites, the renewable energy is emerging as alternative particularly with environmental consequences have become part of global common concern. Countries are under pressure to factor environmental concerns in defining their energy mix. What seems to be the possibility that while the composition of energy mix is going to change, no single form of energy is going to be commanding the dominant position. However unlike past, today the forces of globalisation are contributing to the composition of global energy by making it possible to "to trade any fuel across almost any border, greatly enhancing the prospect that fuels are allocated to their most efficient application. Globalisation allows the diffusion of technology across borders to proceed at unprecedented speed, helping to ensure that fuels compete on true cost. Globalisation also brings standardisation, ensuring efficiency gains and unprecedented flexibility in energy production and consumption—The big picture is again one of convergence, this time across fuels. Not only are oil, coal and gas likely to remain the most important fuels over the next 20 years; their market shares are likely to roughly equalize, at 25 to 30 per cent each. This would be the first time that the world has not been dominated by one single fuel."[30] However it will critically depend upon the way the stake holders steer the transition in terms of policy regime that in turn is going to be determined by the power dynamics of the time.

The widening of resource base of energy supplies from hydrocarbon to renewable is tilting the strategic leverage in favour of those who control technology than resources. America could retrieve its energy salience on the strength of billions spent on energy innovation and research and development. This has accrued it the advantage of not only in bringing non-conventional gas to market but having control over the technologies in the domain of future energy. Similarly the recent breakthrough in Methane Hydrate deposits could change the very dynamics of Japanese energy dependence. Reportedly Methane Hydrates has potential of fifteen times more gas than world shale deposits. Further the Enhanced Geothermal System is likely to make the geothermal energy safe and viable proposition. Along with the technology, the manufacturers of energy infrastructure are going to be the key player too. Significantly China the leading consumer and importer of energy is using its subsidised manufacturing strength to be in the race in energy domain. However the fundamental point needs to be examined whether the emerging trends suggest continuum of zero sum matrix or the possibilities of a positive sum energy security regime? How are the players positioning themselves specially the oil and gas exporters and what implications will it have on leading energy importers from Asia? What could be the advantageous positioning for India and the Gulf in the changing balance of power in energy domain? What are the possibilities of India-Gulf energy engagement to tilt the strategic balance in the making of new global energy regime their favour?

India-Gulf Regional Solar Energy Hub

The energy needs of India and the Gulf countries do converge on diversification of their energy mix by making renewable as significant part of it. In terms of carbon emission both are under pressure. Their recognition of the need also points towards the communion of interest. However the strategy they are pursuing does not promise them position of strength in the emerging global energy regime. It is observed that at this juncture America and China are the leading players who have potential to define the new global regime from position of strength. However despite their power quotient they alone would not be able to provide for a globally sustainable energy regime on the contrary a binary trajectory would lead to competition-conflict possibilities which for countries like India and the Gulf countries is detrimental to their development. The GCC countries are reportedly investing big way in renewable energy like India too. The following table provides the details of GCC investment in the sector.[31]

Table 4: GCC Plans for Investment in Renewable and Impact Assessment on Select Indicators

Country	Current Focus Area	Investment	Private Investment Participation
Bahrain	Solar, Wind, 2 Hybrid Solar cum wind plants	US$ 133 million	Mainly IPP oriented
Kuwait	Solar (Nuclear plans down scaled after Japan solar project disaster)	US$ 600 million	Mainly government
Oman	6 renewable energy Projects Solar, Wind, No nuclear plans for the future	US$ 21 million	Mainly government with private participation
Qatar	7 Solar plants and Wind solar projects	US$ 1 billion	Predominantly government with Scope for private participation at a small level
Saudi Arabia	16 nuclear reactors and Solar	US$100 billion	Government and IPPs to an extent
UAE	4 nuclear rectors, and Solar	US$20 billion	Large avenues for private Investment and IPPs

Note: The project focus is not an exhaustive list of renewable projects.

In making a case for India-Gulf Energy hub, the underlining premise is that given the decentralising nature of renewable there is need to work for a technology regime that promotes a decentralised global energy regime. This can be possible in the framework of Techno-Energy Cooperation. According to Global Trends in Renewable Energy Investment 2012, global investment in 2011 was record with $257 billon a six fold rise over 2004. What is significant that "The $237 billion invested in building these green power plants compares with $223 billion of net new expenditure annually on building additional fossil fuelled power plants globally last year. So we're certainly seeing a green growth trajectory in the power sector, even if we have quite some way to go to achieve an energy mix that is truly sustainable."[32] However the prospects become brighter as cost of technology is declining; it is reported that the price of Photovoltaic module came down by approximately 50 per cent, while onshore wind turbine prices fell by 5 to 10 per cent. Consequently in power sector it is emerging as alternative to fossil-fuel-coal and gas. Apparently the Energy Technology revolution will be the flag bearer of new energy regime and those who invest in the technology will have the corresponding advantage. Among the renewable energy, solar is moving up in its global share. According to IEA solar PV manufacturing industry is now in consolidation stage due to fall in the cost. Estimates suggest that the since 2000the cost of PV has come down from three to four times from $6/Watt to less than $1.5/watt "Preliminary analysis suggests 2012 global solar PV installations near 30 GW, similar to capacity additions in 2011. Generation growth is projected to continue over the medium term, to nearly 280 TWh in 2017, putting solar PV on track to achieve 2020 2DS objectives (380 TWh in 2020). Until recently, deployment was concentrated in countries with strong policy support, such as Germany, Italy and the United States. However, improving competitiveness is helping deployment to spread into Africa, the rest of Asia, Latin America and the Middle East."[33]

Richly endowed with sun shine India and the GCC countries have huge stakes in mainstreaming solar energy in their energy basket due to increasing pressure of rising demand. As observed earlier the mainstreaming will depend upon the cost factor which is a function of R&D and scale. India and GCC combine provide huge market for solar however despite their respective investment, it is not of the magnitude that could pull the string to provide human resources and technological breakthrough. However the two can construct a regional value chain the support of regional engaged in creating new technology and producing in the scale to be not only supplier to their respective demand but to the global market as well. Among the GCC countries Saudi Arabia and UAE are two active players and have huge resources to invest. India is a huge market for solar energy. Under its Jawaharlal Nehru National Solar Mission it proposes the "the installation of 20 GW grid-connected and two GW off-grid solar power, 20 million sq. m of solar thermal collector area and 20 million rural households with solar home lighting by 2022.—The target of JNNSM is to promote grid-connected solar power in a big way with the objective to bring cost of solar power generation to grid parity levels. The immediate aim of the Mission is to focus on setting up an enabling environment for solar technology penetration in the country both at a centralized and decentralized level."[34]

India is investing in big way yet it needs to scale it up to be part of global research orbit. It is precisely for that reason that the government had floated the idea of Special Economic Zones in Chennai. It was envisaged to attract foreign investment to house industrial R & D units, laboratories, testing units, educational and vocational training centre and vending. According one estimate India has been able to attract $ 1.5 billion by 2012 in renewable energy. India allows 100 per cent through automatic route for the project. It also provides fiscal and financial incentives. India has been organising overseas investment meets. It is also pursuing proactive policy of collaboration with foreign countries. Renewable energy is vital to its strategic partnership with many countries. A proactive solar energy engagement between India and GCC could be envisaged in the framework of regional value chain. The employment potential of the sector could be additional region for GCC to look towards this partnership. India could be the location of skills development centre for the region.

Building Strategic Partnership for Sustainable Knowledge Based Economy

Global economy is increasingly becoming knowledge based in its production processes. The knowledge production critically depends upon ideas, innovation, invention, technology and entrepreneurship. It is a process of transformation from intangible to tangible. The value chain in knowledge sector happens to be dynamic in nature, therefore has potential to transform the hierarchical architecture of value chain. From knowledge clusters to its production is a chain that could be locally mediated providing opportunities to move up in its hierarchy. "A knowledge cluster is local innovation system organized universities, research institutions and firms which intends to drive innovation and create new industries. Knowledge hubs are localities with knowledge architecture of high internal and external networking and knowledge sharing capabilities."[35] Such transnational clusters and hubs could be dedicated to specific industry.

During last two decades India has developed knowledge platform to leverage its future growth. India intends to reap the advantage of its demographic dividend by promoting knowledge based economy as the prime mover of its growth. According to a study, "Over the last several years, India has been able to capitalize on its strong capabilities in IT-enabled services sectors to increase its share of services exports to the GCC countries. According to industry estimates, India's IT products and services exports to the GCC countries have been increasing at a growth rate of above 30 per cent annually. Lower costs and English language skills remain the prime advantage for the Indian IT sector. India continues to offer skill-based services at 50-80 per cent lower cost than their source locations and 10-30 per cent cheaper than other low-cost destinations. Consequently, IT sector revenues from exports have risen at a CAGR of 25 per cent over the last 10 years in India."[36] However the high capital intensity has been restricting Indian endeavor to move up in terms of innovation indices.

In diversifying the hydrocarbon economy, the Gulf countries face the deficit in their knowledge account. While it cannot be denied that oil rich region has very high literacy rate yet they face deficit in this domain. GCC countries too recognize that transformation of their oil based economy can take place by research and innovation. GCC needs to move to high knowledge based economy because low end jobs are not acceptable to its people. IMF study points out that between 2000 and 2010 about seven million jobs were created but only two million nationals accepted it.[37] In other words the economy needs to create high skill jobs this means it has to move on knowledge sector. Paradoxically the local human resources pool is not trained to be employable in high end sector. Thus along with moving the economy to high end knowledge sector the region also need to reorient its education system.

Engagement of its young population in economic diversification processes is going to be the key driver of geo-economic transition in the GCC countries. The Gulf youth is finding hard to respond to move away from the comfort of rent based employment. Politically the discomfort of this huge number could be a risky proposition. Estimates suggest that youth under 25 years of age accounts for as high as one third to half of the total population, it constitute more than fifty per cent in case of Oman, Saudi Arabia, around 40 percent in Bahrain and Kuwait and more than thirty percent in Qatar and UAE. Significantly the literacy level in the GCC countries is very high, the governments have been making high investment on education. While the education regime has enhanced the literacy rate but not the skills hence the region is facing unemployment.[38] The generation next thus is facing a unique situation of being co-opted in the system without participating in it. Recognizing the limitations, the governments are reforming the education system but the solution to unemployment lies in diversification of the economy and sustainable development. GCC countries have been attempting to move beyond the rent based economy but the pace needs to be accelerated. Though small size constrains could be addressed by the GCC integration processes, it is equally important that regional integration be conceived as part globalisation processes. Transition of GCC diversification needs to be driven by external sector. The investment trade linkages with emerging Asian economies could replicate the story of Southeast Asia. Indian market size and service sector could be leveraged with growing GCC diversification processes. India story is relevant to the Gulf because, in terms of factor endowment and geo strategic location, the region could define its comparative advantage around the knowledge based service sector. It is argued here that by creating a regional network of research and development incubators along the regional value chain, India and the Gulf countries could augment the knowledge quotient of the region and transform the power hierarchy of global knowledge value chain as well. This provides a rationale that India would like to look at the Gulf region for promoting itself in global knowledge power hierarchy.

Summing-up, in this paper it is argued that in the emerging scenario following the uprising in the neighbouring Arab countries, the political and strategic imperatives in the Gulf region too are asking for correction of structural dynamics than looking for external support systems. Economic participation, social justice and dignity are the new determinants of security and stability. This is a radical shift in regional security discourse which no more remains privileged to external players. However it needs to be emphasized that though domestic has acquired primacy, the external will remain vital in consummating the domestic to contribute to resilience or subversion. External environment remains important but this too is passing through transition. The rise of Asia is pulling the region on its economic strength but has no corresponding military might. The Gulf, in short run does need security support. The Asian countries have to collectively invent a regional security architecture that does share to the security needs but does not escalate 'security temper' by projecting threat perception and arms trade but contributes to its de-escalation. In this paper it is argued that a robust regional inclusive engagement between India and the Gulf in nontraditional security areas may contribute towards systemic resilience which in turn may change the threat quotient of the region because a regime domestically secured does not need to invent security threat for its own security and survival.

NOTES

1. Rami G Khouri, "A second battle also defines the Arabs" at http://www.dailystar.com. June 1, 2013.
2. Colin H. Kahl and Marc Lynch, 'US Strategy after the Arab Uprisings: Toward Progressive Engagement,' *The Washington Quarterly,* 36:2 pp. 39-60.
3. Chris Zambelis and Brandon Gentry, 'China through Arab Eyes'. *The US Army War College Quarterly,* Parameter Spring 2008 pp 60-72. Mohammed Turki Al-Sudairi,'China in the Eyes of the Saudi Media', *GRC Gulf Papers,* February 2013.
4. Elena Maestri,'Schism within the GCC or the Same Old Tribal Politics'? Op-med L. *Istituto Affari Internazionali,* March 2013.
5. Peter Debruge, 'Why 'Wadjda' Matters: Tiny Saudi Movie Makes Waves,' Rearview: *Variety* September 26, 2013.
6. 'Despite Constraints, Saudi women upbeat about empowerment' *Arab News,* September 29, 2013 at http://www.al-monitor.com/pulse/originals/2013/09
7. Christopher Davidson, 'Domestic Dynamics in the Gulf Monarchies After the Arab Spring,' *ISPI No 175,* 2013.
8. *Gulf News,* October 29, 2013.
9. Kenneth Katzman, 'The United Arab Emirates (UAE): Issues for US Policy Congressional

Research Service' October 17, 2013., at http://www.fas.org/sgp/crs/mideast/RS21852.pdf
10. "UAE battle against Muslim Brotherhood extremism continues". *The National* August 25, 2013, at http://www.thenational.ae/news
11. Lori Plotkin Boghardt, 'Youth Activism in the Small Gulf State', at http://www.washingtoninstitute.org
12. 'The Global Strategic Framework for Food Security and Nutrition'. At www.fao.org/docrep/meeting/026/ME498E.pd
13. 'Values-Based Food Supply Chains: Strategies for Agri-Food Enterprises-of-the-Middle', at gwsteven@wisc.edu; rspirog@iastate.edu
14. Andy Spiess, 'Food Security in the Gulf Cooperation Council (GCC) Economies,' GCC Network for Dry lands Research and Development (NDRD), at http://www.ndrd.org
15. "Gulf states are major players in the global land grabs, that diverge considerably from the general pattern, because of their explicit focus on food production. These states are confronting a changed landscape for agro-investments that includes more direct competition from other states and investors, scrutiny by global civil society, and the need to engage in global governance as never before." Eckart Woertz, *The Governance of Gulf Agro-Investments in Globalisations, 2013*, Vol. 10, No. 1, 87–104.
16. At http://www.thehindu.com
17. See Report of the Working Group on Agricultural Marketing Infrastructure, Secondary Agriculture and Policy Required for Internal and External Trade for the 12th Five Year Plan 2012-17.
18. 'UAE's NMC Unit Signs Deal With Indian Food Producer Under the agreement, NMC Trading will introduce Radikal's Basmati rice to the UAE market', at http://gulfbusiness.com 5-12-2012.
19. Thomas Reardon, Kevin Chen, Bart Minten and Lourdes Adriano, *The Quiet Revolution in Staple Food Value Chains Enter the Dragon, the Elephant, and the Tiger*. Asian Development Bank and International Food Policy Research Institute, 2012.
20. *Saudi Arabia Grain and Feed Annual*, at http://gain.fas.usda.gov
21. Setting up Announcement of Eastern Asia Co. for Agricultural Development & Investment., at http://www.mci.gov.sa/en/MediaCenter/Decisions/Pages/28-4-2013-01.aspx
22. Rice prices jump as exporters turn to more lucrative markets, at http://www.arabnews.com, April 6, 2013.
23. *Saudi Arabia Grain and Feed Annual*, at http://gain.fas.usda.gov
24. At http://online.wsj.com/article.
25. 'Future Bright for India Basmati Rice Production, Exports', at http://oryza.com, January 1, 2013.
26. Meeting on Bringing Green Revolution in Eastern India. March 9, 2011,at http://bgrei-rkvy.nic.in/MeetingProceedings/Background.pdf
27. Navneesh Sharma, 'Basmati Rice: Production, Procurement, Processing and Marketing'. The International journal's Research, *Journal of Social Science Management,* Vol. 1, No. 8, December 2011.
28. Enno Harks, 'Transnational Cross Ownership Schemes in Energy Sectors: A Tools for Increasing Energy Security', at http://www.swp-berlin.org
29. At http://www.globalpost.com., April 17, 2013.
30. World Economic Forum, 'Energy Vision 2013,Energy transitions: Past and Future',2013
31. Noriko Suzuk, 'The Role of Renewable Energies in GCC-Japan Relations', March 24, 2013, at http://grc.net.
32. 'Global Trends in Renewable Energy Investment 2012', at http://fs-unep-centre.org
33. IEA, *Tracking Clean Energy Progress 2013.*
34. Jawaharlal Nehru National Solar Mission, Ministry of New & Renewable Energy, at http://www.mnre.gov.in.

35. H.D. Evers, 'Knowledge Hubs and Knowledge Clusters: Designing a Knowledge Architecture for Development' *ZEF Working Paper Series, 27* Department of Political and Cultural Change Centre for Development Research, University of Bonn, p. 4.
36. 'Trade and Capital Flows—GCC and India', May 2, 2012, at www.alpencapital.com.
37. Gulf Cooperation Council Countries: *Enhancing Economic Outcomes in an Uncertain Global Economy IMF, 2011.*
38. "According to the latest available official national data, unemployment rates among people age 15 to 24 between 2001 and 2009 were highest in Bahrain, 31 percent in 2001, followed by Saudi Arabia, 29.9 percent in 2009. Kuwait had 18.4 percent youth unemployment in 2005. In 2008, Qatar reported 7 percent unemployment among its youth. And the UAE indicated in 2005 that its youth unemployment rate was 8 percent. However, a labour force survey conducted in the UAE in 2009 revealed that the unemployment rate in the age group 15 to 19 reached 36.1 percent; for those in the 20 to 24 age group, it was 11.3 percent,"*Youth in GCC Countries: Meeting the Challenge, at* http://www.booz.com.

16

Conflict in WANA Region: Impact on Energy Markets

Shebonti Ray Dadwal

The history of oil is intrinsically linked to the West Asian-North African (WANA) region and any strife, in the area is directly or indirectly, related to the control over these resources. Hence, the recent Arab uprisings, and the face-off between the US-EU and Iran over the latter's nuclear enrichment programme and the impact of ever-stricter sanctions imposed on Tehran on the oil market are not the first time the region has experienced tumult, nor will it will be the last. Each time there has been a conflict, it has been accompanied by oil supply shocks, and fears of global recession. However, the developments emerging from the recent uprisings across the WANA region may have more long term implications, for the oil market—not entirely due to regional factors. Nevertheless, the issues that need to be examined, in the aftermath of recent developments, are: The impact on the uprisings on oil supplies and therefore on prices? How will the world economy react to the ensuing oil-price volatility? And how well can policymakers cope with the above?

The world oil demand in 2013 was around 90.26 million barrels a day, (mbd). China replaced the US as the top oil consumer in 2013 with the US and other three BRIC countries, namely Brazil, Russia and India, as well as Saudi Arabia together occupying five of the next six spots. The top ten consumers, as a whole, account for roughly 60 per cent of total global demand.[1]

In fiscal 2012-13, India imported 184.7 million tonnes of crude as against 171.73 million tonnes in 2011-12.[2,3] In the first quarter of 2013, India's crude oil import bill was Rs 3,654 billion, which is about 18 per cent higher, than the preceding year.[4] If prices or imports or both increase, the bill will be even higher, given that India's oil import bill accounts for almost one third of its total imports. Since fuel prices are subsidised, the government has to bear some of the cost by reimbursing the oil marketing companies for selling fuel at lower prices. As a result, the fiscal deficit target is breached time and again, which in turn increases the government's borrowing costs and keeps interest rates high.

Almost 62.6 per cent of India's imports during April-September 2012 were sourced from West Asia. Saudi Arabia was the largest supplier accounting for 18.3 per cent of the country's total supplies; followed by Iraq that provided 13 per cent of its total requirement during the period. A close third was Venezuela (10.3 per cent); followed by Kuwait (9.8 per cent) and the UAE (9.2 per cent). Iran, which was India's second largest supplier till 2011, slipped to seventh position, after Nigeria, following the more imposition of more stringent US sanctions.[5] This is because the Indian basket of crude oil comprises Oman and Dubai Brent, for sour grades and North Sea Brent, for sweet grade in an approximate 60-40 ratio.

Clearly therefore, developments emanating from the West Asian region has great significance for India, as well as for the world. This paper studies the impact of recent developments in the region on the energy market as a whole, the long term consequences of political factors on the West Asian and North African region's energy sector and the impact on Asia and India, in particular.

WANA Region and the Oil Market

The WANA region is one of the most well endowed insofar as energy (hydrocarbon) resources are concerned. According to 2010 data, the WANA region holds 59 per cent of the world's oil reserves—around 816 billion barrels of oil reserves—20 per cent of which are in Saudi Arabia alone.[6] The region produced 35 mbd, which is around a third of total world production, and exports the bulk of its production, that is, around 40.7 per cent of global oil exports. However, two factors contribute to the region's importance for the oil market: first, the cost of production of oil in the region is the lower than anywhere else at $ 4-6 per barrel.[7] And second, three of the countries in the region, viz., Saudi Arabia, UAE and Kuwait, have excess or spare capacity, that is they do not produce at capacity levels, and this spare capacity, can be brought into production if the need arises. However, it is Saudi Arabia alone, that plays the role of a swing producer, when required, and can bring extra barrels into production at short notice.

Although not all the countries in the region are energy rich, those that are not, are nevertheless largely dependent on the region's energy sector. Most of them are dependent on the revenues accruing from trade, remittances and commodity price channels with the energy-exporting countries, and many of them receive substantial grants and foreign direct investment (FDI) from other states in the region.[8] As a result, when revenues of the energy exporting countries drop, be it due to a fall in production or a price drop, all the countries are affected.

Therefore, whenever there is an upheaval in the WANA region, it becomes a matter of concern for the oil markets. For instance, there have been a number of occasions when the region's oil supplies appeared to be endangered—the Iranian crisis from 1951 to 1954 which resulted in the loss of 924 million barrels; the 1990-91 Kuwait crisis, which took 421 million barrels off the market; and the 2003 US invasion of Iraq which translated into the loss of one billion barrels of oil.[9]

However, other than a relatively brief increase in the price of oil, none of these events affected supplies per se, mainly due to other regional producers increasing output to make up for the lost barrels. Hence, it would appear that often, the price of oil does not reflect the reality. This is because speculators in the futures markets push prices up in the belief that a shortage in physical supplies may be imminent, for various reasons. These can range from lack of timely investment in the face of growing demand and no concurrent production increase by producers, both within and outside OPEC; political turmoil in some oil producing countries; possibility of conflict, such as the Iran-US-Israel stand-off, etc. This disconnect, between actual physical supplies and futures markets, is often the main reason for the volatility in oil prices.

For example, between 2000 and 2005, the price fell rapidly, by around $10 per barrel, from a peak of around $30–40 per barrel. At the end of 2006 prices quickly fell by $20 per barrel from a peak of $70per barrel. The most spectacular example to date, was when the price reached a peak of $147 per barrel in early July 2008, based on the paper barrel markets' belief that there was a likelihood of an imminent shortage. When it was clear this was not the case, the market fell by $40/b within a couple of weeks.[10] Hence, when the paper barrel market realises that there are no shortages, they pull out and the prices collapse. This is what causes the seemingly inexplicable volatility in the oil market.

In many ways, this is what triggered the price rise in the immediate aftermath of the phenomenon popularly known as 'Arab Spring'. On the face of it, the countries that experienced the greatest upheaval, resulting in regime change, namely, Tunisia, Egypt and Libya, are in North Africa, and are not large energy producers or exporters. Egypt has proven oil reserves of 4.4 billion barrels and produces 560,000 barrels a day (bd) of crude oil, in addition to condensates and natural gas liquids (NGLs), while it exports 114,000 b/d—half of it—around 60,000 b/d to India.[11] However, with domestic consumption on the rise, Egypt has turned a net oil importer over the last decade.[12] Libya has proven oil reserves of 47.1 billion barrels, and produced and exported an estimated 1.65 mbd and 1.5 mbd prior to the unrest.[13] The majority of Libya's oil is sold to European countries, namely Italy, France, Germany, and Spain. In comparison, Tunisia's proven oil reserves are only 0.425 billion barrels, and it produces an average of 77,000 b/d, according to the 2012 *BP Statistical Energy Survey.*

On the other hand, the unrest has not been allowed to impact the Persian

Gulf countries. Although sporadic protests were witnessed in Bahrain and Oman, neither of which, are major energy producers or exporters, they were swiftly quelled. In fact, when Libyan production and exports fell after the unrest spread to that country, Saudi Arabia, despite objections from OPEC members like Iran, Venezuela and Algeria, increased output, thereby ensuring that the market was kept well supplied.

On the other hand, the stand-off between Iran and the West, and the threat of an Israeli-US strike on Iran's nuclear facilities, caused the price of oil to escalate. Moreover, the premium on supplies from the region due to the potential threat to shipping through the Strait of Hormuz led to prices remaining high. At the same time, importers of Iranian crude, particularly the Asian countries, were forces to cut their imports to avoid being sanctioned by the US government. Hence, while there was no real threat of supplies being affected from the region, the psychological impact of the region's political developments did impact prices.

Medium and Long Term Implications

Nevertheless, the likely medium and long-term impact of the uprisings continues to worry the oil markets. The reasons for this are various.

When the Arab uprisings began in late 2010—with Tunisia—oil prices were already running high, due to a number of factors. Asian demand, particularly from China and to a lesser extent India, was growing, despite the economic crisis that was slowly engulfing the Eurozone. One of the reasons was the filling up of China's strategic petroleum reserves (SPR), as well as the fact that the effects of the European slowdown were yet to impact the Asian countries in a big way. Beijing has been steadily building up its 500 million barrel oil reserve system, and has finished building four stockpiling facilities with a capacity of around 103 million barrels in the first phase of its SPR plan, and has begun constructing its second phase, which comprises eight storage sites that will reportedly have a combined capacity of around 207 million barrels. Two sites of the second phase were completed in 2011 and a third in Tianjin in 2012, which contributed to the huge demand for oil in the international market. The third and final phase is expected to be completed by 2020.[14] Hence, although demand in the developed countries was gradually waning, Asian countries more than made up for this reduced demand. Moreover, OPEC did not increase output, because of a combination of, fear that the recession in Europe would cause the demand to drop, leaving the market over supplied; and the need to earn bigger revenues to manage their growing public expenditure. And with spare capacity, maintained by only Saudi Arabia, declining, oil prices (Brent) were ruling at well over $100 per barrel.

As a result, when the uprising began in Tunisia and spread to Egypt, the immediate consequence was a five per cent increase in prices. Although Egypt is a not a major oil exporter, concerns were mainly focused on the possibility of closure of the Suez Canal and the SUMED pipeline. According to the US Energy Information Agency (EIA), the closure of the Suez Canal and SUMED Pipeline would add an estimated 6,000 miles of transit around the continent of Africa, raising transportation costs. Moreover, in 2010, petroleum and LNG accounted for 13 and 11 per cent of Suez cargos respectively, and around 5 per cent of seaborne oil trade.[15] Eventually, these concerns were not borne out and the canal was never closed. However, the termination of Libyan exports also sent prices spiralling upwards, particularly following news of international oil companies exiting the country's upstream sector. Although Saudi Arabia increased its output, given the difference in crude quality, Saudi heavy sour crude could not make up for Libya's sweet light crude, which was, in any case, destined mainly for the European market.

Oil prices continued to be volatile through 2010 and 2011, with prices dropping towards the end of 2011. This was due to the declining demand in Europe as the recession deepened; rising production, as OPEC increased output to offset the fall of production in Libya; as well as the surge in US production following the revolution in fracking technology. The US had also cut imports for economic reasons and increased energy efficiency. As a result, speculators were also cutting their net-long positions, resulting in a drop in the price of paper barrels.[16] But at the start of 2012, American and European sanctions on Iran and the resultant threat from Tehran to halt all exports and/or the closure of the Strait of Hormuz, saw tensions rise, along with oil prices, with some analysts predicting that oil could touch the $200/b figure. With Israel also threatening to launch a pre-emptive strike against Iranian nuclear installations, concerns of an imminent conflict grew.

Now two years later, tensions in the region continue to simmer. Three of the countries, including Egypt, have witnessed regime changes although peace is yet to materialise. The verdict is still out on Syria as the civil war rages on in that country, while unrest in Egypt continues following the overthrow of the popularly elected Morsi government by the army. On the other hand, the situation in Tunisia appears to be more optimistic, although the possibility of more regime changes in the region as a whole cannot be ruled out. More importantly, the upheaval in the region is taking place at a time when the US is displaying a marked reluctance to remain as deeply engaged in the region, as it was earlier. Washington's disinclination to prop up its allies, particularly President Mubarak in Egypt, has deeply disappointed the other Arab regimes, and also created concerns regarding their own situation.

There is a view that Beijing may occupy the space created, in the event of a US exit from the region. However, given that China sees the Gulf largely in commercial terms and its relations with the Gulf states are based more on ensuring its energy supplies than for strategic reasons, it is unlikely to provide any overarching security to the Gulf states. A clear indication of this was that while it initially defied the sanctions regime against Iran, it subsequently made substantial cuts in its imports and investments, in order to stay off the US list of countries sanctioned, for doing business with Iran. At the core of China's external energy policy are three basic issues: security of supply, diversity of supply and reducing price risk exposure through acquisition and equity deals. This does not include intervening in the internal affairs of producer states. Moreover, while the Persian Gulf oil producing states will remain important for Beijing, it is also investing heavily in the Americas, including the US, and will support an increase in North American supply, as it provides downward pressures on prices.[17]

Currently, the West Asian monarchs have suppressed domestic and regional unrest by clamping down on protestors, on the one hand and increasing social welfare schemes and distributing largesse that have cost their exchequers billions of dollars, on the other. Nevertheless, tensions in these countries are likely to simmer.

This, in turn, creates an uncertain environment for the future of the critical investments necessary to maintain, and for that matter, increase supply. International oil companies (IOCs) generally prefer to invest in stable regions. Hence, although attractive opportunities have not deterred IOCs from investing in unstable regions, they may move away to less turbulent regions/countries.[18] This would lead to under investment in the WANA region. Already, there has been a decline in the investment in oil production projects in the West Asia, due to prohibitions imposed on foreign investment in many of these countries.

Meanwhile, thanks to the higher spending, domestic sources of investment are, and may be constrained, as social programmes eat into investment in production capacity. Moreover, domestic oil consumption in these countries is growing rapidly, both due to an increase in population, and hence demand. Subsidised prices lead to an increase in consumption, apart from prompting these countries to diversify their economies, by encouraging industries that create more jobs, many of which are energy intensive.

Second, the Iran will take a long time to recover from the impact of the economic sanctions, although a glimmer of hope has emerged following the recent deal between the US and Iran on suspension/halting of the latter's nuclear enrichment programme. Nevertheless, if and when sanctions are officially lifted, restoring Iran's oil—and natural gas—production to levels prior to the sanctions will take several years. A case in point is Iraq, where even after the lifting of the sanctions imposed on the country during the Saddam Hussein regime, could not see the country regaining production to pre-war levels. This is partly, because wells have not been producing to capacity for years, as well as financial constraints and lack of access to requisite finances, technology and machinery.

Third, if prices fall, due to the influx of unconventional oil from non-OPEC producers, it may have the following consequences: a price war initiated by Saudi Arabia to capture larger market share, thereby forcing prices even lower. This may in turn see a period of internal repression, as lower revenues would not be able to sustain welfare schemes that are used to buy compliance of the populations in the Gulf countries. Eventually, this could lead to a tight supply situation, which would then see prices bouncing back. But the precarious investment climate in the WANA states would see investment flowing into unconventional oil and gas, which would become competitive vis-à-vis conventional oil and, as was seen in the 1980s, whereby investors prefer to put their money in less risky—that is non WANA—countries/projects.

Fourth, the increase of demand within the oil-producing states would impact prices as well as supply. The slew of subsidies and welfare schemes that have been introduced in the West Asian countries to ward off opposition to the regimes will have a deleterious impact on both supply as well as prices. Subsidised prices would increase demand while the need for more revenues to sustain these welfare schemes would require higher prices being set by the OPEC countries to fund the same. When limited supplies are available for export, the only option for generating additional revenue would be to increase prices. But can the West Asian producers afford to allow prices to escalate?

The Saudi Dilemma

In as far as the oil market is concerned, no country plays a bigger role, than Saudi Arabia. With the largest conventional oil reserves in the world, all of which are firmly under the control of the royal family, concerns regarding the contagion that has engulfed neighbouring countries, spreading to the GCC countries, and particularly Saudi Arabia, is the single biggest factor in changing the dynamics of the oil market. The Saudi regime, worried that the current unrest in the region may lead to a repeat of the 1994 protests, that questioned the legitimacy of the regime itself, initiated a series of populist measures to quell any potential discontent. While these have succeeded in staving off unrest for the time being, there is no surety that the regimes will not face more opposition in the future unless real reforms and changes take place, be it in governance or politics. In the absence of reforms, they will have to continue to dole out unsustainable subsidies and wage bills. And in order to do that they will need crude to sell at record highs. But in the face of the changes that are taking place in the energy sector worldwide, can high prices be sustained? If not, what will the consequences? And if oil prices continue to be bullish, then what will be the impact on (a) oil-importing nations, including India; and (b) the economies which are trying to recover from the recession?

The Saudi regime created new jobs in the public sector, gave salary bonuses to government officials and raised minimum public-sector wages at a cost of

$130 billion, besides constructing 50,000 homes and undertaking other infrastructural projects.[19] Similarly, Bahrain, Libya and Kuwait increased domestic spending or handed out as much as four per cent of their GDP in cash, outright, to their citizens. The Qatar government too is planning to spend $225 billion over the next five years on new infrastructure projects including road and rail networks.[20]

Much of this was possible due to the huge revenues that had accrued from the high price of oil over the last few years. But the crux of the problem is, that the economies of all the Gulf producers are overwhelmingly dependent on oil exports. Although they have been attempting to diversify their economies since the 1970s, and some of the countries did succeed in developing industries, both in the services and other sectors, their overall dependence on the oil sector, remains unchanged.

Nevertheless, given that most of the oil producing giant wells in the Gulf countries have been discovered and it is only a matter of time before production from these fields starts dropping, it is in their interest, to ensure high prices to make up for diminishing exports. Moreover, with the US now declaring that it is on the verge of attaining energy independence on the back of the hydraulic fracking technology and the huge reserves of shale plays of both oil and gas, there are concerns regarding a flood of new supplies coming into the market. The only option for the conventional oil producers is to ensure that prices remain low enough to make shale oil uncompetitive, given that shale oil costs around $50-60 a barrel to produce. On the other hand, although production costs for West Asian oil vary, the difference typically, is not more than $10 per barrel.[21] Hence for oil companies to invest in shale resources, oil prices need to stay relatively high.

At the same time, there are indications that conventional oil supplies will increase, with Iraq's re-entry into the market as a major oil producer. Baghdad has already increased its output to 3.7 mbd and is exporting 2.6 mbd, and has plans to further increase production to 6.1 mbd by 2020 and 8.5 mbd by 2035.[22] Moreover, Libya too plans to produce 1.8 mbd this year and 2 mbd by 2015, compared to the current 1.5 mbd.[23]

In the short and medium term, however, Saudi Arabia is the only country with enough spare capacity to be a swing producer. Moreover, having created a large fiscal buffer by accumulated large revenues over the last few years due to high oil prices, Saudi Arabia, more than the other OPEC members, can afford a period in which prices range between $75-80 a barrel, but in order to fund its social welfare spending, it needs to increase prices to around $98-100 a barrel.[24]

However, to maintain its control over OPEC and global supply, Saudi Arabia needs to keep prices "affordable" as it realises that higher prices would make unconventional as well as non-OPEC oil production competitive, whereas, lower prices would make them uneconomic. Secondly, till recently, Saudi Arabia's special relationship with the US prevented it from increasing prices which would harm the latter's economy. Following the first oil shock in 1973, Washington and Riyadh came to an agreement that henceforth, all Saudi oil would be sold in dollars in exchange for protection against any threat to the regime. Subsequently, in 1975, the other OPEC members also came to a similar agreement with the US. The agreement ensured that all oil money would flow through the US Federal Reserve, creating a demand for both US dollars, and also allowing the US to control the world's oil.[25]

Since the onset of the global economic recession, the demand from the developed countries have been declining; however, this decline has more or less been offset by the growing demand in the Asian developing countries, which in turn ensured that oil prices hovered around $100 a barrel, after the sudden drop in prices in 2008-09. The events following the Arab unrest also ensured that from end-2010, prices remained over $100 a barrel. Moreover, the sanctions on Iran and threats by Israel to attack Iran's nuclear installations, and Tehran's counter-threat to close off the Strait of Hormuz in the event of any attack, has also contributed to the high prices. But now, there are some ominous signs that prices may drop in the near future.

First, the economic recession in Europe is showing little signs of early recovery, which means the demand for oil will be less in 2013-14. The Energy Information Administration also expects US oil imports to decline from 8.3 mbd to 6 mbd by beginning of 2014, when the domestic conventional and unconventional oil production comes in. US refineries have been upgrading their facilities in order to be able to process heavy, sour crude from the tar sands of Canada, Venezuela and Mexico, as well as domestic shale formations, against imports from Africa. And finally, should Iran resolve its standoff with the international community over its nuclear programme, it will start pumping oil at pre-crisis levels and resume exports at pre-sanctions levels as well. At the same time, with Chinese demand showing signs of dropping in 2013-14, the scenario for supplies seems more than comfortable.

To stave off the coming "crisis", the Gulf producers can, either limit production and risk losing market share, or increase production to a level which will make production from non-Gulf competitors uneconomical. But there is a problem. In the aftermath of the uprisings, the Gulf countries have, and will need to continue, increasing their spending to stave off increasing domestic discontent. It is interesting to note that some of the regimes with little or no oil wealth, including Tunisia's Zine el-Abidine Ben Ali, Egypt's Hosni Mubarak and Yemen's Ali Abdullah Saleh, like their larger oil-producing neighbours, also made similar gestures by providing social welfare packages to their citizens, but since the packages they offered were much less generous, they proved less effective, and these regimes were eventually overthrown.[26] Therefore, maintaining higher oil prices are in Riyadh's interest. At the same time, Saudi Arabia, more than the other regional oil producers, is wary of driving prices so high that it benefits rival non-OPEC producers, including unconventional oil producers. Therefore, it prefers to sell oil directly to its customers and ensures that its production does not end up in the spot market, or contributes to global stocks. This way, it ensures that its customers are well supplied, and prices are maintained at a level that suits its interest.[27]

At the same time, several Arab countries, including the oil exporting ones, are aggressively pursuing a renewable and nuclear energy programme. Saudi Arabia plans to generate 16 GW of solar PV and 25 GW of concentrated solar power (CSP), by 2032 to reduce oil-based generation. Domestic natural gas is also not being seen as an option as much of it is earmarked for various domestic industrial sectors. The UAE has set a target of generating seven per cent of its electricity from solar energy as well as wind power, while Qatar plans to generate 20 per cent of its power from mainly solar energy by 2030.[28]

Implications of High Prices on Importing Countries

Speaking at a meeting in IDSA in 2013, India's National Security Advisor Shiv Shankar Menon said:

> The Western developed countries can now afford the chance that the so-called Arab Spring is bringing to the Middle East. They can actively encourage regime change in the area. The main victims of uncertainty in supply will be emerging economies like China and India who are still to diversify their sources of supply into long-term flexible contracts with others outside the region.

It is in this context that India's energy supply imperatives have to be situated. The inter-relationship between energy, resources and national security underscores the country's policy approach to the region. India's domestic demand for oil, which was 3.58 mbd in 2012, has been growing exponentially year-on-year. However, internal production during the same three-year period has been growing marginally—0.86, 0.9 and 0.92 mbd in 2010, 2011 and 2012, respectively. This increasing shortfall is being met largely from imports from West Asia, which account for two-thirds of India's oil trade. And this dependence on West Asia for its energy is likely to continue.

Hence, India's energy situation means that it cannot afford uncertainties of supply, both for its own use as well as for the larger oil market. For example, although India is not a major importer of Libyan oil, the fall in Libyan production and exports did affect India, because of resultant higher prices. Oil prices touched $120 to a barrel in 2011 for the first time since 2008. And the market remains wary, with speculators envisaging prices rising to $200– 300/barrel, if Saudi Arabia experiences serious political unrest.

A rise in international oil prices translates into a higher import bill, worsens terms of trade and consequently results in a deterioration of the trade balance as well as a squeeze in overall demand, as people—households as well as corporates—try to balance the rise in expenditure. According to some analysts, large increases in the price of oil depress the future marginal product of capital, thereby impacting investment and the future capital stock, and thus can have a long-term effect on output. Moreover, given the preponderance of oil imports in the import basket of developing countries like India, an increase in oil price would lead to a worsening of trade balance, in view of the fixed exchange rate.

India being one of the largest oil consumers and importers in the world—currently the fourth largest importer of oil—and given its year-on-year growth in demand, any increase in crude prices can affect the government's fiscal calculations. In the last two years, India saw its average cost of importing crude rise by \$27 per barrel, bloating the oil import bill to \$140 billion from \$100 billion.[29] Moreover, high international oil prices could result in lower growth and higher inflation, albeit based on whether such price increases are passed on to the consumer. For instance, a 10 per cent rise in international oil prices would cause a decline in real growth of 0.9 per cent and an increase in inflation by 0.6 per cent. If there is no pass-through, inflation does not rise as the government absorbs the entire shock; however if there is a decline in growth because of a rise in the current account deficit the fiscal deficit to GDP ratio will increase marginally. In a partial pass-through scenario, a 10 per cent rise in international oil prices brings down growth by 0.6 per cent and raises inflation by 0.3 per cent. Over the period of the 12th Plan, the adverse impact of oil price shock on macro variables is reduced in both the cases of no pass-through and full pass-through.[30]

Therefore, if prices were to fall, either as a result of lower price postings, or a supply glut driven by the introduction of unconventional resources, it would bring about a change in the geopolitics of the region. Not only would it be beneficial for India, and other oil-importing countries in terms of cheaper supplies; the Asian, including Indian, markets would become preferential destinations for OPEC/West Asian producers.[31]

Hence, while the short term fallout of the developments of the Arab uprisings may be detrimental to the oil market and India, as a large oil and gas importer from the region, in the long term, it could bring some benefits. India is a growing market and a stronger energy partnership would be beneficial for the GCC states, as well as India, particularly in the energy sector. India is fast developing into a petroleum refinery export hub, with a capacity increase of almost 50 per cent in the last five years. Much of the expansion came in the private sector, which now has a third of the country's total refining capacity. In fact, this boom in refinery exports has contributed to the increase in India's total oil demand of 3.7 mbd.[32]

Nevertheless, the current energy relationship between the West Asian countries and India, which is more akin to a buyer-seller arrangement, needs to change to a more substantial one, based on cross-investments and joint ventures in each other's economies and across sectors, including energy, industry, infrastructure and services for mutual benefit. While it would allow India access to investments, for its energy and infrastructure sectors, it would allow the GCC countries to not only invest in an emerging market but also to diversify their economic partnerships eastwards. At the same time, India should explore whether it can assist in ensuring secure transport of supplies through turbulent sea lanes and chokepoints, particularly in the event of a reduced US presence in the region. After all, notwithstanding its energy diversification strategy, the West Asian region will remain India's most important and largest energy supplier in the foreseeable future, and it is therefore in its interest to contribute towards the region's security.

NOTES

1. Oil Market Report, International Energy Agency, February 13, 2-12 http://www.iea.org/publications/freepublications/publication/name,38112,en.html
2. Indian Petroleum & Natural Gas Statistics, 2012-13, Government of India, Ministry of Petroleum & Natural Gas Economic Division
3. Richa Mishra, 'Crude oil sourcing: Iran slips to sixth position from second', *Business Line,* October 8, 2012, www.thehindubusinessline.com/industry-and-economy/crude-oil-sourcing-iran-slips-to-sixth-position-from-second/article3975135.ece
4. Indian oil and gas sector- upstream [H1 2012-13 update], *ICRA Research Services*, December 2012, www.icra.in/Files/ticker/Indian_O&G_Sector.pdf
5. Ruchir Mishra, 'Iraq, Venezuela emerging top crude oil suppliers for India', *Business Line,* November 18, 2012, www.thehindubusinessline.com/industry-and-economy/iraq-venezuela-emerging-top-crude-oil-suppliers-for-india/article4108788.ece
6. Hakim Darbouche and Bassam Fatouh, 'The Implications of the Arab Uprisings for Oil and Gas Markets' *The Oxford Institute for Energy Studies,* September 2011, MEP2, http://www.oxfordenergy.org/wpcms/wp-content/uploads/2011/09/MEP_2.pdf
7. FACTBOX-Oil production cost estimates by country, Reuters, July 28, 2009, http://www.reuters.com/article/2009/07/28/oil-cost-factbox-idUSLS12407420090728
8. 'Middle East and Central Asia: Regional Economic Outlook':, *World Economic and Financial Surveys* International Monetary Fund, November 2012, www.imf.org/external/pubs/ft/reo/2012/mcd/eng/pdf/mreo1112.pdf
9. Hakim Darbuche and Bassam Fatouh, 'The Implications of the Arab Uprisings for Oil and Gas Markets', *Oxford Institute for Energy Studies, MEP 3*, September 2011, p.3, www.oxfordenergy.org/wpcms/wp-content/uploads/2011/09/MEP_2.pdf
10. Oil Price History and Analysis, 2011, *WRTG Economics*, http://www.wtrg.com/prices.htm
11. *Egypt, Country Analysis Briefs*, Energy Information Administration, US Department of Energy, July 18, 2012, www.eia.gov/cabs/Egypt/Full.html
12. Farah Halime, 'Egypt Struggles to Pay Oil Bill', *New York Times*, October 3, 2012, www.nytimes.com/2012/10/04/world/middleeast/egypt-struggles-to-pay-oil-bill.html?pagewanted=all&_r=0
13. *Libya, Country Analysis Briefs*, Energy Information Administration, US Department of Energy, June 2012, www.eia.gov/cabs/libya/Full.html
14. IEA Report on People's Republic of China: Oil & Gas Security: Emergency Responses of IEA Countries, 2012, p.3, www.iea.org/publications/freepublications/publication/China_2012.pdf

15. *Suez Canal/SUMED Pipeline,* World Oil Transit Chokepoints, US Energy Information Administration, August 22, 2012, www.eia.gov/countries/analysysbriefs/World_Oil_Chokepoints.wotc.pdf
16. Matthew Philips, 'Falling Oil Prices Are No Mystery' *Business Week,* June 4, 2012, www.businessweek.com/articles/2012-06-04/falling-oil-prices-are-no-mystery
17. Matthew Hulbert, 'Why The Middle East has a Big Oil Problem: Squaring Obama's Xi Circle', November 26, 2012, http://www.forbes.com/sites/matthewhulbert/2012/11/26/why-the-middle-east-has-a-big-oil-problem-squaring-obamas-xi-circle
18. Gawdat Bahgat, "Preliminary assessment of Arab Spring's impact on oil and gas in Egypt, Libya", *Oil and Gas Journal,* January 9, 2012, http://www.ogj.com/1/vol-110/issue-1a/exploration-development/preliminary-full.html
19. Simeon Kerr, 'Saudi Arabia sets lavish figure', *Financial Times,* December 27, 2011, www.ft.com/intl/cms/s/0/582e70d2-30a5-11e1-b96f-00144feabdc0.html#axzz2IEVSJFGn
20. 'Oil-rich nations focusing more on domestic spending, analysis shows', *Arabian Business.com,* July 16, 2011, www.arabianbusiness.com/oil-rich-nations-focusing-more-on-domestic-spending-analysis-shows-410613.html
21. Kevin Bullis, 'Shale Oil Will Boost US Production, But It Won't Bring Energy Independence', *MIT Technology Review,* November 15, 2012, www.technologyreview.com/news/507446/shale-oil-will-boost-us-production-but-it-wont-bring-energy-independence/
22. 'Will Iraq be the next oil superpower?', *Petroleum Economist,* December 2012.
23. Libya targets oil production increase to 1.8 million b/d in 2013, *Platts,* September 24, 2012, www.platts.com/RSSFeedDetailedNews/RSSFeed/Oil/8749925
24. Paul Stevens, Mathew Hulbert, "Oil Prices: Energy Investment, Political Stability in the Exporting Countries and OPEC's Dilemma", *EEDP Programme Paper: 2012/13,* Chatham House, October 2012, www.chathamhouse.org/sites/default/files/public/Research/Energy%20Environment%20and%20Development/1012pp_opec.pdf
25. Ibid.
26. Michael L. Ross, "Will Oil Drown the Arab Spring?:Democracy and the Resource Curse", *Foreign Affairs,* Vol. 90, No. 5; September-October, 2011: p.2-7
27. Derek Bower, "Saudi Arabia's quantitative oil easing", *Petroleum Economist,* October 2012, Vol 79, No. 8, p. 21.
28. James Montgomery, "Inside MENA Countries' Solar Energy Plans", Renewable Energy World.com, January 15, 2013, http://www.renewableenergyworld.com/rea/news/article/2013/01/inside-mena-countries-solar-energy-plans
29. "India's crude oil import bill jumps 40 per cent to $140 bn in FY12", *Business Line,* June 13, 2012, www.thehindubusinessline.com/industry-and-economy/article3523827.ece
30. N.R. Bhanumurthy, Surajit Das, Sukanya Bose, 'Oil Price Shock, Pass-through Policy and its Impact on India', *Working Paper No. 2012-99,* National Institute of Public Finance and Policy, March 2012, www.nipfp.org.in/newweb/sites/default/files/wp_2012_99.pdf
31. Adith Charlie, Decoding India's Response to the Arab Spring, *Journal of Turkish Weekly,* 24, 2013, www.turkishweekly.net/news/146679/decoding-india%E2%80%99s-response-to-the-arab-spring.html
"Private refineries lead export boom for India", *IEA,* December 20, 2012, http://www.iea.org/newsroomandevents/news/2012/december/name,34513,en.html
32 "Private refineries lead export boom for India", *IEA,* December 20, 2012, http://www.iea.org/newsroomandevents/news/2012/december/name,34513,en.html

17

India and the GCC: Prospects for an Enhanced Security Partnership

Sami Alfaraj

It is quite interesting that the recent quest by the US for a redistribution of power in the Indian Ocean region and the adjacent regions became the reason for India and the GCC to re-examine their roles in the area, and to search for new possible security cooperation between them. India's relations with the Gulf States go back to the period of Silk Road. The trade ties existed historically between India-China-Arabia via the Silk Route and in the present day via the sea route across South East Asia (See Maps 1, 2 and 3). It is this historical relationship on which the new strategy to deal with the strategic problems in the Gulf needs to be built.

The impact of 'Arab Spring' has resulted in the retrenchment of established powers into new roles and a shift from the earlier mercantilist approach to the new methodology. Here the objective is to find different solutions to problems that have been there in the region and could flare up any time. In the current context, the Gulf countries are trying to make the Gulf as real hub for finance and investment and for other nations to participate. The current security challenges demand new solutions by the new rulers and existing players in the region. In this new security paradigm the Gulf countries are looking and examining what role they can play with their existing partner or the new partners. New opportunities are opening up in the Indian Ocean for India and Gulf countries to cooperate. The paper examines the prospects of India-GCC cooperation in the light of recent changes which are unfolding in the region. It analyses the GCC countries view of present Indian role in the Gulf region providing options for India to play a role in the Gulf security.

Map 1: The Gulf and the Indian Ocean

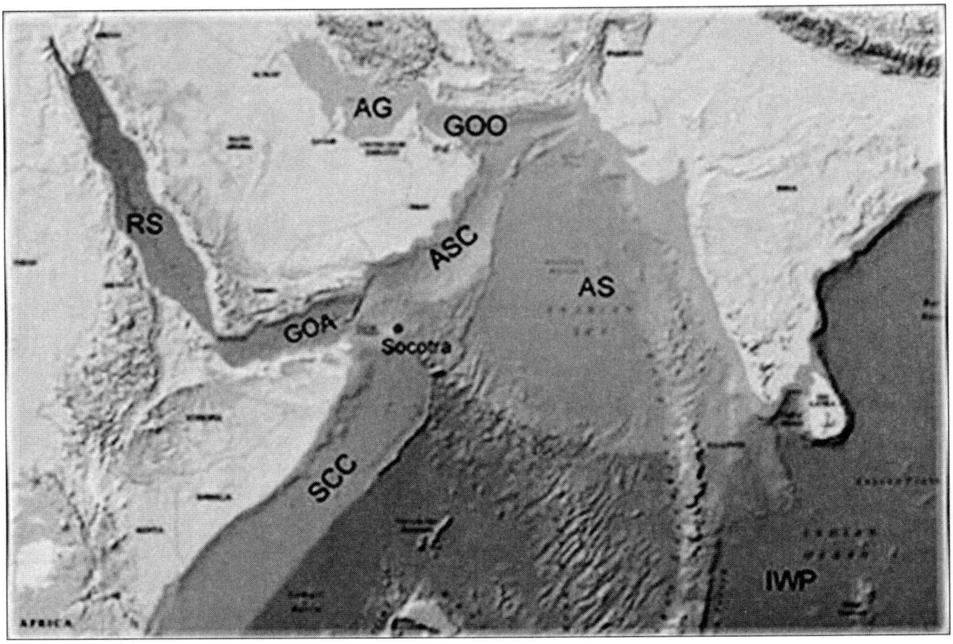

Source: http://www.socotraproject.org/index.php?page=content&id=10

Map 2: The Geographical Components of the Silk Road

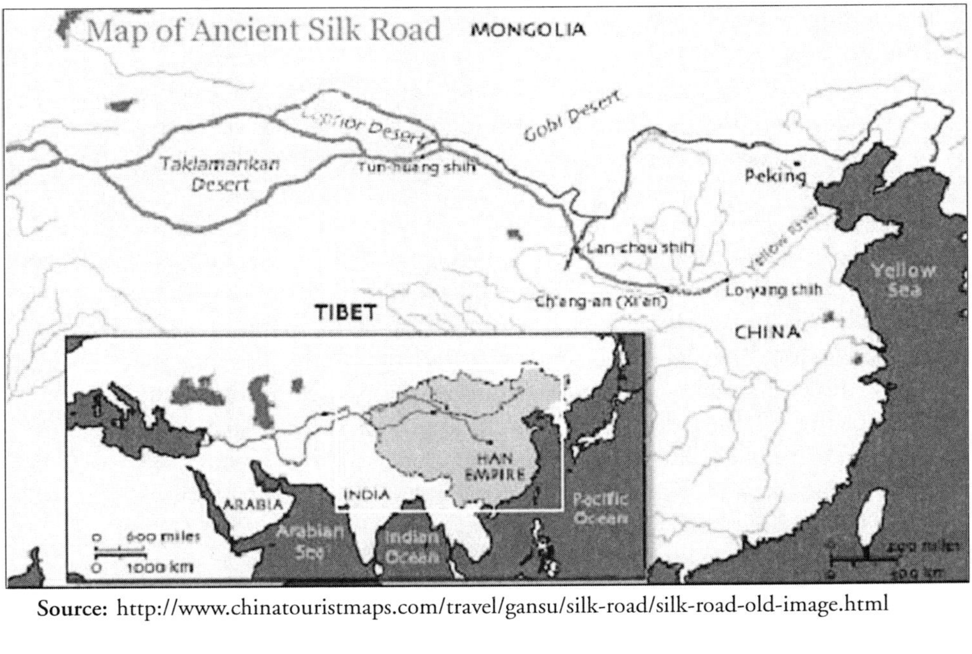

Source: http://www.chinatouristmaps.com/travel/gansu/silk-road/silk-road-old-image.html

Map 3: Maritime Routes Between India and the Gulf During the Age of the Silk Road

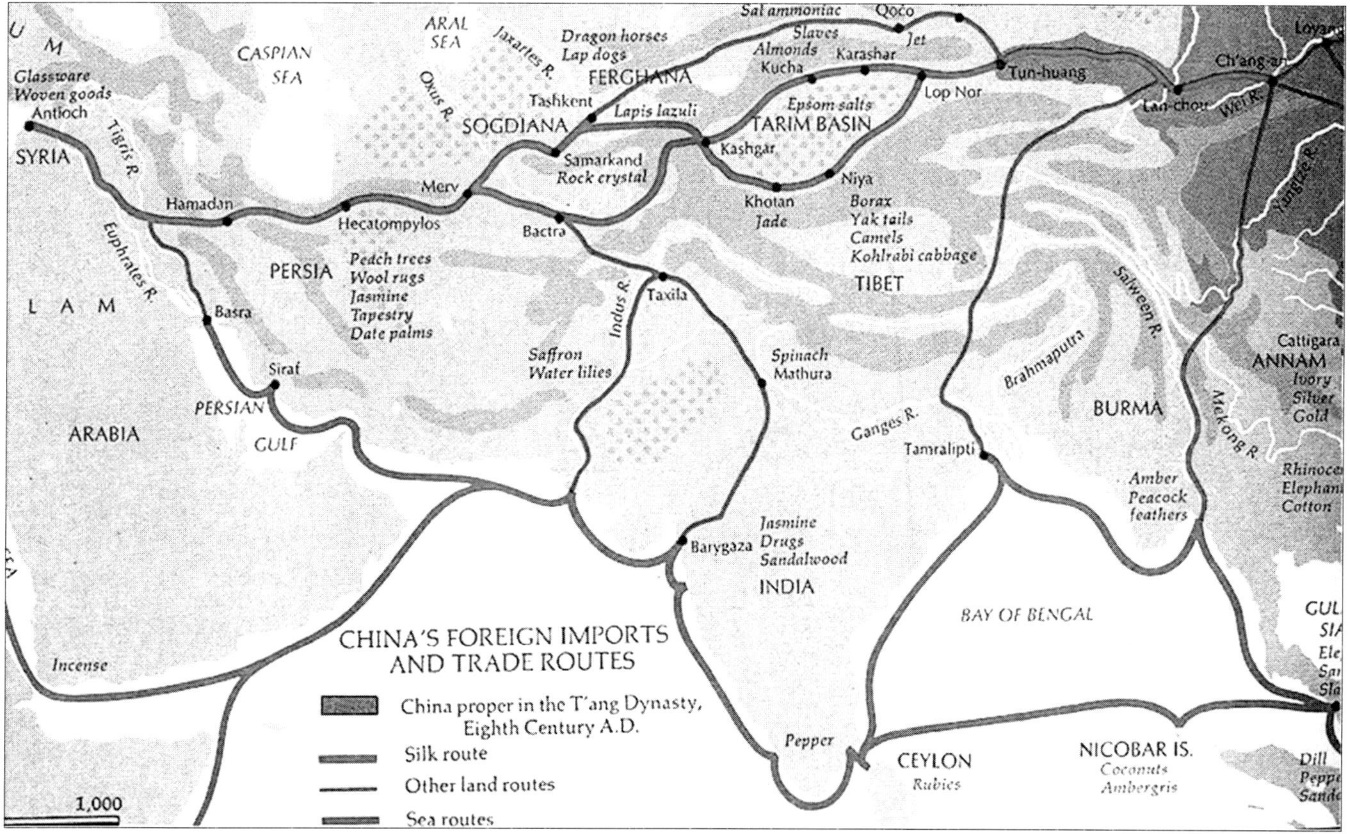

Source: http://aldworthapworld.wikispaces.com/

India's Present Strategic Interests in the Gulf

India's interests in the region are wide and varied. These are mainly:

Labour

The migration of Indian workers to Gulf countries increased from a trickle in 1976 to reach a peak level of 2,72,000 in 1981 after which it declined slowly till 1986.[1] Indian workers in the Gulf have always been the largest source of inward remittances in the country, of which over 45 per cent comes from the GCC countries. According to RBI estimates, India topped globally in 2012 with total remittances of $70 billion.[2]

Crude Oil Imports

India's other important interest in the region is related to its increasing energy demands and its import from the Gulf region. India's crude oil imports increased in November 2012 both on a monthly and an annual basis. Month-on-month, the increase was equal to 298 tb/d, or 9 per cent, while year-on-year it saw a slight increase of 1.5 per cent to average 3.69 mb/d. India's product imports increased as well in November 2012 by 15 tb/d, or 5.1 per cent, to average 310 tb/d, a drop of 15 tb/d, or 5 per cent, from an annual perspective. The product imports' monthly gain came as a result of increased imported volumes of fuel oil, naphtha and LPG. Fuel oil saw the greatest increase in the monthly import volume, growing by 68 per cent from the previous month as a result of its increased usage for power generation.[3]

Middle East oil producers export more oil to Asia than to Europe and North America combined. In fact, about two-thirds of GCC oil exports are channeled to the Asia. The Asian Pacific countries, individually and collectively, are heavily dependent on oil from the Gulf. According to the US Energy Information Administration (EIA) Japan sources roughly 80 per cent, South Korea 75 per cent and India imports almost two-thirds of its oil from the GCC states. The International Energy Agency (IEA) forecasts that China will import 70 per cent of its oil from the GCC by 2015. India is projected to replace Japan and emerge as the third-largest consumer of energy (after the United States and China) by that time. The bulk of Indian supplies come from the Gulf and in particular Saudi Arabia; this dependency is expected to change only marginally in the next decade.[4]

Economic Partnership with the GCC

From India's point of view the GCC offers huge opportunity of enhancing economic partnership. It is important to highlight the vision that Kuwait has for the future. The New Kuwaiti-established Northern Gulf Economic Zone and the development of new cities in other GCC nations open new opportunities for economic cooperation. The goal is to rebuild aging infrastructure in order to make the GCC a financial centre, and the potential for it to become one of the world's leading centres by 2025. The GCC as a hub of trade and as the largest global logistical hub makes it attractive economic partner for India and other Asian countries. Equally important is to bring out that a historical rivalry always existed between Persia, Mesopotamia and Arabia, and it was highly likely that Kuwait could be the theatre for present day conflict to unfold. To prevent the recurrence of 1990 war, the solution is to create a second Kuwait City. The project has already commenced with the building of an expressway and is to be followed by a super railway link in 2015. About $132 billion has been earmarked for the project and an elaborate four Five-Year Plans are to be drawn in order to show their seriousness for the project. There is attempt to help develop southern Iraq though there is an unresolved dispute over the Bubiyan Island. Another important factor which makes Kuwait an attractive country to its neighbours and other countries is that it intends to pursue a Kuwaiti form of socialism in which any new born would be given shares in a company regardless the fact if he is Shia or Sunni. It was likely that the Chinese, considering their experience in the construction of high-speed rail, were to build a similar link in Kuwait in the coming years. From India, Kuwait expects not just unskilled labourers but also skilled labourers like managers, etc. It is significant to point out that the share markets in the Gulf were inflated as investments have not been made seriously. Thus there are possibilities for India to actively participate in this new vision of Kuwait.

Why would the GCC Develop an Interest in a Greater Indian Role in Gulf Security?

Following factors make a case for greater Indian role in Gulf Security:

- The need to augment the balance of power
- Because India is a nation that has a high moral standing
- Because it has a long historical bond with the GCC
- Because India has no strategic differences with the GCC
- India believes in the stability of the Gulf for its own core strategic interests
- India has a popular acceptance on both banks of the Gulf
- India has or will have the strategic means to either deter, or project power adequately when needed

A GCC View of Present Indian Role in the Gulf Region

The GCC strategic planners see similarity of strategic position between India and Saudi Arabia as both are flanked by two large bodies of water. This fact may play a role in devising common plans to deal with the security issues related to the Gulf, the Arabian Sea, Indian Ocean, and the Strait of Bab-el-Mandab. It is important to point out that India increasingly depends on oil supplies from Saudi

Arabia, and that the two nations have similar views on Afghanistan. These facts may augment the case for a larger security partnership between them. However, the idea that India plans to cooperate with Iran over Afghanistan after the US departure is quite unsettling for GCC planners. They regard that there is more of a state of affinity of interests with Saudi Arabia and the UAE to form a partnership to manage Afghanistan based on their influence in the country, than with Iran. Iran, they reason, has had its past dealings with both Pakistan and the regime of *Taliban.* Moreover, the passive role by a historic trading nation like Iran in the security of the Arabian Sea and fighting piracy in the Horn of Africa does not bode well for a larger security partnership between India and Iran. Further, if the security of the Indian Ocean region is the prime strategic interest for India, then the current Iranian intelligence and power projection operations in the Arabian Sea and the Gulf of Eden to support the *Hothies* in Yemen, not only threaten the GCC, but also hit at the very core of this Indian objective.

Can India Play a Role in Gulf Security?

For India, Gulf is not just about presence of its labour and import of oil but it is much more, as new opportunities are opening in the Gulf region in huge infrastructure projects where region needs development oriented nations to participate in these projects. In addition to economic partnership, India can play role in the GCC security. But to play a role in GCC Security it must:

(a) Develop further a common interest, or at least affinity of interests with the GCC
(b) Maintain an adequate deterrent posture
(c) Develop power-projection capabilities
(d) Synchronize crisis-response measures based on the principle of burden-sharing
(e) Establish forward operations areas
(f) Agree to an agenda similar to the *Istanbul Declaration of Cooperation* that starts with intelligence-sharing and ends with interoperability.

In addition, India can plan strategically to send its first Air Craft Carrier in 2017 in the waters of the Gulf. This would be its insurance policy. It is important to note that the Gulf region not only needs its existing insurance policy which is Western alliance, but it also requires its Asian partners to be there. Need is to maintain the old alliance and augment it on a knowledge sharing basis. Now, there are lots of stakes for India, for the Gulf region and also for the rest of the world. What is important to note is that despite differences with Iran, the Gulf countries basically cooperate with Iran on most of the issues. The region needs to cooperate with Iran to stop, for instance, drugs, human trade, piracy, and pollution. To maintain peace and security in the region cooperation with Iran is important. Therefore, the regional countries should not only work together to maintain peace and security in the region, but also invite all others who are the cores of instability in the Gulf to be partners in this scheme of developing constructive security and economic partnership in the Gulf region.

India's high standards in education, training and its professional services are seen as potential sources of investment and partnership for development within the West Asian region. There is huge potential of engagement between India and the GCC countries in these sectors. Despite these strengths and potential, India is reluctant to intervene in Gulf issues, it is perceived in the region to be a moral power and its diaspora is a much respected community. The other potential area of cooperation is technology. Here India has got a special role to play. India can produce different levels of technology that are more suitable for smaller states like the Gulf.

Conclusion

India and the Gulf region have a long historical bond to the level that it is considered as part and parcel of the Gulf. The Gulf countries are greatly influenced by Indian culture and civilisation. There are a lot of customs coming from India and Persia to this region and now these have to be built on. The acceptance of these linkages is not only by the two banks of the Gulf, but also by the region as a whole. India has got a standing in the Arab world, in the Arab-Israel conflict. Both are facing similar challenges. But the main complaint from the region is that it's not doing enough to negotiate with regard to the Iranian issue, the Arab-Israel conflict, and many other issues in which India is viewed as accepted partner. While the case for India is very strong in the Gulf region, it will need to play more pro- active role in the region.

NOTES

1. At http://www.epw.in/roots/indian-labour-migration-gulf-countries.html
2. Duttagupta, I., *The Economic Times,* ET Bureau, January 13, 2013, 04.00AM IST
3. OPEC January 23, 2013, Location: Asia.
4. Altamimi, N., *Alarabiya News,* February 11, 2013.

PART VI

Nuclear Issues in West Asia

18

Nuclear Issues in West Asia: Egyptian Perspective

Mahmoud Karem

Security concerns in Middle East deserve careful perusal and a quick solution. The region at present lacks a clear across the board definition of security. Military doctrines remain divergent and sometimes conflicting. As long as this is the case, there is no multilateral track or venue for discussions like the 1993 Madrid Peace Conference. There are no Confidence Building Measures (CBMs), no collateral measures or track two events to tackle difficult issues in a non official setting. The Israelis are largely responsible for this by not acceding to the NPT and preventing its universality; despite the fact that since 1995 all the remaining Arab countries signed the Non-Proliferation Treaty (NPT), Israel refused to even discuss the nuclear file on the account of the so called "slippery slope" syndrome. Then we attend conferences of this kind and listen, as we did yesterday, to an Israeli presentation presenting a supra racist view depicting Israel as surrounded by a sea of hostile nations. At the same time the region is rich with initiatives such as the 1974 initiative on the establishment of a nuclear weapon free zone in the Middle East, a zone free of weapons of mass destruction, the alternate Blix ideas and the NPT Helsinki conference for a nuclear and a zone free of weapons of mass destruction in the Middle East which did not convene last December 18, due to the US position. The region is fearing a possible attack on Iran, and its repercussion for the economies of the region. Other complex matters such as smuggling of destabilising weapons the possibilities of smuggling components of Weapons of Mass Destruction (WMD's), missile proliferation, disintegration of strong armies while some armies are entangled in political and domestic affairs etc...impact on the security setting of our region and create the present confounded security paradigm.

The generic outline of disarmament initiatives in the this region necessitates the study of Zonal Approach and the 1974 Nuclear Weapons Free Zone (NWFZ) initiative in the United National General Assembly (UNGA). The 1974 initiative presented by Iran and Egypt to establish a Nuclear Weapons Free Zone in the Middle East was later cold shouldered by Egypt due to the changes brought about by the 1979 Iranian revolution. No longer could the consultations between both delegations move smoothly as the new policies of Iran following the assumption of power by Ayatollah Khomeini created a new dictum and the stance of Iranian delegations in multilateral diplomacy and UN related organisations had changed. One major fact needs to be underscored; that the 1974 initiative was a by product of both diplomacies. Both the Egyptian mission to the UN in New York in 1973-1974 as well as the Iranian mission were consulting each other on the language and phraseology of the text. This detailed account outlines the historical unfolding of the initiative in order to understand the dynamics of subsequent initiatives and to make clear that the idea itself cannot be attributed to one diplomacy alone, be it Iranian or Egyptian. In order to clarify some points, a number of historical facts need to be reiterated

The document bearing the title "Establishment of a Nuclear Free Zone in the Region of the Middle East" was included in the General Assembly's agenda in the twenty-ninth session. In response, on July 15, 1974, Iran dispatched an Explanatory Memorandum (A/9693) in which it stated:

First, developments in the region imparted a sense of urgency to this proposal because "greater access by states to nuclear technology has rendered the danger of nuclear weapon proliferation and a concomitant collapse of the non-proliferation structure, a more acute problem".

Second, the General Assembly was the most suitable forum where a proposal of this nature could be discussed.

Third, as a result of the ambiguity surrounding the geographic designation of the region and its security interests, the decision on the precise delimitation of such a zone should be left to the General Assembly. Iran, however, asserted that the preference was for the zone to include "as wide an area as possible".

Eight days later and following extensive consultations between Egypt and Iran, Egypt decided to co-sponsor the Iranian request (A/9693/Add. 1 of July 23, 1974). These consultations resulted in a bilateral understanding between both countries to change the title of the item from "Establishment of a Nuclear Free Zone" to "Establishment of a Nuclear Weapon Free Zone" (A/9693/Add.2 of August 22, 1974). Both countries had agreed that the thrust of the initiative should be directed against the dangers of nuclear weapons and should not hamper their mutual quest for the use of nuclear energy for peaceful purposes, which resulted in adding the word 'Weapon' to the title of the item. A message sent by the Shah of Iran, Mohamed-Reza Pahlavi, to the UN Secretary General clarified that position:

> Atomic science represents man's best hopes for survival and his worst fears

> of doom. If coming generations are to enjoy the blessing of that technology and be free of its burdens, if we want to open new doorways to peace, we must be as bold and as imaginative in curbing the spread of nuclear arms as we have been in creating them.

This same letter went on to discuss the conditions governing the proliferation of nuclear technology and to caution against processing fissile material and the wider dissemination of scientific knowledge that could make acquisition of nuclear weapons a "less burdensome undertaking". It is interesting to compare this statement with Iran's present policy. However, several conditions at that time governed the position of both Egypt and Iran and served as an incentive for the introduction of this item. These include:

> First, the emergence of a conducive climate of understanding, between Egypt and Iran, following the 1973 Arab-Israeli war. The late President Anwar el-Sadat described this new relationship in his book In Search of Identity. He explained how the relationship evolved from one of animosity between both countries under Gamal Abdul Nasser to that of mutual understanding under his own presidency.

Sadat asserted:

> "Today, I am proud to state that Egypt's relations with Iran and with the whole world are based on mutual respect and trust. I shall never forget the day when the Egyptian Petroleum reserves fell to a dangerously low level, after the October 1973 War due to the closure of our oilfields. I sent word to the Shah of Iran and he immediately supplied us with more than 500,000 tons."

He actually ordered Iranian oil tankers that were at sea to change course and go directly to Egypt to offer help. The Shah responded by stating that: 'El-Sadat is a brother to me, I shall respond to his request on the spot'.

Second, it became evident during, and following, the 1973 Arab-Israeli war that the region was at the brink of a nuclear exchange. This was underscored by the fact that Israel did not altogether dismiss the nuclear alternative as a last resort, in the event of a defeat with conventional weapons or in a situation whereby the heart of Israel became endangered. Reports to this effect were cited by *Time magazine* (April 12, 1976:39), in which it was reported that thirteen Israeli nuclear warheads were "hastily assembled at a secret underground tunnel during a 78-hour period at the start of the 1973 October War and were sent to desert arsenals where they remain today, still ready for use". During that phase of the war, Israel faced an unprecedented defeat on the Egyptian and Syrian fronts, compelling Israeli Prime Minister Golda Meir to cable Washington on the fourth day of the war to "Save Israel".

Third, the 1973 war also demonstrated the dangers of drawing both the Soviet Union and the United States to the edge of a nuclear holocaust. Both superpowers airlifted supplies and supplied military hardware and technology to the opposing sides, and were thus drawn into the war. The global perspective of that war was in essence one of East-West confrontation through third parties or "pawns". Perhaps the most dangerous moments of that war came when the United States ordered a worldwide general mobilisation of its forces. As US President Richard Nixon 1980 described the situation:

> Egypt's airlift to Israel and the alert of Egyptian forces which was ordered in 1973 with the knowledge that these actions might lead to an Arab oil embargo were a demonstration of how far the United States will go to keep Egypt's commitment to Israel's survival.[1]

Henry Kissinger observed that the American worldwide alert prompted the Soviets to place elements of the East German army on alert. This in turn forced the United States, according to Kissinger, to alert the 82nd Airborne Division and to dispatch two aircraft carriers, the F.D. Roosevelt and the J.F. Kennedy, to join the carrier Independence east of the Mediterranean. The US forces were ordered to a state of alert, known as DefCon III, which "increases readiness without the determination that war is likely". Nixon cabled Sadat, requesting him "to consider the consequences for your country if the two great nuclear countries were thus to confront each other on your soil".

Finally, the period of the early 1970s coincided with the launching of ambitious programmes by Egypt and Iran for the peaceful use of nuclear energy. Both countries had requested nuclear-power reactors from the United States and thus were in need of demonstrating the seriousness of their intentions to the American legislative branch. The pro-Israeli lobby in the US Congress argued against the approval of the sale of reactors to Egypt. John F. Roehm, Professor of Military Science (cited in Spanier and Nogee, 1981) demonstrated how the Egyptian request for a nuclear reactor "raised a storm of controversy in Congress," which resulted in a provision in the 1974 Foreign Military Sales Act (the Nelson-Bingham bill), authorising Congress to "veto US arms sales to foreign governments of $25 million or more".

The introduction, therefore, of the Nuclear Weapons Free Zone (NWFZ) initiative by both Egypt and Iran could be viewed as a means of demonstrating the good will of both parties, thus, softening opposition to their demands for peaceful nuclear reactors. (Egypt at that time, it may be recalled, had not yet ratified the Non-Proliferation Treaty).

In 1974 a draft resolution was presented to the First Committee of the UN General Assembly by Egypt and Iran. Egypt argued that there were three fundamental principles pertinent to any discussion on Middle East NWFZ:

(1) States of the region should refrain from producing, acquiring, or processing nuclear weapons;
(2) Nuclear-weapon states should refrain from introducing nuclear weapons

into the area or using nuclear weapons against any state of the region; and

(3) Effective international safeguard system affecting both the nuclear-weapon states and the states of the region should be established. Egypt also emphasised that the establishment of a NWFZ should not hamper states from benefits of peaceful uses of nuclear energy, especially given the needs of the developing countries. At this juncture it was interpreted that an Israeli vote against the resolution might direct world attention to its unsafeguarded nuclear facilities. On the other hand, a vote in favour would have dissipated Arab fears, thus minimising the psychological effect of deterrent. Hence, the abstention provided a convenient way to reiterate the original Israeli position, that the countries concerned, in the Middle East must conduct direct preparatory negotiations.

The Israeli abstention in the United Nations was explained in terms of the necessity of holding direct consultations between states in the Middle East and Egypt and introduced an amendment calling for a "preliminary process of consultations between the Secretary General and the states of the region."[2]

In 1980 the Israeli position changed, and Israel agreed to pass the resolution in the General Assembly by consensus. This came one year after the signing of a peace Treaty with Egypt. The resolution enjoys a consensus until today but without any pragmatic action being taken on the ground. Today many analysts point to environmental threat to the region, the safety of the aging nuclear reactor, Dimona that has never been placed under IAEA safeguards. Activists inside Israel warn against radioactive leaks in the Negev; while Green Peace and local Israeli civil societies warn against rise in nuclear radioactive levels in surrounding forests. Others warn against dilapidated radioactive waste storage containers and reports of leakages affecting underground water resources. The rise in intensity of seismic activities, earthquakes in the Negev also increase regional concerns.

The 1990 WMD Free Zone Initiative

The Initiative was launched in Baghdad, Iraq on April 9, 1990 with the Egyptian delegation arguing that such an initiative should add two other components of WMDs to the already set initiative of establishing a nuclear weapon free zone in the Middle East. The banning of chemical and biological weapons as zonal obligations made the initiative more effective. Although the host nation of the Arab summit, Iraq, was recalcitrant and rejected the initiative from the start, the Egyptian delegation underscored the following obligations: 1. All weapons of mass destruction, nuclear, chemical, biological, etc. without exception, should be banned in the Middle East; 2, All states of the region, without exception, should make an equal and reciprocal commitment in this regard; 3. Verification measures and modalities should be established to ascertain full compliance by all states of the region with the full scope of the prohibitions without exception.

While elaborating on the initiative, the foreign minister of Egypt added some other ideas. He: (a) Called upon the major arms producing states—and particularly the permanent members of the Security Council—as well as Israel, Iran and the Arab states, to give undertakings to the Security Council in which they clearly and unconditionally endorse the declaration of the Middle East as a region free of weapons of mass destruction and commit themselves not to take any steps or measures which would run counter to, or impede the attainment of this objective. (b) Called upon the arms producing states and the parties to the NPT to step up their efforts to ensure that all regional states that have not yet done so, to adhere to the Treaty. (c) Called upon the nations of the Middle East region, that have not yet done so, to declare their commitment: (i) Not to use nuclear, chemical or biological weapons, (ii) Not to produce or acquire any nuclear weapons, (iii) Not to produce or acquire any nuclear materials susceptible to military use and to dispose of any existing stocks of such materials, (iv) To accept the International Atomic Energy Agency safeguards regime whereby all their nuclear facilities become subject to international inspection. (d) Called upon those nations of the region which have not yet done so to declare their commitment to adhere to the Treaty on the Non-Proliferation of Nuclear Weapons, as well as to the Convention concerning the prohibition of biological weapons of 1972, no later than the conclusion of the negotiations on the prohibition of chemical weapons being conducted by the Conference on Disarmament in Geneva.

Following the adoption of Security Council Resolution 687 in 1991, which ordered the dismantling of WMDs in Iraq as per paragraph 14 (which underscored that the resolution represented a step towards the goal of establishing in the Middle East a ZFWMD and their delivery missiles), the then minister of foreign affairs of Egypt, Amre Moussa, forwarded a letter to the UN Security Council whereby he pointed out that events in the Middle East had induced many states to endorse Egypt's latest Initiative, which was also endorsed by the Security Council in the context of its resolution 687 (1991).

As years went by, the Initiative enjoyed considerable success and worldwide attention. The fact that it dealt with all components of weapons of mass destruction in a volatile region such as the Middle East, focused world attention on a new global threat especially if tied to illicit trade and surreptitious activities or worldwide networks such as that of A.Q. Khan. Security Council resolution 1540 underscored the same focus and actually created a road map for collective efforts in this regard. NATO also inspired by the WMD free zone initiative put in place a new mechanism, "Active Endeavour", in the Mediterranean, to interdict illicit transportation of WMD components. The Arab world had high expectations that with the entry into force of the work of the UN inspection and monitoring activities in Iraq following a SC resolution, the actual initiative itself would enter the implementation stage. There was great disappointment when this never happened and the Commission focused on Iraq alone without any regional arms control dimension. Some Arab states argued that the Blix Commission and its findings did little to foster regional efforts to establish such a zone. While no WMDs have been discovered in Iraq till today, some believe that this was a pretext, to gain international legitimacy to invade Iraq. This was different from the previous efforts to garner international legitimacy for freeing Kuwait. Arab countries were fully on board with regard to the freedom of /or the liberation of Kuwait, and in fact an Arab League resolution paved the way for a UNSC resolution onward.

In 2010 the NPT RevCon final document suggested the convening of a conference, devoted to exploring the possibility of establishing a nuclear and weapons of mass destruction free zone in the Middle East. The NPT final document in 2010 outlined a specific action plan mandating several international WMDs banning organisations such as the Organisation for Prevention of Chemical Weapons (OPCW), International Atomic Energy Association (IAEA), and the Comprehensive Nuclear-test-ban-treaty Organisation (CTBTO), to prepare relevant documentation on the modalities of the proposed zone. This proposed conference augured well with Arab demands to respect the NPT indefinite extension package of 1995, which included a specific resolution on the Middle East, cosponsored by the three depository countries of the NPT. It was this resolution that made the indefinite extension of the NPT Treaty in 1995 possible. A senior diplomat from Finland was elected as a "facilitator" for the convening of the conference in Finland, and since 2011 Ambassador Jaako Laajava and his devoted team have made considerable efforts, travelled extensively and undertaken rigorous consultations with all the parties concerned, to convene a successful conference in Helsinki in mid-December 2012. In February 2013, the United States officially requested the deferral of conference. The high level expert group of the Arab League met in Cairo on December 18, to discuss contingency plans amidst a great deal of regret for the US decision. The civil society and several NGO's who had planned to meet in Helsinki a few days before the conference announced that they would go ahead with their planned meeting in Helsinki as a gesture of support for the initiative and as a message to the US administration. In the Arab world a consortium of 19 Arab NGOs expressed strong regrets for this delay, refuting the argument that the Arab spring made circumstances inopportune for the implementation of strong arms control initiatives. They called for a withdrawal from the II Prepcom of the NPT that will convene next April in Geneva, and are also considering withdrawal from the NPT Treaty itself as per Article X of the NPT which allows this, if supreme national interests are threatened.

Hence it is necessary to arrive at a definition of security as equal security for all, as the current security asymmetry has pushed military doctrines away from reconciliation and cooperative security towards the doctrine of confrontation. Today in the absence of a negotiating process or a venue where parties can discuss their security concerns, some have attempted to achieve parity by non-traditional means i.e. the poor man's nuclear weapon- such as what transpired in Iraq and Libya. This has forced experts to conclude that the Israeli policy of nuclear ambiguity or nuclear veto has created mistrust instead of building confidence. In this respect, what the region needs at this stage is the revival of arms control discussions such as the ACRS talks that started after the Madrid peace conference in the 1990s.

Other Zonal Approach Initiatives

A zonal WMD free zone is not the only option. Hans Blix the former DG of the IAEA advocates a zone that also does not have facilities for the enrichment of uranium, reprocessing plants, and production of plutonium. Blix argues that the present nuclear fuel cycle is making Iran a "near nuclear weapon state" positing that any zonal approach in addition to WMD should encompass the nuclear fuel cycle itself as with the case of North and South Korea agreeing in 1991, to forgo the construction of enrichment and reprocessing plants. Blix argues that concessions from Iran in this field may lead to reciprocal measures from Israel in a specific and agreed to time frame, and within the purview of IAEA safeguard measures, security guarantees, and an agreed-to, geographic scope definition of the region. Adding to the urgency of implementing the Zone Free from WMD's initiative is the Syrian factor and the threat of possible use of chemical weapons on a civilian population. Had regional efforts to establish such a WMD free zone in the Middle East succeeded, a destruction schedule for chemical weapons and a rigorous role for the OPCW would have been in place for inspections.

The Arab Spring and its Implications for Regional Security

The Arab Spring or Arab awakening, should not be used as a pretext or alibi by any party to hamper efforts to deal with illicit nuclear capabilities in our region, even if some proclaim that the Arab world is over burdened or short circuited because of its transition towards democracy.

A zone free from weapons of mass destruction including their delivery systems should be part of the solution, and a part of the restructuring of the security setting of the region. Democracy, human rights, and good governance are all central and objectives that the Arab revolutions strive to achieve. However, democracy without a sound and proper security setting is unlikely to succeed. It is essential to build a democracy where the security of one nation does not draw from or comes at the expense of the security of other nations. An unresolved Arab Israeli conflict, or lack of legitimate Palestinian rights, will create strong pressure that may hamper a stable political climate necessary for democratic reform. The advent of political Islam does not warrant Israel conducting a hostile policy of aggression against the Palestinians. On the contrary it warrants peace talks, a clear road map that gives the Palestinians and the entire Arab world, the hope of a just and lasting peace. Exaggeration of threats should be replaced by working on the solution. Any Israeli policy of brinkmanship, military, nuclear or political gambling, will have devastating effects on both regional and international peace and security. An arms race may become the alternative and calls for jihad may prevail. Once again solving the Palestinian problem will always remain the crucial prerequisite for regional peace and security.

Iran

As far as Iran is concerned, the Gulf countries will not agree to be crushed between a nuclear Iran and a nuclear weaponised Israel. Additionally a nuclear weapon Iran will pose a threat to neighbouring Turkey and to NATO territories and frontiers. Europe will feel threatened since European territory remains within the range of Iran's newly developed Shihab III missiles capable of carrying a nuclear warhead. This will force Western military strategists to redraw, reassemble, reorganise their flanks, move the nuclear theatre or strike force closer to the Middle East region, and make crucial adjustments in their military and rapid response deployment capabilities.

Such a scenario may also push Gulf nations to seek security guarantees; military or even nuclear assurances from the West, enhance foreign military presence in the region, as what recently transpired in Kuwait which granted military facilities to NATO within the Istanbul NATO initiative; increase dependence on missile protection umbrella systems from the West; raise the probability of incidents or accidental warfare; endanger the safety of navigation in the straits, enable the Hezbollah in Lebanon to become emboldened by a nuclear Iran, and finally increase the possibilities of nuclear hedging. Complicating this scenario is the fact that Iran continues to occupy three UAE islands and continues to threaten regional security in this regard. Undoubtedly if Iran goes nuclear the NPT will face a test of survivability. It may mean the end of the NPT, rendering it worthless, and pushing Gulf states to seek other extra regional security protective measures.

These conditions never existed in South Asia when India and Pakistan embarked on a series of nuclear explosions when deterrence theorists posited that deterrence will force both India and Pakistan to behave rationally causing a nuclear standoff. The difference in the case of Iran is that Iran may use the nuclear reality to augment its policy of territorial protection, indulge in territorial expansion, employ a policy of deterrence against a possible foreign strike or invasion, use this leverage as a negotiating tool vis-à-vis international sanctions, and finally as a means for acquiring regional hegemony and exporting the Shia doctrine.

However forcing the region into denying Iran's legitimate rights to the peaceful uses of nuclear energy in accordance with Article IV of the NPT, pushing for a military confrontation, or even a surgical strike against Iran, will have a devastating effect on the stability of the region, the price of oil, the safety of navigation in major sea lanes, as well as the emerging economies in the Gulf region. It is essential to visualise its impact on the stock markets in GCC countries, investment in Dubai, energy security lines and the international price of oil. One element that should be kept in mind is Iran's success in tying the legitimacy of its nuclear programme with strong popular domestic support, even linking it to religious jihadism.

The Need for a Sound Middle East Security Setting

In conclusion, the Middle East, in the absence of a sound security framework, lack of arms control and non proliferation agreements such as the establishment of a NWFZ or a Zone Free of WMD is doomed to failure. The lack or absence of political arms control initiatives, negotiations, collective talks and efforts, may even lead to military escalation in the region, as well as a harsh ideological conflict. The worse outcome will be if all these become entangled with religious fundamentalist doctrines and beliefs—between the die hard religious doctrines of Israel, the Shia ideology, and fundamentalist tenets of the countries of the Arab awakening.

GCC Policy Options and Alternatives

Today the salient factors, if not challenges, affecting the unfolding security situation in the Gulf are, influenced by three basic elements:

- a progressive turn towards peaceful uses of nuclear energy,
- an existing nuclear threat from Israel and Iran and a search for protection security measures against,
- a procedural dilemma; should GCC countries move collectively towards the comprehensive approach of a Middle East Zone Free from all weapons of mass destruction (WMD), and their delivery systems, or move separately on a sub regional basis alone? What are the pros and cons of each approach?

All these elements place considerable onus on GCC countries. Prescriptively, several proposals or expectations from the GCC nations in this regard can be as below:

> Telling the world that regional security is closely linked to international peace and security, and therefore given the volatile situation in the Arabian Gulf there is a need to uphold regional security; desist from use of conventional

weapons or maritime escalation in the region; request Iran to cooperate by resolving all pending issues relating to the UAE islands; reassuring Bahrain with regard to foreign intervention, addressing religious disparities and confrontation between minorities; since such provocations in a nuclear environment increase the risk of escalation and war.

In this regard it is important to persuade Iran to clear any misconceptions relating any possible military nuclear activities in order to consolidate international confidence. Iran could invite a high level delegation from GCC countries to alleviate doubts regarding the Parchin site. This happened earlier in the case of Argentina and Brazil, which before signing the NPT, undertook reciprocal and reassuring visits to each other's sites. Procrastination or prolonging of this opaque environment will only exacerbate the distrust that is poisoning regional security building efforts.

Iran must commit itself to transparent and more rigorous cooperation with the International Atomic Energy Association (IAEA). The GCC could also call on Iran to settle all this matters in preparation for the first Preparatory Committee of the NPT, enabling Iran to create the necessary conducive conditions for the smooth operation and review of the treaty to which Iran is a party.

Concluding Remarks

In conclusion, I wish to underscore that the Egyptian revolution of January 25, 2011 had several banners; "Bread, Freedom, Human dignity and social justice". These fundamentals have not yet been realised and some feel that the revolution is taking a different direction, or is even being hijacked towards a path, never planned for, when spontaneity and deprivation as well as injustice led millions of people and youthful revolutionaries to take to the streets demanding the overthrow of the Mubarak regime. But the pertinent question is: What do we expect from your part of the world? What lessons can be emulated? What do we expect from, India in particular, to do through this period of democratic transition in the Arab world? What are the negative implications of it and what measures do we need to take to redress these together?

First, we note an extreme focus on the Gulf region, and we understand the important economic implications for India basically in terms of energy security, assurances of supply, apart from guaranteeing the steady flow of the $32 billion expatriate remittances. However the security problem in our region, if allowed to disintegrate, will threaten all the aforementioned elements of relevance to India. This intertwined security setting, cannot be seen singularly, or dealt with in isolation. Hence, India's definition of national security should not be confined to West Asia, alone. Nor should diplomatic initiatives be once again governed by slow responses and long periods of situation assessments. A destabilised Egypt will impact negatively on India's national security and its implications will spill over, beyond doubt. What this means is that defining India's national security as stopping at the periphery of "West Asia", may mean that India's engagement beyond these geographic delineations will cease to exist. This is not commensurate with the global role India deserves. India should not slip into a mode of passive diplomacy or be content with rhetorical denunciations alone. We, in our region, need India's quick, assertive, vibrant diplomacy and positive engagement. India's strong ties with all countries in the region can be better leveraged to promote our much needed peace and stability.

Second, India can offer valuable and irreplaceable lessons in democracy building to our part of the world. A sound domestic political setting, party building, role of religion, role of minorities, the continuity of democratic are all issues that India succeeded in sorting out many decades ago. These are the lessons that need to be presented to Arab societies struggling for citizenship, secularism, fair and active political participation. India's leading role in party platform building, political domestic outreach, political participation and Institutional building can serve as a strong example of democratic transformation in our part of the world. Today in the Arab world, much is said about the need to emulate Malaysia, when in reality the Indian example can offer a plethora of rich lessons. I argued many years ago that cooperation in the field of election monitoring especially between the Egyptian and the Indian election committees, building capacities of observers, could be a fertile area of cooperation, and I am glad it is now taking place.

Third, India's close partnership with Egypt—since Bandung—to establish a historic world movement of the non aligned is now low on India's national priorities and foreign policy objectives. While India's focus remains towards the east and the China dimension, its identification with NAM disarmament and nuclear non-proliferation issues is waning. In contrast China is seemingly upholding its "joint ownership" and identification with the third world and developing countries. India acts more as a nuclear super power, seeking nuclear club recognition and a permanent seat in the Security Council at the expense of its leading and historic role of establishing non alignment and furthering its longstanding principles. If the movement in the eyes of some is dead, positions taken by key and founding states will remain forever. This is a lofty goal still pursued by our movement and the issue relating to Article VI of the NPT on nuclear disarmament is still being debated in all UNGA sessions, NPT review conferences and resolutions.

Fourth, the zonal approach to establish a nuclear weapon free zone in the Middle East and a Zone Free of Weapons of mass destruction requires India's partial support. Whenever there is a paragraph in these resolutions on the NPT, India requests a separate vote on such references either in the General Assembly or in the IAEA. Over many years Egyptian diplomacy tried to explain that such a reference is only being made in the Middle East context and is more aimed at Israel as a non NPT regional actor in the Middle East. Not all these attempts succeeded. Since the seventies when Pakistan invoked the introduction of a resolution in the UNGA on the establishment of a NWFZ in South Asia, India has consistently voted against this resolution. We tried to explain, on several occasions, that regional considerations in South Asia should not prevent or inhibit India, from supporting the establishment of similar NWFZ's elsewhere and particularly in a region striving for peace and security such as the Middle East. In essence we need India's support in the West Asian region to strengthen the regional efforts to establish such a ZFWMD. India's support will carry a strong message as well as give credence to our efforts in this regard. Additionally India is well situated to play a proactive diplomatic role on the Iranian nuclear dilemma. India is an actor widely accepted in Iran and in the Gulf region. Why such a reclusive diplomacy of non engagement? Why leave the talks to the 5+1 parties alone? India is well situated with its historical and cultural assets, amongst both parties, to play a more predominant and catalytic role.

Fifth, despite India's strong achievements in the nuclear field and especially within the sphere of peaceful uses of nuclear energy, little support has been given by India to the West Asian region in this regard. Cultural proximities, historical binding elements, user friendly technology based on self reliance, and a cogent Indian industry of R&D as well as significant IT achievements, have not led to closer long term industrial relations between India and the Arab world. Many Arab including Gulf countries, are opting for nuclear power for energy needs. India is regarded as a great market for power and electricity network cooperation, human capacity training and capacity building, research, dissemination of information on the prerequisites of an interactive societal coexistence scheme with nuclear reactors, and water desalination technology in a region in dire need of fresh water.

Sixth, securing trade sea lanes is also a matter of priority. These sea lanes are crucial for energy security. India's trade with the GCC accounts for $120 billion and 63 per cent of the hydrocarbon supplies that flow through these lanes, yet little cooperation is seen between India's naval forces, GCC nations, and also other nations, especially for combating piracy. Political and strategic discussion must begin and expand to include joint exercises, training, interdiction, naval escort, search and rescue.

NOTES

1. The order for Egypt's airlift to Israel and the alert of Egyptian forces was ordered in 1973 by the author in his official capacity.
2. Mahmoud Karem, *A Nuclear-Weapon-Free Zone in the Middle East: Problems and Prospects*, 1988, Greenwood Press New York, pp. 92-117.

19

Nuclear Issues in West Asia: An Indian Perspective

Rajesh Rajagopalan

Introduction

Iran's nuclear pursuit is one of the key problems facing the Middle East. This paper briefly outlines the current status of Iran nuclear weapons programme, the international responses to the programme, the debate around the likely impact of Iran's nuclear weaponisation on regional stability, and India's likely policy.

The Status of Iran's Nuclear Programme

It is difficult to state with any certainty what the current status of the Iranian nuclear programme is or what its purported end-state would be. Much like other states, Iranian objectives appear to have changed over time, with weapons development being one very distinct and likely possibility. Iranian leaders have repeatedly and publicly rejected nuclear weapons, which includes a fatwa against nuclear weapons by Iran's Supreme Leader Ayatollah Ali Khameini. This fatwa came after Iran decided to come clean on the weapons related aspects of its programme in 2003 but its relevance to Iranian behaviour has been questioned by analysts.[1] While some of these criticisms might indeed be valid, the problem with the fatwa is much simpler: it does not explain why Iran clearly pursued nuclear weapons technology research until 2003.

What can be stated with some confidence is that Iran's nuclear programme has become larger and much more complex and sophisticated over the last several years. Most Western intelligence agencies as well as the International Atomic Energy Agency (IAEA) accepted the American intelligence community's conclusion in a 2007 National Intelligence Estimate (NIE) "that until fall 2003, Iranian military entities were working under government direction to develop nuclear weapons."[2] This NIE stated that in 2003 Iran had stopped its covert weapons programme, though these conclusions were much more complex and circumspect than generally reported.[3] This conclusion was largely reiterated in a February 2011 NIE but this new NIE suggested that Iran had restarted some of its nuclear weapons work, though there was also evidence of an internal debate about the nuclear weapons programme in Iran.[4] A significant IAEA report six months later went further, suggesting that since 2003, Iran had engaged in a wide array of research that had military applications, including nuclear components for an explosive device and warhead design.[5] Though there was apparently a subsequent special intelligence estimate provided to President Obama by the American intelligence community in August 2012, its contents are unclear.

The most serious aspect of Iran's nuclear programme is its increasing potential for uranium enrichment. Though all of Iran's known uranium enrichment facilities are under IAEA safeguards, there are concerns that Iran might have covert facilities that have not yet been uncovered, a suspicion that has its basis in repeated Iranian efforts to hide its nuclear facilities. Facilities such as the ones at Natanz, Fordow and Arak were originally built covertly before being revealed by outside intelligence agencies. Even Iran's known uranium enrichment capabilities have been growing at a very fast pace. Indeed, the growth in these capabilities, more than anything else is the most likely trigger for further crisis in the region.

Iran has been producing 20 per cent enriched uranium for several years now. If this stockpile grows, it could lead to a crisis between Iran and Israel and the US. Israel has set its red lines as 240 kilograms of 20 per cent uranium, which Israeli officials believe will be sufficient for at least one weapon. As Iran ramps up its production of 20 per cent enriched uranium, Iran will have to choose whether to ignore the Israeli red line or take steps to ensure that they somehow do not cross it. So far Iran has been prudent: in 2012, as Iran's enriched uranium stockpile increased, it decided to convert a significant amount of the fuel to reactor fuel. Of the almost 190 kilograms of 20 per cent enriched fuel that it had produced as of August 2011, almost half had been removed and converted to reactor fuel, reducing Iran's stock of 20 per cent enriched uranium to about 91 kilograms.[6] Such conversion seems not to have been conducted over the next few months according to the subsequent IAEA Report in November 2012. Thus, by November 2012, Iran's stock of 20 per cent enriched fuel had increased to about 135 kilograms, slightly more than half of the Israeli red line.[7] The next IAEA report, due in end-February, should clarify whether Iran's stock of 20 per cent uranium has increased or whether it has resorted to converting some of this to reactor fuel in order to not cross the Israeli red line. Early reports suggest that additional conversions have indeed taken place.[8] A key problem here is that Iranian officials do not accept how serious and political (rather than legal) the issue of uranium enrichment is. Seyed Hossein Mousavian, a former Iranian diplomat, argued recently that Western demands such as capping the uranium enrichment levels at 20 per cent go far beyond the NPT "which permits member states to enrich to any level and places no limits on stockpiling enriched uranium."[9] The problem is that while it is legally true that there are no such limits, the political consequences can be serious.

Of course, Iran's stock of enriched uranium is only one issue. The IAEA reports also indicate that Iran has been continuing to install additional centrifuges for uranium enrichment. These have almost doubled in the last three years, going from about 5000 centrifuges in 2009 to almost 10,000 currently. In addition, Iran's work on long-range missiles and reported work on warhead designs suggest a fairly robust programme that has not been slowed down despite years of sanctions. The extensive and comprehensive nature of these programmes suggests that even if Iran has not formally made a decision to build nuclear weapons, it is amassing all the necessary capabilities to make a rapid breakout possible.

International Responses and Iran's Nuclear Weapons Pursuit

One of the key problems with the Iranian nuclear issue (as with the North Korean nuclear issue) is that there is little consensus among the great powers about how to manage the crisis. Indeed, it would not be an exaggeration to suggest that some of the great powers, especially China and Russia, might see in these crises a way to constrain American power. 'Soft balancing' has been recognized for some time as a means by which many of the other global powers have sought to prevent the unipolar power from becoming too domineering.[10] Indeed, from Tehran's perspective, the international circumstances might have become sufficiently less threatening for it to cautiously pursue a strategy that pushes the envelope with regard to its nuclear programme.

The most important reason why Iran pursues nuclear weapons is, of course, its security. Nuclear weapons will give Tehran immunity from the threats it perceives from Israeli and the US. Even if neither the US nor Israel represent a direct military threat, the fact that they have nuclear weapons and that Iran has had an adversarial relations with both for decades means that Iran faces an implicit threat that nuclearisation could correct.[11] This is the logic of the nuclear imbalance that is the centre-piece of Kenneth Waltz's much publicised argument, though Waltz considers only the threat that Iran perceives from Israel (the regional nuclear imbalance) rather than the Iranian threat perception from Washington which is equally relevant.[12] The logic of proliferation here is different from that of Israel or India and closer to that of Pakistan and North Korea. In the case of Israel, nuclear weapons are the necessary means of ensuring the survival of the nation-state, a concern that has its roots in both Jewish history and the imbalance of wealth and power in the region. In the Indian case, its lackadaisical pursuit of nuclear weapons represented the clearest indication that New Delhi had sufficient margin of security at least until Pakistan's nuclear advances were undeniable. But in the case of Pakistan and North Korea and Iran, the perception of insecurity (either general or specifically nuclear) has been overwhelming because each perceived a significant and relevant conventional and/or nuclear imbalance. For states which perceive such insecurity, nuclear weapons represent the clearest path to security. Assuming that such states also have the technical capacity and material means to pursue it, it is unlikely that they can be peacefully convinced to renounce such weapons.

But perception of nuclear insecurity is only one reason why it is rational and understandable for Iran to pursue nuclear weapons. Such pursuit will also require a permissive international condition. Concerted opposition from more powerful actors can ensure both the slowing down and even ending of such nuclear pursuits. Several states including Iraq, Taiwan and South Korea have sought to develop nuclear technology which could have led to nuclear weapons but were eventually 'persuaded' to end such efforts because of various forms of coercive international action. But such action requires, at the least, consensus between the major powers about the necessity for stopping such programmes. Indeed, such concerted action might have been responsible for the reported suspension of Iran's nuclear weapons programme in 2003.

But from Tehran's perspective, the international situation could have become increasingly more permissive over the last several years. Washington, as the dominant power in the global system, has taken the lead in the negotiations with Iran. However, since 2006, the five permanent members of the UN Security Council and Germany (P5+1) have conducted several rounds of joint negotiations with Iran. The idea was to convince Tehran that it was not just the US and Israel that were concerned about Iran's nuclear pursuit but also other global powers. The P5+1 format was designed to demonstrate to Iran that the global community was united in its opposition to Iran's nuclear weapons programme. But the format could not paper over key differences between these powers. Though P5+1 have been negotiating with Iran for several years now, there are significant differences between Washington and Beijing and Moscow about how to proceed even as they apparently agree on the broad outlines of the end goal of the negotiations. China has clearly and consistently opposed international sanctions on Iran. The Chinese Foreign Ministry spokesperson Hong Lei stated the Chinese position at a press conference in October 2012: "(W)e oppose unilateral sanctions against Iran since we believe that pressuring and sanctions cannot fundamentally settle the Iranian issue, but will only complicate and compound it, exacerbate confrontation and undermine regional peace and stability... There is still room for diplomatic efforts. China always maintains that dialogue and cooperation is the only correct way to properly settle the Iranian nuclear issue."[13]

Russia also has differences with the US and the European powers on the Iran issue though Russia does probably have some concerns about the prospect of a nuclear-armed Iran. But senior Russian government officials have stated they "do not see any signs that Iran's Nuclear Programme has military dimension (sic)."[14] Nevertheless, he went on to add that Iran does have obligations too, including to satisfy the questions that the IAEA has. But Russia also apparently sees Iran in the light of its relations with the US. According to one Russian analyst, "the rules of this game are simple. Moscow will be more flexible and ready to discuss the Iranian problem if US authorities demonstrate a constructive approach in resolving issues irritating the Russians."[15] Such dissonance between the great powers increases the incentives for Iran to seek nuclear weapons. For Tehran, it would be foolish to let such opportunities go; indeed a rational actor would pursue such a course given the disagreement among the great powers.

A final reason why it might be rational for Iran to pursue nuclear weapons today is because the chances of a pre-emptive military attack on Iran's nuclear facilities appear to be diminishing. The state with the greatest incentive to strike at these capabilities is obviously Israel. Israel has repeatedly warned that it would not tolerate Iran getting nuclear weapons. It has also demonstrated what might be characterized as 'commitment credibility', a willingness and capability to not make empty threats and to follow through on the threats it does make, destroying Iraq's Osirak reactor in Iraq in 1981 and an under-construction Syrian nuclear reactor in 2007.[16] On the other hand, any pre-emptive attack on Iran's nuclear facilities would be very complicated because of the distances involved, the number of targets that would have to be attacked and the lack of any strategic surprise with regard to Israel's plans (because Iran is well aware that Israel might attack and has taken measures to harden potential targets). Internal divisions within Israel at both the political level and apparently within the Israeli military and intelligence services also make an Israeli decision harder.[17] None of this means that Israel will not resort to a preventive attack; just that from Iran's perspective, it would appear that Israel might not be able to attack it thus increasing Iran's incentive to continue with a weapons programme.

The US has far greater military capabilities to attack and degrade the Iranian nuclear programme, as American officials have apparently informed Israel.[18] The Chairman of the US Joint Chiefs of Staff, General Martin Dempsey, stated that Israel's military only has the capacity to "delay, but not destroy Iran's nuclear capabilities."[19] The key question with the US however is regarding its intentions, not its capabilities. President Obama said in 2012 that he has Israel's 'back' and that US policy with regard to Iran's nuclear weapons programme is one of prevention rather than of 'containment' of Iran's nuclear weapons programme. Nevertheless, there are, as the *New York Times* put it in 2012, "lingering suspicions" in Israel "that the White House would rather contain a nuclear Iran than go to war to prevent it."[20] Relations between the US and Israel have cooled somewhat under President Obama and there appears to be considerable domestic political opposition in the US to going to war yet again in the Middle East. Again, this does not mean that the US will not eventually decide that it has no choice but to go to war if negotiations with Iran do not lead to a satisfactory conclusion. But from Iran's perspective, the considerable domestic opposition in the US to go to war might be seen as an indication that Iran can safely proceed with its nuclear programme.

Nuclear Deterrence and Stability in the Middle East

One of the key issues of debate in Iran's nuclear pursuit is the question of the consequence for nuclear deterrence and regional stability: What is the likely effect of Iran's nuclearisation on stability in the region? Traditionally, the spread of nuclear weapons has been seen as destabilizing, which is the logic behind the nuclear non-proliferation treaty (NPT). This logic was challenged by Kenneth Waltz who argued that the spread of nuclear weapons could stabilize regional conflicts because the same deterrence logic that applied in the Cold War between the US and the Soviet Union would apply in the case of regional bilateral conflicts.[21]

Waltz has reprised that argument in the context of the Iranian nuclear issue. In a short essay in *Foreign Affairs* in 2012, Waltz argued that a nuclear-armed Iran might be the best possible outcome because it is "the one most likely to restore stability to the Middle East."[22] It is worth exploring his argument in some detail because Waltz states lucidly the best case for what is characterized as the 'containment' strategy vis-à-vis Iran and because of the influence Waltz has at the intellectual level in international relations scholarship and, equally importantly, because these arguments are repeatedly used by other opinion-makers.

Waltz argues that the nuclear imbalance is the key factor that has led to the current crisis: as he puts it, "It is Israel's nuclear arsenal, not Iran's desire for one, that has contributed most to the current crisis."[23] Iran desires nuclear weapons "for the purpose of providing for its own security, not to improve its offensive capabilities (or destroy itself)." If Iran acquires nuclear weapons, it is likely to use them no differently than other nuclear powers have in the past. Iran's leaders, Waltz goes on, "are perfectly sane ayatollahs who want to survive just like any other leaders." Whatever their revolutionary rhetoric, states become less bellicose after they get nuclear weapons because they become potential targets of the major powers. Dismissing another often expressed concern, Waltz argues that Iran would be unlikely to pass nuclear weapons to terrorist groups because they cannot fully control what such groups might do with those weapons. Finally, Iran's nuclearisation is unlikely to lead to a nuclear arms race in the region because nuclear proliferations threats are much exaggerated. Waltz's arguments are radical. Even an acolyte like Stephen Walt disagrees with Waltz about some of the likely pacifying effects of a nuclear Iran. For one, as Walt correctly points out, if nuclear weapons were really so stabilizing then it would actually be logical for the US to give Iran nuclear weapons.[24]

Waltz is correct to argue that Iran's nuclear pursuit is driven by security concerns, as are the nuclear pursuits of most countries. Most strategic policies are not monocausal and are driven by multiple factors including fear and pride, though fear tends to predominate over other factors. In that sense, Iran's nuclear weapons programme is understandable. Waltz is also correct to dismiss some of the arguments about what Iran might do with its nuclear weapons, such as the fear that Tehran might pass on these weapons to its client terrorist groups like Hezbollah and Hamas. This is an unfounded but often stated fear: In an essay, Matthew Kroenig argued that in order to constrain its adversaries "Iran could choose to spur proliferation by transferring nuclear technologies to its allies—other countries and terrorist groups alike."[25] Waltz points out that countries have an incentive to keep control over the nuclear weapons that they have worked so hard to get and it would make little sense to transfer it to groups whose behaviour they cannot fully control.

But Waltz's other conclusions are more problematic. The most serious problem is with the consequence to deterrence and stability. Waltz tends to assume that the same logic that prevented war between the superpowers during the Cold War will work in the case of regional adversaries. He expects even deadly enemies become more circumspect after acquiring nuclear weapons. For example, Waltz points to the India-Pakistan nuclear equation arguing that "India and Pakistan have become more cautious since going nuclear."[26] Waltz's understanding of the South Asian nuclear situation is somewhat simplistic. But the India-Pakistan nuclear equation is a good indicator of the kind of deterrence problems that will face the Middle East and specifically Israel, should Iran manage to become a nuclear weapon power.

The key problem that India has faced vis-à-vis Pakistan will likely be the same problem that Israel will face should Iran get the bomb, the problem that is sometimes mistakenly characterized as the 'stability-instability paradox'.[27] Since Pakistan acquired nuclear weapons in the late 1980s, India has found itself severely constrained in responding to Pakistani provocations, including in episodes such as the Kargil war in 1999 and in dealing with Pakistan-sponsored terrorism in India such as the attack on the Indian Parliament in December 2001 and the Mumbai terror attacks in 2008, as well as a large number of other terror bomb attacks in major Indian cities throughout the last decade. But the limits of the deterrence effects are most evident in the Kargil episode, in Operation Parakram after the attack on the Indian Parliament and in the Indian response to the 2008 Mumbai attack.

The Kargil war, occurring less than a year after India and Pakistan went overtly nuclear, demonstrated the limits that both sides faced. On the Indian side, the constraint related to India's inability to cross the Line of Control (LoC) to conduct military operations, forcing the Indian military to pay a higher cost in rooting out the Pakistani forces dug into the mountains on the Indian side of the LoC. But just as there were limits on India, there were some limits on Pakistan too. Pakistan could do little to openly and directly help its forces trapped on the Indian side of the LoC. While Pakistan exhibited recklessness in crossing the LoC to conduct military operations, it could not do so openly. The lessons from Kargil were that both sides faced some constraints but also opportunities. On the Pakistan side, the opportunity was in conducting covert military operations and triggering a limited war. On the Indian side, the opportunity was the ability to conduct a full-scale war, including the use of air power, as long as it was limited to the Indian side of the LoC. Yet another lesson of the war was that nuclear weapons do not obviate all kinds of war and that escalation is not automatic, unlike in the Cold War US-Soviet nuclear confrontation. Hence, the likelihood for the Middle East is not that Iran might launch a premeditated, unprovoked nuclear attack on Israel or that it might give nuclear weapons to terrorist groups such as Hezbollah or Hamas but that nuclear weapons will provide a shield that would allow Iran to continue sponsoring such terrorist groups without the fear of retaliation. This is quite different from the nuclear equation during the Cold War, and it is likely to intensify the secret war between Israel and Iran rather than lead to a direct war, leading to what Ashley Tellis has characterized as 'ugly stability' in the context of South Asia.[28]

Waltz is also wrong, and indeed contradicts himself, when suggesting that Iran's nuclearisation will not lead to any further proliferation in the Middle East. By his own argument, it was Israel's nuclear weapons that drove Iran's weapons programme, but he dismisses that Iran's programme will lead other countries such as Saudi Arabia to seek nuclear weapons. But senior Saudi personalities have repeatedly suggested that Saudi Arabia might seek nuclear weapons if Iran acquires them. The former head of Saudi intelligence Turki al-Faisal said as much publicly in December 2011;[29] and former Obama administration official Dennis Ross confirmed that King Abdullah II had explicitly warned him of the same possibility in 2009.[30] And of course, the WikiLeaks cables revealed that King Abdullah (as well as senior officials in Jordan, Bahrain and Gulf states) had repeatedly urged the US to attack and destroy the Iranian nuclear weapons programme, to "cut off the head of the snake", in the King's words.[31]

The Impact on Global Nuclear Non-proliferation Norms

Iran's nuclear weapons programme could have a direct impact on further nuclearisation in the Middle East, but not necessarily elsewhere. The consequences of regional nuclear proliferation tend to be limited to the region because it primarily impacts on the security of the neighbours of the nuclearising power, irrespective of the original cause of the nuclearisation. Thus, in both the North Korean case and that of Iran, though a reasonable argument could be made that the primary impetus came from the insecurity that these regimes felt from the US, the consequence will be on the region rather than outside the region. Though non-proliferationists have repeatedly argued that there is a likelihood of a 'demonstration effect' of nuclear proliferation that will lead to copycat behaviour in other parts of the world, we have yet to see any such demonstration. Nuclearisation is a dangerous and difficult path both in terms of technology and politics and a path that states are likely to choose only under duress.

But there is another way in which nuclear proliferation could become a more prominent trend. What the Iran (and North Korean) nuclear issues demonstrate is that the great power consensus that was the basis for building and sustaining the nuclear non-proliferation regime is breaking down. During the Cold War decades, both the US and the Soviet Union strongly supported the regime and cooperated in ensuring its tightening. But the last decade shows a significant breakdown in that consensus, with both Russia and China preventing action against Iran and North Korea. To some extent, it does appear that these two powers see these issues as ways of undermining Washington's interest. International norms and regimes are difficult to sustain in the absence of great power consensus, even if the system is unipolar, because of the enormous political and material cost of maintaining these regimes. The US mistake in going to war in Iraq has meant that the US has become even more wary of bearing these costs, thus in essence requiring greater contribution and coordination with Russia and China. Thus, one likely effect of Iran acquiring nuclear weapons is indirect, in indicating the decline of the nuclear non-proliferation regime and norms (as was also the case with North Korean nuclear weapons and the US-India nuclear deal). The long-term consequence of this decline in great power consensus is likely to be quite dire, with the slow dismantling of the nuclear non-proliferation regime and greater spread of nuclear weapons.

The Impact on India's Policy

Foreign policy is always a luxury in a democracy, and India is no different. Moreover, India is sufficiently large and secure that it faces little threat from global developments. Thus, India is likely to continue to sit on the fence on the Iranian issue because it has no good choices and also there are countervailing pressures on the policy-makers.

For one, domestic pressures—the perception of Indian political parties about Muslim views and voting behaviour—are likely to make all major Indian political parties support Iran, or at least stay neutral. Indian Muslims have rarely voted as a bloc and foreign policy is as much of a non-issue to them as to any other

Indian demographic but perceptions of political parties about Muslim preferences are difficult to shake. In addition, the likelihood that coalition governments will continue to rule Delhi will make all political parties risk averse. There is little reason for political parties clinging on to power by their fingernails to pursue a foreign policy that might be risky in the short-run even if it is in India's long-term interest. On the other hand, India is likely to face pressure from the US and Israel but this will be less important than other domestic political pressures. Indeed, it might actually become an opportunity for various Indian governments to demonstrate their 'strategic autonomy' by standing up to Washington. On the whole though, these countervailing pressures will most likely mean that India will seek to continue fence-sitting on the issue. Thus, India will continue to reiterate Iran's right to nuclear technology but also Iran's obligations to live up to the terms of the NPT. This is likely to satisfy neither Iran nor Washington, but probably not irritate them too much either.

Conclusion

The evolution of Iran's nuclear efforts suggests that Iran is intent on developing nuclear weapons, but that it might also recognize the realities of the circumstances it faces and thus might stop just short of the precipice. Hence, it is possible that 2013 might not after all be 'the year of decision'. Nevertheless, it is difficult to see conditions under which Iran might peacefully give up its nuclear weapons potential. If Iran does acquire nuclear weapons, the consequences for the region (and Israel) might not be as dangerous as is sometimes suggested but neither is it likely to lead to greater stability.

Addendum

This paper was originally written for the 2013 Asian Security Conference and completed in January 2013. As this book goes to press in January 2014, there have been dramatic changes regarding the Iran nuclear issue. Hassan Rouhani's election as Iran's President in June 2013 led to a significant shift in Iran's nuclear policies, though it remains to be seen if this shift is a tactical one—the consequence of the biting international sanctions—or a more strategic decision that Iran does not need to build nuclear weapons for its security. In all likelihood, it is somewhere in between, possibly a decision that since Iran now has all the wherewithal for a nuclear breakout whenever it wants to, there is little harm in accepting to negotiate with the international community about Iran's nuclear programme. Washington has clearly accepted that it does not have a military solution to the Iran problem and it does not appear as if Israel has one either. Thus, on both sides, there is an incentive to negotiate an end to the continuing crisis. While no final agreement has been reached as of mid-January 2014, there is still time for such an agreement to be reached, though there are also significant difficulties with reaching a final agreement. But on a crucial issue, that of Iran's right to enrichment, the US and its partners have already agreed that Iran has the right to enrich its uranium. Thus a significant obstacle to the final agreement has already been overcome. The debate and negotiations will thus revolve around how much Iran is allowed to enrich and how much stockpile of enriched uranium it is allowed to hold which will facilitate any potential nuclear breakout. Washington has already indicated that its primary objective is not to eliminate any Iranian capacity to breakout but simply to increase the time Teheran will need for any such breakout. In consequence, even if the negotiations between the P-5+1 and Iran were to be successful, it is unlikely that this will be the end of the Iran nuclear crisis. In addition to Israel, Saudi Arabia and other Gulf states have publicly expressed deep concern about the prospects of a nuclear Iran. It is unlikely that these states will feel secure with an Iran which has a latent nuclear capability. While it is unclear what options they might have to respond to the situation, their need to respond will be yet another reason why the Iranian nuclear issue will continue to remain a significant problem for the region and the world.

NOTES

1. Michael Eisenstadt and Mehdi Khalaji, *Nuclear Fatwa: Religion and Politics in Iran's Proliferation Strategy,* Washington Institute for Near East Policy, Washington D.C., Policy Focus # 115, September 2011.
2. *Iran: Nuclear Intentions and Capabilities*, National Intelligence Council, November 2007.
3. Jeffrey Lewis, "The Ayatollah's Pregnant Pause," *Foreign Policy*, August 15, 2012, http://www.foreignpolicy.com/articles/2012/08/15/the_ayatollahs_pregnant_pause?page=0,0&wp_login_redirect=0
4. Unlike in 2007, the 2011 NIE was not accompanied by a declassified version, though press reports revealed key elements. Greg Miller and Joby Warrick, "US Report Finds Debate in Iran on Building Nuclear Bomb," *The Washington Post*, February 19, 2011.
5. IAEA, *Implementation of the NPT Safeguards Agreement and Relevant Provisions of the Security Council Resolutions in the Islamic Republic of Iran*, Gov/2011/65, November 8, 2011.
6. IAEA, *Implementation of the NPT Safeguards Agreement and Relevant Provisions of the Security Council Resolutions in the Islamic Republic of Iran*, Gov/2012/37, August 30, 2012, pp. 7-8; and *ISIS Analysis of IAEA Iran Safeguards Report*, Institute for Science and International Security, August 30, 2012, pp. 5-6.
7. IAEA, *Implementation of the NPT Safeguards Agreement and Relevant Provisions of the Security Council Resolutions in the Islamic Republic of Iran*, Gov/2012/55, November 16, 2012, pp. 3-4; and David Albright, Christina Walrond and Andrea Stricker, *ISIS Analysis of IAEA Iran Safeguards Report, Rev. 1*, Institute for Science and International Security, November 16, 2012, pp. 5-6.
8. Myra MacDonald and Fredrik Dahl, "Insight: Iran Nuclear Fuel Move May Avert Mid-Year Crisis," *Reuters*, February 10, 2013, http://www.reuters.com/article/2013/02/10/us-iran-nuclear-conversions-idUSBRE91907O20130210
9. Seyed Hossein Mousavian, "Embrace the Fatwa," *Foreign Policy* at http://www.foreignpolicy.com/articles/2013/02/07/Embrace_the_Fatwa_Iran
10. T.V. Paul, "Soft Balancing in the Age of US Primacy," *International Security* 30(1), Summer 2005, pp. 46-71.

11. This was most famously indicated by General K. Sundarji's comment about the lesson of the first Gulf War, which has found resonance in surprising places. Hugh Gusterson, "US Nuclear Double Standards," *Bulletin of Atomic Scientists*, February 20, 2008, at http://www.thebulletin.org/web-edition/columnists/hugh-gusterson/us-nuclear-double-standards
12. Kenneth N. Waltz, "Why Iran Should Get the Bomb: Nuclear Balancing Would Mean Stability," *Foreign Affairs*, July/August 2012, http://www.foreignaffairs.com/articles/137731/kenneth-n-waltz/why-iran-should-get-the-bomb
13. "Foreign Ministry Spokesperson Hong Lei's Regular Press Conference on October 16, 2012, Ministry of Foreign Affairs of the People's Republic of China, at http://www.fmprc.gov.cn/eng/xwfw/s2510/t980569.htm
14. "Interview of Deputy Foreign Minister of Russia S.A. Ryabkov to the Interfax agency, Moscow, September 6, 2012," The Ministry of Foreign Affairs of the Russian Federation, at http://www.mid.ru/bdomp/Brp_4.nsf/arh/9309A17C259EF02244257A92003B22AA?OpenDocument
15. Nikolay Kozhanov, "Russia's Position on Iran's Nuclear Program," The Washington Institute for Near East Policy, April 19, 2012, http://www.washingtoninstitute.org/policy-analysis/view/russias-position-on-irans-nuclear-program
16. There are some questions about the success of the Osiraq attack, though that does not detract from the point I am making which deals with public/elite perception rather than academic assessment. See Dan Reiter, "Preventive Attacks Against Nuclear Programs and the 'Success' at Osiraq," *The Nonproliferation Review* 12 (2), July 2005, pp. 355-71.
17. Chuck Freilich, "Striking Iran: The Debate in Israel," *Survival: Global Politics and Strategy* 54(6), December 2012-January 2013, pp. 93-106; and "To Strike or Not to Strike," *The Economist Online*, August 17, 2012, http://www.economist.com/blogs/newsbook/2012/08/israels-debate-over-iran
18. Jodi Rudoren and David E. Sanger, "Report on Iran Nuclear Work Puts Israel in a Box," *New York Times*, August 30, 2012.
19. "DOD News Briefing with Secretary Panetta and Gen. Dempsey from the Pentagon," US Department of Defense, August 14, 2012, at http://www.defense.gov/transcripts/transcript.aspx?transcriptid=5099
20. Mark Landler, "US Aides in Israel Give Assurance about Iran," *New York Times*, June 6, 2012.
21. Kenneth N. Waltz, *The Spread of Nuclear Weapons: More May Be Better*, Adelphi Paper No. 171, International Institute for Strategic Studies, London, 1981.
22. Waltz, "Why Iran Should Get the Bomb," *Foreign Affairs*, July/August 2012 issue at http://www.foreignaffairs.com/articles/137731/kenneth-n-waltz/why-iran-should-get-the-bomb
23. Ibid. Subsequent quotes in this section are from the same source.
24. Stephen M. Walt, "Should We Give Iran the Bomb?," *Foreign Policy*, June 26, 2012, walt.foreignpolicy.com/posts/2012/06/26/waltz_weighs_in_on_iran?wp_login_redirect=0
25. Matthew Kroenig, "Time to Attack Iran: Why a Strike is the Least Bad Option," *Foreign Affairs*, January/February 2012, http://www.foreignaffairs.com/articles/136917/matthew-kroenig/time-to-attack-iran.
26. Waltz, No. 22.
27. For a more sophisticated overview, see S. Paul Kapur, "India and Pakistan's Unstable Peace: Why Nuclear South Asia is Not Like Cold War Europe," *International Security* 30:2 (Fall 2005), pp. 127-52.
28. Ashley J. Tellis, *Stability in South Asia,* RAND, Santa Monica, CA, 1997.
29. "Prince Hints Saudi Arabia May Join Nuclear Arms Race," *New York Times*, December 6, 2011.
30. Landler, No. 20.
31. Ian Black and Simon Tisdall, "Saudi Arabia Urges US Attack on Iran to Stop Nuclear Programme," *The Guardian*, November 28, 2010.

20

The Iranian Nuclear Challenge

Ephraim Kam

The Iranian threat has become a key issue in the Middle East since the early 1990s, mainly because many governments are concerned about Iran's nuclear activities. Moreover, the Iranian strategy has several threatening dimensions. First, Iran is making huge efforts to attain hegemony in the Middle East, as well the Moslem world. Being the largest Shiite state, Iran is leading the Shiite camp to challenge the Arab Sunni bloc. Towards this end, Iran, during the last decade, has formed a Shiite-radical axis extending from western Afghanistan, through Iran, Iraq, Syria (which is not Shiite, but its Alawite regime is close to the Shiites), and Lebanon, and supplies arms to Hamas and other Islamic Jihad organisations in the Gaza Strip. Second, Iran is deeply involved in terrorist and subversive activities in many countries. Iran is widely believed to be a major sponsor of terrorism, and moderate Islamic regimes are concerned about its drive to export the Iranian model of Islamic revolution to other Moslem countries. Third, since 1987 Iran is making major efforts to pursue a nuclear military programme. If Iran manages to acquire a nuclear weapon, the Middle East will be changed drastically and for the long term.

The possibility of Iran acquiring nuclear weapons is taken so seriously that the American and Israeli governments were considering undertaking a military operation to destroy Iranian nuclear sites. The leaders of Saudi Arabia and smaller Gulf states too have been urging the US administration to do everything, and anything, to put an end to the Iranian nuclear programme.

About seven-eight years ago there was an intense debate among governments, intelligence communities and experts, regarding Iran's drive to acquire nuclear weapons. While the American and Israeli governments believed, that Iran had been making serious efforts, to develop nuclear weapons, since the early 1990s, other governments claimed that Iran had neither the capabilities nor the intentions to produce nuclear weapons. This debate is long over, since so many details about the Iranian nuclear programme have emerged that they leave no room for doubt that Iran is close to building nuclear weapons. These details have been revealed by Western intelligence communities, the International Atomic Energy Agency, and the Iranians themselves.

Thus, for the last few years, there is almost an international consensus, that Iran has made a very significant progress toward acquiring nuclear capabilities. There is even a consensus on the timetable of the Iranian nuclear programme. Leading Western intelligence agencies estimate that at present Iran has probably decided not to make a break for the nuclear bomb, for two reasons: they want to minimise the costs of building the bomb and are therefore waiting for the best time to do so; and second, they want not only one bomb but an arsenal of several bombs, and therefore they are simultaneously acquiring a wide range of nuclear capabilities that will allow them to produce a number of bombs within a short time. According to Western intelligence reports, once Iran decides make the bomb, it will technically be able to so within about a year of taking the decision.

How to Stop Iran: The Diplomatic Option

The current debate on the Iranian nuclear issue is focussed on; can Iran be stopped from acquiring nuclear weapons? There are two main ways to stop Iran. The first option is diplomatic efforts and negotiations to convince Iran to suspend its uranium enrichment programme. While all the concerned governments prefer this option, since it involves no risk, there is an understanding that mere negotiations will not convince Iran to suspend its programme. The negotiations between Iran and the P5+1 governments (the permanent UN Security Council members plus Germany) began in 2002-2003, yet no real progress has been achieved. Iran has shown no signs of agreeing to compromise, and has used the negotiations to gain time to advance its nuclear programme.

In the background of this experience, there is today an international consensus that it is necessary to impose economic sanctions on Iran in order to induce it to compromise. Even the Russian and Chinese governments supported four resolutions to impose sanctions on Iran, in the UN Security Council between 2006-2010. But the Security Council sanctions were light, and until the summer of 2010, the sanctions had no real impact on the Iranian economy. There are two main reasons for this. First, there is no agreement regarding the severity of the sanctions and it is difficult to build a broad international consensus on the issue, in view of the economic and political interests of various governments with regard to Iran. The governments that have reservations, regarding sanctions, are mostly East Asian governments, that are importing increasing amounts of Iranian oil, as well as the Russian government which has close relations with Iran due to political and economic considerations. And second, Iran has been under Western economic sanctions since 1979. During this long period of time Iran has learned how to live with the sanctions, and has devised various ways that enable it to evade the sanctions and minimise their impact. Clearly, the fact that Iran is a major exporter of oil helps it to cope with the sanctions.

Since the summer of 2010, and especially since the summer of 2012, the American administration has imposed fresh and more severe sanctions on Iran. These sanctions have affected two of the most sensitive sectors of the Iranian economy: the oil sector and the banking system. Moreover, the European governments have also played their part in these sanctions, which has hurt the Iranians. The European governments have imposed an oil embargo on Iran, which—together with the isolation of the central bank of Iran—have hit the oil exports of Iran, and hence reduced the foreign currency revenues of the Iranian government. Many international companies have withdrawn from the Iranian economy and reduced their investments there, especially in the energy sector. As a result, the value of the Iranian currency, the Rial, has fallen, and the prices of many basic commodities have risen.

Yet, despite these painful sanctions, so far, there are no signs of Iran being willing to compromise. Iran is only indicating that it is ready to resume the negotiations on its nuclear programme, and perhaps might consider some arrangement regarding the enrichment of uranium to the level of 20 per cent conducted by Iran during 2011 to early 2013. But there is no suggestion, that Iran is willing to give up its efforts to develop nuclear weapons. It seems that at this stage the Iranian regime is willing to deal with the economic distress in order to acquire nuclear weapons, as long as the sanctions do not lead to domestic unrest, or as long as there is no imminent threat of a military attack against its nuclear sites.

The Military Option

The other option is the military option: a military operation against Iran's nuclear sites. There is no doubt that this is a problematic and controversial option. The operation is very complicated from the military viewpoint. The Iranians will probably respond by firing ballistic missiles and carrying out terror attacks against Israel and the United States, and perhaps against America's allies in the Gulf region. The Iranians might then try to rebuild their nuclear sites, and go all out for the bomb. Many governments will condemn the attack, and the Iranians might use it to get the sanctions lifted. The attack might also lead to a rise in oil prices. Such an operation is feasible: the United States is better equipped to carry it out, yet Israel claims that it can do it as well, although there are prominent political and military figures in Israel who are against such an operation.

Before taking the decision to attack, Israel will be required to answer a series of critical questions: What are the chances that the economic sanctions will prove to be effective? Are its military capabilities sufficient to carry out a successful operation? Is the intelligence needed for such an operation accurate enough?

How will Iran respond to such an attack, and what will be the impact of its response? How much time can be gained by destroying the nuclear installations? What will be the international and regional response, to the attack—including the reaction in Arab states? Will the American administration decide to carry out the attack? If it decides not to attack, will the administration give the "green light" to Israel to launch the attack? Can Israel initiate an attack without receiving the "green light" for the operation from the US administration? What is the optimal timing for the operation? How to balance the advantages and disadvantages of the operation? And finally, what is the alternative to a military operation? In other words, can Israel live under the shadow of nuclear Iran? This is a cluster of very difficult questions—each question is difficult to answer, and calculating the bottom-line answer to the entire set of questions, is even more difficult.

Due to the difficulties of a military operation, only two governments have even considered a military option—the American and the Israeli. All the other governments oppose such an operation and will not be a part of it. There is disagreement even between the Israeli government and the US administration. While the American administration maintains that all the options regarding Iran are on the table, including the military one, it also emphasises that current conditions are not ripe for a military attack on Iran. It claims that the economic sanctions route has not yet been exhausted, and that a military attack might not achieve its aim, because it will only delay the Iranian nuclear programme and will not stop it altogether; moreover the attack will have negative consequences in the Middle East, such as an Iranian response against US targets and its allies and a rise in oil prices.

On the other hand, Israel claims that the sanctions have not proved effective, since there are no indications that Iran has changed its mind regarding an agreement to suspend its nuclear programme. Moreover, Israel emphasises that time is running out and in the coming months Iran will enter what Israel has defined as the "zone of immunity", for two reasons: first, once Iran acquires its first bomb, or even produces enough fissile material for a bomb, it will be too late to attack; and second, Iran is constantly improving the security of its nuclear installations, and before long it will be very difficult to attack them—if at all. Moreover, it is clear that once Iran gets the bomb, there will be no chance, not only to attack it, but also to convince it to give up its nuclear weapons, which will then be a fait accompli. Hence, in 2012 Israel declared that it cannot wait indefinitely to undertake a military operation, and has asked the American administration to set a clear timetable for negotiations with Iran, after which a military operation will become inevitable. Israel has also asked the US administration, not to question the viability of the military attack, and avoid undermining it by highlighting the difficulties of the operation.

It should be emphasised that Israel is not alone in underscoring the serious need for considering the military option. The Wikileaks documents have revealed that in the last few years, several leaders of the Gulf states, and most importantly King Abdullah of Saudi Arabia, have been asking the American administration to make all necessary efforts to stop the Iranian nuclear programme, including a military operation. In addition, in the United States itself, a number of political and ex-military personalities have been saying that a nuclear Iran is more dangerous than a military attack against it.

Currently, the Obama administration is inclined to wait to assess the effectiveness of the sanctions and the outcome of the pressures exerted on Iran, and may try once again to negotiate with Iran. The administration is not very optimistic with regard to the outcome of future negotiation, for at least three reasons. First, Iran is still insisting that the European governments recognise its right to enrich uranium and lift the economic sanctions imposed on it. In other words, Iran wants to retain its capability to produce fissile material and develop the bomb. Second, during the last round of talks with Iran, in the spring of 2012, the Western governments insisted, among other demands, that Iran will close its nuclear site in Fordo—one of the most critical sites for Iran. Iran of course rejected this demand among others. And third, there is not even a minimal degree of trust between the parties, especially between Iran and the United States. Without trust, future negotiations are expected to fail as well.

So far, the strategy of the Obama administration has been to prevent Iran from acquiring nuclear weapons, not to contain it. This is a strong commitment. It means that Obama is committed to ensure, by all means, that Iran does not get the bomb; the US rejects the strategy of containment, which means that if Iran gets the bomb, it will make all efforts to deter Iran from launching a nuclear attack against any country. However, if the administration concludes that it has exhausted all diplomatic efforts, it might be faced with two very difficult options: to accept the fact that it cannot prevent Iran from going nuclear; or to carry out a military operation against Iran.

The Implications of a Nuclear Iran

The fact that until now diplomatic efforts have not managed to persuade Iran to suspend its nuclear programme; and that the military option is controversial and is strongly opposed even within the United States and Israel, has given rise to concerns that Iran will manage to acquire nuclear weapons despite pre-emptive efforts. This raises a very important question: what are the implications of a nuclear Iran? The prevailing view is that the acquisition of nuclear weapons by Iran will significantly contribute to the instability in the Middle East. A nuclear Iran might pursue a more aggressive policy—towards moderate Arab and Moslem regimes, as well as the American military presence in the Gulf. Iran is also likely to strengthen its position as the cornerstone of the radical Islamic camp, and pressurise the moderate regimes in the Middle East to adapt their policies to Iran.

And above all, other Middle East countries—especially Egypt, Syria, Saudi Arabia, Turkey, and in the longer run Syria and Iraq—might join the nuclear race and seek to develop their own nuclear capabilities. Until now only a few Arab states have tried to develop a nuclear military programme. The most advanced attempts were made by Iraq under Saddam Hussein during the 1970s and 1980s. Yet his nuclear facility was destroyed twice—by an Israeli aerial attack in June 1981 and by the US forces during the First Gulf War in 1991. Syria also tried to develop a nuclear programme, with North Korean assistance, in the early 2000s, but it too was destroyed in an Israeli aerial attack in September 2007. A few other Arab states, like Libya, also made the effort to do so but these were stopped in the initial stages.

It should be noted, that the fact, that Israel was assumed to have built a large arsenal of nuclear weapons since the 1960s, was not a reason for the Arab states to develop their own nuclear arsenals, perhaps with the exception of Syria. The reason for this is that Arab leaders are convinced that Israel is maintaining its nuclear arsenal only to thwart an extreme threat to its existence, and it does not intend to use it against Arab states under any other circumstances; since such extreme danger to Israel's existence was not expected, due to its military superiority over the Arab armed forces. Moreover, Arab leaders are aware that the United States would exert a heavy pressure on Israel to avoid using nuclear weapons, and would even send American forces, to defend Israel, in order to prevent an Israeli nuclear strike against the Arabs.

But the Arab leaders have a different view with regard to Iran. They are not concerned about an Iranian nuclear attack on their territories. Yet they are concerned about the regional implications of a nuclear Iran as mentioned above. Hence, one should take into consideration the fact that some Middle East governments could decide to follow the example of Iran, the more so, since if Iran goes nuclear, there will be two nuclear players in the Middle East—Iran and Israel. Each of these countries might have a different motivation for developing a nuclear weapon. For Egypt, the leader of the Arab world, it will be difficult to accept that not only Israel, but also Iran has acquired nuclear weapons. The same will also be true for Turkey. Saudi Arabia will face a new strategic threat emanating from Iran, and might need a deterrent in the form of a nuclear weapon. Iraq might choose to revive its programme, as might Syria.

The Implications for Israel

Israel is a unique case in this framework. In addition to all other implications, a nuclear Iran will exacerbate Israel's security concerns. By acquiring nuclear weapons Iran will create an additional layer of deterrence against Israel and the United States. Even the United States will find it more difficult to deter Iran once it possesses nuclear weapons, and its freedom of action vis-à-vis Iran will be reduced. If Iran obtains nuclear weapons it might provide Syria with a nuclear umbrella, in case of a confrontation with Israel. If this happens, it might encourage Syria, in the long run, to consider a military attack against Israel, and limit Israel's freedom of action and strategic deterrence in case of a military confrontation with Syria.

In addition, a nuclear Iran might limit Israel's freedom of action against the Hezbollah, and encourage that organisation to undertake military activities against Israel. Some observers suggest that Iran might provide terror organisations like Hezbollah with nuclear weapons. Yet the probability that Iran would do so seems low. It is doubtful what Iran can gain from doing so. If Iran arms Hezbollah with nuclear weapons, it will be immediately clear, that the weapons came from Iran. If the purpose is to defend the Hezbollah, Iran can do it by itself. Moreover, the possession of nuclear weapons might lead to the Hezbollah getting out of control, and in any case Syria would probably be opposed to the idea, that an organisation in its backyard should possess nuclear weapons.

More importantly, Israel has a unique perception of the threat emanating from nuclear Iran. As has been mentioned above, many governments are concerned about nuclear Iran, especially because of the element of instability that will be introduced into the Middle East. Yet none of these governments believes it is likely that Iran would attack their territory with nuclear weapons. Israel is different because the possibility of an Iranian nuclear attack against its territory is very real. This threat perception has two roots. First, if Iran goes nuclear, it will be the first time in the history of Israel, that an enemy country will acquire the capability to inflict a fatal blow against Israel. And second, Iranian top leaders are quite open about the need to eliminate Israel. The combination of these two elements—the future lethal capabilities and the intentions, as expressed by Iranian leaders—is the reason why many Israelis believe that nuclear Iran might pose a threat to Israel's existence.

Will Iran launch a nuclear attack against Israel? At the moment there is no clarity regarding the future Iranian nuclear policy, and it is possible that the Iranian regime has not decided, how it will use its nuclear weapons, once it acquires them. If Iran, however, chooses to be a rational player, it will probably not attack Israel, or any other country, with nuclear weapons. There are three reasons for this. It appears that Iran decided to build nuclear weapons for deterrence and defence—against Iraq in the past, and against the United States in the present. Though the Iranian leaders would like to wipe Israel off the map, as they suggest, they do not appear to have decided to develop nuclear weapons in order to achieve this aim. Moreover, the Iranians, like everybody else, believe that Israel has a large arsenal of nuclear weapons, and that probably Israel also has second strike capability. Hence, if Iran launches a nuclear attack against Israel, Israel would respond in the same coin, and the impact of a nuclear attack on Tehran—a capital with 14 million people—will be devastating for the Iranians. And finally, Iran is very much aware of the special relationship between the United States and Israel and that the American administration is committed to the existence and security of Israel. Hence, Iran will have to take into account, especially if America makes it clear, that a nuclear attack against Israel would be followed by an American nuclear attack against Iran.

This conclusion has three caveats. First, the assessment, that Iran possibly will not carry out a nuclear attack against Israel, though rational, could be baseless as such strategic assessments often are—more so, since there is no solid basis, for judging intentions. These assessments are based on assumptions, not on facts, because there are no indications with regard to its future nuclear policy. Second, it is difficult to judge the role of religious, ideological and fundamentalists in Iranian decision making. Iran has a unique leadership: It is the only regime where the supreme leader is not a politician or a military man, or an ex-military man; he is a religious leader, and religious leaders may have a different set of considerations, which may include religious motivation. In other words, the Iranian regime might be rational—but rational in Iranian terms, not necessarily in Western or democratic terms. Thus, one should not altogether rule out the possibility that the Iranian leaders might decide to carry out a nuclear attack against Israel, though the probability seems to be low.

And third, even if Iran does not decide to launch a nuclear attack against Israel, one should be wary of an unintended nuclear confrontation. Until now there has been no communication or dialogue between Iran and Israel, because Iran does not recognise Israel's right to exist and hence has rejected all such attempts. The acquisition of nuclear weapons by Iran will create two nuclear players in the Middle East—Iran and Israel—who have no communication between them. The outcome could be a rapid deterioration in the environment, even a nuclear confrontation, due to a misunderstanding, miscalculation or any other mistake. It should be emphasised that such a complete lack of dialogue between nuclear players, in the same neighbourhood, has never been seen in any other part of the world.

Israel is not alone in the front against nuclear Iran. Yet since Israel is in a unique position, the threat posed by a nuclear Iran will require Israel, together with other governments, to make all efforts necessary, to prevent Iran from acquiring nuclear weapons. At the same time, Israel and other Middle East countries will have to prepare themselves for such a scenario, and strengthen their deterrence against Iran. This will require also special efforts by the United States and other powers to make sure that Iran will never use its nuclear capabilities.

Finally, the regime change in Iran in August 2013 and the current interim agreement between Iran and the P5+1 has raised some hope regarding the disputed Iranian nuclear programme. It could be concluded that nuclear weapons in the hands of a moderate regime might be perceived as less threatening.

21

US Missile Defence in the Gulf

Rajendra Abhyankar and Weston Merrick

The United States and its allies in the Middle East have endeavoured to construct a regional missile defence system to limit the influence and deter aggression from the Islamic Republic of Iran. The perception among US foreign policy planners is that the construction of such a system will offer a credible commitment to US allies in the region. It is aimed at protecting population centres, military bases, and oil facilities from ballistic missile strikes. However, in the haste to complete the network, the US has not sufficiently answered whether they can overcome regional rivalries to create the network or indeed if the system will be effective in neutralising potential threats.

The project appears to have disregarded Henry Kissinger's cautionary note in *Diplomacy* that "American leaders have traditionally viewed diplomacy and strategy as separate activities. In the conventional view of the American military, they first achieve their outcome and then the diplomats take over; neither ever tells the other how to pursue its objectives… if military and political goals are not synchronized from the beginning, there is always a danger of doing either too much or too little."[1]

The construction of this network also suffers from the misperception among American military planners that missile defence is a "cure without side effects."[2] The deployment of this system in the world's most volatile region, almost certainly, will have profound unintended consequences: destabilizing the existing military balance, initiating a broader arms race and reducing the incentives to find diplomatic solutions to on-going conflicts. Lastly, this deployment will spark questions from Russia and China about the America's broader intentions.

The increasing militarisation of the Gulf and ratcheting up of tensions which the system represents will jeopardize Gulf security and could directly impact oil flows to India as well as the future of its large Diaspora in the region. The system itself also represents a 'technology demonstrator' for India in the context of its defence posture vis-à-vis Pakistan and China.

Background

The Islamic Republic of Iran has been increasingly building offensive ballistic missiles that threaten US strategic interests (including allied territory, military assets, and economic interests) in the Middle East (Figure 1). To blunt the threat posed by Iran, the US is attempting to knit together a system of ground and sea-based early warning radar sites and missile interceptors in the Gulf. Presently, the US is negotiating bilateral missile defence sales with Gulf Cooperation Council (GCC) countries, including Bahrain, Kuwait, Oman, Qatar, Saudi Arabia, and the United Arab Emirates (UAE), as well as Turkey and Israel.

At this time, the most sophisticated missile defence system in the region belongs to Israel. After their experience with scud missile attacks in the Gulf War and the constant harassment by elements of Hamas Israel has spared no expense in creating a multi-level defensive system called the "Iron Dome" which is a joint US-Israel venture that pairs land-based interceptors with naval and land-based radar systems. The US has already contributed more than $275 million to its construction.[3] In late November 2012 this system was tested against thousands of rockets launched by Hamas. Overall, the system was extremely effective in defeating short and middle range missiles. The Israeli Government claimed that the system was able to shoot down 84 per cent of missiles that posed a threat to civilians though these numbers are contested.[4] Nevertheless, it should be pointed out that the system is yet to be tested against more sophisticated long range missiles.[5]

Unfortunately, this success, coupled with the likely success of Benjamin Netanyahu at the forthcoming general elections, may produce the unintended consequence of limiting the desire of Israel to engage in diplomatic efforts to address the source of these attacks: the two-state solution on the Israel-Palestine conflict.

Iranian Perception

Tehran views America's offensive ballistic missile capabilities as an instrument of Western aggression and imperialism in the region which raises the ante beyond their existing army base facilities in Saudi Arabia, UAE, Qatar and Kuwait and naval base facilities in Bahrain. Iran also believes that American intentions are to overthrow the theocratic regime and thus maintaining a credible threat becomes a priority to thwart that ambition.

Iran also suffers from the animosity of Western powers displayed through the wide range of United Nations and United States' sanctions currently in place on export of oil, banking, and import of spares for US-made aircraft and other machinery and foreign travel of selected Iranian nationals. Furthermore, while other countries in West and Central Asia benefit from Western arms sales and military aid, Iran has powerful sanctions levied on it preventing the acquisition of convention weapon systems. To make up for this lack of conventional strength, Iran has built up power asymmetric weapons that give it material and psychological power disproportionate to their actual military prowess (see Table 1 for regional military expenditures).[6] Therefore, any weapons system that is able to dampen the effectiveness of Iranian's asymmetric military ability will be viewed by Iran as a hostile attempt at subjugation.

Most Salient Challenges

Mistrust in the Region

The major practical difficulty in implementation of an integrated missile defence is the traditional rivalry amongst the Gulf countries involved in the system. The regional architecture, which the US has been advocating since the Clinton Administration, will raise the effectiveness of the entire system by more readily and rapidly sharing data. As noted by one senior US official "No one nation can protect itself. It needs to rely on its partners in order to have an effective missile defence system."[7]

The sanguine appearance that the GCC presents as unified front in promoting the well-being of its member-states belies the sense of unease between the nations in the pact. Realism and balance of power remain the dominant paradigm in the region and none of these states are keen on seeing any other become too powerful.[8] A state impermeable to offensive weapons because of the missile defence system could upset the balance of the region. This worry is particularly acute for small countries like Dubai, Bahrain, Qatar, and most importantly, Kuwait which remembers the lessons of the Gulf War, namely, what occurs when one state unbalances the system.[9]

As such regional prestige and competition should not be discounted as a factor in the unease between these countries. Brian Pellot, a Marshall Scholar and MENA journalist noted, in a recent interview, that the GCC countries are presently engaged in "culture wars"; with each nation vying for an expansion of their soft power.[10] Pellot pointed out this competition is tied deeply to honour and these fissures are unlikely to abate in the near term.

The US has taken some steps to ameliorate the frictions inside the GCC such as the US-GCC Strategic Cooperation Forum (SCF) hosted in March of 2012 by the State Department. The conference aimed to "[provide] a more structured framework for ministerial meetings and for guiding the work of a set of committees to take coordinated steps across the security, political, and economic realms."[11] While these talks bode well for greater regional integration, press releases from SCF meetings are notably vague on concrete steps to increase cooperation.[12]

Even more acute a problem is the mutual animosity between GCC member-states and Israel. The US believes it is critical to integrate the Israeli missile defence shield in to the broader regional network; however, cooperation between Arab nations and Israel on a defence project is virtually unthinkable. Pellot points out that this disdain stems not only from religious differences but also from jealousy over Israel's technological prowess and special relationship with the US.[13] The acrimony may be at an all-time high with Israel's recent aerial offensive in Gaza. In fact, many GCC countries, like Qatar, rushed to the aid of Palestine after the attack.[14] If the GCC is to cooperate with Israel on missile defence it may need to be part of a larger framework that resolves the Palestinian statehood question.

Lastly, the presence of US facilities and personnel is a continuing sore point for Islamic factions in the allied Gulf countries. In fact, this presence of "infidels" in Saudi Arabia during the Gulf War was one of the major grievances of Osama Bin Laden against the United States.[15] The GCC nations will have to weigh whether or not the safety provided by American military forces is worth antagonising their populations. In context of the misnamed 'Arab Spring', the United States also needed to consider contingency plans in case any participating government was to falter.

Actual Effectiveness of Missile Defence System

Another challenge is the technological dimension: whether the missile defence will actually be successful in shooting down all potential targets. There are several difficulties implicit here. First, the technology has not been effective in even ideal practice conditions, let alone in real life against medium and long-range ballistic missiles. These failures largely come from the difficulty of identifying, locating and targeting a missile in time to shoot it down.[16] In the US Department of Defense tests SM-3, the most sophisticated of the missile interceptors, failed to destroy 8 out of 10 targets.[17]

Second, any ballistic missile fired will likely have counter-measures that could render the interceptor ineffective.[18] In fact, Iran has already demonstrated that their rockets have this highly effective technology. The US Department of Defense test included no such counter-measures.

Third, missile interceptors are much more expensive than building ballistic missiles themselves. Therefore, Iran may simply build and launch more missiles than the US and her allies have the capacity to shoot down. Interceptors, not including the fixed cost of launchers and radars, cost near $50,000 a piece[19] while ballistic missiles cost much less (as little as $800 for short-range rockets used by Hamas). A 2008 article in *Janes Weekly* indicated this may already be the case as Iran has reportedly increased the size of their Shahab-3 long-range missile arsenal from 30 to 100 missiles in 2008 alone.[20] Furthermore, Iran understands from its experience observing US "Scud-hunting" in the Gulf War that as soon as it would launch its first strike there would be a swift retaliation against all remaining missile sites.[21] Therefore, Iran may be in a "use them or lose them scenario" where it launches a massive barrage all-at-once to overwhelm the defences.

This difficultly dovetails with the larger problem of regional mistrust and presents a classic prisoners dilemma. If, for example, Qatar detects a Shabab-3 launch and determines the target is a strike of the F-22 stealth fighters housed at the Al Dafra Air Base in the UAE, Qatar may be reluctant to launch its missiles in defence of UAE knowing that any effort to protect its neighbour will limit its own defensive capacity.

Key Undercurrents

Iran's Nuclear Ambitions

United States' haste to build a comprehensive missile defence network in the Gulf is accentuated by recent revelations that Iran may well possess nuclear weapon capability in the next two to five years.[22] The UN's nuclear watchdog, the International Atomic Energy Agency (IAEA), published a report in late 2011 that Iran has enriched uranium to 19.75 per cent, which can quickly be converted to weapons grade (85 per cent). The report also noted that the amount of uranium Iran presently has, if further refined could produce five nuclear bombs. Iran may have enough fissionable material to create a bomb by 2013 and the expertise to put it in a warhead by 2015.[23]

China and Russia

Latent in this argument is that this missile defence system could also be used to reduce the effectiveness of nuclear weapons possessed by Russia and China. This is particularly clear when we consider that this missile system is being built concurrently with systems in Europe and Japan. The United States contends that these systems are necessary as Iran's missiles can presently reach NATO allies like Turkey and Poland and will in the future be able to hit all of Europe.[24] The recent stationing of US Patriot missile batteries in Turkey on its border with Syria in response to the on-going civil war there represents the moving of one more chip in this nascent defence framework.

The Japanese system is being built under the guise that North Korea Taepodong-2 missile can presently strike Japan and in the future will soon be able to reach America's west coast.[25] However, Russia and China believe this to be a thinly veiled attempt to shift the balance of Nuclear Détente.[26] The fact that these missile defence systems are being erected simultaneously with the US 'pivot' towards Asia only raises further questions in China. America needs to work to clarify their intentions with Russia and China to lower tensions arising from the proposed deployment of the system.

Regional Arms Race

The last undercurrent is that increased Iranian weapons capabilities could lead to a regional arms race. This could happen in three ways. First, Iran could increase its stock of ballistic weapons so as to defeat the interceptors. This may spark fear among other countries in the region that missile defence will be ineffective prompting the Gulf countries to acquire more first and second-strike weaponry, like attack aircraft and cruise missiles, thus fuelling the arms race.

Second, if Iran were to approach or declare success at nuclear weaponisation, Israel or even the United States, may launch a first-strike in an effort to destroy as much fissionable and offensive weaponry as possible (for more discussion on the likelihood, viability, and impacts of this assault see the footnote).[27]

Third, if Iran were to acquire nuclear missiles, and it was determined that missile defence would be ineffective in halting a missile salvo, then major regional players (like Saudi Arabia, and Egypt) may attempt to acquire their own nuclear capabilities.[28]

Implications for India

Military and political developments in the Gulf directly impinge on India's security perimeter and are of priority concern. India has been following the United States aim to install a missile defence system in the Gulf. However, it has yet to fully discuss it in its strategic dialogue with the United States. India's view on the setting up of the system would be informed by the following considerations:

1. The primary goal of the missile defence system in the Gulf is to deter an attack by Iran on the GCC countries and represent a ratcheting up of tensions in the Gulf. India has prolific and friendly relations with both the GCC states and Iran and it would be loath to have to choose between either. India has strictly observed UN sanctions and has gone some distance in accommodating US sanctions on Iran. There are limits to the extent beyond which India cannot go given the criticality of both the Gulf countries and Iran to its energy security.
2. Any increase in military tensions or a military conflagration involving Iran will negatively impact the five million strong Indian diaspora living and working in the GCC. India will be forced to act to assure their safety even if it means bringing large numbers back to the country. The logistics of such a large displacement apart, its social and political effects domestically and its adverse impact on inward remittances will be massive.
3. The use by Israel of its 'Iron Dome' missile interceptor system in the recent conflict with Hamas proved a 'technology demonstrator' not only from India's point of view but from that of the GCC countries as well. Notwithstanding its current deficiencies the system works. India would be well aware that in a medium to long-term sense such a system has value for its defence posture vis-à-vis Pakistan and China.

Recommendations

It takes merely a cursory glance at past trends and currents strategic capabilities to see that any future military confrontation in region could involve the use of ballistic missiles so long as the US continues to pursue installation and integration of defensive missile systems in the Gulf. The US would need to seek a transparent and binding multilateral agreement among Middle East allies to create a unified missile system that will allow for certainty that all countries in the missile pact will act in the collective interest in preventing missile strikes.

While missile defence may have a strong future in protecting bases and populations from attack, it does nothing to fix the root of these conflicts. Missile defence is merely a tourniquet being applied to more systematic diplomatic woes. The US two-track model of harsh sanctions for pursing nuclear weapons and economic inducements, if Iran cuts their nuclear weapons programme, will have limited success as Iran crosses the nuclear weapon threshold. The US must do more to remedy the source of the problem through diplomacy and multilateral peace agreements. To this end, the US needs to engage in direct dialogue with Iran. Missile defence should be simultaneously pursued with an open dialogue with China and Russia even though they will be comfortable with US's continuing efforts to create a missile defence programme. This dialogue will at minimum reduce the likelihood of misunderstanding that leads to conflict. Similarly, the United States needs a similar dialogue with India given it will directly impact its security, both military and energy.

In the end, America's ability to sync both the military and diplomatic components of the Middle East missile defence system will determine whether this system decreases conflict in the region or accelerates it.

NOTES

1. Kissinger, H., *Diplomacy*, 1994, New York: Simon & Shuster, p. 479.
2. Senn, M., *The Arms-Dynamic Pacemaker*, Retrieved November 1, 2012, from MEPC: http://www.mepc.org/journal/middle-east-policy-archives/arms-dynamic-pacemaker-ballistic-missile-defense-middle-east, p. 1.
3. Shanker, T., and Broad, W., "Israel's Antimissile System Attracts Potential Buyers", *New York Times*, November 29, 2012.
4. Ibid
5. See no. 2.
6. Ibid.
7. *Travels with the Secretary, Press Briefing En Route Riyadh*, March30, 2012, at http://www.susrisblog.com/2012/03/30/travels-with-the-secretary-press-briefing-enroute-riyadh/, accessed on November 19, 2012, from Suris Blog.
8. Walt, S., *The Curious Case of Small Gulf States*, at http://walt.foreignpolicy.com/posts/2012/11/12/the_curious_case_of_small_gulf_states, accesed on November 12, 2012.
9. Ibid.
10.. Pellot, B., "Media and Culture in GCC Countries", November 7, 2012, (W. Merrick, Interviewer).

11. *Senior Administration Officials Preview of the US-GCC Strategic Cooperation Forum,* (September 2, 2012), at http://www.state.gov/r/pa/prs/ps/2012/09/198424.htm., accessed on November 1, 2012, from US Department of State.
12. *Joint Communiqué from US-GCC Strategic Cooperation Forum*, October 1, 2012 http://translations.state.gov/st/english/texttrans/2012/10/20121001136929.html#axzz2CaXHg3aY, accessed from US Embassy Press Release on November, 2012.
13. Pellot, B., no. 10.
14. Shavit, A., "Gaza's Ghost", *The New Yorker*, November 21, 2012.
15. Slate, "Why US Military Bases are Good for Mecca and Medina?", *Slate Magazin,* October 15, 2001.
16. Inexplicably the official DOD report called these tests a success. Haddick, R., "This is Not a Test", *Foreign Policy,* August 17, 2012, at http://www.foreignpolicy.com/articles/2012/08/17/this_is_not_a_test, accessed on October 22, 2012.
17. Postol, G.L., *A Flawed and Danger US Missile Defense Plan*, May 2010, at http://www.armscontrol.org/act/2010_05/Lewis-Postol/., accessed on November 2012, from Arms Control Association.
18. Sessler, A., Cornwall, J., Fetter, S., and Wright, D., *Countermeasures,* April 2012, http://www.ucsusa.org/assets/documents/nwgs/cm_all.pdf, accesed on November 12, 2012, from UCSUSA.
19. Defence Professionals., May 17, 2009, *Protection for Israeli citizens against rocket attacks.* at http://www.defpro.com/daily/details/277/., accesed on November 20, 2012.
20. Ben-David, A., *Iran accelerates missile production in preparation for possible conflict*, December 11, 2008, at http://www.janes.com/products/janes/defence-security-report.aspx?id=1065927081, accessed in November 2012, from Janes.
21. Boxx, E., *Countering the Iranian Missile Threat in the Middle East*, October 18, 2012, http://www.washingtoninstitute.org/policy-analysis/view/countering-the-iranian-missile-threat-in-the-middle-east., accesed on November 1, 2012, from *The Washington Institute.*
22. "Sticks Now, Carrots Later", *The Economist,* May 19, 2012, at http://www.economist.com/node/21555540., accessed on November 2, 2012, from *The Economist.*
23. Kerr, P. K., *Iran's Nuclear Program: Status, October 17, 2012,* at http://www.fas.org/sgp/crs/nuke/RL34544.pdf, accessed on November 20, 2012, from Congressional Research Service.
24. See Figure 1 for map of range of Shabab-3 Missiles.
25. Ryall, J., "North Korea Claims US is within Missile Range", *The Telegraph*, October 9, 2012.
26. WSJ., "Panetta Announces US Expansion of Missile Defense", September 17, 2012.
27. For more discussion see "Why Iran Should Get the Bomb" by Kenneth Waltz, "Time to Attack Iran" by Matthew Kroenig, and "The Israeli Debate on Attacking Iran is Over" by Shai Feldman.
28. Cook, S., *Don't Fear a Nuclear Arms Race in the Middle East*, April 2, 2012 http://www.foreignpolicy.com/articles/2012/04/02/don_t_fear_a_nuclear_arms_race, accessed on November 12, 2012, from Foreign Policy; Many Middle East experts doubt that Egypt or Saudi Arabia would seek nuclear weapons in this scenario. For more discussion see, Leiber, K., & Press, D., "The Rise of US Nuclear Primacy", *Foreign Affairs, 85*(46), 2006.

Appendix

Table 1: Regional Military Expenditures

Year	Iran		Saudi Arabia		Kuwait		UAE	
	constant (2005) $ millions	% of GDP	constant (2005) $ millions	% of GDP	constant (2005) $ millions	% of GDP	constant (2005) $ millions	% of GDP
1995	1,753	1.8	13,099	9.3	4,525	13.6	3,011	5.5
1996	1,948	1.9	13,078	8.5	3,848	10.3	2,982	5.1
1997	2,171	2.1	17,760	11	2,933	8.1	3,016	4.8
1998	2,290	2.4	20,513	14.3	2,735	8.8	2,986	5.1
1999	3,200	3	18,260	11.4	2,658	7.6	2,950	4.3
2000	4,731	3.8	20,125	10.6	3,082	7.2	2,876	3.4
2001	5,220	4	21,434	11.5	3,029	7.7	2,836	3.4
2002	3,926	2.5	18,817	9.8	3,126	7.4	2,862	3.3
2003	4,594	2.9	18,956	8.7	3,369	6.5	2,807	2.8
2004	5,816	3.3	21,074	8.4	3,679	5.9	2,585	2.3
2005	7,213	4.6	25,393	8	3,909	4.7	2,559	1.9
2006	7,677	4.6	28,926	8.5	3,909	4	—	—

Source: http://www.mepc.org/journal/middle-east-policy-archives/arms-dynamic-pacemaker-ballistic-missile-defense-middle-east

Figure 1: Range of Shabab-3 Missiles

Sources: ESRI, US Department of Defense; Graphics reporting by Tom Reinken; Mark Haper, *Los Angeles Times*.

Figure 2: The Gaza Case Study

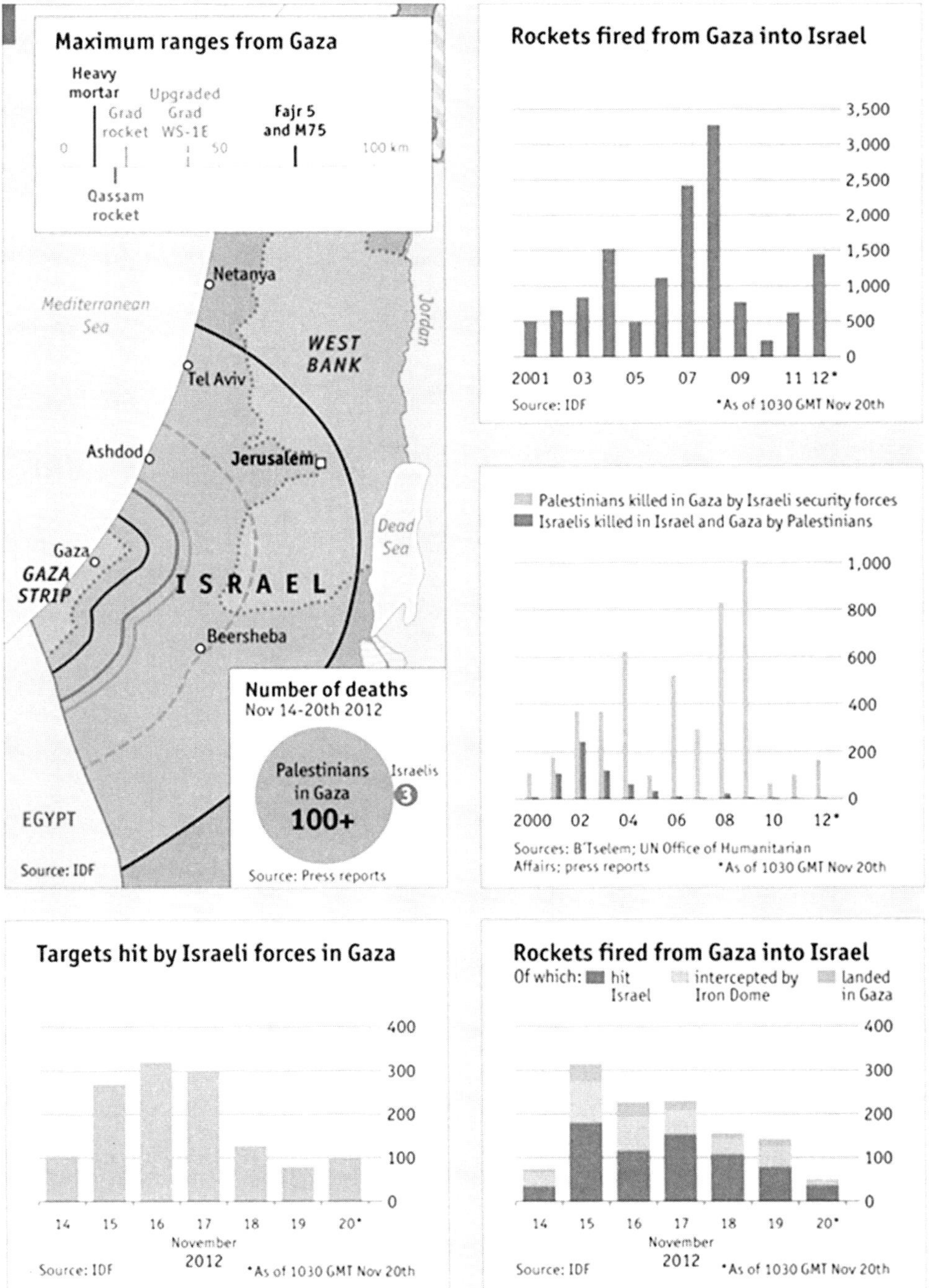

Source: Economist.com/graphicdetail.

PART VII

Role of Asia in Evolving Security Dynamics and Architecture of the Gulf Region

22

Role of Asia in the Evolving Security Dynamics of the Gulf Region

Ranjit Gupta

Introduction

For purposes of this essay, the Gulf region consists of the six GCC countries, Iran and Iraq; and, West Asia, of which the Gulf region is a sub-region, that is considered to be an integral geographical part of "Asia".

This paper is in the nature of an essay with three components: first, it makes an assessment of the main security challenges currently facing the region; second, it reviews the current security architecture in the region; third, it assesses the need for new approaches in the region and particularly examines the possibilities of Asia's potential involvement in the security dynamics of the Gulf region.

Asia currently has no meaningful involvement in security arrangements, in and of the Gulf region. Thus, this paper explores the possibilities of something that does not yet exist. Therefore, the conclusions of the essay constitute a throwing up of ideas and possibilities for discussion rather than those of a research paper. The paper is written from the perspective of a diplomatic practitioner, rather than that of an academic or scholar.

Security Challenges in the Gulf Region

Beyond the standard normative definitions of what constitutes national security and regional security, each region of the world has security issues that are unique to that particular region. Four factors stand out in relation to security in and of the Gulf region in the current context.

First, the emergence of the Islamic Republic of Iran in 1979 completely changed the existing security dynamics of the Gulf region by introducing three new factors: firstly, the more or less dormant historical Shia-Sunni and Arab-Persian divides were resurrected and have since occupied centre stage of the intra-regional security scenario. Secondly, Saddam invaded a perceived unstable Iran in 1980 starting the decade long Iraq Iran war, which ended in a stalemate despite Iraq being supported by the GCC and the Western countries; however, apart from greatly weakening both countries, this further accentuated the sectarian divide and confirmed Iran's isolation within the region. Thirdly, to collectively face the new challenge posed by an assertive, ideologically hyperactive Iran the six Arabian Peninsula monarchies established the Gulf Cooperation Council (GCC) in 1981. In the past three years, these sectarian antagonisms have acquired menacing new dimensions in view of the events set in motion by the Arab Spring.

Within weeks of the protests in Tunisia and Egypt the wave hit Bahrain. The protest movement in Bahrain was not originally motivated by sectarian considerations but by a quest for dignity and equality through greater economic opportunities and political freedom for all its citizens. However, alarm bells rang out loudly in Saudi Arabia as Bahrain is less than 30 kms off its oil rich eastern seaboard where both Saudi Arabia's oil riches and its disenchanted Shiite population are concentrated. The hard line Bahraini prime minister, the King's uncle who has held this job since Bahrain's independence in 1971, Saudi Arabia and the UAE, immediately accused Iran of instigating the huge daily demonstrations. Bahraini police and security forces came down hard on them. Saudi Arabia and the UAE dispatched troops to Bahrain soon thereafter. Saudi Arabia has made it abundantly clear that the monarchy in Bahrain—or indeed in any other GCC state—will not be allowed to fall. The GCC collectively endorsed the hard line Saudi and UAE approach. Both the Western allies of the GCC countries as well as the major Asian countries chose not to get involved in the Bahraini imbroglio.

The estimated Shiite population percentages in GCC countries are: Bahrain around 68 per cent; Kuwait about 30 per cent; Saudi Arabia about 18 per cent; Qatar and UAE about 10 per cent; and, Oman about 8 per cent. About 65 per cent of Iraqis are Shia. Including Iran—which is 90 per cent Shia—more than 60 per cent of the combined populations of the 8 countries of the Gulf region are Shia. Yemen has a 35 per cent Shia population. More than 50 per cent of the Arab Gulf region's oil reserves are located in the Shiite populated parts of the region. Following the US engineered downfall of the Sunni regime in Iraq, Shia political forces emerged as the predominant component of the country's ruling dispensation for the first time in modern history. Iran now has much more influence in Iraq than its fellow Arab countries. The Shias of Iraq and the GCC countries have been consistently discriminated against and treated as second class citizens. Furthermore, there is a huge and unbridgeable asymmetry between the GCC countries' national power and that of Iran in terms of demography, institutional capacity, military manpower strength and indigenous technological capabilities. All these features give Iran the enormous potential leverage of exploiting Shiite grievances, using the bond of overarching Shiite identity, to disturb, even reshape, the balance of power in the Arabian Peninsula and the Gulf region. Saudi Arabia is acutely aware and traumatically afraid of these possibilities and realities. It has thus adopted the principle, that offence is the best form of defence. Hence, the happenings in Bahrain prompted Saudi Arabia to launch a high profile campaign against Iran, once again actively supported by the GCC. This has been mostly egregiously manifested in Syria.

Syria has been Iran's longest standing and staunchest ally in the Arab world. Alone amongst Arab countries it had supported Iran in the Iran-Iraq war. Syria has been the main conduit of Iran's formidable influence in the Levant, providing it vital connectivity enabling it to create the Hezbollah, between 1982-85, and sustaining it in Lebanon and supporting the Hamas in Gaza, both of which have acquired 'halo' status on the 'Arab Street' due to their uncompromising opposition to Israel. Iran has thus projected itself as the main defender of Palestinian rights and interests and undermined the credibility of Arab regimes in the eyes of their own peoples. If Assad's regime were to fall Iran would find it virtually impossible to support Hezbollah and Iranian influence in the sensitive Levantine region would be dealt a virtual death blow. Iran's ability to play an intrusive role in Arab politics would also be severely curtailed. Hamas has already moved under the umbrella of the Muslim Brotherhood of Egypt, of which it was originally an offshoot. The issue is no longer about political reform or democracy in Syria but about staunching Iranian capabilities and influence in the Arab world. Therefore, the overthrow of the Bashar al-Assad regime became the publicly proclaimed Saudi/Qatari objective and that of Western nations too. At stake is the future balance of power in West Asia as a whole, with obviously important ramifications for the Gulf region.

The 'Arab Spring' arrived in Syria in March 2011. Once Assad had decided that he was not going to depart like Mubarak or Ben Ali, overthrowing his regime was never going to be easy, as, unlike them, he had reasonably strong broad based support in the country, despite heading a despotic regime. Eight months ago it seemed that the balance was tilting against Assad, and it was only a question of time when he would be overthrown; but equations started changing perceptibly in favour of the Assad regime due to growing disunity within opposition ranks and the rising doubts in the minds of external supporters due to the increasing strength of radical elements, in particular the Al-Qaeda linked Islamic state of Iraq and the Levant (ISIL) and also another Al-Qaeda linked entity the Jabhat al-Nusrah. Current estimates suggest that between them they have more than 20,000 fighters and are the best armed and equipped rebel groups in addition, there are the fighters of other Islamists groups, numbering another 40,000 or so. Together these Islamists outnumber other opposition groups, who have a numerical strength of about 40,000, but are splintered into a large number of factions. They have broken away from the Syrian National Alliance and the Syrian National Army whose credibility has progressively diminished and is increasingly restricted to their GCC, Jordanian, Turkish and Western patrons.

Britain, France and the US threatened to intervene militarily following the alleged use of chemical weapons by the Assad regime; this lead to Russia and Iran bolstering support to Assad and very strong dissenting voices within the three Western countries against military intervention. Russia persuaded Assad to surrender Syria's entire arsenal of chemical weapons and this finally led to an agreement for a peaceful resolution of the issue endorsed by the U.N. Security Council. This has prevented an already serious security situation in Syria from worsening further. The opposition groups within Syria have opposed this solution insisting that Assad be punished for use of chemical weapons; Saudi Arabia and other actively involved GCC countries are disappointed that there was no military action against Assad. These reactions are a clear giveaway of their essential agenda of regime change, an issue that still remains on the table. Given Syria's complex ethnic and religious mix, the situation on the ground is likely to be much worse than that in post-2003 Iraq, if Assad is overthrown, with unpredictable consequences for West Asia as a whole, but particularly the Levantine region. If Assad remains the civil war will continue. The only way that peace will be restored in Syria will be if either outcome is the result of a negotiated settlement. In this context, the recent Russian initiative was welcomed around the world with a loud sigh of relief, and together with positive Western responses, represents the first sign of international cooperation in the Syrian context. The exchange of letters and a telephone conversation between the Iranian and US presidents, a 30 minute tete-a- tete between the US secretary of state and the Iranian foreign minister and the meeting between the Iranian foreign minister and the foreign ministers of the P-5 plus Germany, are particularly positive developments. Hopefully, all this will lead to the convening of the Geneva Conference in which all the countries directly involved in the Syrian imbroglio can participate to hammer out a solution. Whatever the outcome in Syria, for the Gulf region, the major consequence of the turmoil in the Arab world over the past three years, has been the open no-holds-barred eruption of a particularly nasty power struggle between Saudi Arabia/the GCC countries and Iran. This is the single most important security related issue in the region. Russia has made a dramatic re-entry into the West Asian security arena, thus injecting an important new element into the region.

Second, Arab countries have rarely, had other than autocratic regimes. This has been particularly the case in the countries of the Gulf region where the absolute rule of monarchs, military and other dictators, tribal sheikhs, Imams, etc. has been the norm.

In the past three years, strong and unfamiliar winds of change have been gusting through the Arab world and except for Qatar, all Arab countries have witnessed anti-government demonstrations and protests of varying intensity. Five countries were engulfed by particularly tumultuous convulsions. Two strongly entrenched ruthless autocratic dictators—in Tunisia, in power for 23 years, and in Egypt, in power for 32 years—were overthrown quickly and with surprising ease because the army chose not to confront the people. There has been regime change in another two—Libya (after 42 years of Qaddafi's dictatorial rule) and Yemen (after Ali Abdullah Saleh had been in power for 33 years) following civil wars and due to foreign intervention. A fifth—Syria—is in the throes of an escalating and devastatingly destructive civil war. In Bahrain, the revolt has for all practical purposes been squelched but smaller demonstrations continue to underscore the uneasy and tense coexistence between the regime and the Shia majority of the population. The main fear in GCC regimes is not of the people revolting per se, but of Iranian inspired and instigated subversion by Shia minorities, jointly with other Islamist elements.

Petrified regimes in the GCC countries have carefully observed the evolving events and drawn lessons from the outcomes. Regime preservation and regime security, always paramount, have now become the obsessively preeminent priority for the ruling monarchs in GCC countries, whatever the cost, in blood and treasure. A significant consequence has been that the decades old security dependence of the regimes of the GCC countries on the United States, which had come under increasing internal questioning in the GCC countries due to US policies in the region post 9/11, has acquired a renewed salience.

Third, turmoil in broad swathes of the Arab world involving protests by the masses in unprecedentedly large numbers has resulted, inter alia, in the emergence of Islam as an increasingly significant strategic factor in the region. This has two dimensions—political Islam and militant Islam.

Banned, exiled and persecuted Islamic entities were neither in the vanguard nor even active participants in the protest demonstrations, but the so-called 'Arab Spring' resulted in their emergence into the open. Their underground organisational networks were activated and they were thus much better placed to take advantage of the newly emerging political opportunities. Another bonus was that unlike in the past when their electoral success in Algeria was violently overturned, or, as in the case of Hamas in Gaza, greatly emaciated, due to a boycott by most Arab and Western countries who are the major players in the region; this time around, the electoral success of Islamic parties was accepted both domestically and by the world at large. Tunisia is ruled by Islamic parties. The Muslim Brotherhood, the oldest Islamist political entity in the Arab world, which had heretofore perforce played the role of agitator, assassin, insurgent and opponent, came to power in Egypt through the ballot box. However, it clearly lacked any mandate to make Egypt an Islamist state, but nevertheless attempted to impose its Islamist agenda on the country in a hurry and incurred the wrath of vast swathes of the people and the army and was packed off. How the situation will evolve in the immediate future is uncertain but Islam as a political factor in Egypt can no longer be suppressed. An Islamist party won the largest number of seats and heads the governing coalition in Morocco. Post Qaddafi Libya rapidly slipped into chaos and though elections have been held with the moderate pro-business National Forces Alliance winning an unexpected landslide victory, against the Islamist parties, the country is infested by numerous armed militant groups, many of them salafists; the country continues to be wracked by instability with the government's writ being very weak in most parts of the country, and therefore the Islamists will inevitably play an increasing role sooner rather later. Irrespective of the outcome of the civil war in Syria, given the predominance of hard line extremist Islamic elements amongst the rebels and the fact of Syria being a Sunni majority country, the Islamic factor will inevitably and to a considerable extent shape the composition of any new ruling dispensation.

Apart from the domestic socio-political consequences of the rule of Islamist parties, there will certainly be foreign policy reorientations. Egypt is poised to reclaim a central role in the Arab world. Egyptian foreign policy under Morsy had exhibited a marked contrast with that of Mubarak'. Egypt's unmitigated hostility of the past towards Iran was replaced by a policy of engagement. President Morsy and President Ahmadinejad exchanged visits albeit in multilateral contexts. Iranian military vessels now pass through the Suez Canal routinely. Even after Morsy's ouster the deep animosity of the past is unlikely to be revived.

While the world has little option but to engage with the new Islamists, there are reasons for regimes, particularly in Arab countries ruled by monarchs, to be concerned. Even as Qatar is flamboyantly courting the Muslim Brotherhood and similar Islamist groups, Jordan, Kuwait, Saudi Arabia and the UAE are clamping down strongly on local Muslim Brotherhood cells that are allegedly actively engaged in regime threatening and destabilsing subversive activity. Kuwait, Saudi Arabia and the UAE actively supported the army's overthrowing of the Muslim Brotherhood regime in Egypt. The Muslim Brotherhood is once again been comprehensively targeted and persecuted in Egypt and this is a recipe for continuing instability as the Islamist genie cannot be put back into the bottle.

Governments of Islamist parties are, almost certainly, likely to shed the erstwhile overly pro-Western orientations, bring the Palestinian issue back to centre stage and have foreign policies that are more in the national interest and imbued with pan-Arab nationalism. All this will inevitably have, security related implications in the longer term.

Like the rest of the world, Al-Qaeda was surprised by the extremely large, and what were initially essentially secular and nonviolent revolutionary movements, that toppled dictators in Tunisia, Egypt, Libya and Yemen. Like its political counterparts such as the Muslim Brotherhood and the Ennahda, Al-Qaeda exploited the chaos and turmoil to infiltrate the protest movements. Though Al-Qaeda is an extremist movement that appeals only to a small minority, numbers in themselves are not important as their terrorist attacks have widespread destabilising impact.

Al-Qaeda is now operating in Algeria, Egypt—in the Sinai Peninsula, Iraq, Libya, Syria and Yemen. In Yemen, the Al-Qaeda in the Arabian Peninsula (AQAP) has established several secure enclaves and is posing an increasing threat to normalisation. In North Africa, the Al-Qaeda in the Islamic Maghreb (AQIM) has become strongly entrenched especially around Benghazi and a faction led by Mokhtar Belmokhtar staged the recent deadly attack in Algeria, from Libya. It has successfully aligned itself with a local extremist group in Mali named Ansar Dine, or Defenders of the Faith, and together they had effectively taken control of the northern two-thirds of Mali, until the French intervention. In Somalia it has been in active partnership with the local militant outfit Al Shabab. The Al-Qaeda continues to be an active force in Iraq against the Shia government of Maliki. The Al-Qaeda in Syria and the Levant (ISIL) and the Jabahat al Nusra have become and the most lethal elements of the armed struggle against the Assad regime.

The resurgence of militant Islam in the guise of Al-Qaeda and a host of related local militant Islamic groups is a matter of increasing concern both to the governments of Arab countries as well as those of the wider world.

Fourth, in December 2010 in Tunis, and in January 2011 in Cairo, people rose up spontaneously and in unprecedentedly large numbers demanding not merely reform but regime change. In the Arab context this was REVOLUTION in capital letters. There is still no rational explanation why this eruption took place when it did, or for the sudden realisation by the common people that their destiny is in their own hands and they will no longer permit it to be determined by their dictatorial rulers or by foreigners. Before regimes can be overthrown or dislodged, people must overcome their fear of the regimes, even of the most autocratic ones, and must even be ready to die. Astonishingly, that is what happened and once again there is no explanation of why and how. The Arab world has been changed fundamentally and forever.

This popular upsurge had several other unique features: it began without known or identifiable leaders; without the banner of any specific ideology or organisation; and without instigation and incitement from abroad. It was preeminently a movement spearheaded by the younger generation and was consciously inclusive of all the diverse elements that constitute a national society. The unrest, initially began everywhere as a peaceful, non violent protest against autocratic, corrupt and brazenly repressive rule and the lack of economic development and opportunity for the people at large while the ruling elite lived in luxury. The focus of the protests was almost completely domestic—a demand for democracy, for fundamental political, economic and social reform, for basic human freedoms and dignity and had little or nothing to do with external relations. No government, no intelligence agency, no expert on the Arab world anywhere, had anticipated even the remote possibility, of anything like this happening.

Four long entrenched ruthless dictators in Egypt, Libya, Tunisia and Yemen were overthrown. Islamist regimes were voted into power in Egypt, Morocco and Tunisia—this could not possibly even have been imagined just three years ago. In Egypt the Muslim brotherhood government was overthrown by the army just one year after it took power. But in this case the army acted on behalf of the people. Despite 91 per cent of Egypt's population being Muslim and an even higher proportion of the army being Muslim, people did not want an Islamic state but good governance. They had come out on the streets against Morsy's government in numbers larger than when they rose up against Mubarak. People had not got rid of Mubarak and later the armed forces junta to live under an Islamist dictatorship. They wanted true democracy. Raw 'people power' had won three times against heavy odds, exhibiting that the country's political landscape has changed dramatically, perhaps irrevocably. A strange a spectacle is unfolding in Egypt, a standoff between Muslims and Islamists! Egypt is the largest, most populous and most powerful country in the Arab world; it is also its cultural heart and soul—what happens in Egypt will have an impact throughout the Arab world.

Having said this, it must be kept in mind that while change across the Arab world is inevitable in the longer term, its content, speed and direction will vary from country to country; it is likely to be the slowest in the GCC region. There are plausible reasons for that—monarchies are, at the end of the day, a modern version of the rule of tribal sheikhs with which the people have lived throughout history; before the oil era, peoples of the Arabian Peninsula, were amongst the poorest in the world, while today the general conditions of life, for the people at large, are unimaginably better than their forefathers could ever have dreamt of and incomparably better than anywhere else in the rest of the Arab world, indeed even when compared with most parts of the Third World; the regimes have the resources to pamper their relatively manageable populations or, to put it more crudely, buy off their loyalties. People are seeing the chaos, death, destruction and economic collapse in other countries. Why should they risk their comfortable and enviably peaceful lives?

In any case, regimes in the GCC countries will increasingly band together to ensure that monarchical regimes are not allowed to be overthrown in any GCC country. Unambiguously strong Saudi rhetoric and the dispatch of troops to Bahrain, along with those from the UAE, were not only are consciously thought out signals to the world and but also to their own people. Overcoming the inertia of the past, GCC countries, individually and collectively, have been playing uncharacteristically proactive and substantive roles in supporting and helping each other and taking adversaries head-on. Saudi Arabia has been leading the way with huge packages of financial aid to poorer brother monarchical states. If any monarchical regime falls in the near future it will be more due to the internal politics within royal families on issues of succession rather than by public demonstrations.

Fifth, the GCC countries' current hypersensitivity regarding Iran's nuclear programme is direct fallout of the 'Arab Spring' induced standoff between the GCC countries and Iran, though it has been a regional security concern for nearly a decade. Iran has long suspected that the issue is being used as an alibi for regime destabilisation if not regime change. Rouhani's election as Iran's new president has dramatically changed the atmospherics of Iran's interaction with the world particularly in relation to the nuclear issue. Talks have been under way between Iran and the P-5 plus Germany at the foreign ministers level, the highest level ever. An interim agreement has been reached and its implementation has begun.

A concluding thought regarding the 'current security challenges' strongly merits mention. If this interim agreement is successfully implemented there is every likelihood of a comprehensive agreement on the nuclear issue being negotiated leading to a rapprochement between Iran and the United States, which could transform the strategic landscape of West Asia in general, and the Gulf region in particular.

The Current Security Architecture in the Gulf Region

The key element of the security arrangements in the Gulf region, since World War II, has been the United States acting as the security overseer of the region, determined to ensure that no external power challenged the pre-dominance of US influence in the region. This began by establishing of a path breaking security relationship with Saudi Arabia. On February 16, 1943 President Roosevelt said that, "the defence of Saudi Arabia is vital to the defence of the United States." This led to a meeting on February 14, 1945 and the personal rapport between the President and King Abdul Aziz bin Saud established a strong and enduring foundation for the bilateral relationship. Though the West's unilateral creation of Israel effectively constituted a reneging on Roosevelt's assurance to the King, the latter did not revoke the Aramco concession or terminate the air bases agreement with the US nor did he take any other retaliatory action against the United States. In October 1950, President Truman wrote to the King that, "the United States is interested in the preservation of the independence and territorial integrity of Saudi Arabia. No threat to your Kingdom could occur which would not be a matter of immediate concern to the United States."

Having ousted Prime Minister Mossadeq in a coup in 1953, the United States developed an increasingly close relationship with the reinstated Shah of Iran. This also ensured that the historic Shia-Sunni and Arab-Persian divide did not complicate the regional security scenario.

Thereafter, the US approach was manifested in the "Twin Pillar" policy of having Saudi Arabia and Iran as its two key regional allies. However, this arrangement suffered a body blow after the Islamic revolution in Iran in 1979. In January 1980 in his State of the Union Address President Jimmy Carter declared that "an attempt by any outside force to gain control of the Persian Gulf region will be regarded as an assault on the vital interests of the United States," to be "repelled by any means necessary." The Carter Doctrine has defined US approach since the 1980s; it found expression in the "dual containment" policy towards Iraq and Iran in the 1990s and provided the fundamental rationale for military operations in and around the Gulf region starting with the first Gulf War in 1990-91, the war in Afghanistan since 2001 and the second Gulf War in 2003. All this has resulted in a permanent and growing US military presence in the region through the 1990s to the present. All US troops, which had reached a high of over 500000 in 1991, were withdrawn from Saudi Arabia in the summer of 2003 and bases closed. However, last week it came to light that US has been operating drones against Yemen from a secret base in Saudi Arabia. The US troops were finally withdrawn from Iraq in late 2011/early 2012 and are slated to be withdrawn from Afghanistan by 2014. However, US troops are based in the other five GCC countries with Bahrain hosting the 5th Fleet since 1995 and Qatar the Central Command since 2002.

The UK had been involved with West Asia since the 19th century and continued its security oversight responsibilities through changing times and circumstances, assuming in particular responsibility for the security of the Arab littoral of the Persian Gulf. It oversaw the post World War I dispensation in Iraq. With the strong support and encouragement of the US, a new regional security entity was created in 1955—the Baghdad Pact—with Turkey, Iraq, Iran, Pakistan and Britain as members. The Revolution in Iraq in July 1958 led to the overthrow of the monarchy. The new regime adopted a pro Soviet orientation and Iraq withdrew from the Baghdad Pact. In 1959 it was renamed as the Central Treaty Organisation which was dissolved in 1979 following the Revolution in Iran. Britain however continued its suzerainty and security overlordship over the area termed as the Trucial States on the Arabian Peninsula side of the of the Persian Gulf. It continued to do so even after Kuwait became independent in 1961 and Bahrain, Qatar and UAE emerged as independent states in 1971. Oman has enjoyed Britain's protection since World War I. Thus, US involvement and role were supplemented by the active involvement of the UK. Saudi Arabia and these newly independent states joined together to create the Gulf Cooperation Council following the emergence of the Islamic Republic of Iran that spewed revolutionary anti monarchy rhetoric.

The GCC countries have been very large buyers of state-of-the-art defence equipment and weaponry and almost all of it has been purchased from the US, in particular, but also in significant but lesser quantities from the UK and France, who have also entered into bilateral defence agreements with several GCC states.

As will be evident from the foregoing account the US and UK have been long involved and are strongly entrenched in the security architecture of the Gulf region.

Sanctions have been a major feature of US policy towards Iran since the 1979 Islamic revolution. These were supplemented by sanctions imposed under the authority of the U.N. since 2006, in the context of Iran's nuclear programme, and later by other entities such as the EU and bilaterally by some countries. In addition, there are unilateral US sanctions which prevent business entities in third countries from having economic and energy relationships with Iran since they would risk their business and economic links with the United States by doing so. This has, inter alia, effectively resulted in Iran's oil exports plummeting by almost 50 per cent in the past year. All this is designed to cripple Iran economically to pressurise it to change its strategic policies but the unarticulated sub text is regime change. All this is hurting Iran greatly but so far Iran has not caved in.

The standard Western approach of a military response combined with a coercive demands-threats-sanctions oriented diplomacy has not worked and has actually served to increase the growing instability in the region. The reality is that though the United States' energy dependence on the Gulf region is diminishing very rapidly, the United States is not about the leave the region. However, it will have to modify its assertive approach of the past; in fact, this is already evident in the manner in which issues relating to Syria and Iran have been addressed in these past few weeks. However, a security vacuum is dangerous. There is a need for, at least supplementary arrangements, which, inter alia, should involve greater Asian participation, for reasons that are elaborated later in the paper.

Turkey

Spurned by Europe in its endeavours to join the EU, Turkish prime minister Erdogan's Islamist government began to carve a salient role for itself in the Middle East. It accorded high priority to building close relations with the monarchical states, Palestine and Yemen, even as it continued to maintain very good relations with the supposedly pariah states—Egypt, Iran, Iraq, Israel and Syria. Lured by prospects of becoming a significant player in regional security dynamics, Turkey has been proactively involved in the evolution of events in each Arab country, affected by the turmoil of the past three years, in full cooperation and coordination with the GCC countries. However, three years on, things have not quite turned out the way Turkey had expected. In the process its relations with Syria, Israel and Iran have deteriorated dramatically; in Egypt, Turkey and the GCC countries, find themselves on opposite sides of the fence, in the context of the ouster of the Muslim Brotherhood government. Having made these conscious choices the balance sheet is not looking particularly healthy for Turkey and Erdogan himself, is facing unprecedented domestic political challenges. Turkey's changing fortunes highlight the danger that non-regional countries can get badly burnt by inserting themselves in the quagmire of West Asian politics.

Pakistan

Pakistan has a long history of military involvement and training in the Arab world. Its pilots flew warplanes in the 1967 Arab-Israeli conflict and volunteered to serve during the 1973 Yom Kippur War. In 1970, Gen. Zia-ul-Haq, then head of the Pakistani military training mission in Jordan, where he served from 1967 to 1970 as a Brigadier, led the Jordanian 2nd Division and Pakistani soldiers to quash a Palestinian uprising—the Black September operations. Arafat later claimed that the Jordanian army killed between 10,000 and 25,000 Palestinians. Moshe Dayan has written in his Autobiography: "King Hussein with help from Zia-ul-Haq of the Pakistani army sent in his Bedouin army on September 27, to clear out the Palestinian bases in Jordan...and...killed more Palestinians in eleven days than Israel could kill in twenty years."

Saudi Arabia has had a very special relationship with Pakistan ever since the latter came into being, which has no parallel with its relations with any other country. Over the past six decades Saudi Arabia has given billions of dollars of financial aid to Pakistan apart from supplying oil, occasionally free, and very often on highly concessional terms, particularly in times of war between Pakistan and India and/or when Pakistan's financial position became particularly parlous. Saudi financing was pivotal in the creation and financing of thousands of jihadis in Pakistan, without which the Soviet Union could not have been defeated in Afghanistan, and to later sustain Taliban rule in that country. Up to 20,000 Pakistani troops were stationed in Saudi Arabia during the 1970s and 1980s and one of their major assigned responsibilities was the protection of the Royal family. Pakistani troops and air force have taken part in operations on the Yemen Saudi border in the past. Due to the commonality of US supplied weapons systems Pakistani pilots routinely fly Saudi air force planes and have been engaged in training Saudi armed forces personnel in Saudi Arabia. Joint exercises are a regular feature. Saudi Arabia has been a particularly active and very influential player in the domestic politics of Pakistan with Pakistani political leaders being granted refuge when they are out of power. A considerable body of opinion in the global strategic community that tracks Saudi Arabia's relations with South Asia is of the view that Saudi Arabia has at least part funded Pakistan's nuclear programme and its expensive armament acquisitions. Saudi defence minister Prince Sultan was given privileged and complete access to Pakistani nuclear installations in 1999 and soon thereafter the infamous Dr A.Q. Khan visited Saudi Arabia.

Serving Pakistani armed forces officers and men had served in Bahrain, even before its independence in 1971, and have continued to do so since then. According to reports in the Pakistan media the number of retired army and police personnel, mostly Baluchi Pakistanis, serving in Bahrain security establishment at any given point of time has been around 30 per cent of its total strength; emergency recruitment was undertaken in Pakistan after protests erupted in Bahrain in February 2011. The protesters regard Pakistanis as the most brutal part of the security establishment in Bahrain and they are the most hated people in the country.

The UAE military is an all-volunteer force, of which an estimated 30 per cent are expatriates, a significant proportion from Pakistan. Pakistani armed forces contributed significantly during the formative years of the UAE armed forces and remain deeply involved in training. Joint exercises are a regular feature.

Pakistan defence personnel have probably the closest personal interaction and relations with the defence personnel of most of the GCC countries largely because of a common religion and partly because being non-Arab they are less likely to be potential betrayers. In the event of a royal family from one of the GCC countries coming under direct threat, and in case foreign help is needed, Pakistan more than any other country, would probably be the first option to tap.

Future Security Scenario

Given the nature of the current security challenges in the region it is extremely doubtful that direct full scale military intervention by any party could provide a solution to any of the security challenges; indeed such an involvement and action is likely to worsen an already complex and difficult situation. Foreign governmental intervention to protect incumbent regime(s) from large-scale public revolt is entirely different from foreign intervention to support large-scale public revolts to overthrow incumbent regimes. The latter has taken place but it is very difficult to contemplate that the former can realistically happen. Involvement of regional countries sharing a common culture, language and religion could be a possibility but interventions by others are unlikely to be successful in today's environment.

The involvement of non-regional powers in the security dynamics of any particular region inevitably leads to the strategic interests of the external players taking precedence in the shaping of the security environment of that particular region. This may not necessarily be congruent with the long term politico-security interests of the regional countries. Therefore, the time has perhaps come for the regional countries to assume an increasing share of the responsibility for security of their own regions.

The GCC countries need to ponder deeply about how they are going to ensure security for themselves in the light of the factors mentioned above, in view of their own, increasingly uncertain security environment, both regionally and domestically; and in the context of the transforming relations between them and global powers and among the global powers themselves.

GCC Countries as a Security Factor in the Region

Until three years ago the GCC countries were singularly impotent as a being a meaningful security factor in their own region was concerned. They had not been able to devise any significant indigenous security arrangements for themselves. Beyond huge financial assistance and arms transfers to Iraq by some individual members, and rhetorical support, they had remained rather passive during the Iran-Iraq war. Even when, Kuwait, which was one of its members, was invaded and occupied by Iraq, it was primarily the US, helped by its allies, that rescued Kuwait. The Damascus Declaration was abandoned within weeks of it being signed. The Peninsula Shield, their ostensible joint force, is more symbolic than effective. The contrived image of GCC unity that is sought to be projected, masks the endemic border disputes and mutual suspicions; the fear of 'big brother' Saudi Arabia among the smaller GCC countries; and the considerable variations in the approaches of individual GCC countries with regard to their relations and interaction with important regional countries such as Egypt, Iran, Iraq and Israel, etc. These factors have prevented any meaningful political and military integration amongst them.

However, the turmoil in the Arab world during the past three years served to energise them, both collectively and individually, as nothing had done before. They have since been playing an uncharacteristically proactive and substantive role in supporting and helping each other and taking their adversaries head on. They have been in the vanguard on the politico—diplomatic front in relation to events in Libya, Syria and Yemen and have very agilely mended fences with the evolving power structure in Egypt, quickly overcoming their deep disappointment with events and US policy there. They sent troops to Bahrain. They openly supplied arms to the opposition in Libya and Syria. They brokered the solution in Yemen. They have been unusually active in the Arab League and the UN. They have disbursed huge packages of financial aid to poorer brother monarchies and Yemen. A small country with a miniscule population but with very deep pockets and the highest per capita income in the world, Qatar has been assertively hyperactive and been substantively involved in far away Lebanon, Libya, Palestine, Sudan, Syria, Yemen; in bringing the different parties involved in Afghanistan together; and even with the Polisario. The GCC states' involvement has had a direct and manifestly tangible influence in shaping outcomes. They now seem to have developed the self confidence to be players, in their own region in particular, and in the Arab world in general. This is a desirable development from every perspective.

Regimes in the GCC countries will increasingly band together to ensure that monarchical regimes are not allowed to be overthrown in any GCC country. The unambiguously strong Saudi rhetoric and its dispatch of troops to Bahrain, along with those from the UAE, are conscious signals, to Iran in particular, as well as to the world and even to their own people. Many countries have recognised the dangers posed by radical Islam—particularly Kuwait, Saudi Arabia and the UAE. The differences between them and the Qatari approach are on public display in the context of events in Egypt and Syria with Qatar supporting the Muslim Brotherhood and other hard line Islamist forces whereas Saudi Arabia ironically favours secular and liberal factions including, in the case of Egypt, the army. If any monarchical regime falls, it will be more due to internal politics within the royal families rather than because of public demonstrations and protests.

The strategic discourse on regional security in the Gulf region has been obsessively dominated by the GCC-Iran divide but the fact that in the past, both sides have made enormous efforts to overcome mutual suspicions, is almost completely obscured. This is dealt with, in some detail, in the following paragraphs, as this element could be the kernel of a possible détente between the GCC countries and Iran.

Ayatollah Khomeini, the leader of the Islamic Revolution and founder of the Islamic Republic of Iran in 1979, and its first Supreme Leader declared that "the concept of monarchy totally contradicts Islam" and announced intentions of exporting the Islamic revolution to other parts of the Muslim world. The monarchical regimes of the Arabian Peninsula were alarmed and established the Gulf Cooperation Council in 1981. Clashes between Iranian-led demonstrators and Saudi security forces in Mecca on July 31, 1987, left 275 Iranian pilgrims dead and 303 wounded. This led to very strong Iranian invective against Saudi Arabia and its rulers. Khomeini vowed that, "even if it were possible to forgive Saddam Hussein, it would never be possible to forgive Saudi Arabia." Khomeini threatened that Fahd "will not remain alive." Akbar Hashemi Rafsanjani, the de facto commander-in-chief of the Iranian military in the Iran-Iraq war and Chairman of the Iranian Majlis from 1980 to 1989, said that:

> ...the martyrs' blood must be avenged by burning the roots of Saudi rulers in the region....The true revenge is to remove the colossal and precious wealth belonging to the Islamic World which lies under the soil of the Arabian Peninsula from the control of criminal agents of colonialism. The Saudi rulers have chosen an evil path, and we will send them to hell ('Iraqi Invasion of Kuwait as Turning Point in Iran-Saudi Relationship': Reza Ekhtiari Amiri and Fakhreddin Soltani. *Journal of Politics and Law* Vol. 4, No. 1; March 2011).

Diplomatic relations were thereafter broken.

However, just three to four years later the scenario changed dramatically. The end of the Iran-Iraq War in 1988, the death of the extremely hard line Imam Khomeini in 1989 and, most importantly, the Iraqi invasion and occupation of Kuwait provided opportunities for building bridges with the GCC countries. Akbar Hashemi Rafsanjani was elected Iran's president in 1989. Iran's Constitution was modified in July 1989 giving the president more decision-making power. Spouting radically different rhetoric, Rafsanjani proclaimed that "Iran needs to stop making enemies" signalling a substantive shift in foreign policy from promotion and export of revolutionary Islam to pragmatic coexistence with neighbours in particular, and the wider developed world in general, to help Iran's economic growth, development and post-war reconstruction. He condemned Iraq's invasion of Kuwait, demanded Iraqi withdrawal and spurned Iraq's suggestions that Iran could join Iraq and reap huge benefits. Inter governmental interaction between Iran and the GCC states immediately started acquiring the characteristics of normality. The Iranian foreign minister Velayati travelled to GCC countries and met the rulers of Qatar, Oman, UAE and Bahrain. Rafsanjani saw GCC rulers as rich potential investors rather than as pawns to be toppled. Iran created a free trade zone on its islands of Kish and Qeshm. Diplomatic links with Saudi Arabia were restored. Direct air links with several GCC countries were restored. Trade and investment began flowing freely across borders. This prompted a positive response and the GCC Summit in Qatar in December 1990 declared that the GCC "...welcomed the prospect of future cooperation and Iranian participation in regional security arrangements" and said, for the first time, that they regarded Iran as an "acceptable partner" for security of the Persian Gulf. (Amiri and Soltani) However, Egypt and the US were strongly opposed to any Iranian role and involvement and hence Iran was excluded from the new regional security mechanism envisaged under the Damascus Declaration of March 1991. But by May the Damascus Declaration was dead. Sultan Qaboos, the Head of the GCC Committee on Regional Security Arrangements sent Foreign Minister Alawi to Tehran in March 1992 to inform Iran that the GCC wished to give it a role in establishing regional security arrangements. (*Gulf News,* 10 March, 1992). However, the 1992 Abu Musa island flare up between Iran and the UAE put paid to this new initiative. The GCC became convinced that Western military protection was the best way forward for them vis-à-vis both Iran and Iraq.

Notwithstanding the forging of military alliances between the GCC states and the US, there was a renewed thrust to improve relations during Sayyid Mohamed Khatami's presidency, 1997-2005. The first foreign visits by the new Iranian foreign minister Kamal Kharrazi were to several GCC capitals to invite them to participate in the OIC summit in Tehran in December 1997, the singular highlight of which was that it was attended by Saudi Crown Prince Abdullah. In

February-March 1998, the former president, Rafsanjani, then Chairman of the Expediency Council, visited Saudi Arabia and spent two weeks in the country during which he was granted audiences with the King and the Crown Prince. He reiterated, that "relations with neighbours, Islamic countries and Third World countries have top priorities in Iranian foreign policy." On its part Saudi Arabia rejected US accusations of Iranian involvement in the bombing of US military housing at Al-Khobar in Saudi Arabia in 1996, which had killed 19 American servicemen and wounded 370 others. The two countries established an Economic Cooperation Joint Commission. Iran lifted visa requirements for Saudi citizens visiting its country. Later, Rafsanjani's unexpected visit to Bahrain resulted in the establishment of diplomatic relations at the ambassadorial level. President Khatami visited Saudi Arabia and Qatar in May 1999. During the Saudi interior minister's visit to Tehran in April 2001, a Security Cooperation Agreement was signed, thus opening a new chapter in bilateral relations. In addition, Khatami sought improvement of relations with the US giving a path breaking interview with the American television channel CNN on January 7, 1998. Here he made clear his goal of improving Iran's relations with the US through a "dialogue of civilisations." In another positive signal to GCC countries in 2003 Khatami refused to meet militant Iraqi cleric Moqtada al-Sadr.

GCC countries welcomed Mahmoud Ahmadinejad's election as President (2005-13). He too initially accorded importance to relations with GCC countries and visited several GCC countries including Saudi Arabia and became the first Iranian president to visit the UAE (in May 2007). In July 2006 Qatar was the only non-permanent member of the Security Council that voted against a resolution imposing sanctions on Iran. In a highly innovative and path breaking move the Emir of Qatar invited Ahmadinejad to attend the GCC Summit in Doha in December 2007. King Abdullah entered the conference hall flanked by Ahmadinejad and Sultan Qaboos of Oman. He held a bilateral meeting with Sheikh Khalifa bin Zayed al-Nahayan, the president of the United Arab Emirates. At the opening session of the Summit, Ahmadinejad said, "We are proposing the conclusion of a security agreement ...We want peace and security... based on justice and without foreign intervention". He also proposed the formation of an organisation to improve economic cooperation between Iran and the GCC, as well as working towards a free trade agreement. The fact that the final summit statement did not even mention his participation, let alone anything about the proposals he made, does not take away from the significance of the Qatari initiative. Meanwhile, despite major political impediments, the UAE has consistently been amongst the top four of Iran's trading partners, mainly due to trade with Dubai; furthermore, it is estimated that almost 400000 Iranian nationals live in the UAE, mainly in Dubai and Sharjah; there is huge Iranian investment in the UAE, again mostly in Dubai, though estimates vary wildly between \$20-\$300 billion.

Even last year, amidst sharply rising tensions between Saudi Arabia and Iran, King Abdullah convened an emergency OIC Summit where he received Iranian President Ahmadinejad with great cordiality and had him seated next to himself. All GCC countries attended the Non Aligned Summit in Teheran at the end of August, with the Emir of Qatar attending personally. Even though Saudi Arabia was represented at a relatively low protocol level, the choice of the Saudi representative—Prince Abdulaziz bin Abdullah, the deputy minister for Foreign Affairs, son of King Abdullah and a possible successor to Prince Saud as foreign minister, was very significant. He also had a bilateral meeting with President Ahmadinejad.

Iran knows that none of the GCC states individually or even all collectively pose any meaningful security threat to it. Its security concerns basically stem from implacable US hostility and a very strong US military presence in several countries around it. Rhetoric, biases and prejudices apart, the fact is that since the Islamic revolution in Iran, beyond consolidating its hold over Abu Musa and the two Tumbs islands, Iran has not taken any direct aggressive action against any of the GCC countries. The islands were taken over by Iran at the time of the Shah when the Emirates were still under British protection. Following the troubles in Bahrain in 2011 the Bahraini King appointed an independent inquiry commission which in its report said that there was no evidence of Iranian interference.

If great powers do not interfere then accommodation between the two sides is not impossible.

Future Role of the United States

The growing resentment and anger of the people of the Gulf region in particular and the Arab and Islamic worlds in general against the policies of the United States was manifested in spectacular fashion by the attacks in New York on September 11, 2001. In retaliation the United States brought about regime change in Afghanistan and Iraq by military force. Its subsequent lengthy military presence in those two countries, apart from inflicting huge financial cost and leaving many thousands dead, has arguably left the two countries worse off than before, and the region as insecure if not more so. Though US actions and policies vis-à-vis Iran have hurt Iran greatly they have not succeeded in forcing Iran to change its policies. American influence, reputation and standing have diminished very considerably throughout the region. All this has also contributed to increasing domestic financial constraints in the United States and 'war weariness' amongst both the political elite, and certainly the people at large.

Having said this, the reality is that despite their growing disenchantment with the US, the GCC countries are not going to ask that US forces to leave. Another reality is that Iran would have to recognise is that despite America's diminishing influence, the US will remain the most important player in the region for the foreseeable future. The third reality is that despite diminished influence, and its diminishing energy dependence on the region and despite financial constraints, the US is not about to leave the region, whether any country, individually or otherwise, desires it to do so. And finally, in an increasingly uncertain and unpredictable security and strategic environment, if push comes to shove, the US will take any action it deems, necessary according to its assessment of its own national interests and security, irrespective of the views of, even its allies, let alone adversaries.

Other Possibilities

In the light of the foregoing account many questions arise:

> Are the security architectures and arrangements of the past relevant for dealing with the security challenges thrown up by the unfolding events of the past three years, which manifestly pose very different challenges than those of yester years?
>
> Must the security concerns of the region continue to be addressed through military alliances and militaristic approaches? The increasing militarisation of the Gulf provides only illusory security. Is it not time to move beyond Cold War paradigms of exclusive blocs of countries confronting each other? Does the US have the ability and willingness to be able to shoulder regional security burdens as in the past?
>
> Any forward movement on the reconfiguration of the regional security architecture requires that the closed GCC-Iran-US triangle, that has created a strategic gridlock, must be opened up. Is this possible?

The situation is getting much more complex and out of the box unorthodox approaches are needed. A winner take all and loser lose all approach will not work; compromises will have to be made by all players, regional and non-regional. Meeting current and future challenges would need a much more nuanced and consensual approach. While it is almost impossible to even imagine that existing military alliances could be replaced by any meaningful alternative arrangements in any realistic short term time frame, it is doubtful whether these alliances, by themselves will help the region navigate the new and contemporary security problems which have emerged.

The time has come to initiate efforts to craft these new arrangements on priority. However, there must be a clear recognition and acceptance by all concerned that the current arrangements and any evolving new arrangements would have to co-exist for some time. Inevitably, these processes are going to be slow in acquiring traction and require patience and perseverance; meaningful outcomes will take time.

But regional initiatives will be necessary to make this work, however difficult it may be to envisage such possibilities currently; just the attempt in itself may have a salutary effect. Iran is too isolated to be able to make any meaningful moves which would have credibility, and thus it is the GCC countries would have to take the initiative.

Prince Saud Al-Faisal, the Saudi minister of foreign affairs, made a wide-ranging and particularly thought provoking speech in Manama, Bahrain, on December 5, 2004. The subject was 'Towards a New Framework for Regional Security'. He has been foreign minister since 1975 and is currently the world's longest-serving incumbent foreign minister. He has thus seen it all. Therefore, his speech deserves very close attention; in fact, even more so today than when it was delivered 9 years ago. One of several significant sentences from that speech deserves to be highlighted: "...the international component of the suggested Gulf security framework should engage positively the emerging Asian powers as well, especially China and India." Since then prominent personalities of GCC countries have also been expressing such sentiments more and more.

King Abdullah has shown the way. Given Saudi Arabia's longstanding special relationship with the US, King Abdullah's choice of China and India as the first two destinations for state visits after ascending the throne was a deliberate, path breaking development. The frequent exchange of visits by leaders and other high level dignitaries, between China, India, Japan and South Korea and the Gulf States during the past decade, is a very clear indication of new foreign policy related thinking in the GCC countries.

The tragedy is that there does not appear to be any concerted tangible effort on the part of the GCC countries to set substantive objectives and take action oriented initiatives to further Prince Saud's and King Abdullah's path breaking moves. Equally, though this approach has been widely prevalent in strategic discourse since then, Asian countries too have not shown any substantive enthusiasm in this respect.

In any case, the questions that will be asked are: why should non-Arab Asian countries be brought into the picture? What do they bring to the table? The answer is a lot and with very good reason.

First, the key lies in finding interlocutors who have credibility and good relations with the GCC countries and Iran on the one hand and the US and Israel on the other. Asia alone provides such interlocutors—China and India in particular and even Japan; all three are major global powers with rising stature.

Second, Asia is in the process of displacing the West as the fulcrum of the global economy and China and India are its leading locomotives.

Third, major Asian economies, both developed and developing, have collectively become the largest buyers of hydrocarbons from the Gulf region. Their demands are projected to keep increasing—and substantially so. The Gulf region's role as an energy supplier for Asia will therefore continue to grow incrementally for the foreseeable future, even as America's requirements of oil and gas from the Gulf region are projected to diminish dramatically.

Fourth, beyond the hydrocarbons factor, other economic links—trade and investment—between the Gulf region and the rest of Asia are also growing very rapidly and indeed are poised to overtake the economic relationship between the Gulf region and the Western world, in the next few years.

The rapidly strengthening economic relationship (including the hydrocarbon sector) between the four major Asian countries and countries of the Gulf region is brought out with great clarity through tables, charts, explanatory notes, etc, in an excellent article entitled 'The Role of Asian Countries (China, Japan, South Korea and India) in the Evolving Security Dynamics and Architecture of the Gulf Region' by Prof. Tim Niblock presented at Workshop 3 at the Gulf Research Meeting 2013 at the University of Cambridge in July 2013. The contents are indeed enlightening. Niblock contends that:

> The best security setting for the Gulf states is one where they will be collectively responsible for their security (and for the sea lanes leading out into the Indian Ocean), within the framework of a regional collective security organisation. In such a scenario, the framework and the resulting organisation could benefit from the support of external powers, but without any direct security presence. External support, in this case, would need to be balanced, with the involvement of Asian as well as Western powers.

Furthermore, it must also be kept in mind that the Gulf region is an integral cultural and geographical part of Asia. Stronger strategic synergies in the energy and economic domains between countries of the Gulf region and those of the Asia Pacific region are making the Gulf region an integral part of the unfolding Asian growth story. Therefore, the significance of its connections with the rest of Asia is a strategic factor in its growing importance for the Gulf region on the one hand; and peace and stability in the Gulf region are becoming factors of increasing strategic and even existential significance for the major Asian countries on the other. A new regional security framework, more in tune with these current and evolving realities, is needed.

In the light of all these factors, as we go forward, a strategic order in the Gulf region that relies on the West for its security and the East for its prosperity will be increasingly untenable. Western countries have interests in the region and they are not about to go away. Both Western countries and Asian countries are necessary for the security of the Gulf region—Western countries are already involved and Asian countries have to be brought in. That process needs to be initiated now and preferably at the initiative of countries of the Gulf region so that the process can evolve smoothly. Iran is too isolated to take any initiative. The GCC countries have good relations with both the West and the East and could, and should, do so.

Each region has its own specificities. The security related dialogue architecture created by ASEAN through its Dialogue Partners network, the ARF, and mechanisms such ASEAN+1, ASEAN+3, the East Asian Summit, etc, involving all players who have interests in the region, are templates worth examining. Hardly anybody would contest that these arrangements have helped in keeping the Asia Pacific region peaceful despite the existence of a large number of serious disputes. These arrangements could serve as a broad model.

Any architecture that is created would ultimately need to involve the P-5 and the EU; India, Japan, South Korea and Pakistan; Egypt, Israel, Turkey and Yemen and of course Iran and Iraq. The governments of Qatar, Saudi Arabia and the UAE, collectively or individually, could consider commissioning institutions such as the Gulf Research Centre, the Qatar Foundation, the King Faisal Centre for Research and Islamic Studies, etc. to initiate projects charged with (a) reviewing the literature relating to the subject including compiling a list of previous ideas and proposals and culling elements relevant contemporary conditions and requirements; and (b) engage intensively through specially convened workshops to create conceptual security frameworks for the consideration of governments.

These workshops could initially have small teams from Qatar, Saudi Arabia and the UAE, on the one hand, and China, India, Japan and Pakistan on the other as well as Iran. The members ideally would be retired diplomats, retired armed forces officers and academics specialising in regional security issues, to be appointed in consultation with the concerned governments, so that the exercise has some credibility.

23

India-West Asia Relations: Building Inclusive Partnership in the Future

Meena Singh Roy

The political unrest which started in December 2010 in Tunisia and later engulfed the entire West Asian region has now entered in its second phase. Even today, the West Asian region is in the midst of turbulent changes which presage the emergence of a new and different set of security and economic challenges, new patterns of relationships, both within the region and with countries having major stakes and interests in the region. The region is witnessing much more uncertainties with regards to its domestic politics.

The present paper examines India's growing stakes in the region and explores the possibilities of building inclusive partnership with the West Asian countries in the context of emerging security challenges. It argues that from the regional perspective, India is viewed as a reliable partner which can play an important role in the region. However, it has been somewhat reluctant player. There is huge potential for India to build inclusive partnership with the West Asian countries. It is suggested that India should re-articulate its "New West Asia Policy" with a road map for next ten years.

Evolving Geo-political Trends in West Asia

The wave of political change in West Asia and North Africa (WANA) has neither succeeded in bringing desired effective democratisation and modernisation, nor has it created peace and stability in the region. In fact, the much debated phenomenon of change known as 'Arab Spring', 'Arab Turmoil' or 'Islamic Awakening' has resulted in strengthening extremist forces, increasing ethnic tensions and growing sectarian divide in the region. However, this is not to negate some positive developments in the region. In the post 'Arab Spring' period some of the Gulf States mainly—Qatar, Saudi Arabia, Kuwait and UAE, have been able to provide considerable domestic stability and economic prosperity. This has been possible because of the substantial control that regimes exercise over their population and their strong economic might. Some experts are of the view that the wave of change which started in the form of 'Arab Spring' is unstoppable and is irreversible. However the trajectory of this change in the Gulf will be different for very good reasons, first of all, the population of these countries is small, their wealth resources are much bigger and the relationship between the ruler and the ruled is of a different kind then what one would find in the republican dictatorships, Therefore, the 'Arab Spring' in the Gulf can be managed much better.[1] An expert from the Gulf region is of the view that the current wave of change "has nearly ended six decades of political stagnation that the Arab people had to go through and these six decades of political stagnation is what the 'Arab Spring' is all about no more no less, there are no words to explain but at least for now we know almost six decades of political stagnation which led the Arab world from bad to worse and worst have hopefully ended for good."[2] In his view the 'Arab Spring' had unleashed in its own way three big trends; first, it has created a vacuum of leadership; second, it has increased the power of small states and third, it has strengthened the forces status-quo in the six Arab Gulf States.[3]

The main features of the second phase of the political transformation in the West Asian region are mainly, the political uncertainties in Syria and Egypt; fear of growing jihadi/extremist forces; the impact and future of recent interim agreement between Iran and West over its disputed nuclear programme; increasing violence in Iraq; development of new political equation between Turkey and Iran, likelihood of the change in the regional power equations; growing insecurity of Saudi Arabia in the light of Iran's détente with the West and growing stakes of the Asian countries in the West Asian region. More importantly, the Syrian civil war and efforts by international community to find any solution to this crisis through Geneva-II are not very promising. Similarly, Egypt is seen to be heading once again towards government controlled by the military leadership.

At this stage, it is too early to provide definitive answers about the full impact of the political transformation which is taking place in the region but, what can be said with some certainty is that the essence of the socio-political tumult sweeping the region has been such that the people at large have overcome their fear of the existing regimes and called for drastic and fundamental political transformation, including regime change. It has also sent warning signals among the ruling regimes to address the long-standing political and economic demands of its people particularly those of the youth. This has led to dramatic changes in domestic political environments in most of the countries of the region. The impact of these changes is yet to unfold completely but what is predictable is that this period of uncertainties is likely to continue in near future. While one can remain optimistic about the region in long run, but in short and medium term the situation does look extremely grim for the whole region.

The balance of power in the region is also being transformed. Arab uprisings have ensured that the region would never remain the same again. Despite emergence of new actors in the region and regardless of the perceived view that US influence in the region is weakening, America will continue to play a major role in near future as well. The American policy of 'pivot to Asia Pacific' might draw greater attention to Asia but it will not allow Washington to overlook its vested interests in this region. What is important to note is that the new political dispensations will not be forced to follow the 'Accepted Order' laid down by the West for long. Despite championing the cause of democracy in the world, US and the West will be exposed to completely new set of challenges to manage their strategic partnership with the regional countries. The US will continue to find it convenient to deal with the dictators.

The emerging political order in West Asia is also marked by considerable shifts within individual countries as well as at the regional level. In the post Arab uprising scenario economic concerns have risen to the fore internally in these countries. Managing people's welfare and addressing internal economic problems will constitute as major challenge for the new regimes in West Asian region. These changes have implications for both regional and international stake holders.

India's Stakes in the West Asian Region

These changes are likely to affect India. West Asia forms a part of India's extended neighbourhood. The present political transformation in the region as well as the realisation of India's rise in stature as an emerging regional power has necessitated a fresh look at this geo-strategically important region. Already, this region accounts for largest trade volumes for India overtaking India's trade with China. The GCC countries constitute India's largest socio-economic partner. Six set of factors make this region strategically important for India:

1. Approximately six million Indians live and work in the GCC countries. They constitute about thirty five per cent of the total expatriate population, making them the foreign nationality of first preference in this region overall as well as in each GCC country, and the largest chunk of Indian nationals in any region abroad.
2. These Indians living in Gulf region remit more than one-third of the annual $69 billion remittances to India.
3. The GCC countries are India's largest trade partner. The economic ties between India and the GCC countries are moving at a faster pace increasing the mutual interdependence. In 2011-2012, the total value of the trade between the two amounted to US $145.72 billion (See Table 1). In 2012-13, UAE was the top trading partner of India with total trade amounting to US $ 75,455.01 million. During the same period Iraq, Iran and GCC countries were among the top twenty five

Table 1: India-GCC Trade (including oil and gas) Year 2011-12

Values in US$ billion

Country	Import	Export	Total
Saudi Arabia	31.06	5.68	36.74
UAE	35.79	35.92	71.72
Oman	3.32	1.32	4.65
Kuwait	16.37	1.81	17.56
Qatar	12.92	0.81	13.73
Bahrain	0.88	0.44	1.32
Total	100.35	45.36	145.72

Source: Government of India, Ministry of Commerce and Industry.

trading partners of India. (See Table 2). Similarly during April-September 2013-2014 all GCC countries, Iran and Iraq were among the top twenty five trading partners of India (See Table 3).

4. In addition India hosts the second largest Muslim population in the World, which views Saudi Arabia as its important pilgrimage because of the holy Shrines at Mecca and Medina. Therefore, cultural and religious aspect of the people-to-people ties between the two countries form a significant part of the overall relations with Saudi Arabia.
5. For India, the energy resources of the West Asian region are extremely significant because of its growing hydrocarbon demands. At present China is the main driver of increasing energy demand in the current decade, but India is going to take over in the 2020s as the principal source of growth.[4] West Asia has the world's major oil and gas reserves. Four countries in the region—Iran, Qatar, Saudi Arabia and the United Arab Emirate (UAE)—rank among the top ten countries of the world with large proven gas reserves; and five countries—Saudi Arabia, Iran, Iraq, Kuwait and the UAE—rank among the top ten countries of the world having large proven oil reserves. [5] According to recent reports, Saudi Arabia's total capacity, including 50 per cent of the Neutral Zone it shares with Kuwait, is 12.5 million barrels per day (bpd).[6] Saudi Aramco has also begun pumping heavy crude from its huge offshore Manifa oil fields, ahead of schedule, and plans to raise production to 500,000 bpd by July 2013.[7] More importantly, Iraq is likely to emerge as the next oil superpower in the years to come. Its oil production in December 2012 was around 3.2 million barrels per day (bpd)—the highest figure since 1983. Its current exports amount to more than 2.6 million bpd, with the major share of it going to Asia.[8] This makes Iraq a critical source of global oil supplies once again. According to the International Energy Agency (IEA), Iraq's oil output should double by 2020, reaching 6.1 million bpd, and is expected to rise to 8.3

Table 2: India's Top 25 Trading Partners, Year 2012-13

Values in US$ Million

Dated: 04/02/2014

Rank	Country	Export	Import	Total Trade	Trade Balance
1.	**U Arab Emts**	**36,316.65**	**39,138.36**	75,455.01	-2,821.72
2.	China P RP	13,534.88	52,248.33	65,783.21	-38,713.45
3.	USA	36,155.22	25,204.73	61,359.95	10,950.49
4.	**Saudi Arab**	**9,785.78**	**33,998.11**	**43,783.89**	**-24,212.33**
5.	Switzerland	1,117.28	32,166.54	33,283.82	-31,049.25
6.	Germany	7,246.20	14,325.79	21,571.99	-7,079.58
7.	Singapore	13,619.24	7,486.38	21,105.63	6,132.86
8.	**Iraq**	**1,278.13**	**19,247.31**	**20,525.44**	**-17,969.18**
9.	Indonesia	5,331.30	14,879.49	20,210.79	-9,548.19
10.	Hong Kong	12,279.20	7,907.17	20,186.37	4,372.04
11.	Japan	6,100.06	12,412.29	18,512.35	-6,312.24
12.	**Kuwait**	**1,061.08**	**16,588.13**	**17,649.21**	**-15,527.05**
13.	Korea Rp	4,202.25	13,105.12	17,307.37	-8,902.87
14.	**Qatar**	**687.18**	**15,693.08**	**16,380.26**	**-15,005.89**
15.	Belgium	5,507.30	10,046.87	15,554.17	-4,539.57
16.	Australia	2,348.65	13,085.70	15,434.34	-10,737.05
17.	**Iran**	**3,351.07**	**11,594.46**	**14,945.53**	**-8,243.39**
18.	UK	8,612.54	6,293.09	14,905.62	2,319.45
19.	Nigeria	2,740.04	12,086.11	14,826.15	-9,346.07
20.	Malaysia	4,444.07	9,951.06	14,395.13	-5,506.99
21.	Venezuela	234.14	14,117.67	14,351.81	-13,883.54
22.	South Africa	5,106.93	8,887.89	13,994.82	-3,780.96
23.	Netherland	10,565.02	2,379.09	12,944.11	8,185.93
24.	Brazil	6,048.53	4,825.76	10,874.29	1,222.77
25.	France	4,986.03	4,652.36	9,638.39	333.66
	Total of Top 25 countries	*202,658.77*	*402,320.88*	*604,979.66*	*-199,662.11*
	India's Total	**300,400.67**	**490,736.64**	**790,987.00**	**-190,335.97**

Source: At http://commerce.nic.in/eidb/iecnttopn.asp accessed on January 3, 2014.

million bpd by 2035, thus making it the world's fourth largest producer. Despite North America's oil renaissance, West Asia still remains at the core of the world's oil reservoir.[9] West Asia remains the main source of India's imports. Countries like Saudi Arabia, the UAE, Iran, Qatar and Iraq meet India's major oil and gas needs. In recent years, the Persian Gulf region alone has accounted for more than 60 per cent of India's total hydrocarbon imports. India's bilateral ties with most of the countries along the Persian Gulf, such as Iraq, Kuwait, Saudi Arabia and Yemen, have been dominated by energy imports.[10]

6. Over fifty per cent of flight connections between India and the world are between India and the GCC countries. This clearly highlights the growing interdependence between India and the GCC countries.

Table 3: India's Top 25 Trading Partners
Year 2013-2014 (April-September)

Values in US$ Million

Rank	Country	Export	Import	Total Trade	Trade Balance
1.	**U Arab Emts**	**14,952.57**	**17,076.35**	**32,028.92**	**-2,123.77**
2.	USA	19,950.62	11,810.21	31,760.83	8,140.41
3.	China P RP	5,721.15	25,790.60	31,511.75	-20,069.45
4.	**Saudi Arab**	**6,584.41**	**18,185.72**	**24,770.13**	**-11,601.32**
5.	Switzerland	1,206.10	12,744.41	13,950.51	-11,538.30
6.	Singapore	8,159.41	3,335.90	11,495.30	4,823.51
7.	**Iraq**	**498.64**	**10,565.12**	**11,063.77**	**-10,066.48**
8.	Hong Kong	6,534.43	4,050.02	10,584.45	2,484.40
9.	**Kuwait**	**478.31**	**9,397.81**	**9,876.12**	**-8,919.50**
10.	Germany	3,651.57	6,202.17	9,853.73	-2,550.60
11.	Indonesia	2,571.25	7,175.66	9,746.90	-4,604.41
12.	UK	4,745.57	3,703.04	8,448.61	1,042.53
13.	Japan	3,361.83	4,984.11	8,345.94	-1,622.28
14.	Korea Rp	1,992.81	6,302.64	8,295.45	-4,309.84
15.	**Qatar**	**316.91**	**7,620.70**	**7,937.61**	**-7,303.79**
16.	Belgium	2,900.29	4,961.36	7,861.64	-2,061.07
17.	Nigeria	1,235.98	6,508.01	7,743.99	-5,272.04
18.	Venezuela	101.53	7,540.86	7,642.39	-7,439.33
19.	Unspecified	6,020.37	1,017.44	7,037.81	5,002.93
20.	Malaysia	2,143.38	4,802.03	6,945.40	-2,658.65
21.	Australia	1,112.40	5,280.95	6,393.36	-4,168.55
22.	**Iran**	**2,451.24**	**3,926.60**	**6,377.83**	**-1,475.36**
23.	South Africa	2,477.13	3,835.55	6,312.67	-1,358.42
24.	Netherland	3,942.26	1,511.08	5,453.34	2,431.18
25.	Italy	2,477.43	2,057.95	4,535.37	419.48
	Total of Top 25 countries	*105,587.54*	*190,386.26*	*295,973.81*	*-84,798.72*
	India's Total	152,105.39	231,791.63	383,868.63	-79,686.24

Source: At http://commerce.nic.in/eidb/iecnttopn.asp accessed on January 3, 2014.

Re-discovering the Relationship in the New Geo-political Environment

Given these stakes, it becomes extremely significant for India to re-look at its engagement with the West Asian region, especially in the coming decades.

This region is considered as India's "extended neighbourhood". India has been working towards building an inclusive partnership looking for new areas of cooperation not only in economic and energy sector but also in political and strategic arena. At political level, there have been more than fifteen high level visits from both the sides between 2000 and 2012. As mentioned earlier, there has been substantial growth in economic ties between India and the West Asian region.

The significance of India's growing political and economic interaction and emergence of strategically significant relationships with the Gulf countries has been widely acknowledged both by the officials and experts. In the last two decades, India's relations with the West Asian countries particularly with the GCC have been growing both in political and economic arena. A combination of political and economic factors at regional and international levels facilitated India and the countries in West Asia to consolidate their age-old ties.[11] In the post 9/11 period there was noticeable shift in the foreign policy of the Gulf region. The GCC started looking at the Asian countries under the framework of its 'Look East Policy'. This was an attempt to diversify its relations while maintaining its ties with the US and Europe. However, engagement with the Asian countries became the important feature of the Gulf States. This was also driven by the fact that there was growing perception about the negative impact of the US policies towards the West Asian region. It is argued by some experts that since the Americans moved in the West Asia, three wars have occurred which means that the Americans have failed decisively in keeping the Gulf stable and secure in return for oil. This clearly points out that the American policy in the region has resulted in having the negative impact on the Gulf security. This negative impact has been attributed to US thinking of always adopting a military approach for security. It is in this context that Gulf countries started looking at India to develop strategic partnership. While the Gulf region wants India to play much more active role in the region, it laments about India being a reluctant player.[12] From the Gulf perspective,[13] India-Gulf relations are very rich and diverse, where the economic leg of the relationship remains strong and the statistics of its economic ties are impressive and this is likely to grow stronger in the near future as well. However, its political leg is not as strong and promising. There are number of concerns that demand rethinking and fresh approach by India towards this region. These concerns are:

1) One major issue for the Gulf region is of security. For small Gulf States their security is of top priority. In exchange of oil they shop for security. These smaller states live in a tense zone next to tough and expansionist neighbours. An expert from UAE alluded to this concern by stating that "to us security is the sentimental concern. We live in a very tough neighbourhood so our security concern is real not manufactured, the nuclear Iran will nuclearise the Gulf security and that's just qualitatively a different level of Gulf security concern."[14]
2) India is making the mistake like the Western countries of viewing the region through the prism of "oil" and ignoring its rich cultural, diverse and historical relations with the region which has been reduced to mere economic, business and remittances issues. It is argued that the Gulf States relations with the US have been that of investing in the insurance company which in turn provides security to the region. It was noted that "we have always sought an insurance company and we will pay

handsomely for insurance company and that's what the America is all about for us by the way, it's definitely an insurance company."[15]

3) So far, India remains deliberately ambiguous on the elusive formula for Gulf security. The Gulf States view India as a regional probably a global power, therefore, this ambiguity is not befitting a future power. The Arab Gulf States view Iran as a destabilising force that needs to be confronted. However, India does not see Iran as a destabilising force. It was articulated by one expert from the region that "India needs to be more clear in its views and we have not seen that."[16]
4) At the same time Arab Gulf States do not like India's growing strategic relations with Israel. The Palestinian issue has been pushed under the carpet. It is perceived that in past, India used to be different in many ways in dealing with the Palestinian issue. Therefore, it is expected that in future India will be much more caring for the very industrious six million Palestinians. From the Gulf perspective more idealistic India is needed.
5) One of the major concerns is the Indian bureaucracy, who make it overwhelmingly difficult for Gulf particularly the UAE investments to fructify. These investors are frustrated and ready to give up on the lucrative Indian market if their legitimate concern is not addressed.

Options and Opportunities for India

In the light of above, it can be articulated that the Arab Gulf is seeking India's larger and greater role in the region. They also want India to take into consideration their concerns. But the dilemma before Indian policy-makers is to carve out a policy which can address the concerns of smaller Arab States, and at the same time manage its ties with big neighbouring Iran on one hand and its growing strategic ties with Israel on the other hand. In future, India will have to manage the above mentioned complex set of problems in region by adopting an innovative approach. More importantly, given India's historical and cultural ties, expectations from India are high. Hence, it is difficult for India to come up to these expectations. Under these circumstances, the key questions which merit some attention are: what then is the most viable option for India? What role does India want to play? And how best can it contribute to the regional stability? In an attempt to address this complex set of issues some of the suggestions were articulated by experts, officials and academic community from the region and India during the 15th Asian Security Conference in February 13-15, 2013 for enhancing the India-West Asia relations. Following suggestions were voiced:

1) Despite India's increasing dependence on West Asian energy resources, its policy approach towards this region has to go beyond energy. Given its close historical proximity and acceptability in the region India will have to come up with a more holistic approach.

2) India needs to once again factor more idealistic and principled approach propagated by Nehru and Gandhi in its policy.
3) Regional actors to invest in the peace and stability of the region.
4) As the project of creating second Kuwait City has already commenced with the building of an expressway to be followed by a super railway link in 2015, this opens a great opportunity for India to invest and participate in this project. From India, Kuwait expects not just unskilled labourers, but also skilled workers like managers, etc.
5) With respect to India-GCC economic ties, the trade with the region is dominated by exchanges with the UAE (fifty per cent) and Saudi Arabia (twenty five per cent). Therefore, portfolios need to be diversified to maintain desired trade volume. It is important that India leverages its expertise in the knowledge services sector.
6) The potential for creation of a regional supply chain with reference to the convergence in food economy between India and the Gulf States need to be explored.
7) A collective Asian approach towards GCC countries was suggested which could include China, Japan, South Korea, Malaysia and Indonesia, for sustainable security architecture. This security architecture could also factor in non-traditional security concerns.

In addition to above suggestions, a study done by the experts in IDSA has come up with number of recommendations to cement the existing ties with the region in areas of energy, trade, security and people-to-people contacts.[17]

Energy Cooperation

To further cement the energy cooperation it is suggested that the current buyer-seller relationship needs to change into a partnership of criss-cross investments in India and the West Asian oil-exporting countries. This policy will facilitate greater interdependence and also help address the general criticism that India's policy towards the region needs to go beyond energy considerations.

India should look for opportunities for joint ventures in West Asia not only with international companies but also with local companies. Priority should be accorded to projects like LNG liquefaction, fertiliser and desalination plants and other such ventures which will be beneficial for both sides. For attracting investments from the sovereign funds of these countries, India should engage in high-level diplomacy with countries like Saudi Arabia, the UAE and Qatar.

Through a mutually agreed upon mechanism, a share of the oil and gas revenues earned from India should be earmarked for investment in India. The purchase of a minimum fixed volume of oil and/or gas at average monthly prices could be worked out and agreed upon bilaterally.

Iran and Iraq need to be factored in a big way while formulating India's energy policy towards the region. Although Iraq is a high-risk proposition and Iran a problematic one, to ensure its future stable energy supply, India should work on long-term plans to expand its energy cooperation with Iraq and Iran. Food security is a big issue in the West Asian region. Therefore, an energy and food trade-off can be looked upon as a policy option to strengthen India's energy ties with the regional countries.

Surplus refining capacity is India's strength, which should be leveraged through contractual arrangements involving the purchase of crude oil and sale of refined products with as many countries as possible. Some oil-exporting countries may want refining capacities to be created on their soil. India could enter into joint ventures for establishing refineries on their soil.

There could be a structured India–GCC energy cooperation dialogue every year to enhance the energy cooperation between India and the GCC countries. Such a dialogue could cover upstream and downstream hydrocarbon cooperation, energy efficiency, renewable energy, clean technologies and civil nuclear cooperation.[18]

Enhancing Political, Security and Economic Cooperation

In the political arena India should re-articulate its "New West Asia Policy" with a road map for next ten years. Given the complexities of the issues in the region India's policy needs to take into account the concerns of the smaller states and adopt a balanced approach to strengthen bilateral political, economic and security ties with the region. It could in fact play a role of the balancer in bridging the gap between Iran and the GCC, Israel and the Arab countries and Israel and the Palestinians. This could start with the Track-II dialogue leading to Track-I subsequently. Appointing a special envoy for West Asia and setting up of eminent persons group on West Asia will go a long way in creating better understanding between India and West Asia. The current geo-political developments demand India to upgrade its ties with Iran, Iraq and Egypt while continuing to build stronger ties with the GCC countries.

In the security arena, the region wants India to play much more active role. This view thus necessitates forging of new security partnership with the regional countries to address the common concerns like terrorism and extremism, piracy, criminal activity, money laundering and controlling the proliferation of small arms. It will be equally significant on part of India to enhance its defence diplomacy with the regional countries. Some Indian experts are of the view that peace and stability in the Gulf can only be created if it is regional and inclusive security arrangement. This is because of asymmetry in terms of size and power of the regional countries of the region. It is argued that India should develop relations with the Gulf fundamentally on a bilateral basis and if the countries of the Gulf get together and develop regional structures for peace, stability and growth India should be willing to make its own contribution to help in the process. India's relationship, it has been pointed out with all the Gulf countries, should be on a very broad basis and should not just focus on any special sector like oil and gas.[19]

Another view point from Indian perspective is that if the GCC feel strongly about India and its participation in the region, they should support India in the reforms of the global fora including Security Council and redress or offset this great asymmetry which prevails in Asia.[20] There is need on part of the West Asian countries and India to move towards common understanding of each other's security concerns.

To boost existing economic engagement with the region, India could look at diversifying its trade ties. It has to look at enhancing trade with the West Asian countries which are left behind. It also needs to create friendlier, accessible business environment to attract foreign investment from the West Asian region particularly from the Gulf. In the current situation India should take full advantage of opportunities opening in the Gulf Region in the infrastructure, Information Technology and medical sector.

Finally, India should make use of its soft power, which has great potential to boost cooperation between the two regions. This could be done by establishing India Chair in the West Asian countries; opening educational and vocational and cultural institutions and encouraging students exchange programmes and setting up the language labs for better understanding. An annual track-II dialogue among the Indian and regional think tanks will substantially help in better understanding of the problems and concerns of both sides.

Conclusion

It could be concluded that in the current global order, the role of the Asian powers particularly, India and China is likely to grow in West Asian region despite its strong military and strategic ties with the United States. More importantly, the Asian growth story will remain incomplete without West Asia becoming integral part of it. India is perceived by the regional countries as an emerging global power with rising stature and therefore expected to play a larger role not only in the economic sector but also in security arena. Therefore in an attempt to address the new challenges which are still unfolding, India needs to revisit its policy towards this strategically important region. The new approach could explore possibility of looking at the region beyond energy as new opportunities of cooperation open up for India in other areas. This could be done by developing stronger bilateral engagements followed by cooperation at regional level with its Asian partners and pronouncing 'New West Asia Policy'.

NOTES

1. Views expressed by Ambassador Ishrat Aziz during the 15th Asian Security Conference at the IDSA on February 15, 2013.
2. Views expressed by Abdulkhaleq Abdulla, Professor of Political Science and currently Chairman of the cultural committee at the Dubai Cultural and Scientific Association during the 15th Asian Security Conference at the IDSA on February 13-15, 2013.
3. Ibid.
4. World Energy Outlook Report of 2013, IEA, London, November 12, 2013. At www.worldenergyoutlook.org
5. Meena Singh Roy, "India-West Asia Energy Dynamics: Managing Challenges and Exploring New Opportunities", Rumel Dahiya, ed. *Developments in the Gulf Region: Prospects and Challenges for India in the two Decades*, New Delhi, Pentagon Press, 2014, pp. 68-69.
6. *Petroleum Intelligence Weekly*, London, Vol. LII, No. 16, April 22, 2013, p. 7.
7. Ibid.
8. Derek Brower, "Will Iraq be the Next Oil Superpower?" *Petroleum Economist*, December 2012-January 2013, p. 14.
9. IEA, Iraq Energy Outlook: World Energy Outlook Special Report, October 9, 2012, at http://www.worldenergyoutlook.org/media/weowebsite/2012/iraqenergyoutlook/Fullreport.pdf (accessed on May 15, 2013).
10. For detail see Meena Singh Roy, no. 5, pp. 70-71.
11. Prasanta Kumar Pradhan, "India and the Gulf: Strengthening Political and Strategic Ties", Rumel Dahiya, ed. *Developments in the Gulf Region Prospects and Challenges for India in the two Decades*, New Delhi, Pentagon Press, 2014, pp. 1-30; Samir Pradhan, "India-Gulf Trade Relations", Ranjit Gupta, Abu Bagader, Talmiz Ahmad, and N. Janardan, *India and the Gulf: What Next?*, Gulf Research Centre Cambridge, 2013, pp. 123-143.
12. Views expressed by the experts from Gulf Region during the 15th Asian Security Conference at the IDSA on February 13-15, 2013.
13. Ibid.
14. See no.2.
15. Ibid.
16. Ibid.
17. Dr Arvind Gupta, Dr Meena Singh Roy, Rajeev Agarwal, Dr PK Pradhan, Dr M Mahtab Alam Rizvi, "'Arab Spring': Implications for India", Policy Brief, January 2, 2014, at http://www.idsa.in/policybrief/ArabSpringImplicationsforIndia_westasia_020114
18. See no.5, pp. 68-69.
19. Views expressed by Ambassador Ishrat Aziz during the 15th Asian Security Conference at the IDSA on February 15, 2013.
20. Views expressed by Ambassador Sheel Kant Sharma during the 15th Asian Security Conference at the IDSA on February 15, 2013.

Index